DEBUSSY AND HIS WORLD

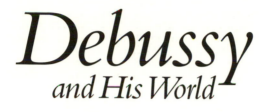

Debussy
and His World

EDITED BY JANE F. FULCHER

PRINCETON UNIVERSITY PRESS
PRINCETON AND OXFORD

Published by Princeton University Press, 41 William Street,
Princeton, New Jersey 08540
In the United Kingdom: Princeton University Press,
3 Market Place, Woodstock, Oxfordshire OX20 1SY

The musical examples from "Les Papillons" in Marie Rolf's essay are reproduced with per-
mission of the Music Division, The New York Public Library for the Performing Arts, Astor,
Lenox and Tilden Foundations. The musical examples from *Daniel* reprinted in John
Clevenger's essay, "Debussy's Rome Cantatas," are reproduced with permission of Jephta
Drachman; those from *Le Gladiateur* are reproduced with permission of the Bibliothèque
Nationale. The photographs of paintings reproduced in Leon Botstein's essay are used with
the following permission: *Nocturne in Blue and Silver* by James McNeill Whistler: Courtesy of
the Fogg Art Museum, Harvard University Art Museums, bequest of Grenville L. Winthrop,
photo by Katya Kallsen; *The Burning of the Houses of Lords and Commons, October 16, 1834*,
1835 by J.M.W. Turner: oil on canvas 92.7x123.2 cm, photograph copyright ©The
Cleveland Museum of Art, 2001, bequest of John L. Severance, 1942.647; *The Old Musician*
by Edouard Manet: 1862 oil on canvas, Chester Dale Collection, photograph copyright
©2001 Board of Trustees, National Gallery of Art, Washington, D.C.; and *Yvonne Lerolle in
Three Poses* by Maurice Denis: oil on canvas, Samuel Josefowitz Collection, Lausanne,
Switzerland. Photograph copyright © 2001 Artists Rights Society (ARS), New York/ADAP,
Paris. Permission to reproduce the documents about Achille-Claude Debussy's Paris
Conservatoire training comes from the Archives Nationales in Paris.

Library of Congress Cataloging-in-Publication Data

Debussy and his world / edited by Jane F. Fulcher.
p. cm. — (The Bard Music Festival series)
Includes bibliographical references and index.
ISBN 0-691-09041-6 (cloth : alk. paper) — ISBN 0-691-09042-4 (pbk. : alk. paper)
1. Debussy, Claude, 1862–1918—Criticism and interpretation. 2. Music—19th
century—History and criticism. 3. Music—20th century—History and criticism.
I. Fulcher, Jane F. II. Series.

ML410.D28 D37 2001   780'.92—dc21   2001027840

British Library Cataloging-in-Publication Data is available

This publication has been produced by the Bard College Publications Office:
Ginger Shore, Director
Mary Smith, Art Director

Designed by Juliet Meyers

Composed in Baskerville by Natalie Kelly

Text edited by Paul De Angelis

Music typeset by Don Giller

Printed on acid-free paper. ∞

www.pup.princeton.edu

Printed in the United States of America

1 3 5 7 9 10 8 6 4 2

1 3 5 7 9 10 8 6 4 2
(Pbk.)

For Carl E. Schorske

Contents

PART III
DOCUMENTS

Acknowledgments

I wish to thank Leon Botstein for giving me the opportunity to explore new aspects of Debussy and his œuvre, together with my colleagues in the field. I am also grateful to the other members of the Bard Music Festival Committee, Robert Martin, Mark Loftin, and Irene Zedlacher for their role in bringing this festival and volume about. In additon, I wish to express my gratitude to those members of the Bard Publications Office with whom I have worked so closely on this volume, and who have provided me with such excellent advice and support—Paul De Angelis, Natalie Kelly, and Ginger Shore. I also would like to thank Don Giller for his expert work in preparing the musical examples, and Fred Appel, at Princeton University Press for all his help in the process of preparing this book. All of us participating in the volume wish to thank those individuals and libraries (cited in the appropriate articles and on the copyright page) which so generously gave us the permission to use their materials. Finally, I wish to thank Arno J. Mayer, of Princeton University, for his willingness to read portions of this manuscript, and especially his excellent advice concerning my introduction and essay.

DEBUSSY
AND HIS WORLD

Constructions and Reconstructions

of Debussy

Jane F. Fulcher

Ever since the seminal insights of Roland Barthes and Michel Foucault, we have been inescapably aware that neither "authors" nor their "oeuvres" are a given, but are "constructed" and reconstructed. Our sense of an artistic achievement, of what constitutes the "mature" or greatest works, as well as of the content and boundaries of an oeuvre, are not self-evident, but culturally imposed. For we periodically redefine and select those works that can be accommodated within a coherent conception of an author's opus, as we construe it, slighting those works that challenge its "unity." A name thus becomes a "classification," presupposing continuity and homogeneity: This "author function" subsequently organizes, limits, and flattens out all contradiction or "polyphony" of intention. In sum, through this process ambiguity of meaning or "multivocality" disappears, as does recognition that an author's identity may be unstable or continually negotiated and evolving in time.[1]

Of no composer, perhaps, are these insights more relevant than Claude Debussy, the constructions and reconstructions of whom were begun by zealous advocates in his own day. His first group of acolytes, the "Debussystes," who flocked around the composer upon the triumph of *Pelléas et Mélisande* in 1902, sought to "freeze" his style with this crowning achievement. Inevitably they felt betrayed when their master refused to remain static stylistically, and eventually redefined his creative identity, even reincorporating academic elements that he had previously reviled.[2]

And yet this misrepresentation endures, for our culture has constructed a facile, "impressionist" Debussy, achieving mastery in his "middle" period, thus implying a devaluation of his earliest and late works. Indeed, in the case of the latter, Debussy's reincorporation of tradition challenges our conception of progress within the canon, or the ineluctable evolution of modern music, of which he has been annointed a "father."[3] Hence, for the sake of coherence we have generally ignored the inconsistency and complexity of Debussy's real development—his tendency to situate himself via both the musical future and past.

One goal of this volume is to capture the complex reality of Debussy's trajectory, or to retrace a creative life, replete with ambiguities and inconsistencies, within its context. For the one continuity that we may recognize in Claude Debussy is his unceasing evolution—his perpetual reinvention and self-exploration, both personal and creative, throughout his life. Always responding to his contemporaries, continually in tense dialogue and competition with them, inherently hostile to dogma or to factions, he stubbornly refused to repeat himself.

Yet this radical independence had a context, one rooted in Debussy's social experience as well as in his training, which impelled him to define himself against the norm, seeking out new sources of artistic inspiration. Moreover, Debussy's ability to "rethink music," as noted so acutely by Pierre Boulez, must be seen against the background of ferment and change in French music from the Franco-Prussian War (of 1870) to World War I. His profound innovations did not occur in a vacuum, as this volume attempts to demonstrate. Debussy's response was however so singular as to raise the question among contemporaries of whether his music was "truly French."[4]

Several of the essays in this volume explore the sources of this unique creativity, or of that which made Debussy, as William Austin has put it, "one of the most original and adventurous musicians who ever lived."[5] Issuing from a background that did not mold his taste, but rather challenged him to define one, Debussy resisted convention from the start, seeking alternatives to the language he was taught at the Conservatoire. Belonging to no one group or class, but crossing many, as Christophe Charle explains in his essay, Debussy abjured "the orthodox," retaining his independence and ability to both assimilate and transform his models. Indeed, each change in Debussy's social and artistic experience was integrally linked with a phase in his perpetually mobile, insatiate aesthetic and musical exploration.

It is precisely this remarkable independence that these essays demonstrate, one which allowed Debussy to redefine those influences with which he came into contact, or to reshape them toward his personal ends. A perpetual maverick who reviled all convention, as they attest, Debussy balked at entering into any situation—salons, musical societies, or factions—that would categorize and therefore distort him. As Gail Hilson Woldu and I argue in our essays, we must approach Debussy's restless search for a music authentically reflecting experience against the background of the litigious, factionalized, and politicized musical world of his period. For in his opinions as well as in his art, Debussy had always to examine all positions for himself, to decide personally what of the established creeds he could accept or had to reject.

Hence another goal of this volume is to attempt to resituate Claude Debussy within the more complete picture of the political, cultural, and musical world of the period now emerging. For Debussy's context was not only artistic and musical, but institutional, political, and social, as Christophe Charle discusses in his panoramic essay on Paris in Debussy's lifetime. Here he traces the social and cultural reality of Debussy's situation, and particularly how his inability to assimilate himself to "categories"—social or musical—both marginalized and injured him financially. Charle similarly explores Debussy's strategies within this world, and the tensions that resulted between his musical, aesthetic ambitions and his concrete social, or professional situation.

John Clevenger considers the institutional context at the very start of Debussy's career, tracing that which he both absorbed from his training and, almost endemically, rejected. Hence both he and Marie Rolf reexamine the emergence of Debussy's creative personality in his early works, as well as their relation to his education, or the "rules" he was taught. But the context shifts as we turn to the period following Debussy's return from Rome and his attempt, as his early biographer Léon Vallas has put it, to "disengage" his personality from all previous influences.[6] Now the context is both musical and social, as Debussy, "consecrated" by the Prix de Rome—and thus "authorized" to enter the world of official and bourgeois culture—emphatically rejects it to seek out "la bohème."

It is against this background that Rosemary Lloyd examines Debussy's entry into that grouping of poets, painters, and musicians who coalesced around Stéphane Mallarmé. This period of entry into the Symbolist aesthetic was also that of Debussy's attraction to and then rejection of Wagner, as well as of his exploration of the alternative world of non-Western music. Within this context, David Grayson discusses a previously slighted example of Debussy's "unorthodox" collaborations in this period—one with his friend (and member of Mallarmé's circle), the writer Pierre Louÿs.

The influence of the other arts in shaping the direction of Debussy's explorations and goals persisted and extended to painting, which throughout his life remained a source of inspiration. This is the subject of Leon Botstein's key essay, which demonstrates how pervasive and continual this influence was throughout the serpentine trajectory of Debussy's career. But as the composer developed, such quintessentially non-academic influences mingled provocatively with elements from his former academic training, as Brian Hart discusses in his essay. Specifically, he considers *La Mer*, which defied generic categorization, partially as a result of its dialogue with the symphonic models taught at the Conservatoire and the rival Schola Cantorum. Moreover, he shows, both here and in the "Documents" section, how this change in artistic direction confounded the critics, which included not only Debussy's former supporters but his more conservative adversaries. Debussy's place within the "French tradition," as it was defined by rival political-musical factions, henceforth became a central issue, and would remain so until the artist's death.

It is within this framework that I examine Debussy's final search for "roots" in the concept of the nation, his only real certitude now, with regard to identity, being that he was "French." As I argue, he continued to reintegrate the past, and specifically that of the French nation itself, but, as always, as he interpreted it personally, regardless of established political doctrines. Not only did this lead to further transformation based upon new poetic and musical models, which included his own personal French canon, but to his critical examination of his own stylistic past. Now Debussy became irrefragably aware of the complexity of his own identity, of the fact that it was inherently pluralistic, having been "reconfigured" or "negotiated" throughout his lifetime. This inner "polyphony," I maintain, emerges in his last compositions, as Debussy, in dialogue with himself, intrepidly debates his own conceptions of France and of "the classic," and confronts his complex personal truth.

Yet as the essays within this volume demonstrate, paradox ran throughout Debussy's career, as he abjured all dogma that risked stifling his ever mobile and restless creativity. A composer who was both sui generis and deeply rooted within a culture and a context, Debussy has continued both to fascinate and perplex his historians and to entice audiences to his "unclassifiable" art.

NOTES

1. On these tightly imbricated concepts, see Roland Barthes, "La Mort de l'auteur," in his *Le Bruissement de la langue* (Paris: Seuil, 1968), and Michel Foucault, "What Is an Author?" in *The Critical Tradition: Classic Texts and Contemporary Trends,* ed. David H. Richter (Boston: Bedford Books, 1998).

2. See Jane F. Fulcher, *French Cultural Politics and Music from the Dreyfus Affair to the First World War* (New York: Oxford University Press, 1999), pp. 179–86.

3. See Pierre Boulez, *Notes of an Apprenticeship,* trans. Herbert Weinstock (New York: Alfred A. Knopf, 1968), pp. 335–57.

4. See Fulcher, *French Cultural Politics*, pp. 154–61.

5. William W. Austin, *Music in the Twentieth Century, from Debussy through Stravinsky* (New York: W.W. Norton, 1966), p. 1.

6. Léon Vallas, *Claude Debussy* (London: Oxford University Press, 1933), pp. 49–65.

PART I

The Evolution

✦

Debussy's Rome Cantatas

by John R. Clevenger

As most knowledgeable musical observers would surely agree, Debussy's
Pelléas et Mélisande marked a radical departure from previous operatic
tradition at the time of its premiere performances in 1902. But because
the majority of Debussy's earlier dramatic essays have remained all but
unassessed by scholars, the composer's circuitous path to the signal
accomplishment that brought him world fame has remained as deeply
shrouded in obscurity as the misty locales and unfathomable characters
of his great Symbolist music drama itself. Indeed, a clear understanding of Debussy's development as a dramatic composer may be achieved
only by examining all his early dramatic compositions. Toward this end,
I have selected for investigation in this study the four early dramatic
works of Debussy that have received the least scrutiny thus far: the
unstaged learning pieces that may be conveniently grouped together
under the rubric of Debussy's Rome cantatas.

Setting aside such fragmentary efforts as *Hélène* (spring 1881),
Eglogue (late 1881), and *Hymnis* (spring–summer 1882), Debussy developed his musical-dramatic style primarily in six substantive dramatic
compositions he wrote before the age of thirty. Of these works, the two
that were composed outside the purview of scholastic officialdom—the
partially complete Parnassian music drama *Diane au bois* (1881–1886),
and the ill-conceived and unfinished grand opera, *Rodrigue et Chimène*
(1890–1892)—have attracted the most attention from scholars in recent
years. Both pieces have been performed recently, *Rodrigue et Chimène*
has been professionally recorded, and *Diane au bois* has been the subject
of extensive published analyses.[1] The three academically constrained
Prix de Rome cantatas, including the incomplete practice cantata *Daniel*
(spring 1882), the second prize-winning cantata *Le Gladiateur* (*The
Gladiator*; May 19 – June 13, 1883), and the first prize-winning cantata,
L'Enfant prodigue (*The Prodigal Son*; May 24 – June 18, 1884), have been
virtually ignored by scholars until now.[2] Debussy's stylistically freer

Rome *envoi* cantata, *La Damoiselle élue* (*The Blessed Damozel*, 1887–1888), which he submitted to the Académie des Beaux-Arts at the end of the third year of his Prix de Rome stipend, and which was therefore still subject to official criticism, is somewhat better known. Of these six dramatic compositions, only *L'Enfant prodigue* and *La Damoiselle élue* were published during Debussy's lifetime; both these cantatas have been professionally recorded.[3]

Debussy's Rome cantatas are remarkably varied. *Daniel* features some inspired pianistic cross rhythms and much sprightly up-tempo music, despite being handicapped by an abysmal libretto. With its dark and dismal story line, *Le Gladiateur* is filled with music of extraordinary violence, to a degree perhaps never again encountered in Debussy's oeuvre, with the possible exception of a few isolated passages such as Pelléas's onstage murder at the end of Act IV of *Pelléas et Mélisande*. The more stylistically polished music of *L'Enfant prodigue*, with its pastoral strains and warm familial sentiments, is imbued with the essence of Debussy's compositional personality, even though it is demonstrably restrained stylistically. *La Damoiselle élue*, the only early cantata for which Debussy was free to choose his own text, exudes all the warmth, refinement, and evocative splendor of which he was capable toward the end of his formative period. The Rome cantatas thus represent widely ranging facets of Debussy's early conception of dramatic composition as it was conditioned by his Paris Conservatoire training, the stringent requirements of the Prix de Rome competition, the equally exacting—though less enforceable—guidelines for the Rome submission pieces, and the state of operatic art in France at the time.

Taken together, the Rome cantatas constitute a particularly important category of Debussy's early compositions: those written under the duress of academically imposed strictures. Because these pieces have consequently been regarded as academically tainted, and because the first two of them have been difficult of access, scholars have been loath to study them. Yet not only do the Rome cantatas comprise a majority of Debussy's early substantive dramatic settings, but the latter three (*Le Gladiateur*, *L'Enfant prodigue*, and *La Damoiselle élue*) were in fact his only finished dramatic compositions before *Pelléas et Mélisande*. Moreover, these works—particularly the three Prix de Rome cantatas, each of which is about twice as long as *La Damoiselle élue*—were among the lengthiest compositions Debussy wrote in any genre during his formative period from 1879 to 1888. There can be little question, then, that these four cantatas deserve the most serious scholarly scrutiny.

Hence it is unfortunate that previous research on Debussy's Rome cantatas has been so scanty. With the exception of my own recent writings,[4] there have been no comprehensive analytical studies of any of the three Prix de Rome cantatas.[5] *La Damoiselle élue* has fared only a little better, having been ably scrutinized by Everett Maurice Alfred in his dissertation on Debussy's choral music.[6]

The present study, then, is the first in which these four important exemplars of Debussy's early dramatic style are considered together. In the process of assessing these cantatas I address, beyond the purely analytical findings set forth, three questions pertaining to Debussy's position within the history of style. First, how stylistically constrained are these early scholastic compositions? Second, when and how obligingly did Debussy submit to Wagner's influence? And third, what was Debussy's point of departure as a dramatic composer, and how did he start to break the molds of tradition to achieve something new? In seeking to answer these questions, I hope that a fuller appreciation may be reached of the true nature of Debussy's achievements as a dramatic composer.

The Prix de Rome and Debussy

In the early 1880s, any French or naturalized French citizen under the age of thirty, not just Conservatoire composition pupils, could compete for the Prix de Rome.[7] The award typically involved a two-year sojourn at the Villa Medici in Rome, optionally followed by a year or two of travel elsewhere, generally to Germany, and a total of four years of state support.[8] The prize was intended to broaden the horizons of the recipients—despite the fact that, as Henri Rebois remarks, "Italian musical activity was almost exclusively concentrated in Milan and Naples," and most certainly not in Rome, during this era.[9] Albert Lavignac, in a chapter of his book on music education entitled "The Creative Faculty and Higher Musical Studies," thoughtfully explains this rationale. In order to "furnish the divine creative faculty with every chance to reveal and assert itself,"[10] he suggests that, beyond carrying out general literary and scientific studies, an aspiring composer should expand his mind through travel:

> One might think that it is not a matter of importance to have traveled much in order to produce beautiful melodies, but this is a mistake, for, without having to regard it as an indispensable condition, yet very often the contemplation of beautiful mountain scenery, the incidents of a sea voyage, the emotion produced by a striking natural phenomenon or the memory that it leaves behind

is the principal cause of the inspiration of a beautiful thought that reflects its grandeur, charm, or local color. It is a sentiment of this nature that explains the sending to Italy and Germany . . . of the winners of the Prix de Rome. . . . In these travels, in addition to all that people learn in traveling, they find the opportunity, as Montaigne says, to rub against other intelligent artists. Inspiration may find its source in everything and everywhere; it is therefore in the most cultivated and best furnished minds that it will most frequently find the opportunity of springing forth, with equal intensity of innate genius.[11]

For Debussy, the Prix de Rome was problematic. Its four-year government stipend, although modest, had to be attractive to him, as it would have been to any Conservatoire composition pupil about to graduate into the real world.[12] The seal of official approval that came with it surely would have held some appeal for him as well, despite any protestations he may have made to the contrary. Yet winning the prize would also mean at least two years' separation from his illicit lover, Marie Vasnier, and a prolonged stay in the smothering, confining atmosphere of central Rome. He had already visited this city with the von Meck family and detested it; and a Rome residency promised no great musical stimulation in any event. Hence it is no wonder that Debussy hesitated even to compete for the prize, as detailed in my documents section on Debussy's Paris Conservatoire training later in this book.

Nevertheless, Debussy took part in the Prix de Rome competition three times, failing the preliminary round in 1882, placing a strong second with *Le Gladiateur* in 1883, and finally taking home the first grand prize with *L'Enfant prodigue* in 1884. He thus endured the difficult six-day sequestration of the preliminary round three times and the grueling twenty-five-day sequestration of the final round twice.[13]

According to the Prix de Rome competition's restrictive regulations, the cantata for the final round was to be composed for two or three characters of unequal voices (typically soprano, tenor, and bass). The text, selected among numerous newly written librettos during a preliminary poetic contest, would provide material for an aria for each character, a duet, and a trio (in the usual case of a scene to be set for three voices), as well as recitatives linking these various set pieces. An instrumental introduction should precede the scene, and the trio, if present, could involve some vocal ensemble passages without accompaniment.[14]

The cantata texts that were selected for the final rounds might often be unsuitable for a composer of refined literary tastes like Debussy. For instance, the libretto selected for the final round of the 1883 competition,

Emile Moreau's *Le Gladiateur*, with its implicit violence and overblown emotions, was a far cry from the delicately nuanced modernist poetry that Debussy was already beginning to set in his early songs and independent dramatic essays. Nevertheless, the assessment undertaken herein of *Le Gladiateur* reveals that Debussy was unquestionably—if surprisingly—inspired by Moreau's unusually fine libretto. Such was decidedly not the case with the laughable libretto of Debussy's practice Prix de Rome cantata, written in preparation for the 1882 contest, Emile Cicile's *Daniel*, which had been used for the 1868 competition. With its silly stage devices (including a burning hand of God and a mysterious message appearing out of thin air) and lame dialogue, this piece of literary hackwork could only have left Debussy disenchanted with the prospect of having to set such Prix de Rome cantata texts to music. Fortunately, the pastoral setting and compelling evocation of peasant life of Edouard Guinand's *L'Enfant prodigue*, selected for the final round of the 1884 competition, may have struck a chord with the young Debussy, given his lifelong love of nature. Indeed, his setting contains some exquisite music with an unmistakably Debussyan flair.

Moreover, Debussy had no choice but to compromise stylistically in order to win the prize, as a well-known anecdote transmitted by Louis Laloy makes clear. Describing an event that transpired in the spring of 1883, as Debussy's compositional training under Ernest Guiraud was just beginning to bear fruit, Laloy writes:

> The taste of this musician [Guiraud] was worth more than his works; he took an interest in the incorrigible youth, and even gave him good advice. One day, Debussy had set to music a comedy of Banville, *Diane au bois,* and had brought it, not without pride, to class; Guiraud read through it and pronounced: "Come to see me tomorrow and bring your score." The next day, after a second reading, [Guiraud asked]: "Do you want to win the Prix de Rome?" "Without a doubt," [Debussy replied]. "Well, all that's very interesting, but you must save it for later. Or else you will never win the Prix de Rome."[15]

Taken together with Guiraud's report on Debussy for the January 1882 composition semester examination, as cited in my documents section later in this book, that his most original pupil is "intelligent, but needs to be bridled," this anecdote points up the considerable extent to which Guiraud helped Debussy not only to learn the ropes of composing music, but also to rein in his radical compositional impulses enough to win the Prix de Rome despite himself.

However trying the sequestrations were for Debussy, however hard he struggled to write cantatas according to official prescriptions to texts not of his choosing, however much anxiety the prospect of an impending separation from his lover and the relative isolation of a lengthy stay in a foreign capital caused him, however much he tried to avoid this separation by attempting (unsuccessfully) to meet the September 29, 1884, deadline for the more lucrative Prix de la Ville de Paris,[16] winning the Prix de Rome was certainly a watershed event in Debussy's life. With the grand prize came his first important official recognition and material support for four years—enough time to make significant headway in his quest to develop a compositional style of sufficient sophistication and subtlety for expressing his unique artistic vision.

Not inconsequentially, these competitions also gave Debussy ample practice in writing for the stage, and they provided him with much early experience in handling the resources of the full orchestra, a craft at which he would come to excel. Indeed, the performance of Debussy's *L'Enfant prodigue* at the Rome prize ceremony of the Académie des Beaux-Arts on October 18, 1884, would have afforded the young composer his very first opportunity to hear his music played orchestrally.

Furthermore, even though Debussy's Rome sojourn was personally trying and quite unproductive in terms of compositional output,[17] he did seize the chance to experiment with new musical and dramatic means, particularly in *Diane au bois*. Debussy's official submission pieces, the dramatic ode *Zuleima*, the orchestral and choral diptych *Printemps*, *La Damoiselle élue*, and the *Fantaisie* for piano and orchestra, also afforded him opportunities to further refine his orchestral technique. Hence if the Prix de Rome competitions—and the grand prize itself—constituted a bitter pill for Debussy to swallow, it was one that must have had beneficial effects, or at least side effects, for his development as a composer.

Daniel

In the Conservatoire composition classes, it was customary to have students write a practice Prix de Rome cantata, the so-called *cantate de travail*, employing a libretto that had been used for a previous competition, as both Gustave Charpentier and Julien Tiersot attest.[18] In the spring of 1882, as Debussy was preparing to enter the Prix de Rome competition for the first time, Guiraud apparently assigned him to set a text that had been used for the 1868 competition, Emile Cicile's *Daniel*. As preserved, Debussy's rendering of Cicile's insipid drama includes some 484 measures of complete but unorchestrated music.

Debussy evidently finished, or at least nearly finished, the piece, since the missing segments clearly result from lost leaves of the manuscript, which is a fair copy, not a sketch, with the music breaking off at the ends of leaves at two points.[19]

Overall, Debussy's setting is remarkably uneven: a few inspired and overtly untraditional set pieces are set off by generally weak dialogue segments; other numbers, particularly the ensembles, are merely formulaic in design. Moreover, the frequently pianistic conception of the accompaniment betrays the composer's immaturity. In composing the cantata, Debussy was faced with the daunting challenge of reconciling his profoundly original artistic impulses with the strictures of academic tradition, while also learning how to create an effective musical drama. The methods he used in attempting to surmount this challenge are telling, for even at this initial stage of his activity as a dramatic composer, Debussy clearly modeled himself after the master of the music drama, Wagner.

The Libretto

Set in a palace in ancient Babylon, Cicile's drama involves three characters, the proud Assyrian king Balthazar, his queen Adéna, and the prophet Daniel.[20] The short Scene 1 is made up simply of Balthazar's drinking song. As the nobles of his court indulge in a sumptuous feast and the din of musical instruments adds to the merriment, the king boisterously sings his song of celebration, leaving to the subjugated crowd the worries and pain of life. Laughing off the sound of distant thunder, he encourages his friends to drink and be of good cheer.

Scene 2 opens as Adéna enters, afraid that what seems to be the rumble of thunder may in fact be the sound of an approaching army. In the ensuing duet, as she expresses her fears of this seeming portent of doom and the perceived threat of divine retribution, Balthazar attempts to comfort her, arrogantly declaring that the God of Israel can do him no harm. He tries, to no avail, to assuage her fears by enticing her with the splendors of the feast: the intoxicating scents of the fragrant flowers and the incense, the enchanting chords of the instruments. In the following dialogue, in order to demonstrate the impotence of the Israelite God against his power, he calls for a stolen sacred chalice to be brought to him and filled with wine. As Adéna warns him not to commit such an act of sacrilege, he drinks from the holy vessel. "J'y bois à Baal!" ("I drink to Baal!") he exclaims, as a violent clap of thunder is heard. Terrified, the queen cries out. On the wall, a burning hand of

God has appeared, writing a cryptic message in strokes of flame. In his turn struck with terror, the king implores his Chaldean sages to explain to him the meaning of the mysterious words.

Daniel enters, as Scene 3 begins. Coming, as he says, on the order of God, the prophet warns the king that he will soon know the meaning of the message. He tells Balthazar that God will destroy his throne and deliver his kingdom to his enemies. Just then, the sound of an approaching army and the blaze of military trumpets is heard, as Medians overwhelm Balthazar's soldiers. As death rains down upon the ramparts of the palace, the trio begins. Balthazar and Adéna beg for mercy; Daniel acknowledges their plea. But it is too late: heavenly justice must be exacted. The palace collapsing around them, the king and his queen reluctantly submit to the power of death, as Daniel looks on unscathed.

Musical-Dramatic Construction

Like Debussy's Prix de Rome competition cantatas, the form of *Daniel* is determined largely by the structure of the supplied text. Consisting essentially of set pieces connected by dialogue segments, the work is entirely conventional in this respect.

In its use of true Wagnerian leitmotives, however, the music of *Daniel* is decidedly unconventional, at least as viewed from the Conservatoire's perspective in the early 1880s, before the Wagnerian system had fully taken hold in France. As shown in Example 1, four separate leitmotives—which may be distinguished from the reminiscence themes of traditional French opera by their generally shorter length and freer and more pervasive employment—occur in the cantata.

Balthazar's two-fold Drunkenness leitmotive and reminiscence theme (Example 1a) is established much in the manner of the more traditional reminiscence theme, occurring throughout Balthazar's Drinking Song at mm. 1–84. Either the accompanimental motive or the vocal theme recur six times during the remainder of the cantata. Adéna's Foreboding leitmotive (Example 1b) occurs first at her entrance immediately following the conclusion of Balthazar's song at m. 87, as he notices her state of alarm. The Doom leitmotive (Example 1c) first appears at mm. 120–22, as Adéna frightfully confesses that she imagines the rumble of distant thunder to be the sound of an approaching army—a presentiment that turns out to be accurate. And the Pronouncement of God leitmotive (Example 1d) first accompanies the ridiculous appearance onstage of a hand of God at mm. 310–11, where it is contrapuntally (if simplistically) combined with Doom.

Example 1. Recurring themes in *Daniel*

Ver - sez;   que de l'i - vres - se, Aux ac - cents d'al - lé - gres - se...
Pour;   *so that from drunkenness,* *To accents of good cheer...*

Example 1a. Balthazar's Drunkenness leitmotive and reminiscence theme

(Elle entre avec les marques d'une vive frayeur.)
(She enters showing signs of vivid terror.)

Example 1b. Adéna's Foreboding leitmotive

(Adéna: "Toujours, comme un sombre présage,
Cette idée en mes sens jette un mortel effroi.")

("Still, like a somber portent,
This idea casts a mortal fear in my senses.")

Example 1c. Doom leitmotive
(See following page for 1d.)

With 11.8 recurring themes per 100 measures of music, *Daniel* is substantially leitmotivic, and hence unmistakably Wagnerian in conception. If Debussy's apprentice-like adoption of the Wagnerian system of musical-dramatic construction is surely less than completely successful either musically or dramatically, his Wagnerian orientation right from the start as a dramatic composer is therefore clear.

Style

Extracts from three set pieces from *Daniel*—Balthazar's opening aria, the Balthazar-Adéna duet from Scene 2, and Daniel's aria from Scene 3—should provide an adequate sample from which Debussy's stylistic

Example 1d. Pronouncement of God leitmotive (combined with Doom leitmotive)

starting point as a dramatic composer may be assessed. As the ensuing analyses of his later Rome cantatas show, the music of *Daniel* is surprisingly radical in certain respects, while entirely conventional in others.

Unlike the later competition cantatas, Debussy supplied no instrumental introduction for *Daniel*, even though musical instruments are mentioned in the stage directions, affording a good scenic excuse for devising a festive prelude, and an instrumental introduction was a requirement of the Prix de Rome competition. Instead, Balthazar's boisterous drinking song serves to set the initial tone for the drama. An extract from this set piece, consisting of the instrumental opening followed by the refrain, is provided in Example 2.

Balthazar

Versez; que de l'ivresse,	Pour; so that from drunkenness,
Aux accents d'allégresse,	To accents of good cheer,
Circulent les doux feux;	Circulate the sweet passions;
Versez, et que l'aurore	Pour, and how much the dawn
Demain éclaire encore	Tomorrow will again light up
Et nos ris et nos jeux.	Both our smiles and our games.

Although this number is set as a conventional five-part refrain form, as Refrain-A-Refrain-B-Refrain, Debussy's compositional ingenuity asserts itself immediately. The lively but tonally abstruse opening vaguely implies D minor through the use of predominant and dominant harmonies at mm. 1–3, forming one of Debussy's stylistic staples, the polyfunctional complex, in which predominant and dominant tonal functions are blended. The opening turns out to be tonally deceptive,[21] as another polyfunctional complex is stated immediately thereafter at mm. 4–8, this one outlining the true key of B-flat major. Although the harmonies in these measures are more clearly syntactical, Debussy's innate tendency toward static harmony and reiterative phraseology is apparent in the bichordal oscillation at this point. Such reiterative construction based on two oscillating chords—a mode of musical continuity that is diametrically opposed to the goal-directed syntactical harmony of traditional tonal music—had been a feature of Debussy's style from his very first known composition from three years before, the song "Madrid" (spring 1879).

The ensuing music of the refrain at mm. 9–23 is only partly syntactical harmonically. The emphasis on what was called, in the Conservatoire harmony textbook of Henri Reber that Debussy had used in Emile Durand's harmony class, the "weak" mediant harmony at m. 10 and again at mm. 14–15,[22] lends a neo-modal flavor to this passage.

Example 2. Balthazar's Drinking Song from *Daniel*, Excerpt (mm. 1–23)

Example 2 continued

Example 2 continued

This implicitly modal sound is intensified by parallel fifths in the bass register (as indicated by parallel lines in the example). The tonally obscure bichordal oscillation at mm. 16–19 and the nonsyntactical chords at m. 20 only temporarily veil the underlying B-flat major tonality, which is quickly clarified by syntactical harmonies leading into the cadence at m. 23. The unusual harmonic retrogression from dominant harmony to subdominant harmony at m. 22 constitutes an early instance of the polyfunctional cadence, involving a fusing of predominant and dominant harmonies—that is, a polyfunctional complex—at the point of cadence, a Debussy trademark throughout his compositional career. This opening set piece, then, is strikingly fresh harmonically, although quite conventional formally.

The duet between the arrogant king Balthazar and his fearful queen Adéna from Scene 2, an extended excerpt from which is provided in Example 3, is by contrast much less Debussyan. This number, in fact, exhibits one of the work's chief weaknesses, for it involves much preconceived melody to which words were evidently only secondarily fitted. In this respect, the duet is symptomatic of a composer who was caught in the grips of stale convention. Here, as generally in his early ensemble passages (including the love duet from *Diane au bois*, which is surprisingly conventional), either the young Debussy had not yet developed sufficient means to break the bonds of tradition, or else he felt compelled to stay within permissible stylistic boundaries. In either case, the crying musical and dramatic insufficiency of such academically restricted settings could only have convinced him that he would have to invent new dramatic forms if he was ever to find sufficient means for expressing, in the operatic medium, his sincere and searing artistic vision.

Balthazar

Bannis le trouble qui te glace,	Banish the uneasiness that chills you,
Bannis une folle terreur,	Banish a foolish terror,
Jamais l'orage et sa menace	Can the storm and its menace
Pourrait-il effrayer ton cœur?	Forever frighten your heart?

Adéna

Si l'orage aujourd'hui me glace,	If the storm today chills me,
Du péril que pressent mon cœur,	Some peril of which my heart has a presentiment,
C'est qu'hélas ! pour moi, sa menace	It is because, alas! for me, its menace
N'est que le signe précurseur.	Is only the harbinger of what is to come.

Balthazar

Que t'importe l'orage ?	What does the storm matter to you?

Adéna

Je tressaille à sa voix.	I tremble at his [God's] voice.

Balthazar

Rappelle ton courage,	Summon your courage,
Il n'atteint pas les rois.	He will not touch kings.

Viens, des fleurs odorantes	Come, from the fragrant flowers
Les senteurs enivrantes,	The intoxicating scents,
Les parfums de l'encens	The perfumes of the incense
Pénétreront tes sens, . . .	Will penetrate your senses, . . .

Adéna

Non, des fleurs odorantes	No, from the fragrant flowers
Les senteurs enivrantes,	The intoxicating scents,
Cet éclat, cet encens	This splendor, this incense
Pénètre en vain mes sens; . . .	Penetrates in vain my senses; . . .

The intense musical interest generated by the pulsating pianistic cross rhythms and changing meters of the introductory segment to this part of the duet beginning at m. 206 dissipates as soon as metrical regularity is tritely recaptured to set the stage for the vocal entrance at m. 211. Harmonically, this introductory passage again involves a polyfunctional complex. Because of its intrinsic tonally defining properties, the primary tonality of E major is unambiguously projected, even in the absence of syntactical harmonic progression.

In the ensuing section of the duet at mm. 211–26, as Balthazar tries to comfort Adéna and she expresses her fears, the music lapses into nearly unmitigated conventionality. This main segment of the duet is based upon entirely syntactical harmonies that hardly go beyond what Debussy learned in Durand's harmony class—or, for that matter, the thoroughly conventional harmonizations of Durand's own vocal and dramatic music.[23] Only the incessant use of enriched and extended tertian sonorities and the two polyfunctional cadential articulations at mm. 217–18 and mm. 223–26, both of which involve parallel fifths in the bass register and are followed immediately by subtonic nullifications (the use of the subtonic degree to weaken tonality, by thwarting the tonally defining effect of the leading tone), point to Debussy as the author of the passage. Phraseologically, this portion of the duet is unwaveringly—even naïvely—foursquare. In fact, in its long-breathed vocal phraseology, its lilting compound metric feel, and its use of pedals and enriched sonorities, the section closely mimics an idiom often found in the operas of Jules Massenet, as detailed later in this essay. This part of the Balthazar-Adéna duet, then, may reflect either a conscious bow to tradition or a genuine Massenet influence.

The following dialogue segment at mm. 227–35 also exhibits two features that are evidently derivative of standard French operatic usages of the era. Whether these stylistic borrowings reflect a conscious stylistic compromise made in view of the conservative nature of the Prix de Rome competition or a genuine influence from the music of the French milieu is difficult to determine. First, the initial lines of the dialogue at mm. 227–29 are underpinned by a diminished seventh chord. This sonority was employed all too commonly in French operas of this period, and Debussy relied on it all too readily to dispose of dialogue passages quickly in each of his three Prix de Rome cantatas. This usage may result simply from his tuition under Guiraud, who frequently composed dialogue segments based on the sonority.[24]

Second, the abrupt transition from a sharp key area (E major) to a flat key area (A-flat major) to set the stage for the ensuing lyrical segment beginning at m. 236 was a device commonly employed in French opera at the time, particularly in love arias and duets, which were almost always set in flat keys.[25] But the overtly pianistic expanding wedge formation introducing the contrasting key area at mm. 233–35, featuring an exhilarating arrival on an extended major dominant ninth chord, with the sonorously enriching element (the major ninth) piquantly isolated registrally and rhythmically, is all Debussy.

The formulaic nature of the accompaniment of the phrases beginning at m. 236 is reminiscent of the simplistic methods of accompanying a melody presented in the piano accompaniment manual of Debussy's harmony and accompaniment professor, Durand, using broken chords and stock accompanimental patterns.[26] Such methods were apparently taught in the Conservatoire composition classes as an expedient to enable young composers to turn out ensemble passages quickly and easily, so that the cantata could be finished in the short time allotted for the Prix de Rome competition sequestration. Such techniques are plainly in evidence in both of Debussy's competition cantatas, in the musically weak trio from *Le Gladiateur* as well as the much finer duet from *L'Enfant prodigue*. But they are absent entirely in *La Damoiselle élue*, which did not have to be turned out under any such severe time constraints.

(Text continues on pg. 34.)

Example 3. Balthazar-Adéna Duet from *Daniel*, Excerpt (mm. 206–43)

Example 3 continued

Example 3 continued

Example 3 continued

Example 3 continued

Example 3 continued

Example 3 continued

Example 3 continued

Other aspects of the concluding portion of the Balthazar-Adéna duet beginning at m. 236 are more musically engaging. Complete pentatonic collections, such as the E♭-F-G-B♭-C incipient pentatonic formation occurring in both voices in octaves at m. 236–37, are occasionally exposed melodically, lending the passage a calming tone and a distinctly Debussyan flair. Parenthetical harmonies following the excerpt provided in Example 3 enliven the harmonic underpinnings of a passage that is otherwise largely syntactical. Phraseologically, this concluding lyrical section is again curtly foursquare, employing phrases and phrase segments that are almost exclusively either four or two measures in length.

Altogether, then, the music of the duet is predominantly traditional, written for the most part according to the compositional prescriptions Debussy was learning at the Conservatoire. As is the case with almost every ensemble passage Debussy wrote during his student years, only a modest admixture of Debussyan experiments may be discerned therein.

Much less conventional is Daniel's aria from Scene 3, an excerpt from which (including the lead-in to the set piece and the first part of the aria only) is provided in Example 4. Here Debussy allows himself much stylistic freedom in order to depict musically the sacred righteousness of a messenger of God. Debussy's experimental side is especially evident in the introductory dialogue segment at mm. 327–31, which features partial triadic planing (triads moving in parallel subsuming part of the musical texture, as indicated by parallel lines in the example). This is a particularly radical usage, favored by such nonconformist and officially scorned compatriots as Edouard Lalo and Emmanuel Chabrier, and Debussy would not dare repeat it quite so brazenly in either of his competition cantatas.

Daniel

Gardez vos présents. Je ne viens	Keep your gifts. I come
Que par l'ordre du Dieu,	Only by order of God,
mon maître.	my master.

C'est la voix du Dieu des combats	It is the voice of the God of battle
Qui gronde ici dans le tonnerre,	That rumbles here in the thunder,
Le Dieu tout puissant dont la voix	The all-powerful God whose voice
Terrasse les rois de la terre.	Overwhelms the kings of the Earth.

Set in a traditional ternary form, Daniel's aria is anything but straightforward harmonically. Employing a veiled tonal basis that may perhaps best be described as a variable mode centered on C, the harmonies of this number are almost entirely nonsyntactical. Only six chords at the

Example 4. Daniel's Aria from *Daniel*, Excerpt (mm. 327–46)

Example 4 continued

end of part B (not included in the example) progress in a logical manner, according to the harmonic precepts of the common practice as codified in the Conservatoire harmony textbooks. The bichordal oscillation at the opening of the aria proper (mm. 332–35) affords another early example of this pet Debussyan constructive device. The coloristic harmonies of the following measures defy classification, although partial planing at mm. 336–37 and approximate planing at mm. 340–42, supporting another vivid accompanimental wedge formation, are familiar facets of Debussy's mature stylistic apparatus. This part of the aria concludes at mm. 345–46 with an utterly nonsyntactical cadence that may be classified as a modal cadence, in which the penultimate sonority contains the anti-tonal subtonic degree, B♭.

Phraseology in Daniel's aria is remarkably fluid. In part A (mm. 332–46), as shown in Example 4, two four-measure phrases are followed by a seven-measure phrase; neither melodic symmetries nor harmonic factors serve in any way to unite these irregular musical utterances. Rather, Debussy has conceived the music flexibly so as to adhere closely to the meaning of the text. Indeed, an obvious musical depiction of thunder occurs in the bass at m. 336, as Daniel sings the line, "C'est la voix du Dieu des combats Qui gronde ici dans le tonnerre" ("It is the voice of the God of battle / That rumbles here in the thunder"). Such an arioso-like manner of constructing set pieces was evidently not characteristic of the stylistically restrictive Prix de Rome cantatas of the era, judging by Paul Vidal's winning setting of *Le Gladiateur* in 1883. In that piece purely musical factors, including symmetrical melodies, highly regularized rhythms, and foursquare phraseology, almost always hold sway in determining the overall musical-dramatic shape.[27]

Le Gladiateur

Composed for the final round of Debussy's first full Prix de Rome competition from May 19 to June 13, 1883, *Le Gladiateur* was performed twice—with the accompaniment arranged for piano four-hands—on June 22 and 23, 1883.[28] In ranking Debussy's cantata second behind Paul Vidal's much less sophisticated and far more conventional setting of the same libretto, the Académie des Beaux-Arts judged the work as follows: "Generous musical nature but ardent to the point of intemperance; some gripping dramatic accents."[29] Press reviews, several of which pointed to Debussy's originality, were mostly favorable: "Debussy's cantata [bears] witness already to a true talent and a certain dose of imagination"; "[Debussy exhibits] a remarkable musical nature, but a rather exaggerated penchant for originality"; "Debussy, . . . less expert than Vidal in the technique of his art, seems to me, on the other hand, to have a more original personality. . . . Debussy's scene was worthy in all respects of the supreme recompense"; "Debussy has a true musician's temperament; but his gifts need to be pondered and he does not have nearly the perfect knowledge of the craft that the young Vidal already possesses to a high degree."[30]

Indeed, Debussy's first complete Prix de Rome cantata—and his first complete music drama—is a creditable work. Far better integrated musically than *Daniel*, *Le Gladiateur* exhibits a striking interpenetration of text and music that may be attributed to Debussy's keen sensitivity to poetic and dramatic values. Although weighed down to some extent by scholastic requirements (particularly in its rhetorically effusive ensemble numbers, which feature tiresome text repetitions to a discernibly greater degree than the ensembles of *Daniel*), *Le Gladiateur* is the work of a composer who is on the verge of achieving stylistic self-assurance. Wagnerian in more than one respect, the piece could almost have been a true Wagnerian music drama were it not for the strictures of the competition as reflected in the structure of the libretto.

The Libretto

Emile Moreau's libretto is notable for its cogent structure and compelling dramatic situations.[31] Press critics applauded its unusually high quality, one even proclaiming that "its harmonious verses . . . have only one defect, that they could almost do without the addition of music."[32] Indeed, as contemporary reports suggest and the exuberant nature of the respective settings confirms, Moreau's fine drama genuinely inspired the contestants. In the words of the reviewer for *Le Ménestrel*, "the beautiful verses of the cantata, *Le Gladiateur*, . . . had really inspired our young Mozarts in training."[33]

The plot is straightforward. Narbal, eldest son of the Numidian king Jugurtha, has been captured in battle by the Roman consul Métellus. As Scene 1 begins, the prisoner sleeps in chains in a cell beneath the Circus Maximus, awaiting the moment of his appearance in the arena. He awakens to the sounds of the clamoring Roman populace already crowding into the circus, and then hears the somber procession of his countrymen being led toward the arena. As trumpet fanfares herald the beginning of the victory celebration, the gladiator intones an impassioned invocation. Calling out to his god Baal for vengeance against the Romans, he imagines the Roman populace, through divine intervention, being thrust into the arena, where they would become fodder for the gladiators' swords. He then falls again into a stupor.

To his surprise Fulvie, the daughter of Métellus, enters as Scene 2 begins. Having witnessed Narbal's courage under the lictor's whip during the victory procession, she has fallen in love with him. Taken aback, the gladiator joins her in a love duet. But despite her earnest pleas that he escape with her, he refuses, saying that to flee would seem cowardly. Embracing Narbal, Fulvie promises to deliver him from his fate one way or another, and they kiss.

As Scene 3 begins her father suddenly appears, enraged at what he sees. In the first trio the proud Roman consul struggles to restrain his fury, while Fulvie and Narbal sing of love's redemption. Then, before Métellus can take Narbal away, Fulvie produces a vial of poison, and the lovers drink from it in turn. In the second trio, Fulvie and Narbal sing ecstatically of his deliverance from the horrors of the arena, while Métellus laments his ruined hour of triumph. Finally, the lovers fall to the floor, entangled in each other's arms, and die in front of a horrified Métellus. Thus the vengeance that had been sought by the gladiator is ultimately delivered through the vehicle of Fulvie's love.[34]

Musical-Dramatic Construction

Like *Daniel*, *Le Gladiateur* is constructed using the Wagnerian system of leitmotives, which appear together with more traditional types of recurring themes. As shown in Example 5, Debussy wields two stage devices, one reminiscence theme, and three leitmotives in the cantata.

The Jeering Crowd stage device (Example 5a) and the Arena Trumpets stage device (Example 5b) occur at appropriate points in the drama to portray events occurring offstage. The Procession Music reminiscence theme (Example 5c) accompanies the gladiators' solemn procession to the arena in Scene 1 at mm. 107–35, and then is recalled in Scene 3 at mm. 540–43 as Narbal defiantly offers the gladiators' traditional salute to his captor as he drinks the poison, "Celui qui va mourir, ô Romain! te salue!" ("The one who is about to die, o Roman! salutes you!").

The true Wagnerian leitmotives in *Le Gladiateur* include Vengeance (Example 5d), Love's Deliverance (Example 5e), and Fight (Example 5f). The Vengeance leitmotive—the sole consistent identifying characteristic of which is the diminished seventh sonority on which it is based—is by far the most pervasive. This central leitmotive is ubiquitous in Scenes 1 and 3, and it appears at appropriate points in Scene

Example 5. Recurring themes in *Le Gladiateur*

Example 5a. Jeering Crowd stage device

Example 5b. Arena Trumpets stage device

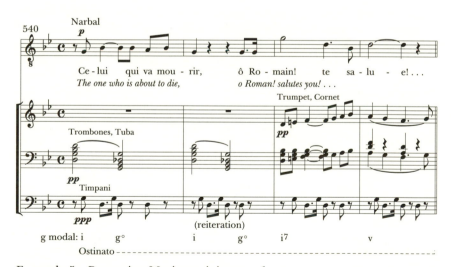

Example 5c. Procession Music reminiscence theme

Example 5d. Vengeance leitmotive

Example 5e. Love's Deliverance leitmotive

Example 5f. Fight leitmotive

2. The association of the diminished seventh sonority with the central dramatic theme of vengeance in the cantata is forged in part through several prominent expositions of the chord directly accompanying or immediately following the use of the word itself. At the climax of the invocation in Scene 1 at mm. 177–79, for instance, soon after the gladiator sings "*venge* tes enfants" ("*avenge* your children"), a diminished seventh chord accompanies his imagined violent fulfillment of that vengeance. Similarly, during Métellus's aria in Scene 3 at m. 481 and m. 485, Métellus sings the word *venger* twice against diminished seventh chords. The simplicity of its physiognomy allows Vengeance to be readily combined with the other leitmotives; one such instance is shown in Example 5d, where the Fight head motive appears within a diminished seventh chord context.

Love's Deliverance first appears, appropriately enough, as Fulvie enters just prior to Scene 2. During her aria, the leitmotive assumes the function of a sectional accompanimental motive, thus cementing its association with the drama's heroine. Love's Deliverance is combined with Vengeance, again simply by being stated in a diminished seventh chord context, at two crucial points in Scene 3: at mm. 533–36, as Fulvie produces the vial of poison, and again at mm. 595–99, as she drinks from the vial, setting the stage for the work's dramatic apotheosis.

Fight occurs first as a primary theme in the latter portion of the Prelude beginning at m. 29; Debussy would repeat this basic prelude design of commencing with mood-setting music and concluding with a primary thematic statement in each of his two later Rome cantatas. The dramatic association of Fight is fixed immediately thereafter at mm. 48–53, for it accompanies Narbal's opening lines as he dreams of the recent battle, "Mort aux Romains! . . . Tuez jusqu'au dernier! Victoire!" ("Death to the Romans! . . . Kill them to the last man! Victory!").

Two subtler musical-dramatic references also occur in *Le Gladiateur*, as shown in Example 6. The first, which might be called the Vehicle of Vengeance motive (Example 6a), appears first during the gladiator's invocation in Scene 1 at mm. 161–62, and then later during his dialogue with Fulvie shortly after she enters early in Scene 2 at mm. 222–24. It involves a hidden melodic echo in the vocal line underpinned by a distinctive neighboring harmonic succession that is recalled at the same tonal level, thereby linking the gladiator's petition to his god Baal for vengeance against the Romans with the eventual vehicle for that vengeance, Fulvie. The second, which might be called the Gladiators' Trumpets motive (Example 6b), involves a similarly concealed reference to the Arena Trumpets fanfare at the climax of the gladiator's invocation at mm. 187–88. Here the trumpets suddenly interject the characteristic $F4$-$F5$ octaves of the trumpet fanfare in a similar dotted figure (compare Example 5b), as if Narbal imagines that the gladiators will have their own trumpets with which to call the Roman populace into the arena, so that the tables may be turned. These remarkably subtle musical-dramatic nuances point up how great was the interpenetration between music and drama that Debussy was able to achieve in this, his first complete music drama.

With 10.0 recurring themes per 100 measures of music, *Le Gladiateur* involves, like *Daniel*, a fairly substantial density of recurring themes. Although this may have been desirable from a Wagnerian perspective, by French standards it was certainly not generally accepted practice in 1883. According to Maurice Emmanuel, in the early 1880s Wagner was viewed by the powers that be at the Conservatoire as "the destroyer of

Example 6. Other thematic references in *Le Gladiateur*

Example 6a. Vehicle of Vengeance motive

Example 6b. Gladiators' Trumpets motive

all tradition."[35] As Martin Cooper has observed, the foremost operatic composer in France at this period, Massenet, employed leitmotives systematically for the first time in *Hérodiade*,[36] which had yet to be played in Paris at the time of the 1883 Prix de Rome competition. Hence Debussy's employment of leitmotives in *Le Gladiateur* may well have been considered too radical by the competition judges, a likely reason why Debussy lost the competition that year.

Le Gladiateur is also Wagnerian in that it exhibits greater continuity than was common for Prix de Rome cantatas in three respects. First, Debussy frequently invests dialogue passages with greater musical import, blurring the distinction between dialogue and set piece. Second, Debussy's set pieces are often wholly or partly through-composed, employing a discrete musical idea for each textual idea contained therein. Third, Debussy's setting, which has thirty-four key and meter signature changes, is quite tonally and metrically fluid. Debussy's great sensitivity to poetic values apparently caused him to mold his music closely to the ebb and flow of the drama, a trait that is even more evident in his contemporaneous setting of the extant scenes from *Diane au bois*.

Le Gladiateur exhibits an overall tonal motion from A minor to A major. It seems clear that this tonal progression is intended to express the underlying dramatic progression from torment and despair at the beginning to triumph—the fulfillment of vengeance—at the end, in the traditional nineteenth-century fashion initiated by Beethoven's Fifth Symphony. Moreover, the cantata plays on this global tonal association by turning to the ultimate major-mode resolution area at strategic points in the interior of the drama. The most sophisticated tonal-dramatic reference occurs in the gladiator's invocation in Scene 1 at mm. 152–98. Debussy renders this segment—a microcosm of the drama as a whole—as a tonal microcosm as well. Beginning in A minor, the invocation reaches a triumphant A major at the climax as Narbal imagines the supremely violent fulfillment of his vengeance. The key of A major is also referenced momentarily at Métellus's entrance at the beginning of Scene 3 at mm. 436–37, when Fulvie realizes that their fate is sealed: a cadential resolution to A major accompanies her line, "C'en est fait ! La mort entre avec lui !" ("Then it is done! Death enters with him!"). The definitive turn to A major occurs, appropriately enough, at the beginning of the death scene at mm. 591–94, as Narbal sings to Fulvie, "Qu'elle est douce, la fin que tu me préparas !" ("How sweet it is, the end that you prepared for me!").

Le Gladiateur even exhibits clear timbral-dramatic associations. Trombones and timpani are associated with the central dramatic theme of vengeance, and the harp is associated with love and comfort. Trombones and timpani are pervasive throughout Scene 1, where they are most prominently featured in the procession music. The harp, appropriately, is inextricably linked with Fulvie, entering for the first time in Scene 2, just before the love duet at m. 252. In Scene 3, the alternation between these opposing timbral forces is especially closely aligned with the dramatic flux. Métellus's bitter reproaches early in the scene are underpinned at first by a chilling low brass choir at mm. 440–62, to which an ominous timpani flourish is added at mm. 454–59, and then by a strident trombone solo at mm. 466–78. The tone changes immediately thereafter as prominent harp arpeggios accompany Fulvie's and Narbal's answering phrases at mm. 488–516, in which they sing warmly of love's redemption. The timbral alternation continues throughout the remainder of the scene, with the harp finally winning out at the end. Within Debussy's oeuvre, such a symbolic exploitation of timbres is not unique to *Le Gladiateur*: in *Pelléas et Mélisande*, as Arthur Wenk has pointed out, horns are associated with darkness and death, and timpani with impending disaster.[37]

Style

Extracts from three set pieces from *Le Gladiateur*—the Prelude, Narbal's Invocation from Scene 1, and the Love Duet from Scene 2—may serve as a representative sample of Debussy's style in his first competition cantata. The Prelude, the beginning of which is provided in Example 7, effectively sets the emotional tone for the work. The first portion, featuring strings in octaves against somber low brass chords, is not thematic; the latter portion (not included in the example), exposes two of the leitmotives of the overall drama that are most germane to Scene 1, Vengeance and Fight. At mm. 1–14 harmonies that are essentially syntactical, yet not tonally transparent, first express the main tonality of A minor, then briefly tonicize C major starting at m. 12. Floating nonsyntactical chords take over for several measures thereafter: trivial planing involving first inversion triads at mm. 15–16 is followed by a pungent bichordal oscillation at mm. 17–18, forming a polyfunctional complex projecting the underlying tonality of A minor. The metrically stressed nonharmonic tones throughout the opening segment of the Prelude, particularly as the first tonal articulation is approached more or less syntactically at mm. 17–22 (where every strong beat carries an appoggiatura, an accented passing tone, or a suspension), call to mind the harmonic style of Wagner. These lazily unfolding non-harmonic formations serve to weaken the clarity of the underlying harmonic syntax, without obscuring it entirely. Though not deeply veiled tonally, then, this opening segment of the prelude is by no means tonally forthright. Not unduly untraditional, it is nonetheless somewhat progressive harmonically.

Much like Daniel's aria in *Daniel* (see again Example 4), Narbal's Invocation in Scene 1 is treated as a continuously evolving arioso passage. In the extract provided in Example 8, small-scale phraseological symmetries are eschewed in favor of flexibly conceived music that is molded closely to the meaning and flow of the text. As in Daniel's

aria, some all-too-literal text-painting is evident in the rapid figurations at mm. 155–56, suggestive in a rather silly way of Baal's godly
powers. Highly irregular phrases are defined by unconventional
cadential formations, including the polyfunctional complex function-
ing as a half cadence at m. 156 and the plagal cadence variant that is
avoided chromatically by resolving to a major-minor seventh chord at

Example 7. Prelude from *Le Gladiateur*, Excerpt (mm. 1–23)

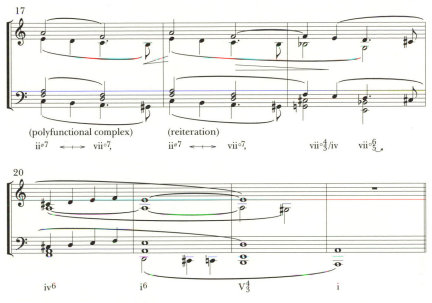

Example 7 continued

mm. 168–69. Like the Prelude, the harmonies are indirectly expressive of the underlying tonality of A minor, in a way that unmistakably transcends the common practice. Following a nonsyntactical neighboring formation at mm. 152–54, the arrival at the polyfunctional half cadence at m. 156, and an arpeggiated nonsyntactical diminished seventh chord at mm. 157–60, C major is tonicized briefly at mm. 161–66, again through the use of a polyfunctional complex. The strong but avoided plagal variant cadence into m. 169 articulates the return to A minor in a subtle but effective manner. Among the more dramatically effective numbers in the cantata, Narbal's Invocation is thus distinctly untraditional.

Narbal

Baal, source du feu que rien ne peut tarir,	Baal, inexhaustible source of fire,
Qui mets le bronze en feu et le granit en poudre,	Who sets bronze ablaze and turns granite to powder,
Ô roi des déserts étouffants,	O king of the stifling deserts,
Toi dont le souffle est l'incendie,	You, whose breath is flame,
Du fond de notre Numidie	From the heart of our Numidia
Viens, Baal ! Venge tes enfants !	Come, Baal! Avenge your children!
Punis ce peuple impie !	Punish this impious people!

Example 8. Narbal's Invocation from *Le Gladiateur*, Excerpt (mm. 152–69)

Example 8 continued

Example 9. "Phrase massenétique" in *Le Gladiateur*: Love Duet, Opening (mm. 255–62)

Debussy's love duet from *Le Gladiateur*, the opening of which is provided in Example 9, employs an idiom overtly borrowed from Massenet: what Rodney Milnes has aptly called the "phrase massenétique," involving compound meters such as $^{12}_{8}$ or $^{9}_{8}$ (and a particular brand of expansive but highly regular phraseology.[38] Beyond an effusive melodic style, other features commonly associated with the phrase massenétique include luxuriant enriched chords, pedal tones in the bass, and an obbligato accompanying instrumental line that adds an elegant contrapuntal touch. All are present in the love duet from *Le Gladiateur*.

Even the key of the love duet, D-flat major, is conventional: as Cooper notes, love scenes in French opera of the era "were almost always in

Example 10. The Grand Melodic Arc in *Le Gladiateur:* Love Duet, close (mm. 293–302)

D-flat or G-flat major."[39] Furthermore, the linking passages leading into such lyrical numbers often involved a more or less abrupt transition from a key with several sharps to a key with several flats. The lead-in to the love duet from *Le Gladiateur* involves a transition from E major to D-flat major. Similarly, the lead-in to the concluding duet from *Diane au bois* involves a transition from D major to G-flat major. Debussy also employed the technique to set off a main lyrical segment in the Balthazar-Adéna duet from *Daniel*, as previously discussed (see again Example 3, mm. 227–32).

Debussy indulged in sweeping melodic arcs at certain points of *Le Gladiateur*, as in the conclusion of the love duet shown in Example 10. Such grandiose melodic gestures—surely antithetical to Debussy's essential compositional persona—must represent yet another stylistic compromise made for the purposes of the competition. Debussy would make the same compromise more successfully in *L'Enfant prodigue*, in both the Lia-Azaël duet, where the climactic passage at mm. 451–60 strikingly resembles the passage shown in Example 10, and the concluding trio, particularly at mm. 621–44. The same sort of overblown melodic rhetoric is found in the incomplete trio of *Daniel*, beginning at m. 68 of the second fragmentary portion of the manuscript.

As can also be seen in Example 10, Debussy's *Le Gladiateur*, unlike his mature vocal works, involves frequent text repetitions, particularly in the ensembles. This may be regarded as a standard feature of French opera of the era, hence to be expected in a scholastic composition—the ensembles in both Guiraud's *Galante Aventure* and Massenet's *Hérodiade*, indeed, contain numerous text repetitions.

Example 11. Incipient Hexatonicism in *Le Gladiateur*: Fulvie's Profession of Love (mm. 235–36)

Compared to his independent compositions of the era, such as the scenes from *Diane au bois*, Debussy's *Le Gladiateur* is not especially radical stylistically. In contrast to the relatively frequent occurrence of such personal experiments throughout *Diane au bois* and in his evidently less restrained—though also less compositionally adept—practice cantata, *Daniel*, his first competition cantata contains only a few Debussyan devices. Debussy flirts only occasionally with exotic pitch collections in *Le Gladiateur*. A characteristic instance is the hexatonic segment so exquisitely traced in Fulvie's vocal line in Scene 2 at mm. 235–36, as shown in Example 11. At other points in the drama, such as during the procession music at m. 122, open fifths are occasionally asserted as sonorous special effects. Very limited instances of partial planing are occasionally found, such as the parallel major-minor seventh chords that occur just preceding the climax of Narbal's invocation at mm. 182–84.

Probably the least fortunate aspect of Debussy's first Prix de Rome competition cantata is its overreliance on bombastic diminished seventh chords to portray moments of great dramatic stress (including calls for vengeance, the specific leitmotivic association of the diminished seventh sonority, as previously explained) and as the chordal basis for many dialogue segments. But given the prevalence of this overworked sonority in contemporaneous French operas (numerous instances may readily be cited in both Guiraud's *Galante Aventure* and Massenet's *Hérodiade*), this may represent either a concession to popular taste grudgingly made for the Prix de Rome competition or a vestige of French compositional practice that Debussy had not yet managed to eliminate from his style.

L'Enfant prodigue

Composed for the final round of Debussy's second full Prix de Rome competition from May 24 to June 18, 1884, *L'Enfant prodigue* was performed twice—with the accompaniment arranged for piano four-hands—on June 27 and 28, 1884.[40] In awarding Debussy's cantata the first grand prize, the Académie des Beaux-Arts judged it as follows: "Very marked poetic sense, brilliant and warm coloring, animated and dramatic music."[41] Press reviews were generally positive. Charles Darcours, writing for *Le Figaro*, applauds the young Debussy's originality, while criticizing the cantata for "defects that characterize the style of dreamers in music," including its often indecisive tonality and formal disorder. The latter feature, he claims, "appears to be one of the principal laws" of the piece.[42] A. Héler, writing for *L'Art musical*, likewise praises Debussy's original approach to dramatic composition: "by making, so to speak, an abstraction of the poetry that was offered to him, he has dared to depict the color of the poetry" in the music. But he also criticizes the work's "excessive means, relative to the nature of its subject," pointing ambivalently to Debussy's "interesting, rather incoherent, but expressive music."[43]

L'Enfant prodigue is perhaps as remarkable for what it lacks as for what it contains, for in it, leitmotives are replaced by more traditional reminiscence themes—thus representing a seeming regression in Debussy's evolution as a dramatic composer. In this respect, indeed, the work is unquestionably the most conservative of all his Rome cantatas. In other respects, though, the piece is quite progressive, and more than a little Debussyan.

The Libretto

Edouard Guinand's rendering of the biblical tale of the prodigal son is no great literary or dramatic masterpiece.[44] Set for three characters, Azaël, a young Galilean; his mother, Lia; and his father, Siméon, the single-scene drama takes place in a calm countryside village near a lake. The story begins as Lia, listening to the joyous singing of children in the distance, wistfully recalls the happy days before her wayward son had departed. Realizing that others in the village are able to enjoy the company of their offspring in their declining years, she cries out, "Azaël! Azaël! Pourquoi m'as-tu quittée?" ("Azaël! Azaël! Why have you left me?") Siméon enters, consoling her. Pointing to a gathering throng of peasant children, he enjoins her to be happy in such joyous surroundings. A gay procession traverses the scene and the peasants start to dance.

Meanwhile, Azaël regards the celebration from afar. He recalls the innocent times of his youth, when, pure of heart, he frolicked in these serene surroundings, cherished by his mother. But he is weary from his long homeward journey, and his feet are bloodstained. Unable to make it to the village, he cries out in anguish as he loses consciousness, falling to the ground by the shore of the lake.

Lia, having fled the festivities, which have only heightened her distress, approaches the lake. Imagining her son, far away, alone and weak as he calls for his mother, she catches sight of what she thinks at first is an indigent traveler lying by the wayside. Moving forward to help him, she recognizes her son. Thinking him dead, she cries out in anguish, beseeching him to open his eyes. He finally awakens, and their duet begins. He asks for her forgiveness, she tells him that the past is buried forever, and they rejoice in each other's company.

Siméon reaches the lakeside scene, unsure at first how to react to his son's return. Lia implores him to set aside his anger and forgive Azaël. Finally, Siméon announces to all in the vicinity: "Frappez la cymbale et le tambourin! . . . L'enfant prodigue est retrouvé!" ("Strike the cymbal and the tambourine!... The prodigal son has returned!") Their trio of celebration concludes the drama, as they give thanks to the Lord for their bountiful natural surroundings and their newfound happiness.

Musical-Dramatic Construction

Musically, there is no question that Debussy's Prix de Rome-winning cantata is the best of his three Prix de Rome cantatas. Yet the music of *L'Enfant prodigue*, while by no means patently traditional, is discernibly less radical than that of *Daniel*, and its musical-dramatic conception is nowhere near as sophisticated as that of *Le Gladiateur*. Clearly, then, Debussy compromised stylistically in order to win the Prix de Rome. But his real achievement in composing *L'Enfant prodigue* was to do so without renouncing his artistic ideals, managing somehow to meet the minimum acceptable academic requirements while still rendering the inner drama of Guinand's text in a sincere and convincing way.

In stark and at first perhaps puzzling contrast to *Daniel* and *Le Gladiateur*, no true Wagnerian leitmotives appear in *L'Enfant prodigue*. Of the recurring themes that do occur in the cantata, as shown in Example 12, some are reminiscence themes, comparable in every respect to those used in traditional French opera. Stated intact as full-blown themes at first, typically within dramatically important set pieces, they are later brought back in fragmentary form to recall the emotions or circumstances surrounding the initial statement. Other recurring themes are straightforward stage devices, directly depictive of events unfolding onstage, such as dance music. Hence at first blush Debussy seems to have taken a giant developmental step backward. But as the preceding analysis of *Le Gladiateur* strongly suggests, this apparent stylistic regression more likely resulted from a further compromise that Debussy realized he had to make in order to win the Rome prize.

The Peasant Revelry reminiscence theme (Example 12a) is first exposed in the Prelude at mm. 3–14 and mm. 37–40. Its dramatic significance is established during Siméon's recitative at mm. 119–22, where it accompanies the approaching procession of peasant children. The Motherly Love reminiscence theme (Example 12b), a chief theme of the cantata overall, is initially exposed as the main theme of the prelude at mm. 19–37. Its dramatic significance is established during Lia's Recitative at mm. 54–55,

Example 12. Recurring themes in *L'Enfant prodigue*

Example 12a. Peasant Revelry reminiscence theme

Example 12b. Motherly Love reminiscence theme

Example 12c. Lia's Despair reminiscence theme

Example 12d. Cortege stage device

Example 12e. Dance Theme A stage device

Example 12f. Dance Theme B stage device and reminiscence theme

as she mournfully laments her lost son. The Lia's Despair reminiscence theme (Example 12c) first appears during her ensuing aria at mm. 66–79, as she plaintively intones the words "Azaël ! Azaël ! Pourquoi m'as-tu quittée ?" ("Azaël! Azaël! Why have you left me?"). The Cortege stage device (Example 12d), which employs the same flowing sextuplet sixteenth note figure that constitutes the head of the Peasant Revelry reminiscence theme (as shown by brackets in Examples 12a and d), first accompanies the peasants' procession at mm. 132–35. The primary Dance Theme A stage device (Example 12e), with its quartal and modal underpinnings, first appears during the dance sequence at mm. 151–58, and the secondary Dance Theme B stage device and reminiscence theme (Example 12f) first appears during the same set piece at mm. 179–94. The two dance themes are eminently Debussyan in their gently flowing, arabesquelike character, with syncopations and ties across barlines occurring in Dance Theme A, and successive two-against-three polyrhythms occurring in Dance Theme B.

With only 4.3 recurring themes per 100 measures of music, *L'Enfant prodigue* exhibits a significantly lower density of recurring themes than either *Daniel* or *Le Gladiateur*. But the recurring themes in *L'Enfant prodigue* are potent enough musically, and their dramatic associations clearly enough drawn, to be used to good effect. Because of their great thematic diversity and richness and even though they do not occur nearly as pervasively in this more traditionally constituted dramatic piece, the result is a conceptually satisfying musical-dramatic whole.

As in *Le Gladiateur,* a clear tonal-dramatic association is employed in *L'Enfant prodigue:* here, B minor represents sorrow, and B major represents joy. Following the B major Prelude, Lia's aria of despair is set in B minor beginning at m. 66. As Siméon tries to console her, the tonality at m. 123 slides into B major, the key of the ensuing joyous procession music. Soon relinquished, this tonality of dramatic resolution is definitively recaptured as Lia and Azaël begin their ecstatic duet of reunion at m. 361. B major then underpins the exultant concluding trio beginning at m. 567.

Style

Extracts from three set pieces from *L'Enfant prodigue*, the Prelude, Azaël's aria, and the Lia-Azaël duet, should suffice to illustrate the nature of Debussy's stylistic achievement in reconciling the stringent Prix de Rome competition requirements with his original, deeply poetic compositional nature. The Prelude, the opening of which is provided in Example 13, is surely one of Debussy's most luminously beautiful early musical inspirations. Like the prelude from *Le Gladiateur* the previous year, it serves to set the emotional tone of the work, while exposing or at least foreshadowing primary thematic materials. Just as the Fight leitmotive, melded with Vengeance, had served as the primary theme of the latter portion of the *Le Gladiateur* prelude, the centrally important Motherly Love reminiscence theme serves as the primary theme of the latter portion of the *L'Enfant prodigue* prelude (not included in the example).

The bagpipe-like D♯–A♯ open fifth at the beginning of the Prelude immediately establishes the cantata's pastoral character, providing a ground for the initial exposition of what will become the Peasant Revelry reminiscence theme, as shown by brackets at mm. 3–6 in the example. At the same time, this nontonic open fifth produces a tonally deceptive opening, which temporarily but heavily veils the primary B major tonality of the piece. The focus in these measures on the weak mediant degree lends this opening a subtly neo-modal flavor, an appropriate musical beginning for an ancient biblical story. As soon as the opening sonority is transmuted into tonic harmony at m. 7, however, it is rationalized retroactively as an enriched sonorous component of the primary tonic, rather than an independent harmony. The reiterative, static harmonic basis of mm. 1–10 and the arabesquelike melodic figurations of the Peasant Revelry motive, spinning out gently over the lazily unfolding line in the bass at mm. 7–10, produce a delicately Debussyan utterance.

Just as the primary B major tonality, which is only weakly projected by diatonic saturation at mm. 7–10, becomes stronger with the first true harmonic progression to the subdominant at m. 11, it is nullified by a fleeting assertion of the subtonic degree. The ensuing, mostly syntactical harmonies make the controlling tonality entirely clear. The major ninth added to the dominant seventh chord at mm. 17–18 is luxuriantly extended, in a manner reminiscent of Reber's suggestion that the "principal charm" of the major dominant ninth chord lies in giving it "a duration sufficiently long so as to allow its resonance to become penetrating."[45] The floating sensation thus produced would become one of Debussy's favorite techniques, used repeatedly and to wonderful musical effect in his earlier, more tonal compositions. The initial confirmation of the primary tonality occurs across a grouping boundary at m. 19, as the main theme of the Prelude, the Motherly Love reminiscence theme, is prominently exposed (in the portion of the Prelude not illustrated here). Altogether, this opening section of the Prelude defies the most fundamental organizing principles of common-practice music: rather than being structured architectonally or periodically, it involves a plastic, almost organic growth of musical materials, a sort of developmental form. Debussy would take such an organic conception of musical structure

Example 13. Prelude from *L'Enfant prodigue*, Excerpt (mm. 1–18)

Example 13 continued

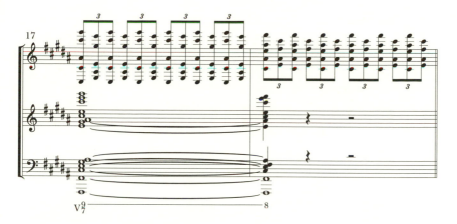

Example 13 continued

much further in his second Rome submission piece of 1887, *Printemps,* and then carry the procedure to its logical efflorescence in his germinal form masterpiece, *Prélude à l'après-midi d'un faune* of 1892–1894.[46]

The primary thematic segment from Azaël's aria, in which the prodigal son laments the lost innocence of a childhood forever gone, is provided in Example 14. Set in a languorous compound triple meter and featuring lush sonorities and multiple pedals, this portion of Azaël's aria reflects, like the Balthazar-Adéna duet from *Daniel* and the love duet from *Le Gladiateur,* a likely direct stylistic influence from the operas of Massenet.[47]

Azaël

Ô temps à jamais effacé,	Oh times forever gone,
Où comme eux j'avais l'âme pure ;	When like them [dancing peasant children] I had a pure soul;
Où cette sereine nature	When this serene nature
Fortifiait mon corps lassé ;	Fortified my weary body;
Où près d'une mère, ravie	When close to a mother, enraptured
De presser mon front sur son cœur,	To press my forehead to her heart,
Je ne connaissais de la vie	I knew of life
Que l'innocence et le bonheur !	Only innocence and happiness!

The harmonies of this section of the aria are primarily syntactical, although a few Debussyan features and stylistic mannerisms creep in occasionally. At m. 244, a standard Debussyan polyfunctional complex appears that could be analyzed as either a single dominant eleventh

Example 14. Azaël's Aria from *L'Enfant prodigue*, Excerpt (mm. 242–57)

Example 14 continued

harmony or, during the latter two beats, a subdominant harmony in the vocal line and the upper parts over a dominant implication in the bass register. At mm. 246–47, a neo-modal succession is underpinned by Debussy's stock parallel fifths in the bass register. At m. 250, a characteristic subtonic nullification initiates what is otherwise a standard Conservatoire compound modulation through m. 257. But the closing gesture leading to the final cadence at m. 257 is built on a lengthy descending fifths cycle such as Debussy would frequently use in his earlier compositions to emphasize points of tonal arrival within tonally fluid passages. Hence this excerpt from Azaël's aria, while finely wrought, is largely traditional in character, offering only a faint taste of the true Debussy.

The Lia-Azaël duet, a portion of which is provided in Example 15, is stylistically closely comparable to both the Balthazar-Adéna duet from *Daniel* (compare Example 3, mm. 236–43) and the love duet from *Le Gladiateur* (compare Examples 9 and 10). Employing symmetrical melody and foursquare phraseology throughout, a sweeping vocal climax in octaves at mm. 412–15, formulaic accompanimental figurations, and ample text repetitions (in other portions of the number not shown here), this lyrical duet surely satisfied all the stuffy stylistic expectations of the Prix de Rome competition. Yet musically, the effect is far superior to that produced by the ensemble passages in the earlier cantatas, indicating that Debussy has finally achieved full mastery of the restrictive Prix de Rome cantata idiom.

Azaël

Heures fortunées !	Happy hours!
Après des années,	After many a year,
Tremblant et confus, je songe	Trembling and confused, I dreamt
au retour ;	of returning:
Et, plein de tendresse,	And, full of tenderness,
Ton cœur qui me presse	Your heart that presses against me
Ainsi qu'autrefois me rend	As of yore gives me its love!
son amour !	

Lia

Heures fortunées !	Happy hours!
Depuis des années,	After many a year,
Dans le désespoir, j'attends	In despair I awaited your return;
ton retour ;	
Et plein d'allégresse,	And, full of tenderness,
Mon cœur qui te presse	My heart that presses against you
Ainsi qu'autrefois te rend	As of yore gives you its love!
son amour !	

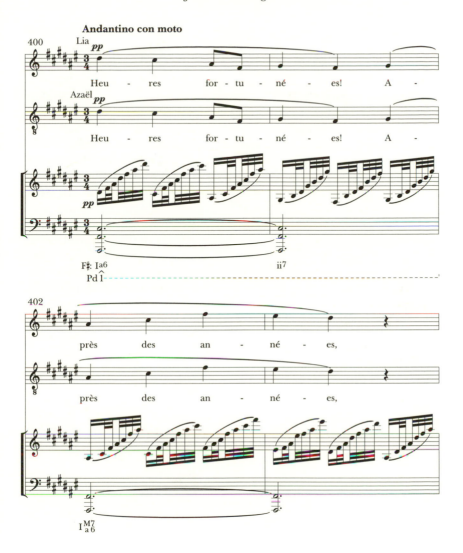

Example 15. Lia-Azaël Duet from *L'Enfant prodigue*, Excerpt (mm. 400–415)

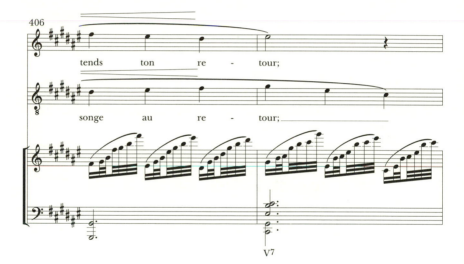

Example 15 continued

Example 15 continued

Example 15 continued

Overall, *L'Enfant prodigue* does contain a few overtly experimental devices. True modal passages appear occasionally, such as the C-sharp dorian setting of the primary theme of the peasants' dance music at m. 151–58, which also involves the daring quartal harmony C♯–D♯–F♯–G♯. Open fifths are employed periodically to evoke the carefree natural life of the peasants, such as at the opening of the Prelude, as previously discussed (see again Example 13, mm. 1–2), and just before Siméon's aria at m. 508. A sudden but very brief bout of emphatic partial triadic planing at mm. 563–64 sets the stage for the beginning of the trio, a usage resembling that found in *Daniel* (see again Example 4, mm. 328–30), which similarly serves to set off the beginning of a lyrical set piece. The melodies of the dance music, as discussed previously (see again Examples 12e and f), involve gracefully undulating arabesques. But in general the music is decidedly restrained stylistically, compared to independent early compositions of Debussy such as *Diane au bois*. In fact, as shown in Example 16, the pervasive hexatonic passage in the familiar 1908 revised version of the cantata, which partitions the dance music at mm. 198–99, was a later substitution for a much tamer incipient hexatonic formation used in the original version. Debussy would not have been foolish enough to tempt fate by employing such a provocative usage in the actual competition.

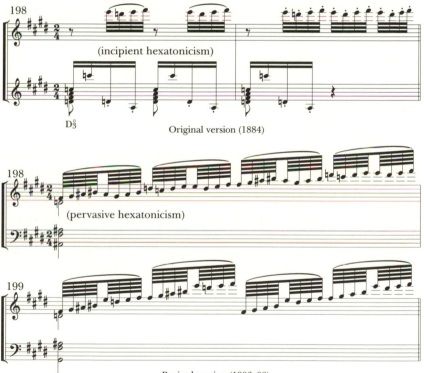

Example 16. Hexatonicism in the Two Versions of *L'Enfant prodigue*: Dance Music, Excerpt (mm. 198–99)

La Damoiselle élue

As Article 33 of the regulations of the Académie de France à Rome states, the Prix de Rome laureate was expected, during the third year of his stipend, to "compose an oratorio on French, Italian, or Latin words; or otherwise, at his choice: either a *messe solennelle* or a Requiem mass, or a Te Deum, or a grand Psalm, or else a vocal and symphonic work with soloists, choruses, and orchestra, in at least two movements, on a new or old poem; or finally an opera, either tragic or comic, in at least two acts, on a new or old libretto." In addition, the Rome pensioner was directed to compose a symphonic work suitable for opening the annual meeting of the Académie des Beaux-Arts the following year.[48]

Ever rebellious against authority, Debussy could bring himself to fulfill only the first part of this requirement,[49] by setting a text that may have been transmitted to him by his teenage brother Alfred,[50] Gabriel Sarrazin's prose translation of Dante Gabriel Rossetti's quasi-religious, erotically tinged English Pre-Raphaelite masterpiece, *The Blessed Damozel*. Composed mostly after Debussy had returned to Paris in early 1887, the oratorio or cantata[51] was finished by early 1888.

There could have been many reasons for Debussy's attraction to both Rossetti's poem and the accompanying painting, a copy of which Debussy also owned.[52] As depicted in the poem and the painting, the sultry maiden with flowing golden tresses and opulent robe was a direct ancestor to the resplendent, sublimely sexual Art Nouveau woman—an aesthetic fixation to which Debussy would return repeatedly throughout his career, from the Scottish lassie with the flaxen hair to Mélisande herself. Rossetti, like Debussy, had been profoundly inspired by the poetry of Edgar Allan Poe. He was a friend and aesthetic forebear of James Whistler, whose monochrome paintings would inspire Debussy's *Nocturnes*. Moreover, Rossetti had broken with established academic traditions in both poetry and painting, much as Debussy was trying to do in music. Hence the young composer must have felt a strong aesthetic kinship with Rossetti; indeed, he would later contemplate adapting another Rossetti poem, in collaboration with Pierre Louÿs, for a piece to be entitled *La Saulaie*.[53]

Judging by the reports on the compositions that Debussy submitted to the Académie des Beaux-Arts during the period of his Prix de Rome stipend, he experimented intensively indeed at this final stage of his formative period. About his first submission piece, *Zuleïma* (now lost), Henri Delaborde, the secretary of the Académie des Beaux-Arts, writes:

M. Debussy, for his first year's submission piece, has written the first part of a symphonic ode, entitled *Zuleïma*. The work that had earned M. Debussy the first grand prize of musical composition in 1884 [*L'Enfant prodigue*] gave the Académie reason to expect that this young artist, endowed with remarkable faculties, would furnish in the future the confirmation of the melodic and dramatic qualities of which he had given evidence in his competition piece. The Académie regrets having to declare an entirely contrary result. M. Debussy seems today tormented by the desire to produce the bizarre, the incomprehensible, the unperformable. Despite some passages that do not lack a certain character, the vocal part of his work offers interest neither melodically nor in terms of declamation. The Académie wants to hope that time and experience will bring, in the ideas and in the works of M. Debussy, some salutary modifications.[54]

As his first germinal form composition, Debussy's second submission piece, *Printemps*, was one of the most important compositions of his formative period; its wordless chorus was a timbral innovation that the composer would use again to exquisite effect in the third of his *Nocturnes*. Delaborde's famous report on this work—involving the first known application of the term "impressionism" to Debussy's music—is telling:

M. Debussy assuredly does not transgress by platitude or banality. He has, quite to the contrary, a pronounced, even too pronounced, tendency toward the pursuit of the strange. One recognizes in his case a feeling for musical color, the exaggeration of which makes him too easily forget the importance of precision of design and form. It is strongly desired that he guard against this vague "impressionism" that is one of the most dangerous enemies of truth in works of art. The first movement of the symphonic piece of M. Debussy is a sort of adagio prelude, of a reverie and affectation that lead to confusion. The second movement is a bizarre and incoherent transformation of the first, which the combinations of the rhythm render at least a little clearer and more perceptible. The Académie expects and hopes for better from a musician as talented as M. Debussy.[55]

The report on Debussy's third submission piece, *La Damoiselle élue*, betrays an unmistakable softening of the official stance toward his experimentation:

The text chosen by M. Debussy is in prose and rather obscure; but the music that he has adapted to it is devoid neither of poetry nor of charm, although it manifests again these systematic tendencies of vagueness of expression and form for which the Académie has already had occasion to reproach the composer. Here, however, these inclinations and procedures manifest themselves with more reserve and seem to a certain point justified by the nature itself and the indeterminate character of the subject.[56]

Debussy intended the *Fantaisie* to be his fourth year's submission piece, but the report for 1888 indicates that he never submitted it.[57]

Thus *La Damoiselle élue* fits seamlessly within a series of radical works in which the composer consciously strove to throw off the shackles of academic tradition, even though the Rome *envois* were still subject to official scrutiny. Indeed, he evidently experimented in these submission pieces just as much as he did in *Diane au bois*, in which he avowedly attempted to "invent new forms."[58] Debussy brought the full force of his inventive powers to bear in his luminescent setting of Rossetti's poem: spurred undoubtedly, in part, by the unusual nature of the text, which is in prose and contains no true dialogue, he entirely eschewed traditional musical-dramatic construction in creating the cantata. There are no set pieces, and very little in the way of symmetrical melody; rather, the music is molded closely to the shape and meaning of the text, spinning out in a freely evolving musical shape that borders on formlessness. Evanescent, floating chromatic harmonies, evocatively veiled tonalities, Wagner-inspired endless melodies, and true Wagnerian leitmotives permeate the composition to a degree not previously encountered in any dramatic composition of Debussy, including *Diane au bois*. In the music of *La Damoiselle élue*, indeed, may be discerned the work of a profoundly original composer standing at the threshold of stylistic mastery.

The Libretto

Rossetti's exquisite poem, which has justly been called "one of the most beautifully versified poems in the [English] language,"[59] was inspired by Poe's *The Raven*, which depicts the torment of a male lover left alone on earth. Rossetti wished to portray the other side of the same theme, the sadness of the deceased maiden in heaven. Although Sarrazin's prose translation ably reproduces Rossetti's voluptuous imagery, the suppleness of the original poem's varied meter, as well as the rhyme scheme linking the even-numbered lines of the six-line stanzas, could not, of course, be maintained. And the poem's gently undulating flow, featuring many well-placed alliterations and much lovely assonance, could at best be merely approximated. Hence it is a shame that Debussy could not set the original text, given his evidently much keener sensitivity to poetic values and text declamation by the late 1880s.

Unlike the Prix de Rome cantatas, for which the texts were furnished intact in a form ready to be set to music, Debussy had to adapt Rossetti's poem, from which several stanzas had already been omitted in Sarrazin's translation.[60] He excised all remaining parenthetical utterances of the earthly lover in order to keep the focus solely on the heavenly scene, while also dropping some extraneous descriptive stanzas to accommodate the necessary balanced dimensions of a musical setting. In lieu of a plot synopsis or any attempt at poetic analysis, it seems best simply to provide the English version of the poem as cut down and used in French translation by the composer:[61]

1. The blessed damozel leaned out   (Chorus)
    From the gold bar of Heaven;
Her eyes were deeper than the depth
    Of waters stilled at even;
She had three lilies in her hand,
    And the stars in her hair were seven.

2. Her robe, ungirt from clasp to hem,   (Narrator)
    No wrought flowers did adorn,
But a white rose of Mary's gift,
    For service meetly worn;
Her hair that lay along her back
    Was yellow like ripe corn.

3. Around her, lovers, newly met   (Chorus)
    'Mid deathless love's acclaims,
Spoke evermore among themselves
    Their heart-remembered names;
And the souls mounting up to God
    Went by her like thin flames.

4. And still she bowed herself and stooped   (Narrator)
    Out of the circling charm;

Until her bosom must have made
    The bar she leaned on warm,
And the lilies lay as if asleep
    Along her bended arm.

5. The sun was gone now; the curled moon   (Chorus)
    Was like a little feather
Fluttering far down the gulf; and now
    She spoke through the still weather.
Her voice was like the voice the stars
    Had when they sang together.

6. "I wish that he were come to me,   (Damozel)
    For he will come," [she said.]
"Have I not prayed in heaven?—on earth,
    Lord, Lord, has he not pray'd?
Are not two prayers a perfect strength?
    And shall I feel afraid?

7. "When round his head the aureole clings,
    And he is clothed in white,
I'll take his hand and go with him
    To the deep wells of light;
As unto a stream we will step down,
    And bathe there in God's sight.

8. "We two will lie i' the shadow of
    That living mystic tree
Within whose secret growth the Dove
    Is sometimes felt to be,
While every leaf that His plumes touch
    Saith His Name audibly.

9. "We two," [she said,] "will seek the groves
    Where the lady Mary is,
With her five handmaidens, whose names
    Are five sweet symphonies,
Cecily, Gertrude, Magdalen,
    Margaret and Rosalys.

10. "He shall fear, haply, and be dumb:
    Then will I lay my cheek

To his, and tell about our love,
    Not once abashed or weak:
And the dear Mother will approve
    My pride, and let me speak.

11. "Herself shall bring us, hand in hand,
        To Him round whom all souls
    Kneel, the clear-ranged unnumbered heads
        Bowed with their aureoles:
    And angels meeting us shall sing
        To their citherns and citoles.

12. "There will I ask of Christ the Lord
        This much for him and me:—
    Only to live as once on earth
        With Love,—only to be,
    As then awhile, forever now
        Together, I and he."

13. She gazed and listened and then said,   (Chorus)
        Less sad of speech than mild,—
    "All this is when he comes." She ceased.   (Damozel, Chorus)
        The light thrilled towards her, fill'd
    With angels in strong level flight.
        Her eyes prayed, and she smil'd.

14. [(I saw her smile.)] But soon their path   (Chorus)
        Was vague in distant spheres:
    And then she cast her arms along   (Narrator)
        The golden barriers,
    And laid her face between her hands,
        And wept. [(I heard her tears.)]

Musical-Dramatic Construction

Set entirely for female voices, including a soprano soloist (the Damozel), a contralto narrator, and a female chorus, Debussy's cantata features a deft interplay of vocal performing forces. The soprano, of course, sings the long monologue of the Damozel, enclosed within quotation marks in the poem, and the narrator and chorus sing the descriptive text more or less in alternating stanzas, as indicated in the English original provided above.

Debussy must have welcomed the challenge of rendering prose in music: with its irregular line lengths and the lack of poetic meter, such a text invited a novel sort of musical setting. It did not lend itself to traditional strophic or refrain forms, or any kind of periodic melodies unfolding in an orderly manner within well-defined set pieces. Indeed, Debussy by this time was ready to discard structural conventions altogether and allow the shape and meaning of the poetry to determine the musical form and substance; or put another way, to render the drama as closely as possible in the music, leaving aside all set forms of traditional operatic practice. If any precedent for the style of *La Damoiselle élue* exists in the Prix de Rome cantatas, it would lie in such arioso numbers as Daniel's aria in *Daniel* (see again Example 4) or Narbal's invocation in *Le Gladiateur* (see again Example 8). Even then, the fluidity of Debussy's musical-poetic rendering in *La Damoiselle élue* transcends anything encountered in the Prix de Rome cantatas by a wide margin. A self-confessed Wagner enthusiast by the late 1880s, Debussy may well have consciously imitated Wagner's conception of endless melody in composing the cantata. He certainly adopted the Wagnerian system of leitmotivic construction to a degree unprecedented in his oeuvre until then: with 38.9 recurring themes per 100 measures of music, *La Damoiselle élue* exhibits a far higher density of recurring themes than any of the Prix de Rome cantatas. Perhaps surprisingly, its leitmotivic density is also more than twice that of *Diane au bois*, which features 16.2 recurring themes per 100 measures.

The recurring themes in *La Damoiselle élue* are shown in Example 17. All of them should be regarded as true leitmotives, since without set pieces, the more traditional conception of the reminiscence theme, originally exposed within a full-length number and brought back in more fragmentary form later, is irrelevant. Nevertheless, two of these thematic elements exist as full-blown themes from which one or more separate motives are extracted and worked at various points of the composition. These recurring themes musically embody the various interwoven images and themes of Rossetti's poem marvelously. Each is imbued with specific textual and dramatic associations, by appearing, at least accompanimentally, at appropriate points in the text. Where the melodic strand of a particular motive is sung and thus emphasized, its poetic association is ineluctably fixed.

The timeless, pictorial Circling Charm leitmotive (Example 17a) evokes the ethereal swirl of the heavens by, appropriately enough, tracing a musical circle. Appearing initially at the opening of the cantata, where it serves beautifully to set the scene, the poetic association of this ubiquitous leitmotive is established at mm. 96–97, where the narrator sings its melodic strand to the words, "En dehors du charme encer-clant" ("Out of the circling charm"). Its timeless effect is generated through the temporally static property of the reiteration on which it is based; the statically unfolding reiterated formation impedes the flow of musical time, producing a sense of an eternal moment frozen in time.

The Hope theme (Example 17b), the head of which is often extracted and used as a leitmotive through the course of the cantata, has a dis-tinctly Wagnerian physiognomy, calling to mind, perhaps, the prelude to *Parsifal*. Also exposed initially during the prelude at mm. 9–14, its textual association, the Damozel's hope that her prayers will finally be answered, is fixed at mm. 135–39, where the Damozel sings its melodic strand to the line, "Deux prières ne sont-elles pas une force parfaite?" ("Are not two prayers a perfect strength?"). A characteristic descend-ing fifths cycle underlies the harmonization of part of this theme.

The Blessed Damozel theme (Example 17c) is another perfect exem-plar of the phrase massenétique, lending further credence to the notion of a substantive and genuine early influence from Massenet's operatic style on Debussy. Two separate motives from this most symmetrical of the cantata's themes are extracted and worked ubiquitously through-out the piece; occasionally they are heavily transmuted and even fused with other motives (such as Wish, as explained presently) to express dramatic nuances. Appearing as the primary theme of the Prelude at mm. 35–42, this theme thus affords essential thematic material for the composition as a whole. Unlike the other motives, the distinctive, expansive melody of the Blessed Damozel theme is never sung intact (although its head motive is sung several times in various contexts), but its textual association is made obvious by its primacy of place.

The Wish motive (Example 17d) musically embodies the work's central theme, the Damozel's fervent wish to be reunited with her earthly lover. Comprised simply of a half-diminished seventh sonority, the very indistinctness of this most nebulous of the cantata's leitmotives serves an important compositional purpose. Much like the diminished seventh sonority that represents the central dramatic theme of vengeance in *Le Gladiateur*, this half-diminished seventh sound is allowed to permeate the composition in a way that a more definitely constituted leitmotive could not. Indeed, much as Vengeance is fused with other leitmotives in *Le Gladiateur* (most notably Love's Deliverance and Fight), Wish is fused with the Blessed Damozel theme at mm. 123–27, just before the Damozel first sings. This is done simply by stat-ing fragments from the theme in a half-diminished seventh chord context, exactly as Debussy had done previously in *Le Gladiateur*, by stating the head of Love's Deliverance in a diminished seventh chord

Example 17. Recurring Themes in *La Damoiselle élue*

Example 17a. Circling Charm motive

Example 17b. Hope theme and motive

Example 17c. Blessed Damozel theme and motives

Example 17d. Wish motive

Example 17e. Lover motive

Example 17f. Christ's Peace theme

context. Moreover, in both *Le Gladiateur* and *La Damoiselle élue*, the first thing the main character sings is a vocal arpeggiation of the primary leitmotive, thus imbuing that leitmotive with great musical and dramatic significance. At mm. 48–50 in Scene 1 of *Le Gladiateur*, Narbal vocally arpeggiates a diminished seventh chord to the words, "Mort aux Romains ! . . . Tuez jusqu'au dernier !" ("Death to the Romans! . . . Kill them to the last man!"). At mm. 128–30 in *La Damoiselle élue*, the Damozel vocally arpeggiates a half-diminished seventh chord to the words, "Je voudrais qu'il fût déjà près de moi, Car il viendra" ("I wish that he were come to me, For he will come"). Indeed, a similar arpeggio of the same half-diminished seventh chord underpins her last words at mm. 254–55 as she sings, "Tout ceci sera quand il viendra" ("All this is when he comes"), producing an effective sense of compositional rounding. And whereas dominant minor ninth chords (of which the diminished seventh sonority is a subset) occur prominently throughout *Le Gladiateur*, dominant major ninth chords (of which the half-diminished seventh sonority is a subset) occur prominently throughout *La Damoiselle élue*. By such means, the sonorities involved really transcend leitmotivic status, becoming part of the sonorous ethos, as it were, of each cantata. Such a symbolic employment of a particular sonority may well have been inspired by Wagner's use of the so-called Tristan chord in *Tristan und Isolde*, which, like Wish in *La Damoiselle élue*, is a half-diminished seventh sonority associated with longing.

The Lover motive (Example 17e) is perhaps the simplest and least conspicuous of the leitmotives in the work. Its association with the Damozel's earthly lover is clearly established beginning with its first appearance at mm. 148–51, where the Damozel sings its filaments to the words, "Lorsqu'autour de sa tête s'attachera l'auréole" ("When round his head the aureole clings"). The motive pervades the accompaniment of stanzas 7 through 10, appearing prominently at the opening of each of these stanzas in which the Damozel imagines her reunion with her lover.

Finally, the Christ's Peace theme (Example 17f) is particularly salient, even though it occurs only three times. Expressive of the resolution that only Christ himself can grant, this touching, stately theme's central role in the cantata is unmistakable. It underlies the work's climax at mm. 231–34, where the Damozel sings its melody to the climactic lines in which she is to appeal directly to Christ: "Alors, je demanderai au Christ, Notre Seigneur, Cette grande faveur, pour lui et moi" ("There will I ask of Christ the Lord This much for him and me"). The theme is also emphasized by virtue of its prominent placement near the conclusion of the cantata at mm. 290–93, just after the final statement of Wish at mm. 286–88, as the Damozel weeps, and just before the final statement of Circling Charm at m. 294–95. This beautifully wrought conclusion tells a wordless story through leitmotivic associations alone: as we leave the timeless, heavenly scene of her despair, we know that, ultimately, the Damozel's wish can only be fulfilled, she can only find peace, through the intervention of Christ himself.

As in *Le Gladiateur,* a clean timbral-poetic association is asserted in *La Damoiselle élue.* The association with the English horn/oboe sound of the Wish motive, which may be postulated as virtually a direct borrowing of the Tristan chord, also lays bare its Wagnerian pedigree. The plaintive oboe sound is of course closely associated with the Tristan chord in Wagner's great chromatic opera, which, with *Parsifal,* exerted the deepest influence on Debussy of any of Wagner's works. In *La Damoiselle élue,* the English horn or the oboe are heard prominently tracing the motive both at mm. 123–27, just before the Damozel starts to sing, and at the final statement of the motive at mm. 286–88, as the Damozel weeps.

Furthermore, just as the Tristan chord is resolved at the apotheosis of Wagner's score (after Isolde's love-death at the end of the opera, the oboe ascends through the B, upon which it had so often gotten stuck previously, to a resolving D♯, which is held prominently as dramatic and tonal resolution is achieved), Wish is resolved at the climax of Debussy's score. As shown in Example 18, the motive is traced linearly as a G-sharp half-diminished seventh chord and then resolved in the normal tonal way as a leading tone seventh chord progressing to an A major tonic chord, as the Damozel imagines her long-awaited reunion with her earthly lover. Thus a remarkably sophisticated, purely musical resolution embodies the dramatic resolution so fervently desired by the Damozel.

Although no obvious tonal-poetic associations are apparent in the cantata,[62] one aspect of the many tonal areas projected in the work warrants mention. Without exception, all the tonalities in *La Damoiselle élue* are major keys (even the phrygian choral passage beginning at m. 48 resolves in the traditional modal manner to an E major final chord). In this way too, perhaps, Debussy sought to evoke the brilliant lights and scintillating colors of the swirling charm of heaven.

Example 18. Resolution of Wish in *La Damoiselle élue*

Style

Two passages from *La Damoiselle élue*, the Prelude (mm. 1–48) and the recitation of the handmaidens (mm. 183–97), should serve as an adequate sample of Debussy's style at this final stage of his formative period, only a few years before he was to compose several of his greatest works. Both extracts well illustrate the highly variegated nature of Debussy's experimental tonal and harmonic idiom as he strove to capture musically every shade of meaning and emotional nuance of Rossetti's voluptuous poem.

The Prelude to *La Damoiselle élue* is provided in texturally simplified form in Example 19. The striking resemblance of this 48-measure prelude, in both length and design, to both the 48-measure prelude to *Le Gladiateur* and the 41-measure prelude to *L'Enfant prodigue*, unequivocally establishes the direct lineage of Debussy's Rome *envoi* oratorio from the Prix de Rome cantatas. Like the preludes to the earlier Prix de Rome cantatas, the prelude to *La Damoiselle élue* serves to establish the mood of the work overall, while also exposing primary thematic materials, to which dramatic significance is to accrue as the body of the piece unfolds. The *La Damoiselle élue* prelude, however, never could have survived the scrutiny of the stodgy Rome prize competition judges. Its heavy doses of nonsyntactical harmony, projecting the controlling tonal framework in an extraordinarily subtle way, give this prelude a degree of tonal and harmonic sophistication beyond anything encountered in the Prix de Rome cantatas.

The opening passage at mm. 1–8, comprising two fluidly evolving statements of Circling Charm, is as supremely evocative as it is tonally veiled. The static initial unfolding of Circling Charm at mm. 1–2 is underpinned by starkly presented partial triadic planing that subtly implies the overall tonality of the cantata, C major. This is accomplished in a totally nonsyntactical way through diatonic saturation. But this weakest of tonal implications is immediately obscured by the sudden turn to an incipiently pentatonic enriched sonority built on the eminently nontonal subtonic degree, B♭. This harmony moves cadentially to project the E-flat major tonal area fleetingly at mm. 3–4. The ensuing restatement of Circling Charm at mm. 5–6 implies the key of A-flat major, again through diatonic saturation. The motive freely evolves as a lovely, arabesquelike filament is added in the horn in m. 6; when this new thread continues on forgetfully to G♭3 on beat 4, the fugitive sense of A-flat major is thwarted through subtonic nullification. Another surprise ensues, as G♭ is enharmonically reinterpreted as F♯ over another luxuriant incipient pentatonic chord built on B. As in the earlier, parallel gesture at mm. 3–4, this chord moves cadentially to project yet another distant key area, E major. Altogether the floating, almost entirely nonsyntactical harmonies of this mystical opening segment of the Prelude serve more to hide the overall tonality of C major than to project it, in so doing foreshadowing the evocative openings of both *Prélude à l'après-midi d'un faune* and *Pelléas et Mélisande*. In this exquisite passage, Debussy has clearly begun to find his style.

Following a discernibly Wagnerian presentation of the Hope theme at mm. 9–14, the development of the Hope motive at mm. 15–28, and the marvelously depictive statement of Circling Charm at mm. 29–32, the

Debussyan aspects of which are indicated in the analysis, the emphatic half cadence at mm. 33–34, involving an extended dominant ninth chord, marks a strong point of tonal arrival at C major. This sets off the presentation of the primary theme of the Prelude, the Blessed Damozel theme, in precisely the same way that the strikingly similar half cadence in the *L'Enfant prodigue* prelude (compare Example 13, mm. 17–18) sets off the initial presentation of the Motherly Love theme. Here, though, the effect is rendered all the more magical by the unpredictable approach to the half cadence through a thoroughly nonsyntactical B-flat major harmony that disrupts what had become a syntactical progression in C major beginning at m. 22, again through Debussy's standard technique of subtonic nullification. Upon its progression to what is immediately heard as a strong dominant function at m. 33, the B-flat chord is retroactively explained as an upper-third decoration of dominant harmony.

The following presentation of the Blessed Damozel theme at mm. 35–42 is, in its periodicity, almost out of place in such a subtly nuanced prelude. Firmly projecting C major and purely diatonic, it is, however, not entirely syntactical. Focusing on the weak harmonic mediant level, consisting entirely of root position chords, and underpinned by a series of organum-like parallel fifths in the bass, this passage suggests modality, yet within an overarching tonal context. The resulting neo-modality is similar to usages scattered throughout both *Daniel* and *L'Enfant prodigue*. The harmonization of the Christ's Peace theme at mm. 231–34 is similarly neo-modal, and a true phrygian choral passage also occurs later in the cantata at mm. 49–57. Hence Debussy employs such neo-modal and modal harmonizations as special effects to evoke the quasi-religious nature of the poetic subject. Similar usages are found occasionally in *Pelléas et Mélisande* and other mature compositions, where they similarly serve typically to evoke either religious sentiments or antiquity.

The close of the prelude at mm. 43–48 also involves two favorite Debussyan devices, the subtonic nullification at m. 43 and the nonsyntactical bichordal oscillation at mm. 43–46. The concluding cadence serves a transitional function: standing in temporarily as a plagal cadence in C major, the final resting point on E octaves pivots immediately to E phrygian for the ensuing true modal choral passage alluded to above.

The recitation of the handmaidens at mm. 183–97—perhaps the most acclaimed passage in Rossetti's poem, for one of them, Rosalys, has both roses and lilies hidden in her name—is provided in Example 20, again in texturally simplified form. The scintillating harmonies of this passage well illustrate the considerable extent to which Debussy was willing to experiment harmonically in order to evoke his subject musically.

Not quite representative of Debussy's mature harmonic style, the passage is filled with boldly coloristic harmonies and fluid tonal shifts. As stanza 9 of the Damozel's monologue begins at m. 183, the tonality is firmly ensconced in A major. The essentially syntactical harmonies,

Example 19. Prelude from *La Damoiselle élue* (mm. 1–48, texturally simplified)

Example 19 continued

Example 19 continued

Example 19 continued

Example 19 continued

underpinned by the parallel fifths of the unfolding Lover motive, dissolve into nonsyntactical harmonies beginning at m. 187, at the start of the recitation proper. Just as quickly, these harmonies coalesce into G major, featuring the major submediant harmony at m. 189 directly preceding the minor subdominant harmony at m. 190. After a functional cadence at mm. 190–91, the recitation of the handmaidens' names is rendered through an equal-interval succession by major thirds. Starting at G major in m. 192, this equal-interval succession continues through B major at m. 193 to settle upon E-flat major at m. 194, a tonal goal that is confirmed once again through an authentic cadence over very Debussyan parallel fifths in the bass at mm. 196–97. The manner in which these three successive fleeting tonal areas are projected is also characteristic for Debussy. At first the brilliantly dissonant formations might be interpreted as plagal progressions in which the subdominant harmony is enriched by added seconds, but they actually represent yet another variant of Debussy's favorite cadence, the polyfunctional cadence. At m. 192, for instance, the added second, D, is really just the dominant note in G major, projecting ever so slightly the dominant tonal function; in its combination with subdominant harmony, the requisite functional fusion of the polyfunctional cadence is achieved in a remarkably subtle way. Thus Debussy's setting of the ninth stanza of the poem is anything but tonally sedentary: beginning on A major, the setting wanders all the way to E-flat major, a tritone removed.

Example 20. Recitation of Handmaidens from *La Damoiselle élue* (mm. 183–97, texturally simplified)

Example 20 continued

Summary

The accompanying table provides a summary of the Debussyan features found in all four Rome cantatas and *Diane au bois*. It shows that Debussy's style in his Rome *envoi* cantata was decidedly more radical than that in his Prix de Rome competition cantatas and moderately more radical, in most respects, than that in *Diane au bois*. In the crucial realm of nonsyntactical harmony, only *Daniel* and *Diane au bois* compare with *La Damoiselle élue*; in terms of enriched sonorities, only *Diane au bois* does. More important, the tallies of reiterations show that *La Damoiselle élue* is far more reiterative, and thus much more temporally static, than any of the other works. The totals for text repetitions are

Table 1
Debussyan Features in the Rome Cantatas and *Diane au bois*

	Daniel (incomplete; spring 1882): 1535 beats, 484 mm.	*Le Gladiateur* (19 May–13 June 1883): 2169 beats, 629 mm.	*L'Enfant prodigue* (24 May–18 June 1884): 2217 beats, 644 mm.
Enriched Sonorities	20.2%	20.7%	24.4%
Independent Non-Tertian Sonorities	0.00 per 100 beats	0.28 per 100 beats	0.50 per 100 beats
Hexatonicism	0.00 per 100 beats	0.41 per 100 beats	0.27 per 100 beats
Pentatonicism	0.52 per 100 beats	0.18 per 100 beats	0.22 per 100 beats
Reiterations	20.7% of measures reiterative	16.1% of measures reiterative	20.1% of measures reiterative
Text Repetitions	33.1% of words repeated	46.6% of words repeated	23.9% of words repeated
Nonsyntactical Successions	59.4%	31.9%	30.1%
Planed Successions	5.02 per 100 beats	1.43 per 100 beats	1.26 per 100 beats
Parallel Fifths	1.56 per 100 beats	0.37 per 100 beats	1.16 per 100 beats
Subtonic Nullifications	0.98 per 100 beats	1.84 per 100 beats	1.07 per 100 beats

	Scenes from *Diane au bois* (1883–86): 1795 beats, 500 mm.	*La Damoiselle élue* (1887–88): 877 beats, 298 mm.
Enriched Sonorities	51.0%	40.8%
Independent Non-Tertian Sonorities	0.00 per 100 beats	0.00 per 100 beats
Hexatonicism	1.23 per 100 beats	1.82 per 100 beats
Pentatonicism	0.67 per 100 beats	0.80 per 100 beats
Reiterations	39.0% of measures reiterative	51.3% of measures reiterative
Text Repetitions	21.2% of words repeated	0% of words repeated
Nonsyntactical Successions	40.2%	48.8%
Planed Successions	1.95 per 100 beats	1.48 per 100 beats
Parallel Fifths	0.78 per 100 beats	4.33 per 100 beats
Subtonic Nullifications	2.17 per 100 beats	2.62 per 100 beats

equally telling, for while text repetitions are rampant in *Daniel* and especially in *Le Gladiateur*, they are discernibly less pronounced in *L'Enfant prodigue* and *Diane au bois*. That they are altogether absent in *La Damoiselle élue* indicates that by the late 1880s Debussy had finally managed to expunge this artifice from his style altogether.

In the introduction to this essay, three questions were posed for which answers may now be supplied. First, how stylistically constrained are these early scholastic compositions? The Prix de Rome cantatas, at least the competition cantatas, are quite constrained stylistically, although each of them contains at least a few unconventional elements. The evidence suggests that Debussy consciously restrained his progressive Wagnerian inclinations in *L'Enfant prodigue* in order to win the Prix de Rome. In other ways too, Debussy seems to have made progress in reverse in each successive Prix de Rome cantata setting, an apparent stylistic regression that may reasonably be ascribed to his perceived need to compromise stylistically in order to win the competition. That *La Damoiselle élue*, by contrast, is not at all constrained stylistically demonstrates that Debussy had no fear of flaunting vested academic authority when he knew he could get away with it.

Second, when and how obligingly did Debussy submit to Wagner's influence? The presence of true Wagnerian leitmotives in *Daniel*, *Le Gladiateur*, *Diane au bois*, and *La Damoiselle élue*, as well as his use in the two competition cantatas of clear tonal-dramatic associations (another, less obtrusive Wagnerian trait), proves that Debussy submitted totally and willingly to Wagner's influence from the very outset of his activity as a dramatic composer. These discoveries, moreover, support François Lesure's contention that Debussy's immersion in Wagnerian ideals during his stay with Madame Wilson-Pelouze (a Wagner enthusiast who helped found the *Revue wagnérienne*) at Chenonceaux in the summer of 1879 may have led to his decision to become a composer in the first place.[63] Given the great sophistication of Debussy's employment of leitmotives in *La Damoiselle élue*, it is apparent that, as he approached maturity, he had thoroughly mastered the Wagnerian system. It is therefore ironic that Debussy, even though he made ample use of Wagnerian techniques in *Pelléas et Mélisande*, achieved greatness only by turning his back on Wagner in other, more fundamental ways.

Third, what was Debussy's point of departure as a dramatic composer, and how did he start to break the molds of tradition to achieve something new? Given the existence of certain discernible influences from the operatic styles of both Guiraud and Massenet on Debussy's Prix de Rome cantatas, and the presence of the distinctive *phrase massenétique* even in the more personal *La Damoiselle élue*, it seems clear that Debussy's point of departure as a dramatic composer was conditioned to a considerable extent by what he had learned at the Conservatoire, as well as what he had absorbed from the prevailing French operatic idioms of the day. But Debussy quickly started to break the molds of that tradition, prodded, no doubt, by his native sensitivity to poetic and dramatic values. His desire to capture all the nuances of a drama musically, along with his evident interest in finding more natural means to render text vocally, led him eventually to eschew overt tonality, predictable harmony, periodic forms, symmetrical melody, and artificial text repetitions. Indeed, he began sporadically to transcend tradition even in his Prix de Rome cantatas, including *L'Enfant prodigue*. By the time Debussy set to work on *La Damoiselle élue*, he was ready to break free of conventional musical strictures altogether. When carried forward to his Symbolist compositions of the late 1880s and 1890s, particularly *Pelléas et Mélisande*, this same tendency led him inexorably to make striking advances in every musical parameter as he sought to forge purely musical correlates for Symbolist poetic techniques. In so doing, Debussy the dramatic composer—or better, Debussy the *poetic* composer—changed the face of musical composition forever.

NOTES

1. No thoroughgoing analysis is undertaken of either of these works in this study, although *Diane au bois* is tangentially considered for purposes of comparison. Comprehensive analyses of *Diane au bois* may be found in the following two sources: James R. Briscoe, "'To Invent New Forms': Debussy's *Diane au bois*," *Musical Quarterly* 74 (1990): 131–69; and Chapter VII of my dissertation, "The Origins of Debussy's Style" (Ph.D. diss., University of Rochester, 2001). The complete but unorchestrated scenes from *Diane au bois* were performed, in an arrangement by James Briscoe, at the meeting of the American Musicological Society in Cleveland in 1986. The recently revealed early overture for the work, as composed for piano four-hands, has been recorded by Christian Ivaldi and Noël Lee (Arion ARN 268128). *Rodrigue et Chimène*—which Debussy disavowed entirely, effectively deeming it fit for the fireplace—was reconstructed by Richard Langham Smith and orchestrated by Edison Denisov. It has been performed and recorded by the Opéra de Lyon (Erato/Radio France 4509-98508-2).

2. I helped to mount two performances of *Le Gladiateur* on March 1–2, 1997 in Chico, Calif. Overseen by Sylvie Beaudette, musical director, and Gwen Curatilo, Chico State University Opera Workshop director, the production featured Aaron Scheidel, tenor, as Narbal; Tamara Allspaugh, soprano, as Fulvie; and Daniel Elias, baritone, as Métellus. The Chico Symphony Orchestra, conducted by David Colson, provided the accompaniment.

3. *Daniel*, about seven-eighths of which has been preserved in a manuscript reduced score, is held in the Gregor Piatigorsky collection maintained by his daughter, Jephta

Drachman, in Stevenson, Maryland. I am deeply indebted to Mrs. Drachman for allowing me to visit her home to finalize my edition of the piece. I also consulted the microfilm
of the manuscript, held at the Library of Congress in Washington, D.C., as Microfilm
86/20, 244 (item 14). The manuscript full score of *Le Gladiateur* is held at the Bibliothèque
Nationale in Paris as Ms. 969. Photocopies of nine leaves containing fragments from the
manuscript reduced score are held at the Centre de Documentation Claude Debussy in
Paris, in Box 21. The remaining twenty-eight leaves of music from the *particelle*, to which
I have not yet had access, have recently surfaced and were sold at auction in Paris in
April 1999. The manuscript full score of *L'Enfant prodigue* is held at the Bibliothèque
Nationale as Ms. 968; the piano four-hands–vocal score was published by Durand,
Schoenewerk in 1884. The original version of the cantata has been consulted in prepar-
ing this study, not Debussy's 1908 revision. Both the original 1893 Librairie de l'Art
Indépendant piano-vocal score and the revised 1903 Durand full score of *La Damoiselle
élue* served as sources for this essay. Among other recordings, *L'Enfant prodigue* is available on Orfeo C 012821 A, and *La Damoiselle élue* is available on IMP Classics PCD 1037.

4. My article on *Le Gladiateur* focuses primarily on an analytical and stylistic comparison with Paul Vidal's Prix de Rome–winning setting of the same libretto, in order to
assess the extent of Debussy's stylistic compromise for this scholastic competition. See
John R. Clevenger, "Debussy's First 'Masterpiece', *Le Gladiateur*," *Cahiers Debussy* 23
(1999): 3–34. The three Prix de Rome cantatas together are treated, somewhat less com-
prehensively than in the present study, in Chapter IV of my dissertation, "The Origins
of Debussy's Style."

5. Briscoe's dissertation on Debussy's formative works, for instance, contains only
sketchy commentary about *Daniel* and *Le Gladiateur*; he cites only two short passages
from the latter work as examples of Debussy's "grandiose rhythmic style." *L'Enfant
prodigue* is dealt with primarily as a source for short examples, with no thoroughgoing
analytical treatment being undertaken. See James R. Briscoe, "The Compositions of
Claude Debussy's Formative Years (1879–1887)" (Ph.D. diss., University of North
Carolina, 1979).

6. Although Alfred correctly identifies the textual associations of the work's leitmotives, important analytical insights remain to be unearthed; and of course the piece
has yet to be considered in relation to the Prix de Rome cantatas, from which it sprang
in a demonstrably direct line of descent. See Everett Maurice Alfred, "A Study of Selected
Choral Works of Claude Debussy" (Ph.D. diss., Texas Tech University, 1980). Richard
Langham Smith's study of Debussy's Pre-Raphaelite contacts provides useful historical
background; the author also postulates (correctly, in my view) that the pervasive half-
diminished seventh sonority in the work is an unabashed borrowing of Wagner's famous
Tristan chord from *Tristan und Isolde*. But Langham Smith's analysis of the piece is not
comprehensive. See Richard Langham Smith, "Debussy and the Pre-Raphaelites,"
Nineteenth-Century Music 5 (1981): 102–04.

7. Constant Pierre, *Le Conservatoire National de Musique et de Déclamation: documents
historiques et administratifs* (Paris: Imprimerie Nationale, 1900), p. 275.

8. Some confusion encountered in the biographies about the duration of Debussy's
Prix de Rome stipend may have arisen from information supplied in Henri Rebois, *Les
Grands Prix de Rome de musique* (Paris: Firmin-Didot, 1932), p. 31, where the foreign
sojourn is reported to have lasted only three years beginning in 1876, with two years
spent in Italy, followed by a one-year stay elsewhere. But whereas the time abroad may
typically have been three years, the stipend in fact lasted four years. Therefore Debussy
continued to receive his modest stipend through the end of 1888, even though he had
returned to Paris in early 1887. Indeed, Debussy's fourth year of support is mentioned

in Henri Delaborde, "Rapport sur les envois de MM. les pensionnaires de l'Académie de France à Rome en 1889," *Journal officiel* 22 (1890): 1100–1102.

9. Rebois, *Grands Prix de Rome*, p. 35. Albéric Second's parody, reviewed in the 21 June 1868 issue of *Le Ménestrel*, humorously portrays the Prix de Rome winner's predicament, while questioning the rationale behind the Rome sojourn for musicians: "Why was I supported in Italy for two years, at three thousand francs per year? Was it to study under the eyes of an illustrious master there? . . . But the director of the Académie is a painter, not a musician. To form my taste by constantly hearing beautiful music there? But in Rome the theaters are open only four months out of twelve. To inspire me by the performance there of the works of great contemporary composers, interpreted by the great modern singers? But the various Italian opera stars prefer Paris, and disdain the Italian theaters." See Albéric Second, "Misères d'un prix de Rome," *Le Ménestrel* 35 (1867–1868): 236.

10. Albert Lavignac, *Musical Education*, trans. Esther Singleton (New York: Appleton, 1922), p. 243.

11. Ibid., pp. 245–46.

12. At the time, Rome pensioners in music received 4,085 francs per year, over 1,200 francs of which was earmarked for food and music copying expenses. See *Le Ménestrel* 50 (1883–1884): 142.

13. The conditions of these sequestrations are described in my documents section later in this book.

14. Pierre, *Conservatoire National*, p. 277.

15. Louis Laloy, *Claude Debussy* (Paris: Dorbon, 1909), p. 14. That Debussy dedicated the overture of *Diane au bois* to Guiraud lends credence to this oft-quoted account.

16. The first prize for the Prix de la Ville de Paris competition at the time was a hefty 10,000 francs, the second prize 6,000 francs, in contrast to the annual Prix de Rome stipend of less than 3,000 francs once food expenses had been deducted. But Debussy could not meet the deadline, which followed too closely on the heels of the Prix de Rome competition sequestration. As François Lesure notes, Debussy's incomplete lyrical scene, *Hélène*, for soprano, mixed chorus, and orchestra, fits the restrictive and rather unusual specifications for this competition—a piece written for solo voices and chorus with orchestral accompaniment, but neither intended for the theater nor of religious character. See François Lesure, "Achille à la Villa (1885–1887)," *Cahiers Debussy* 12–13 (1988–1989): 15. *Choeur des brises*, for a Marie Vasnier–like agile high soprano and chorus, may meet these criteria as well, although the accompaniment, such as it exists in preliminary form in the preserved sketches held at the Stanford Memorial Library, is for piano.

17. A detailed record of Debussy's experiences in Rome has been provided in François Lesure, *Claude Debussy: biographie critique* (Paris: Klincksieck, 1994), pp. 75–89.

18. Françoise Andrieux, *Gustave Charpentier, lettres inédites à ses parents: la vie quotidienne d'un élève du Conservatoire, 1879–1887* (Paris: Presses Universitaires de France, 1984), pp. 92–93; Julien Tiersot, "Œuvres de première jeunesse de Berlioz et de Debussy," *Le Ménestrel* 95 (1933): 3.

19. The missing segments include perhaps a single leaf of dialogue just before the trio in Scene 3, and perhaps two or three leaves of music comprising the end of the trio and the concluding short dialogue. Certain portions of Balthazar's opening aria that seem incomplete actually represent restatements of the refrain, and hence are easily reconstructed. Other portions of this number lack accompaniment, but the set piece may well have existed in complete form in a separate manuscript of nine leaves that was once held in the Legouix collection but is now lost. See François Lesure, *Catalogue de l'œuvre de Claude Debussy* (Geneva: Minkoff, 1977), p. 31.

20. The libretto is held at the Archives Nationales in Paris, in document AJ[37] 258/2 (unpaginated). It has been published recently in Martine Kaufmann, ed., *Debussy: Textes* (Paris: Radio France, 1999), pp. 148–51.

21. The deceptive nature of the passage is enhanced upon its approximate restatement at mm. 32–35, where false reprises of the opening vocal motive (the ascending perfect fifth) are presented a major third too low, as F#-C# instead of B♭-F. Here Debussy has skillfully dovetailed the end of part A with the beginning of the second refrain.

22. Henri Reber, *Traité d'harmonie*, 4th ed. (Paris: Colombier, n.d.), p. 19.

23. The music of Debussy's professors is treated in Part Two of my dissertation, "The Origins of Debussy's Style."

24. See, for example, the dialogue passages in the love duet of Bois-Baudry and Armande in Guiraud's 1882 opera, *Galante Aventure*, particularly pp. 161 and 174 of the Durand, Schoenewerk piano-vocal score.

25. For instance, an almost identical turn from a sharp key (E major) to a flat key (G-flat major) sets off the beginning of the love duet proper in *Galante Aventure* at p. 170 of the piano-vocal score.

26. Emile Durand, *Traité d'accompagnement au piano* (Paris: Leduc, [1884]), pp. 246–47.

27. See my recent article, "Debussy's First 'Masterpiece'."

28. The performers, who were likely recruited by Guiraud, included the famous Viennese soprano Gabrielle Krauss as Fulvie; the tenor Antoine Muratet, a gifted Conservatoire pupil, as Narbal; and the baritone Alexandre Taskin as Métellus. See Lesure, *Biographie*, p. 61. Taskin had sung the role of Vigile in the Parisian première of Guiraud's *Galante Aventure* at the Opéra-Comique the year before, as indicated on the title page of the piano-vocal score.

29. Quoted in Lesure, *Biographie*, p. 61.

30. *Le Ménestrel* 49 (1882–1883): 246; Charles Darcours, "Notes de musique," *Le Figaro*, 27 June 1883: 6; W. B., "Concours de l'Institut," *L'Art musical* 22 (1883): 201; Ernest Reyer, "Revue musicale," *Journal des débats* (28 October 1883): 2.

31. The libretto is held in the reference section of the library of the Institut de France, in *Académie des Beaux-Arts: les Comptes rendus des séances publiques annuelles* 17 (1880–1886). It has been published recently in Kaufmann, *Textes*, pp. 158–61.

32. *Le Ménestrel* 49 (1882–1883): 231.

33. Ibid., 246.

34. A Latin epigraph placed at the head of Moreau's libretto emphasizes Fulvie's pivotal role in the drama. It reads: "Quid fœmina possit" ("What woman can do").

35. Maurice Emmanuel, *"Pelléas et Mélisande" de Debussy: étude et analyse* (Paris: Mellottée, 1950), pp. 36–37.

36. Martin Cooper, Kenneth Thompson, Stella J. Wright, and David Charlton, "Massenet, Jules (Emile Frédéric)," *The New Grove Dictionary of Music and Musicians*, vol. 11, ed. Stanley Sadie, (London: Macmillan, 1980), p. 801.

37. Arthur B. Wenk, *Claude Debussy and Twentieth-Century Music* (Boston: Twayne, 1983), p. 44.

38. Rodney Milnes, liner notes to the 1995 EMI recording of Massenet's *Hérodiade*, p. 20.

39. Martin Cooper, *French Music from the Death of Berlioz to the Death of Fauré* (London: Oxford University Press, 1951), p. 112.

40. The performers, recruited by Guiraud, included the soprano Rose Caron as Lia, the tenor Ernest Van Dyck as Azaël, and the baritone Alexandre Taskin as Siméon. See Lesure, *Biographie*, pp. 68–69. Taskin had sung the role of Métellus in Debussy's *Le Gladiateur* for the competition the previous year.

41. Quoted in Lesure, *Biographie*, p. 69.

42. Charles Darcours, "Notes de musique: le prix de Rome," *Le Figaro*, 2 July 1884: 6.

43. A. Héler, "Concours de l'Institut," *L'Art musical* 23 (1884): 73–74.

44. The libretto has been published recently in Kaufmann, *Textes*, pp. 162–66.

45. Reber, *Traité*, 93.

46. Germinal form and other facets of Debussy's technical apparatus in the late 1880s and 1890s are treated in the Introduction to my dissertation, "The Origins of Debussy's Style."

47. The claim that Debussy consciously imitated Massenet in composing *L'Enfant prodigue* has often been made but almost never backed up with concrete technical evidence. In this respect, at least, Debussy's Prix de Rome-winning cantata is clearly indebted to Massenet's operatic style.

48. Pierre, *Conservatoire National*, p. 278.

49. Scattered throughout the official reports on the submissions of the Prix de Rome laureates in music during the period of Debussy's stipend are pointed reminders—undoubtedly directed at none other than Debussy—to adhere more closely to the statutory requirements regarding what sorts of compositions should be submitted. Evidently, Debussy never once satisfied these requirements completely.

50. As Lesure points out, Alfred Debussy translated another Rossetti poem into French for publication by the *Revue indépendante* in November 1887, and Debussy is known to have corresponded with his younger brother during his Rome sojourn. So it seems logical to conclude that Alfred may have alerted his elder brother to the fanciful and inspiring poetry of Rossetti—unless it was the other way around. See Lesure, *Biographie*, p. 92.

51. The terms are essentially synonymous, although "oratorio" is usually applied to religious unstaged dramatic works, while "cantata" is usually applied to secular ones. Although it has religious overtones, the text of *La Damoiselle élue* is by no means sacred.

52. Richard Langham Smith, "La Gènese de *La Damoiselle élue*," *Cahiers Debussy* 4–5 (1980–1981): 11. The Pre-Raphaelite technique of using pure colors over a white ground makes their pictures appear stunningly bright; when used in female portraiture, the resulting Pre-Raphaelite image of woman is striking and unmistakable.

53. The project never came to fruition. See Lesure, *Biographie*, p. 167.

54. Henri Delaborde, "Rapport sur les envois de Rome en 1886," *Journal officiel* 18 (1886): 6082.

55. Henri Delaborde, "Rapport sur les envois de Rome en 1887," *Journal officiel* 20 (1888): 977. As is widely accepted by now, if a generic label must be affixed to Debussy's music, it should be musical symbolism, not musical impressionism. He was demonstrably far more deeply influenced by symbolist poetry than by impressionist painting.

56. Henri Delaborde, "Rapport sur les travaux de MM. les pensionnaires de l'Académie de France à Rome, en 1888," *Journal officiel* 21 (1888): 468.

57. Henri Delaborde, "Rapport sur les envois de MM. les pensionnaires de l'Académie de France à Rome, en 1889," *Journal officiel* 22 (1890): 1100–1102.

58. The revealing phrase ("d'inventer de nouvelles formes") comes from a letter Debussy wrote to his mentor, Henri Vasnier (the very man he was in the process of cuckolding), on 19 October 1885. See François Lesure, ed., *Claude Debussy: correspondance, 1884–1918* (Paris: Hermann, 1992), p. 38.

59. Joseph F. Vogel, *Dante Gabriel Rossetti's Versecraft* (Gainesville: University Press of Florida, 1971), p. 91.

60. Debussy's primary source was Gabriel Sarrazin, *Poètes modernes de l'Angleterre* (Paris: Ollendorff, 1885), pp. 263–69.

61. The stanzas are numbered for convenience, and the performing forces in Debussy's setting are shown to the right. Text omitted by Debussy but necessary to appreciate the metric flow of some stanzas is included in square brackets. The French text has been published recently in Kaufmann, *Textes*, pp. 167–68.

62. However, because A major underlies the initial statement of the Hope theme at mm. 9–14 of the Prelude, and because the Wish motive resolves to an A major tonic chord at the climax of the work at m. 244 (see again Example 18), a case could be made for a rather tenuous tonal-dramatic association in this respect. And just as both competition cantatas begin and end at the same tonal level (*Le Gladiateur* beginning in A minor and ending in A major, and *L'Enfant prodigue* beginning and ending in B major), *La Damoiselle élue* begins and ends in C major. Debussy clearly composed each of these works with a primary tonal centricity in mind.

63. Lesure, *Biographie*, p. 40. Debussy must have acquired the use of leitmotives directly from Wagner, not indirectly through Massenet (by way of *Hérodiade*), as Briscoe has claimed, since Debussy almost certainly did not know *Hérodiade* when he composed either *Daniel* or *Le Gladiateur*. See Briscoe, "'To Invent New Forms'," 166.

Debussy, Gautier, and "Les Papillons"

Marie Rolf

Imagine my surprise when, a decade ago, I was contacted by John Shepard, Head of Rare Books and Manuscripts in the Music Division of The New York Public Library for the Performing Arts, asking me to authenticate a recently acquired manuscript. Although the manuscript was signed by "Ach. Debussy," the song was not cited in any catalog or other published list of works by the composer. Imagine my delight when, upon examining the document in New York, I was able to confirm not only that was it a bona fide manuscript by Debussy, but that it was essentially a newly discovered composition as well.

The provenance of Debussy's manuscript is impressive. "Les Papillons" was originally given by the composer's widow, Mme Emma Debussy, to Arturo Toscanini, an active champion of Debussy's works.[1] Toscanini in turn gave the manuscript of "Les Papillons" to the Canadian conductor, Wilfrid Pelletier, in the early 1950s. According to Pelletier, the autograph score was a birthday present, and it remained in his collection until his death in 1982. Toscanini and Pelletier had become friends through their mutual association with the Metropolitan Opera, where the Canadian was a regular conductor from 1929 to 1950.

Pelletier was best known for his profound knowledge of the French and Italian repertoire. He conducted the Canadian première of Debussy's *Pelléas et Mélisande* in 1940, and introduced Canadian audiences to numerous other contemporary French works as well. His support for young musicians was realized in many ways;[2] among these, he served as a judge for The Joy of Singing competition in New York. On February 18, 1962, that year's winner of the competition, Billie Lynn Daniel, sang the world première of "Les Papillons," accompanied by pianist Lowell Farr, in Town Hall. Daniel was a graduate of the Juilliard School of Music, where she had studied with Rose Bampton, the dramatic soprano who sang at the Metropolitan Opera from 1932 to 1947 and who had married Wilfrid Pelletier in 1937. It is likely that Pelletier shared the manuscript of "Les Papillons" with his wife and her most gifted pupils. Pelletier wrote a brief note for the program of Billie Lynn Daniel's recital, recounting the provenance of the manuscript and adding that "to my knowledge, this song has never been mentioned by any biographer, nor sung in public." In his review of the recital for *The New York Times* (19 March 1962), Eric Salzman cited Debussy's "charming, graceful setting of a Gautier poem."

Upon Pelletier's death in 1982, the autograph score of "Les Papillons" remained in Rose Bampton's possession. In 1990, she donated it to the Music Division of The New York Public Library for the Performing Arts. A published facsimile of the manuscript, in addition to my transcription and commentary on the song, is forthcoming from The New York Public Library.

Following a brief description of the manuscript, some of the principal issues surrounding this piece—including the question of dating the song, its stylistic features, and the music's relationship to Gautier's text—will be discussed; at the end of this study, the work will be positioned in historical context. Of course, no amount of prose can replace the experience of listening to the song, so I encourage readers to take advantage of any opportunity to hear the piece, including the performance that will surely accompany the launching of The New York Public Library's facsimile publication in the near future.

Debussy's manuscript consists of a single bifolio, 35 cm by 27 cm. Each page contains twenty-four staves and, although there are no watermarks, each folio carries an embossment of "LARD ESNAULT / Paris / [the beginning of the bottom line is obliterated, but presumably it is 25, RUE] FEYDEAU."[3] Black ink is used throughout the manuscript, which consists of a title page, music on the two inner pages of the bifolio (written upside down in relation to the title page), and a final, blank page. Three corrections in lead pencil (not in Debussy's hand) appear on the second page of music: the word *irai* is corrected to *irais*, and two accidentals are added.

In addition to the song's title, the title page bears a charming dedication to Mme Marie-Blanche Vasnier, replete with misspelled name and missing accents: "à Madame Vanier / qui a seule la voix assez legere / pour chanter des melodies ou il est / question de papillons. / Les Papillons. / Pantoum de Th. Gautier. / Empapilloné par Ach. Debussy." (to Madame Vanier / who alone has a voice light enough / to sing songs about butterflies. / The Butterflies. / Pantoum by Th. Gautier. / Set aflutter by Ach. Debussy.) This dedication, followed by a relatively clean musical score, indicates that the manuscript was probably prepared as a presentation copy to Mme Vasnier, Debussy's *inspiratrice*.

The two met in 1880 while Debussy was serving as accompanist for the voice classes of Mme Moreau-Sainti, with whom Mme Vasnier studied. Soon the youthful composer would be spending time in the Vasniers' homes, both in Paris and at Ville d'Avray in the country. Young Achille, as he was known in those days, was completely infatuated with the older, married woman, and she in turn must have been flattered by the attention of the promising composer, who eventually wrote twenty-seven songs for her. The depth of his affection for Mme Vasnier is revealed in a collection of thirteen songs, entitled simply *Chansons*, presented to her before he left Paris for his two-year stay at the Villa Medici in Rome. Now know as the Vasnier Songbook, this manuscript is dedicated "à Madame Vasnier. Ces chansons qui n'ont jamais vécus [sic] que par elle, et qui perdront leur grâce charmeresse—si jamais plus elles ne passent par sa bouche de fée mélodieuse, l'auteur éternellement reconnaissant." (to Madame Vasnier. These songs that lived only through her and that will lose their charming grace if they nevermore issue from her melodious fairy mouth, the eternally grateful author.) Note the similar language, although perhaps more intense, used by the composer in this dedication to Mme Vasnier, penned before his departure for Rome in January 1885. Notice also that he had learned to spell her name correctly by that time!

Although Debussy signed his name as "Ach. Debussy" a second time at the end of "Les Papillons," he did not date this manuscript. Several clues suggest that the piece was probably composed during the fall of 1881. First is Debussy's telltale reference to himself as "Ach. Debussy." Born Achille-Claude in 1862, he was invariably called "Achille" throughout his student days until around 1890, when he adopted the name of "Claude-Achille" along with a change of chirography. It was not until 1893 or 1894 that the composer became known simply as Claude Debussy. Second, Debussy's signatures on the manuscript of "Les Papillons"—specifically, the shape of the *A* and its separation from the *ch*, the squared *D*, and the flamboyant *b* and *y* at the end of his name— closely resemble those on the manuscripts of the song "Triolet à Philis"[4] (dated 12 October 1881) and *Ouverture Diane*[5] (dated 27 November 1881). Finally, two other unpublished songs from 1881—"Rondel chinois" and "Tragédie"[6]—bear dedications that are strikingly similar to that on the manuscript of "Les Papillons." In both of them, Debussy misspells Mme Vasnier's last name, and in both of them, he uses the same grammatical construct, referring to his muse as "la seule" who can sing them or inspire him.[7] The "Rondel chinois" is dedicated "A Madame Vanier [sic] la seule qui peut chanter et faire oublier tout ce que cette musique a d'inchantable et de chinois. Ach. Debussy." (To Madame

Vanier [sic], the only one who can sing and make forgettable all that this music has that is unsingable and Chinese. Ach. Debussy.) And the manuscript of "Tragédie" reads: "A Madame Vanier [sic] la seule muse qui m'ait jamais inspiré quelque chose ressemblant à un sentiment musical (pour ne parler que de celui-là)." (To Madame Vanier [sic], the only muse who has ever inspired in me anything resembling musical feeling [to mention only that one].)

Most helpful in our quest to date "Les Papillons" are the manuscripts of "Rondeau," "Zéphyr," and "Souhait,"[8] composed during Debussy's journey with Mme Nadejda von Meck in fall 1881. In that year, as in the summers of 1880 and 1882, the young Achille was hired by Tchaikovsky's well-known patroness to teach piano to her children and to play piano duets with her. On October 2, 1881, he traveled with Mme von Meck's entourage from Moscow through Vienna, Trieste, and Venice, en route to Rome and Florence, returning to Paris in early December.

The manuscript of "Rondeau," although not dated, was dedicated to Mme von Meck's son, Alexander. Based on a poem by Alfred de Musset, it was composed in the same key as "Les Papillons" (F-sharp major) and bears some stylistic similarities to it. "Zéphyr" and "Souhait," both based on poems by Théodore de Banville, are dated "Rome, November 1881" and "Florence, 1881," respectively. The poetic images of "Zéphyr," composed in E, are very similar to those in "Les Papillons." Banville writes "Si j'étais le Zéphyr ailé, J'irais mourir sur votre bouche" (If I were the winged Zephyr, I would go to die on your mouth) while Gautier's persona asks "S'ils me pouvaient prêter leurs ailes, Dites, savez-vous où j'irais? . . . J'irais à vos lèvres mi-closes, Fleur de mon âme, et j'y mourrais." (If I had their [the butterflies'] wings, do you know where I would go? . . . I would go to your half-closed lips, flower of my soul, and there I would die.) "Souhait" is more adventurous in its harmonic conception. Although it ends in B major, it artfully evades that goal, spending a good deal of its time in F sharp and slipping into B only at the end of the song.[9]

Although "Rondeau" and the bulk of "Souhait" share the same F-sharp tonality as "Les Papillons," and the texts of "Zéphyr" and "Les Papillons" are similar, these features do not, in themselves, prove that "Les Papillons" was composed contemporaneously. When considered in combination with the stylistic issues that will be discussed shortly, however, these observations do present a compelling case for ascribing the date of "Les Papillons" to fall 1881.

Issues such as paper type and handwriting weigh heavily in authenticating and dating a manuscript such as "Les Papillons," but stylistic matters also play an important role in this process. An examination of the text setting, the form of the song, the characteristic figurations given to the piano, and the treatment of the vocal line help to confirm the authenticity of the work, and to place this song in the context of Debussy's oeuvre.

To facilitate our study, let us first review Théophile Gautier's poem (translation is my own).

Les Papillons	Butterflies
Les papillons couleur de neige	Snow-colored butterflies
volent par essaims sur la mer;	fly in swarms over the sea.
Beaux papillons blancs, quand pourrai-je	Beautiful white butterflies, when can I
prendre le bleu chemin de l'air.	take the blue path in the air?
Savez-vous, ô belle des belles,	Do you know, oh most beautiful of all,
Ma bayadère aux yeux de jais,	My bayadere with jet-black eyes,
s'ils me voulaient prêter leurs ailes,	if they gave me their wings,
dites, savez-vous, où j'irais?	tell me, do you know where I would go?
Sans prendre un seul baiser aux roses,	Without taking a single kiss from the roses,
à travers vallons et forêts,	across vales and woodlands,
j'irais à vos lèvres mi-closes;	I would go to your half-closed lips,
Fleur de mon âme, et j'y mourrais.	Flower of my soul, and there I would die.

Gautier's "Les Papillons" first appeared as the translation of a mysterious "indostani" song in chapter 7 of his short novel *Fortunio*, published in 1837.[10] The next year, "Les Papillons" was published in a volume in the collection entitled *La Comédie de la mort et poésies diverses*. It is possible that the first two lines of Gautier's poem were inspired by the first two lines of a "Pantoum malais" by Victor Hugo,[11] published in 1829: "Les papillons jouent à l'entour sur leurs ailes; Ils volent vers la mer près de la chaîne des rochers." (Butterflies flutter around on their wings; They fly toward the sea near the rocky cliffs.)

Understanding the relationship between Debussy's musical form and Gautier's poetic structure provides a context for the song within the composer's oeuvre. Gautier cast "Les Papillons" in three four-line strophes, with each quatrain containing alternating end rhyme (abab cdcd eded). Debussy followed this tripartite division, but he imposed a return of musical material in the final section, resulting in an overall ABA form. Manipulating the text to fit this musical structure was a device commonly used among composers of the time, presumably to unify their works, and Debussy's early songs often rely on this convention.[12] Debussy's mature settings generally adhere more closely to the formal structure of a poem; that is to say, he repeats musical material only if and when the passage returns in the poem. His setting of Baudelaire's "Harmonie du soir" (composed in 1889) epitomizes a completely faithful musical response to the poetic structure. Baudelaire's poem is a pantoum, where the second and fourth lines of each strophe become the first and third lines of the next; each time a poetic line returns, Debussy weaves into the musical fabric the same melody, often linked with its original harmonies and countermelodies.

Gautier calls "Les Papillons" a pantoum as well, but it does not follow the common form of a pantoum favored by Baudelaire and other, younger poets who were writing just before the turn of the century. Rather, Gautier's pantoum harkens back to the older, Malayan genre, which includes not only the quatrain with an alternating end-rhyme scheme but which follows other, more general principles as well.[13] In the Malayan pantoum, the first two lines of a quatrain often evoke an image, typically borrowed from nature, that symbolizes the idea contained within the last two lines. The correspondences between the first two and the last two lines may involve their rhyme schemes, the number of syllables in each line (typically between eight and ten), or even the occasional repetition of consonants; in each of these cases, the first and third lines reflect each other, as do the second and fourth lines. In each quatrain of the octosyllabic "Les Papillons," the first and third lines are always feminine, ending in mute *e*, while lines 2 and 4 are masculine. Some repetition of similar sounds occurs—in the first strophe, the *papillons* of line 1 return in line 3, for example, and in the third strophe, the consonant *f* appears in lines 2 (*forêts*) and 4 (*fleur*)— although this aspect of the pantoum form is not featured by Gautier. In addition, each strophe displays the alternating end-rhyme scheme. Perhaps most important, however, the passive images portrayed in the first two lines of each quatrain (the butterflies, the bayadere, and the landscape of valleys and woodlands) shift to a more active stance—that of flight—in the last two lines of each quatrain.

To summarize briefly, Debussy's musical response to the structure of Gautier's "Les Papillons" was less strict than was his setting of Baudelaire's "Harmonie du soir." Nevertheless, the composer's nascent respect for poetic form is apparent from his careful acknowledgment of Gautier's "Pantoum" both on the title page and at the top of the first page of music, just under the title, in the manuscript of "Les Papillons."

Debussy's approach to prosody in "Les Papillons" is only partially successful. He attempts to reflect the spoken rhythm of Gautier's verse by varying the note lengths of the melody, as for example in the line, "Volent par essaims sur la mer" (Example 1).[14] At other times, however,

Example 1. "Les Papillons," mm. 4–5

key words do not consistently fall on strong metric positions; the placement of the word *lèvres* in the middle of a bar (Example 2) is a case

Example 2. "Les Papillons," m. 24

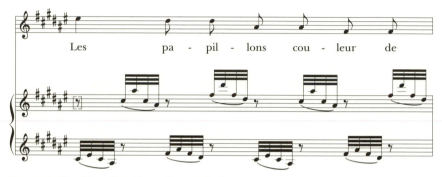

Example 3a. "Les Papillons," mm. 1–2

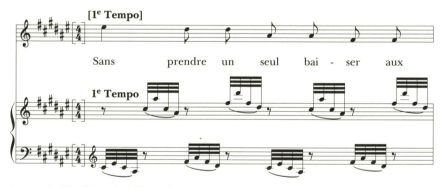

Example 3b. "Les Papillons," m. 20

in point. Unimportant words, such as articles and prepositions, often receive undeserved emphasis in their strong metric placement. "*Les papillons*" in the second measure (Example 3a), or "*Sans* prendre un" in measure 20 (Example 3b), are two examples of such inappropriate emphasis; these secondary words not only receive a metric accent, but they also fall on the highest melodic point of each of these lines, thus stressing them even more. In most cases, awkward constructs such as these result from the composer's conceiving a melodic line first and then fitting the poetic text to it.[15] This melody-based compositional approach, characteristic of many earlier French composers of song (Jules Massenet, for example), does appear in Debussy's early songs, but it is a procedure from which he gradually tried to break away during the 1880s.

Debussy's more mature songs—both series of *Fêtes galantes* (published in 1903 and 1904, respectively) and the *Chansons de Bilitis* (published in 1899), for example—serve the poetry first and foremost. Neither single words nor complete lines of the poem are repeated by the composer in order to accommodate a melodic repetition or sequence. Word accent is carefully respected. The melodies themselves become less melismatic and more syllabic. Their contour is often less distinctive; Debussy will even set entire lines of text on a single pitch, often in a low tessitura. His mature melodies follow speech so closely that they approximate recitative; by the time Debussy began composing his opera *Pelléas et Mélisande* in 1893, this recitative-like style was part and parcel of his compositional technique.

Three aspects of "Les Papillons" anticipate Debussy's mature approach to prosody. In this song, the composer repeats no portion of the text, unlike many of the other songs he composed in the early 1880s. For the most part, Gautier's poem is set syllabically, that is, with one note of music for each syllable of text. In addition, Debussy employs recitative for exclamatory passages or for lines whose importance he wishes to underscore. The recitative-like setting of Gautier's second stanza, beginning with "Savez-vous" in measure 10 and continuing through the "Dites" in measure 16 to "Savez-vous où j'irais?" (Example 4), features shorter melodic gestures, punctuated by frequent rests in the voice, and a reduced texture in the piano, ending with simple block chords. At the end of the song, on the words "fleur de mon âme, et j'y mourrais," the piano drops out altogether, leaving the singer virtually unaccompanied. The freer rhythm, indicated by a fermata on the word *âme*, followed by a slower tempo for the last measure, carries dramatic impact, reflecting the intensity of the text.

Such recitative-like passages are found in many of the other songs from 1881 already mentioned: "Tragédie," "Rondeau," "Zéphyr," and "Souhait"; these passages interrupt the predominant texture of figural patterns in the piano. In both "Zéphyr" and "Souhait," the opening flourishes in the piano prolong a lush sonority (the tonic with an added sixth), setting the stage for the vocal entrance. "Les Papillons" follows this same formula, although the actual figuration is lighter, resembling the flutter of a butterfly's wings.

Example 4. "Les Papillons," mm. 10–18

Debussy himself was a pianist and, consequently, his piano accompaniments are generally quite idiomatic. There is a strong preference for keys like F sharp, a key that lies well in a pianist's hands and which, in addition, probably suited the range and bright timbre of Mme Vasnier's voice. Virtually half of the songs thought to have been composed in 1881, including "Les Baisers," "Tragédie," "Rondeau," "On entend un chant," and "Les Papillons," were conceived in F sharp (or G flat). Two songs Debussy composed in the following year—"Les Roses"[16] and the first version of "Clair de lune"[17]—were also cast in the key of F sharp (G flat) and with similar figural patterns in the piano.

Although chordal arpeggiations often set the atmosphere in Debussy's early songs, the piano may also project melodic material, often doubling the vocal line. As Debussy's contrapuntal skills develop, the melodies he writes for the voice and for the piano gain independence from each other. Passages where the piano doubles the voice one octave lower (such as those in measures 6–7, 10, and 24–25 of "Les Papillons," illustrated in Example 5a–c), become more and more rare in Debussy's later songs.

Like many of the twenty-seven songs that Debussy wrote for Mme Vasnier before 1884, the melody of "Les Papillons" exploits the upper range of her voice. The peak of this song occurs on a high a#2 in measure 15, on the phrase "S'ils me pouvaient [sic] prêter leurs *ai*les"; seconds later, on the word *ro*ses, the singer is required to dip down to a low d#1. An overall range of an octave and a fifth—from d#1 to a#2—is quite demanding, requiring a vocal technique that Mme Vasnier apparently possessed. While the tessitura of "Les Papillons" is not as consistently high as that of several other songs that Debussy wrote for his muse, it is nevertheless clear that he had her vocal abilities in mind while composing this song.

Some parallels exist between Gautier's and Debussy's artistic technique and development. The poet's insistence on strict rhyme, especially the octosyllabic quatrain (which is the predominant scheme used in his mature collection, *Emaux et Camées*), and his devotion to the sonnet were characteristic features of his style. Gautier's early poems are miniatures, precious and fanciful in nature, often focusing on microscopic details of flora and fauna. Similarly, Debussy began his compositional career working on a small scale; the preponderance of his early compositions are songs. Partly because so many of them were inspired by Mme Vasnier and partly because of the poetry Debussy chose, their subject matter invariably deals with love in the context of nature. It is now clear that these text-based works served as a fertile training ground for the composer to cultivate his compositional vocabulary and technique. As both Gautier and Debussy matured, their work evolved from representational, nature-inspired miniatures to larger, abstract froms; compare, for example, Gautier's jewel-like "Les Papillons" (first published in 1837) with his philosophical "L'Art" (published in 1857), and Debussy's purely melodic, naturalistic setting

Example 5a. "Les Papillons," mm. 6–7

Example 5b. "Les Papillons," m. 10

Example 5c. "Les Papillons," mm. 24–25

of Banville's "Nuit d'étoiles" (composed in 1880) with his abstract, syntactical response to Mallarmé's "Soupir" (composed in 1913).

Such parallels may appear superficial, however, in comparison with the profound aesthetic link between the two artists. Limitations of space prevent a detailed discussion of symbolist philosophy in this essay.[18] Suffice it to say that, as one of the first proponents of "l'art pour l'art" (art for art's sake), Gautier prepared the way for the symbolist writers. And, more than any of his contemporaries, Debussy worked at giving symbolist ideals a musical voice. Given their mutual involvement with symbolist values, it is no surprise that Debussy would be attracted to Gautier's work.

When viewed through a stylistic lens that is informed by an understanding of Debussy's other songs, "Les Papillons" emerges as a work that is not only certainly composed by Debussy, but one that fares well, both technically and aesthetically, in the context of his other early songs. Debussy's fascination with the pantoum form of Gautier's poem is evident, although its musical application is not yet fully developed. The song's prosody reveals a composer who is struggling with issues such as word accentuation and appropriate melodic shape, but who is responding respectfully to the poem in a treatment that involves predominantly syllabic setting, no text repetition, and an idiomatic use of recitative. The pianistic figurations in "Les Papillons" create an arpeggiated, chordal backdrop for the voice, as in many of Debussy's other early songs. Even the choice of key—F sharp—is characteristic. The basic texture and the occasional doubling of the voice in the piano indicate, as well, that this song is early. Compared with other songs composed for Mme Vasnier, the tessitura of "Les Papillons" is typical, although not extreme. Most telling is Debussy's attraction to literature that is inherently symbolist in nature; ultimately, this type of poetry served as a catalyst for the development of his unique compositional style.

At least forty-eight composers chose to set Gautier's "Les Papillons" to music.[19] Among them, Ernest Chausson's setting has the most potential bearing on Debussy's. Composed on June 6, 1880, Chausson's "Les Papillons" became the third in a collection of seven songs that were published as his Opus 2, completed in 1882. (Incidentally, the fourth song in this collection, "La dernière feuille," was also based on a poem by Gautier.) It is unlikely that Debussy knew Chausson's setting of "Les Papillons" before he began to work on his own setting, especially since the two composers did not know each other personally until the late 1880s.

Chausson's setting of "Les Papillons" resembles Debussy's in several ways. An ostinato pattern establishes and maintains the atmosphere of a fluttering butterfly throughout Chausson's song; the regular sixteenth-note motion halts only for the recitative-like setting of the final line, "Fleur de mon âme, et j'y mourrais." Chausson's tuneful melody is clearly influenced by Massenet. Unlike Debussy's vocal line, however, Chausson's melody remains within a moderate tessitura, and its overall range is only from d^1 to f^2. Although Chausson's harmonic vocabulary is simpler than Debussy's, his approach to prosody is much more successful. Like Debussy, Chausson sets his song in three sections; but instead of imposing an artificial return to the A section, Chausson pursues a more natural, through-composed treatment of the text.

Debussy eventually set two other poems by Gautier, each quite different in character and written within two years after setting "Les Papillons." "Séguidille" remains unpublished[20] but it, like "Coquetterie posthume" (composed on March 31, 1883 and notated as the sixth entry in the Vasnier Songbook),[21] is vintage Debussy writing for Mme Vasnier. The extraordinary range of "Coquetterie posthume"—from d^1 to c^3—would challenge the technique of any soprano, and the enormous leap from g^1 to $b\flat^2$ on the final words of the song, "quand je mourrai" (when I die), is emotionally arresting (Example 6). In this poem, Gautier merges the themes of love and death, flirtatious beauty and religious piety. Debussy's musical response is typical of many of his early songs, where voice and piano often double each other, where the text is treated as an appendage to a preconceived melody, and where handling of prosody is awkward at best. Debussy casts "Coquetterie posthume," like "Les Papillons," in a large-scale ABA form, but he achieves the ternary structure through a full-scale repetition (a technique he avoided in "Les Papillons") of Gautier's first quatrain, specifically lines 1, 2, 3, 4, and then lines 2 and 1 again. Perhaps the most tantalizing connection between the two songs, however, involves Debussy's use of the pitches f^1—$b\flat^1$—d^2—$c\sharp^2$ for the

Example 6. "Coquetterie posthume"

words "quand je mourrai" at the beginning of the song and at its return for the last A section (see Example 7a); these pitches are exactly the same as those used for the final line of "Les Papillons" on the words, "Fleur de mon âme, et j'y mourrais" (see Example 7b). Two lines about death, penned by Gautier, although from different poems, are given precisely the same pitches by Debussy in his musical settings of them. Aural associations such as these are no mere coincidence; in fact, they abound in Debussy's music.

In summary, there can be no doubt, given the overwhelming physical and musical evidence of the manuscript of "Les Papillons," that this virtually unknown song is Debussy's authentic work. How very fortunate we are to be able to celebrate its appearance during our lifetime.

Example 7a. "Coquetterie posthume," mm. 1–6

Example 7b. "Les Papillons," mm. 26–27

NOTES

1. Toscanini conducted Debussy's *La Mer* at a concert at the Théâtre des Champs-Elysées in Paris on June 17, 1932, held in conjunction with the unveiling of a monument dedicated to Debussy. It is possible that Emma gave the manuscript of "Les Papillons" to the conductor on this occasion, in thanks for his participation in this event; the following year, in December 1933, she would sell many of Debussy's manuscripts at auction.

Toscanini's personal copy of *La Mer*, which he conducted on numerous occasions and recorded as well, is now housed in the Toscanini Collection in the Music Division of The New York Public Library for the Performing Arts. It bears witness to his lively interest in Debussy's score, for it is filled with Toscanini's annotations for conducting and even some suggestions for revised orchestration.

2. Pelletier founded and directed the Metropolitan Opera Auditions of the Air in 1936; he conducted the Children's Concerts of the New York Philharmonic in 1952–1957; and he became the first director of the Conservatoire de musique du Québec à Montréal in 1943, holding that position until 1961.

3. This embossment, discussed on pp. 540–41 in Marie Rolf, "Orchestral Manuscripts of Claude Debussy: 1892–1905" (*The Musical Quarterly* 70/4 [1984]), is present on many of Debussy's manuscripts through the mid-1890s.

4. Debussy's setting of Banville's poem "Triolet à Philis" was published as "Zéphyr."

5. Yves Lado-Bordowsky reproduces these signatures in his excellent article chronicling the changes in Debussy's autograph signature from about 1880 to 1884, and showing how a calligraphic analysis can help date a work; see his "La chronologie des œuvres de jeunesse de Claude Debussy (1879–1884)" in *Cahiers Debussy*, nouvelle série no. 14 (1990): 3–22.

6. I am grateful to John R. Clevenger for sharing his transcription of these two unpublished songs, as well as those of "Les Baisers" and "On entend un chant."

7. By 1884, Debussy had composed about forty-three songs; twenty-seven of these were specifically dedicated to Mme Vasnier. Debussy misspelled her name in at least six of these dedications; in all of his manuscripts penned after January 1882 and that involved Mme Vasnier's name, the spelling is correct. The manuscripts of "Les Papillons," "Rondel chinois," and "Tragédie" bear the only dedication in which he used the identical grammatical construct of "la seule," suggesting that these three songs were composed in close proximity to one another.

8. "Rondeau" and "Zéphyr" were published in 1932 by B. Schotts Söhne in Mainz. The reader may consult a transcription of "Souhait" in James R. Briscoe's edition of *Sept Poèmes de Banville* (Paris: Editions Jobert, 1984).

9. The rather unorthodox manner in which Debussy belatedly slides into B major—from a French augmented-sixth chord with a C♮ in the bass—is a device he will exploit in many later works, vocal and instrumental.

10. *Fortunio* appeared in installments (*feuilletons*) in *Le Figaro*, between 28 May and 24 July 1837, under the title "L'Eldorado." Its exotic subject matter concerns an Indian prince living in Paris. I am grateful to Professor Andrew G. Gann for alerting me to the early publication history of "Les Papillons."

11. Gautier and Hugo met in 1829, the same year in which Hugo's "Pantoum malais" was published; on Gautier's death in 1872, Hugo penned one of the finest of his later poems, "À Théophile Gautier."

12. For example, in "Les Roses," very likely composed just a few months after "Les Papillons," Debussy again superimposed an ABA form on the text. In "Zéphyr," also an

ABA song from 1881, the musical return is apparently motivated by the text; Banville repeats the first two lines at the end of his poem.

13. See Henri Lemaître, ed., *Dictionnaire Bordas de littérature français* (Paris: Bordas, 1994), p. 631.

14. Permission to reproduce from the author's transcription all examples from the manuscript of "Les Papillons" has been kindly granted by the Music Division, The New York Public Library for the Performing Arts, Astor Lenox and Tilden Foundations.

15. In his early songs, Debussy often repeats portions of the text in order to accommodate melodic sequences, a practice that reinforces our notion that he composed these melodies first and then worked with the text. A study of the later songs, especially those that involve a new setting of the same text, reveals a completely different compositional approach, one that assiduously avoids text repetition and that is far more sensitive to matters of prosody; for one such comparative analysis, see pp. 227–33 of Marie Rolf, "Debussy's Settings of Verlaine's 'En Sourdine'," in *Perspectives on Music*, ed. Dave Oliphant and Thomas Zigal (Austin: Humanities Research Center, The University of Texas at Austin, 1985): 205–33.

16. "Les Roses" was published as one of the *Sept Poèmes de Banville*.

17. This song was originally published in the musical supplement of *La Revue musicale* (1 May 1926), but it is more readily available in the *Quatre Chansons de jeunesse* (Paris: Editions Jobert, 1969).

18. General sources on symbolist literature and art are readily available. The first penetrating study of Debussy and the symbolists is Stefan Jarocinski's *Debussy: Impressionisme et symbolisme*, translated from the Polish by Thérèse Douchy (Paris: Editions du Seuil, 1970). François Lesure and Guy Cogeval edited a catalog on *Debussy et il simbolismo* (Rome: Fratelli Palombi Editori, 1984), and Lesure's seminal biography is entitled *Claude Debussy avant Pelléas, ou les années symbolistes* (Paris: Klincksieck, 1992).

19. I am grateful to Professor Andrew G. Gann for bringing this fact to my attention.

20. The current owner of the Piatigorsky collection generously allowed me to study the manuscript of "Séguidille."

21. Six previously unpublished songs from the Vasnier Songbook were edited by Arthur Hoérée and published in 1983 as a collection entitled *Chansons* by Editions Salabert in Paris. Soprano Dawn Upshaw has recorded twelve of the songs from the Vasnier Songbook (including "Coquetterie posthume"), accompanied by James Levine, on a CD entitled *Forgotten Songs* (Sony, SK 67190, 1997).

Bilitis and Tanagra: Afternoons
with Nude Women

DAVID GRAYSON

There is a long tradition of using antique subjects to confer respectability to erotic art, but for his *Chansons de Bilitis*, Pierre Louÿs took the subterfuge even further, claiming that his book of erotic prose poems was actually a translation from the Greek of the writings of a recently discovered poetess of the sixth century B.C. The title-page of the original edition, published in December 1894 but dated 1895, did not even divulge the author's name but rather read *Les Chansons de Bilitis. Traduites du grec pour la première fois par P. L.* ("The Songs of Bilitis. Translated from the Greek for the first time, by P. L.")[1] Louÿs had the Hellenic credentials to venture such a prank, having recently published translations of Meleager and Lucian, *Les Poésies de Méléagre* (1893) and *Scènes de la vie des courtisanes* (1894), respectively. To lend credibility to the hoax, he prefaced the book with a biography of the fictitious author ("Vie de Bilitis"). Born in Pamphylia to a Greek father and a Phoenician mother, Bilitis enjoyed the pastoral life until an unhappy affair left her with a daughter, whom she abandoned when, at age sixteen, she traveled to Mytilene, the capital of Lesbos. There she befriended Sappho and enjoyed a ten-year relationship with a younger woman named Mnasidika. When her jealousy led to a break-up, Bilitis left for Amathus, on Cyprus, where she became a temple courtesan in the service of Aphrodite. Louÿs's preface credited the discovery of Bilitis's songs to an equally fictitious German scholar, a professor of archaeology and philology with the suspicious name G. Heim (as Louÿs later pointed out, "G/Heim=Geheim=Le mystérieux").[2] Heim supposedly unearthed Bilitis's tomb near Amathus and found her sarcophagus adorned with three epitaphs and the walls of her tomb covered with black amphibole plaques inscribed with her poems. A note at the end of the volume cited Heim's imaginary book *Bilitis sämmtliche Lieder, zum ersten Male herausgegeben, und mit einem Wörterbuche versehen* (Leipzig, 1894) as Louÿs's source and described a forthcoming companion volume, in which Heim planned to offer fifty-two plates reproducing Bilitis's sarcophagus, its contents, and the plaques. Louÿs published his "translation" at his own expense (with help from his brother Georges); it was issued by Edmond Bailly's Librairie de l'art indépendant in an edition of five hundred copies.[3] The poems themselves were divided into three groups following a narrative consistent with the three phases of Bilitis's life: "Bucoliques en Pamphylie" (Bucolics in Pamphylia), "Élégies à Mytilène" (Elegies at Mytilene), and "Épigrammes dans l'île de Chypre" (Epigrams in the Isle of Cyprus). A fourth section, "Le tombeau de Bilitis" (The Tomb of Bilitis), contained the three sarcophagus epitaphs. In yet another mischievous gesture, Louÿs listed the titles of one hundred songs in the table of contents but included only ninety-three in the collection; the other seven were marked "non traduite," the implication being that their sexual content prevented their publication. Writing in 1898 to an unidentified "erudite" correspondent, Louÿs explained that naming these untranslated songs was necessary to the organization of the volume and that he planned to add them as soon as the law permitted it.[4] Of course, these poems were never actually written, although Louÿs did produce an enormous body of unpublishable erotic literature.[5]

This first edition bore the enigmatic dedication: "À / ANDRÉ GIDE / M.b.A. / Champel, 11 juillet 1894." Gide later explained that it was on this date at Champel, a spa on the outskirts of Geneva, that he told Louÿs about Meryem bent Ali (M.b.A.), a sixteen-year-old girl who had been his mistress in Biskra, Algeria, the previous winter.[6] It was customary in her tribe, the Oulad Naïl, for girls to earn their dowries through prostitution, and in this capacity Meryem had enabled Gide to enjoy relations with a woman, even if he initially had to fantasize about her brother in order to consummate the act.[7] In response to Gide's enthusiastic reports, Louÿs changed his plans (he was on his way to Bayreuth) and traveled to Constantine and Biskra, where he too became involved with Meryem. According to Gide, she was the inspiration for many of the *Chansons de Bilitis*. Louÿs had begun to write the *Chansons* on March 5, 1894, and his records indicate that he had completed about two-thirds of them by May 23, that is, prior to meeting her. But he also indicated (in a copy of the 1914 edition, which he annotated for his brother) that from the day he first laid eyes on Meryem, he recommenced the *Chansons* entirely with her in mind. He described her there as "a marvel of grace, of delicacy, and of antique poetry."[8]

Writing to Gide on August 10, 1894, he effusively compared her to a Javanese, an American Indian, the Virgin Mary, and most evocative of Bilitis, a Tyrian courtesan bedecked with jewels like those found in antique tombs.[9] In a letter to Debussy dated July 31, 1894, he was less poetic but more explicit, describing her as having "the most depraved morals": "her French is so good that, in a situation that I cannot describe without becoming indecent, she lets loose with this declaration: 'Tarrarraboum!! ça y est' . . . [. . .] It is hot, the light is amazing, and all of the women resemble Bilitis, at least the little girls do . . ."[10] Louÿs returned to Paris in late August. In the manuscript *Notes pour Bilitis*, he indicated that he completed the *Chansons de Bilitis* on September 8 (at 3:25 in the morning), then worked every day correcting them until October 7.[11] Revision continued in the proofs, which he did not return to the printers until mid-November.[12]

Almost immediately following publication, Louÿs began a second series of Bilitis songs, which he wrote in several installments: December 19–23, 1894; January 6–November 30, 1895; July 29–October 31, 1896; and March and October 1897.[13] For the second, expanded edition of the *Chansons* Louÿs interspersed these new songs with the old, many of which were revised or corrected. Louÿs's name now appeared on the title page, but he was still identified merely as the translator: *Les Chansons de Bilitis. Traduites du grec par Pierre Louÿs et ornées d'un portrait de Bilitis dessiné par P.-Albert Laurens d'après le buste polychrome du Musée du Louvre*. The painter Paul-Albert Laurens, who provided the portrait of Bilitis, had accompanied Gide on his 1893–1894 trip to North Africa. It was actually he who "discovered" Meryem bent Ali, employed her services, and then offered to share her with Gide.[14] The second edition of the *Chansons de Bilitis* was issued by the Société du Mercure de France on November 30, 1897 (though with a publication date of 1898), and comprised 146 songs, with a further 12 that were "not translated." (Amusingly, the "untranslated" songs of the second edition were entirely different from those of the first.)

Although the second edition buttressed the connection to Meryem through Laurens's portrait of Bilitis, Louÿs had new muses for some of his new poems, written in March and October 1897. On March 15, 1897, while living in Algiers and recuperating from a bout with pneumonia, Louÿs met Zohra bent Brahim, a young Moor who had been a model for the painter Louis-Édouard Brindeau. The two soon began a passionate relationship. Although illiterate, Zohra spoke perfect French, having been brought up by French nuns. Nevertheless, references to her in his correspondence—"this little savage," "the Barbaresque slave," "this academic monkey child"—reveal racist and colonialist attitudes. In a letter of April 9, Louÿs confessed to his brother that he loved her beyond measure, and on April 15, he wrote to Debussy of their relationship: "We are stuck together like two dogs in the street. . . . You cannot imagine how brown she is, you see; and it's lovely, on white sheets, a woman's body in chocolate."[15] To prove his point, he took a photograph of her (doubtless one of many), lying nude in bed.[16] Zohra accompanied him when he returned to Paris (on May 5, 1897), but life quickly became complicated. In October a second love consumed him—for Marie de Régnier, the sister of his future wife and the current wife of his friend, the poet Henri de Régnier. Louÿs's interest in her actually dated back to 1894 and flared up periodically over the years; their affair lasted four years, until November 1901. She, too, became the subject of numerous nude photos[17] and was presumably the inspiration for "Le Chevelure," No. 31 of the *Chansons de Bilitis* (1898 edition): an annotated copy of the 1914 edition bears the cryptic comment: "Paris, 189[7]. To conceal the name better, I do not give the date. Everything is true, down to the last detail."[18] Louÿs was thus caught between two mistresses as the new edition of the *Chansons* was being prepared for publication. This complicated the matter of the volume's dedication, which in any case needed to be changed: His friendship with Gide had come to an end, and Meryem had been replaced in his affections. He considered "To the girls of our era and to one of them in particular," which would have allowed him to tell both Zohra and Marie that he had had them in mind, but he settled on something more general and visionary: "This little book of antique love is respectfully dedicated to the girls of the society of the future."[19] Louÿs could not have foreseen, but doubtless would have enjoyed the fact that his invention would lend her name to the American lesbian organization, the Daughters of Bilitis, which was founded in San Francisco in 1955.[20]

Some months before the publication of this new edition, on May 9, 1897, Debussy wrote to Louÿs, asking his permission to set one of the *Chansons de Bilitis*. The journal *L'Image* wanted to print a piece of music by him, and Debussy was particularly interested in "La Flûte de Pan," No. 20 in the original edition.[21] Louÿs responded very positively, but suggested instead the unpublished "La Chevelure," the recent Bilitis poem apparently inspired by Marie de Régnier. Clearly this poem held a special, personal meaning for him, and having just returned to Paris, he must already have had her very much on his mind. He thus sent Debussy a manuscript copy of the poem.[22] Debussy decided to set both poems, one for himself and the other for Louÿs. He completed "La Flûte de Pan" on June 22 and "La Chevelure" by July 5, on which date he wrote to Louÿs, offering to play him the two songs.[23] The poet was delighted with the settings, writing to Debussy on July 8: "What you have done with my *Bilitis* [poems] is delightfully good; you cannot imagine the pleasure they give me."[24] Perhaps to please Louÿs, who may have wanted to send Marie an overt message in a covert manner,[25] Debussy submitted "La Chevelure" to *L'Image*, which printed the song under the title "Chanson de Bilitis" in its October 1897 issue, with decorative illustrations by Kees van Dongen and with Louÿs identified as the author, rather than the translator, of the poem. This indiscretion was probably inadvertent. The earliest edition of the *Chansons de Bilitis* to name Louÿs as the author was that published by Librairie Charpentier et Fasquelle in 1900, although the conceit that they were translated from the Greek was perpetuated in this, and even in several subsequent editions. By December 1897, Debussy had decided to set a third Bilitis poem, "Le Tombeau des Naïades," and he completed the song by March 1898.[26] Debussy's *Trois Chansons de Bilitis*, published by Fromont in August 1899, thus comprise three songs whose texts all derive from Part I of the collection (in the second edition they are Nos. 30, 31, and 46, the last being the final poem of the section). In tracing the arc of Bilitis's ill-fated heterosexual love affair—seduction, consummation, and the aftermath of the breakup—they reflect Louÿs's narrative structure. The première, on March 17, 1900, was sung by Blanche Marot, accompanied by the composer, at a concert of the Société nationale de musique at Salle Pleyel.

Debussy's next Bilitis composition, the incidental music for *Les Chansons de Bilitis*, was instigated by Louÿs. Writing to Debussy from Barcelona on October 25, 1900, Louÿs described a forthcoming performance of the *Chansons de Bilitis* at the Salle des Fêtes of the newspaper *Le Journal*, in which selected poems were to be recited and mimed. Fernand Samuel, director of the Théâtre des Variétés, wished to repeat the performance at his theater but wanted music to be incorporated into the production. He recommended the composer Gaston Serpette, many of whose operettas had been performed at the Variétés. Louÿs understandably preferred that Debussy write the music and jokingly described the task as involving no more than "eight pages of violins, silences, and sonorous chords." He urged Debussy to accept: "I ask this of you because, *if I were in your position I would do it*, and I am convinced that you could thus write pages that are 'absolutely your own' while keeping the audience of the Variétés in the state of excitement that it requires. —And besides, old chap, that will spare you from having to worry about the quarter's rent, coming due in January."[27] Louÿs's "hard sell" was no doubt conditioned by his prior unsuccessful attempt, in November 1897, to persuade Debussy to write a ballet or pantomime based on his novel *Aphrodite* for the Olympia music hall. The composer apparently considered it beneath his dignity to entertain music-hall patrons, leading Louÿs to argue that, though there may be a lot of prostitutes in the audience at the Olympia, there were even more in the amphitheater of the Opéra.[28] In the case of Bilitis, however, Debussy accepted Louÿs's offer, even though, as he explained in his reply of October 28, there was little time and he did not even know how many *chansons* were to be included.[29] Shortly thereafter Louÿs returned to Paris, and the two collaborators must have quickly worked out the details. Above all, they apparently decided that Debussy's music should be used for both performances—not only at the Variétés but also at the Salle des Fêtes. Repeated postponements by *Le Journal*, for which Debussy was initially grateful, gave him more time to write the music, which he scored for two flutes, two harps, and celesta.[30] There is a question, however, as to how many *chansons* were included in the single performance that was eventually given on February 7, 1901 at *Le Journal*. In a letter of January 23, 1901 Louÿs told his brother that there were to be eleven; the sole review of the event, which appeared in *Le Journal* under the initials Ed. L. the day after the performance, names ten; and the surviving parts of Debussy's music include twelve. Only three parts are extant: flutes 1 and 2 (in a single part), harp 1, and harp 2.[31] The score and the celesta part are missing, although two celesta cues are present in flute part, representing the first two measures of No. 8 and the first measure of No. 12.

The twelve *chansons* in the surviving parts are listed below, where the numbers in parentheses are those of the 1898 edition of Louÿs's *Chansons de Bilitis*. Seven of them (Nos. 2, 3, 5, 7, 9, 11, and 12) originated in the first edition, and the careful reader might seek to distinguish the Meryem- from the Zohra-inspired *chansons*.

1. Chant pastoral (2)
2. Les Comparaisons (12)
3. Les Contes (18)
4. Chanson (23)
5. La Partie d'osselets (28)
6. Bilitis (38)
7. Le Tombeau sans nom (59)
8. Les Courtisanes égyptiennes (105)
9. L'Eau pure du bassin (112)
10. La Danseuse aux crotales (123)
11. Le Souvenir de Mnasidika (148)
12. La Pluie au matin (154)

The review in *Le Journal* omitted Nos. 4 and 11 from its list of *chansons*, and inverted the order of Nos. 8 and 9. The parts, however, give no indication that Nos. 4 and 11 were skipped, but the latter *chanson* is unique in that all three extant parts are entirely in Debussy's hand rather than that of the copyist who prepared the material. Debussy's letters to Louÿs indicate that the parts were copied only shortly before the performance, probably no sooner than the last week of January.[32] When the copyist laid out the parts, he numbered and titled all twelve *chansons*, and copied the music to the extent that it was finalized. Wherever there was a lacuna (or questions) he left blank space or empty measures, which Debussy later filled in. The composer presumably completed No. 11 so late that he had to fill in all of the parts himself.[33] Louÿs, when writing to his brother on January 23, might have assumed that No. 11 would not be ready in time and therefore thought the performance would include only eleven *chansons*. Perhaps it *wasn't* ready in time or due to its late completion was left off the printed program (assuming there was one). Either scenario would explain its absence from the review in *Le Journal*. On the other hand, the omission of No. 4 from this same review may simply have been an error, perhaps resulting from its "generic" title ("Chanson"). The key point is that, regardless of what was performed, the parts unambiguously call for twelve *chansons*.

The question of order raised by the review is pertinent, however, since the numbering of the *chansons* in two of the three parts (flutes and harp 1, but not harp 2) was altered in a manner consistent with the review, with the order of Nos. 8 and 9 reversed. True, a subsequent effort was made to reinstate the original order, but it was done incompletely, with ambiguous results. Thus, although the original intent is patent, it is certainly possible that Nos. 8 and 9 were reversed for the 1901 performance and even that this reversal represents final intentions. The list of *chansons* reproduced above shows that the original order followed that of Louÿs's poems (as was also true of Debussy's *Trois Chansons de Bilitis*), but *musical* considerations might have prompted a departure from that sequence. There are only two points in the entire work where the music of consecutive *chansons* is contiguous, that is, one directly follows the other without an intervening poetry reading: between Nos. 3 and 4 and between Nos. 9 and 10. In the latter instance, the tonal progression is somewhat jarring, and a more pleasing effect is achieved when No. 10 follows No. 8. Naturally, there are also literary consequences. While the *Trois Chansons de Bilitis* drew all three poems from Part One of Louÿs volume, the *Chansons de Bilitis* incidental music spans all three parts, though not in equal proportions: Nos. 1–6 relate to Bilitis's pastoral life and incipient (hetero-) sexuality (her ill-fated affair, which was the subject of the *Trois Chansons*, is bypassed here), No. 7 pertains to her lesbian relationship, and Nos. 8–12 reflect the courtesan life. This distribution seems to neglect Bilitis's lesbian relationship, even if it is recalled in No. 11. However, in keeping with Louÿs's decision to use an all-female cast, most of the *chansons* deal with interactions between women, and are sexually charged to varying degrees. Louÿs regarded his portrayal of lesbianism as one of the chief novelties of the book. As he explained to his brother in a letter of December 22, 1897: "In particular, I believe that the *second* part will seem very novel. Till now, lesbians were always portrayed as *femmes fatales* (Balzac, Musset, Baudelaire, Rops) or profligate (Zola, Mendès, and in comparison with them, a hundred others of lesser importance). Even Mlle de Maupin, who is not at all diabolical, is still not an ordinary woman. 'This is the first time' (I sound like Landouzy) that *an idyll* has been written on this subject."[34] Louÿs based his portrayal of the relationship between Bilitis and Mnasidika on personal observation, which he described to his brother in a letter of December 12, 1894: "The feeling that Bilitis has for Mnasidika is a deformation, not of love, but of the maternal instinct. *Always* (in these sorts of households) one of the two has toward the other an attitude of boundless *protection* and compassion. The weaker is regarded as a little child who must be preserved and cared for."[35] This viewpoint is explicit in "La Berceuse de Mnasidika" (not selected for musical setting). The most overtly lesbian of the *Chansons de Bilitis* (incidental music) is No. 11, "Le Souvenir de Mnasidika" (The Remembrance of Mnasidika), in which two female dancers finally succumb to their mutual attraction and "consummate their tender dance upon the earth." In comparison, No. 7, "Le Tombeau sans nom" (The Nameless Tomb), the single "lesbian" *chanson*, is relatively chaste: Bilitis and Mnasidika gaze at a tomb holding hands, and Bilitis, trembling, leans against her lover's shoulder. Switching the order of Nos. 8 and 9, as may have been done at the première, alters the way in which the latter may be understood. No. 8, "Les Courtisanes égyptiennes" (The Egyptian courtesans), marks the transition to Bilitis's courtesan phase, and in No. 9, "L'Eau pure du bassin" (Pure Water of the Basin), she stares at her reflection and surveys the signs of vigorous lovemaking that mark her body. Reversing the sequence creates the presumption that it was a female, not a male, lover who had this effect on her.

The *Chansons de Bilitis* were staged with *tableaux vivants*. The format was for the recitation of each poem to be followed by a short piece of music, during which female models held poses suggested by the poem. (This arrangement is analogous to the dramatic tableau or "tableau curtain" in stage dramas, especially melodramas—when the characters froze the action in poses that epitomized the dramatic situation. The device was particularly effective at the ends of acts.)[36] Some of the poems were preceded by a short prelude (Nos. 1, 4, and 10) and some had either one or two short interludes separating sections of the poem (one interlude in No. 4, and two in No. 7). The parts are unambiguous regarding the alternation between text and music, which is for the most part accurately represented in the 1971 Jobert edition of the score.[37] At no point should there be reading *over* the music, in the manner of a melodrama.[38] Some confusion has arisen from the fact that three different locutions precede the music that follows each poem. In No. 1 there is a specific textual cue: "après les mots: 'Il faut chanter un chant pastoral, invoquer Pan, dieu du vent d'été.'" In Nos. 2–4 and 11 it is marked: "après la Récitante" (after the reciter). And in Nos. 5 and 7–10 there is the indication: "pendant le Tableau" (during the *tableau*). All seem to be indicating the same thing—that the music accompanies the *tableau* and begins once the recitation of the poem has ended. The differences in the instructions probably reflect nothing more than different compositional periods. (The chief anomaly, No. 11, is the only *chanson* for which all of the music was copied by Debussy himself.) In Nos. 6 and 12 the music is unlabeled but should surely be performed like all the others. In No. 12 the concluding portion of the music (mm. 13–21) is signaled by a tempo change and a cyclic recollection of No. 1. In the Jobert edition, Arthur Hoérée inserted the poem at this point (between mm. 12 and 13), even though the original parts indicate no break in continuity.[39] It would seem to make more sense to adhere to the pattern established in the other *chansons*: after the recitation of the poem, the *tableau* would be accompanied by the music (mm. 1–12), then at m. 13 the curtain would be lowered, allowing the cyclic return of the music of No. 1 to serve as a purely musical postlude to counterbalance the prelude that opens the work.

The review in *Le Journal* offered a brief but vivid account of the program, which it described as "a private soirée that brought together an élite audience" to hear "the 'Chansons de Bilitis' by our brilliant associate, Pierre Louÿs; and may we say right away that it was one of the most artistic performances that has ever been put on view." The remark acknowledged Louÿs's long and valued association with the newspaper, which had serialized two of his novels, *La Femme et le pantin* (May 19 – June 8, 1898) and *Les Aventures du roi Pausole* (March 20 – May 7, 1900), and had more recently begun to publish a series of articles by him, beginning on November 24, 1900 with "Liberté pour l'amour et mariage." No doubt this literary association was crucial to the paper's decision to sponsor the performance. While the reviewer ranked Louÿs "among the Masters," on account of his novel *Aphrodite*, he identified the composer merely as "M. de Bussy, Prix de Rome." The review is worth quoting at length:

> The "Chansons de Bilitis," accompanied by *tableaux vivants* that were painstakingly arranged by Pierre Louÿs himself and by captivating music by M. de Bussy, received an enthusiastic reception.
>
> Pierre Louÿs is no longer among those who need to be introduced to the literary world. His "Aphrodite" has at once established him as one of the Masters. Those who then read his *chansons* had the pleasure yesterday of savoring them recited, marvelously recited by Mlle Milton. Graceful music, cleverly archaic, composed by M. de Bussy, Prix de Rome, accompanied Mlle Milton's voice and created together with it a soothing rhythm, whose charm added to the antique beauties of the poetry.
>
> The verse, the music, which would have been enough to enchant us, were enhanced by the most artistic *tableaux vivants* that have ever been offered up for our applause. . . .
>
> For the disposition of these diverse tableaux, Mlles Loulii, Marcel, Darcy, Marie Chaves, Lucienne Delbeau, etc., brought to bear the exquisite arrangement of their impeccable figures, and a mighty striving toward the ideal envisioned by the poet. To gaze upon these marvelous academy-figures, sometimes slender, sometimes sturdy, always pure and artistically draped, the spectators could believe themselves transported to the great epochs of pure nudity.[40]

Further details of the visual aspects are contained in Louÿs's correspondence. On January 23 he wrote to his brother about the rehearsals: "This week I am spending every afternoon with nude women. It's nice. It has to do with models who will portray eleven *Chansons de Bilitis* on the stage of *Le Journal*, sometimes with draped veils, sometimes in Kos-type robes, sometimes with nothing at all except their two hands or their stance, three-quarters from behind."[41] After the first rehearsal he wrote to Debussy: "Aside from a blue plush back-cloth, irritating enough, which gives the naked flesh an unfortunate 'Carolus Duran' look, all the rest is praiseworthy: proper costumes, correct props, a heavy gauze full of good intentions, poses without posing (without lifting the fifth finger, if you see what I mean), and finally three out of the five women are good-looking. On the whole, a powerful artistic impression."[42]

Although neither Louÿs nor the reviewer described the actual poses, one can probably get a fairly accurate idea of what the *tableaux* looked like from reading the texts. They begin quite innocently: Bilitis and Sélénis watch their flocks, then engage in various pastoral activities—Sélénis lies in the meadow, hunts grasshoppers, picks flowers, and washes her face in the brook, while Bilitis spins wool. But eroticism is quickly introduced, starting with the second *tableau*: Bilitis and Melanthô, an older friend who has larger breasts, compare their physical attributes by displaying their nude bodies to the other girls. Succeeding *tableaux* continue in the same vein: the girls fondle Bilitis, kiss her cheek, rest their heads on her breasts, and beg her to tell them stories; Bilitis is bedecked with necklaces hanging to her breasts, flowers in her hair, pearls along her legs, and two arms encircling her waist; Bilitis has won at dice and whispers consolation into the ear of her opponent, whose neck she clasps; Bilitis flaunts her nude body; Bilitis grasps Mnasidika's hand and leans on her shoulder as they gaze at a marble stele; Bilitis and Plango visit the Egyptian courtesans and have uneasy exchanges; Bilitis examines the reflection of her (nude?) body in a basin of water; Myrrhinidion, nude, dances for Bilitis; Bilitis watches two women dance, kiss, brush up against one another, and fall to the earth to "consummate their tender dance," reminding Bilitis of her relationship with Mnasidika (a recollection signaled by the return of music from "Le Tombeau sans nom"). The final *chanson*, like the first, eschews eroticism: while the courtesans are entertaining their paramours, Bilitis, sad and alone, writes verses in the sand and imagines immortality through her poetry—after she is gone, those who love will sing her songs. The *Chansons* thus begin and end with appeals to song, but between them a lifetime's experience has intervened, calling for different music. In the first *chanson*, Bilitis spoke of the need to "sing a pastoral song to invoke Pan, god of the summer wind" (the line both begins and ends the *chanson*). In the last, she is writing the songs and only imagines their future performance. When the music of the opening *chanson* is recalled in the postlude to the final one, it does not return in its original form, but is presented explicitly as a recollection, transformed in the light of a new-found wisdom. The melody is no longer carried by the sensuous flutes, but by the more ascetic and incorporeal harps, and the naïve oscillating root-position harmonies give way to more sophisticated chords, directed by a linear bass line that rises knowingly. This remembrance intermingles with residue of the final *chanson* until the music completely evaporates, as both past and present drift into eternity—like the mortal remains of Bilitis herself, the discovery of which Louÿs chronicled in his prefatory "Life of Bilitis": "so soft and so fragile that the moment it was breathed upon, it fell to dust."[43]

Beyond mentioning that the performance was a "private soirée," the review in *Le Journal* accentuated the social nature of the event by devoting nearly half of the column to a listing "at random" of the names of more than two hundred audience members who were gathered in the "stylish Salle des Fêtes." (Altogether, Louÿs had expected an audience of three hundred.[44]) "Privacy" was a concern since the *tableaux* featured so much nudity and erotic contact between women. While the pseudo-classical subject gave Louÿs some latitude in this regard, the fact that it was a private soirée made the work less vulnerable to moral censure than it would have been had it been a public entertainment. But even this could not insulate the *Chansons de Bilitis* from attack. According to Louÿs, Senator René Bérenger, a self-styled guardian of public decency, learned of the impending performance and threatened the editor of *Le Journal* with legal action if it took place. The threat was simply ignored, and Louÿs defiantly pledged that the performance would take place without the slightest change, which, as far as we know, is what happened.[45] Louÿs's stance was both artistic and political, and part of an ongoing crusade. His article, "Plaidoyer pour liberté morale" (Speech in defense of moral liberty), published in the *Mercure de France* in October 1897, challenged the prevailing attitude that nudity and love were scandalous subjects and wondered why nudity created a furor onstage but was glorified in the plastic arts.[46]

It is important to recall, however, that the *Chansons de Bilitis* were conceived for performance, not only at *Le Journal*, but also at the Théâtre des Variétés, a music hall which, along with the Folies-Bergère, Moulin Rouge, Olympia, and Bobino, specialized in *tableaux vivants*, typically based on familiar artworks and featuring nudity.[47] As it turned out, the *Chansons* were not repeated at the Variétés, but the original plan to do so may explain the balance of the program, which resembles a music-hall variety bill and may even have been selected in consultation with the director of the Variétés. Although *Bilitis* was clearly the centerpiece of the evening's entertainment, the review in *Le Journal* briefly described the "acts" that framed it:

> Before the curtain fell, Mlle Loulii reappeared before us as "Tanagra," after the sculpture by Gérôme, during which Mlle Milton recited to us verse by M. Paul Bilhaud, which captivated the listener.
>
> At the beginning of the soirée, we applauded Mlle Arlette Dorgère, marvelously singing an élégie by Massenet, accompanied by that exquisite artist, M. Petitjean; then Mlle Luz Chavita, in the "zest" of her Spanish dances, dances that would have made Saint Anthony himself swear.[48]

Massenet's "Élégie" of 1875, conventional and sentimental, would seem to be an odd complement to the Debussy-Louÿs *Chansons*, but it was very popular in its day and was probably selected for that reason. It was also apparently an effective vehicle for the music-hall singer and actress, Arlette Dorgère, a stunning blonde whose shapely figure and vivacious personality were beautifully captured in colorful posters by Jacques Chéret for the Scala music hall in 1904.[49] According to the caption of a photograph of her that adorns a postcard advertisement for Vin Désiles, a tonic wine, she was associated with the Théâtre des Variétés,[50] and she also performed at the Cigale.[51] Massenet was probably as high-brow as she got. The Spanish dancer, that irresistible blend of exoticism and eroticism, was also a standard music-hall act,[52] and judging from the critic's comments, Señorita Chavita admirably filled the bill with her "spicy" numbers. (Later in the year, on November 22, 1901, she made her debut at the Opéra-Comique, dancing "La Flamenca" in Act 2 of Bizet's *Carmen*.[53])

Jean-Léon Gérôme's *Tanagra* (1890), the subject of the evening's other *tableau vivant*, celebrates the ancient Greek city of Tanagra, where, beginning in 1871, graverobbers and, soon thereafter, archaeologists unearthed thousands of painted terra-cotta figurines. By 1872 many were put on the market, and a number were purchased by the Louvre. These figurines were so popular and so easily copied that forgeries were already common by the middle of the decade.[54] Gérôme's sculpture is of a nude woman, seated on a pile of excavated rock and dirt, with figurines visible in the soil and a pickax leaning against the pile. She sits with her knees nearly touching, the balls of her feet on the ground, and her left hand extended to display or offer the statuette of a hoop dancer, fashioned somewhat in the manner of a Tanagra figurine. Originally, the white marble sculpture was lightly tinted, but most of the color has since faded.[55] It was exhibited at the Salon of 1890, purchased that year by the state, and is currently at the Musée d'Orsay, Paris.[56] The sculpture seems to be not an imitation of the ancient sculptures, but a celebration of the archaeological discovery that brought them to light. The nude woman looks modern, not Tanagran, and her polychrome more like makeup than Tanagra-style decoration. She is clearly not an excavated statuette—she is too large for that, and moreover, she was not *placed* on the dirt pile but rather has seated herself on it. Furthermore, the figurine she holds is not a copy of a Tanagra statuette, but a modern sculpture by Gérôme inspired by the Tanagra finds. Gérôme made this point explicit by sculpting a separate polychromed marble of the *Hoop Dancer* ("La Joueuse de cerceau") the following year.[57] The *real* Tanagra figurines are in the earth at her feet.

What we have, then, is neither an excavated antiquity nor an imitation of one, but a modern nude given an antique aura, much like Bilitis herself. Louÿs was well aware of Tanagra, and in his preface to the *Chansons*, compared a particular courtesan's robes to those of the Tanagra figurines. Was he hoping, through this allusion to Tanagra, to remind his readers of the recent unearthing of authentic antiquities and thereby give credence to his fabricated tale of Prof. Heim's discovery of Bilitis's tomb? Perhaps, but even so, by 1901 the cat was already out of the bag.

Gérôme's interest in Tanagra—and his mystification of antiquity and modernity—extended to three paintings. *Painting Breathes Life into Sculpture* ("Sculpturae vitam insufflat pictura") and *View into a Ceramic Shop in Tanagra* ("Atelier de Tanagra"), both of 1893, are ostensibly historical paintings that depict a woman in a Tanagra ceramic shop painting terra-cotta statuettes, but instead of Tanagra figurines they are multiple copies of Gérôme's own *Hoop Dancer*![58] Moreover, the shop's shelves are stocked with both authentic antiquities and works by Gérôme himself, including *Tanagra*. His 1895 painting *The Artist's Model* ("Le Travail du marbre" or "Le Modèle de l'artiste") is a self-portrait sculpting the life-size *Tanagra* from a live model.[59] Here Gérôme confounds not only antiquity and modernity, but art and life. In the painting, a painted sculpture of the hoop dancer seems to be leaning forward to get a better view of the live, nude model, while the sculptor, in a state of reverie, caresses the thighs of his plaster statue. His thoughts are revealed by the erotic painting on the wall behind him, his own *Pygmalion and Galatea* of 1890, which shows the sculptor Pygmalion kissing his statue of Galatea and in so doing, bringing her to life.[60]

Gérôme's *Tanagra* was a white marble sculpture, tinted to make it appear as lifelike as possible.[61] Its presentation as a *tableau vivant*, as was done at *Le Journal*, fulfilled the sculptor's fantasy by literally bringing the statue to life. In that sense, as well as in others, described above, it was a perfect complement to the *Chansons de Bilitis*. There the held poses represented "arrested motion," more in the manner of a dramatic tableau, while *Tanagra* was the true *tableau vivant*: "stillness brought to life."[62]

According to the review in *Le Journal*, the evening's entertainment ended at 12:30 A.M. Was there more on the program than the four relatively brief "acts" discussed in the review? In a letter to his brother regarding the soirée, written about two weeks before the event, Louÿs mentioned only the *Chansons de Bilitis*, but said of it: "Music by Debussy, lecture by [Georges] Vanor, recitation by Mlles Moreno [Marguerite Moréno?] or de Sivry."[63] Presumably the two actresses were being considered for the role ultimately taken by Mlle Milton, unless there was also recitation of other poetry. But if Georges Vanor gave a lecture about Bilitis, the reviewer did not consider it worthy of mention.

Prior to the performance, Debussy promised to give Louÿs "the slight and hasty manuscript of the music for the *Chansons de Bilitis*."[64] This gesture may explain the disappearance of the score and consequently the absence of a celesta part, assuming Debussy (or somebody else) played this part from the score. In another letter dealing with preparations for the performance, Debussy asked Louÿs to remind the concert organizers at *Le Journal* that they still needed to hire the instrumentalists: two flutes, two harps, and a Mustel celesta.[65] By naming the manufacturer of the celesta, he may have been referring to the rental of the instrument rather than the hiring of its player, but even if he intended to engage a celesta player, he might not have found one. Debussy was not listed in the review as being in the audience, though his wife was (as was Paul Bilhaud—member of the artistic circle known as the Hydropathes—whose poem accompanied *Tanagra*), but this is hardly conclusive evidence that he was playing the celesta.

Even if Debussy gave the score to Louÿs, he must have kept a copy, since he used the music of seven of the *Chansons* (Nos. 1, 4, 7, 8, and 10–12) in his *Six Épigraphes antiques* for piano duet or piano solo, which date from July 1914.[66] It is inconceivable that he reconstructed the music from memory. This self-borrowing, together with the celesta cues in the flute part, constitute the primary evidence toward a reconstruction of the missing celesta part. But the *Épigraphes antiques* also reveal something else about the *Chansons de Bilitis*, having to do with musical continuity. The music for the fourth *Chanson*, titled "Chanson," consists of three segments: a prelude, an interlude, and a closing section for the *tableau*. When Debussy borrowed this music for the opening of his third *Épigraphe antique*, "Pour que la nuit soit propice," he simply arranged the three segments of "Chanson" in succession, inserting only a half bar of rest between the interlude and closing segment. By implication, then, Debussy conceived his incidental music as essentially a continuous and coherent unit that was twice interrupted for the insertion of verse. A similar phenomenon is apparent in "Le Tombeau sans nom," the seventh *Chanson*, where the music of the closing segment consists essentially of a linking together of the two preceding interludes, with elaborated textures, an ostinato bass, and an explicit motor rhythm reinforcing the continuity. Again, the interludes are revealed to be, not isolated fragments, but a continuous music that has been interrupted by verse. It is true that when Debussy borrowed this music in "Pour un tombeau sans nom," his second *Épigraphe antique*, he inserted statements of the ostinato bass between the three borrowed *Bilitis* segments. But doing so was necessary in order to reveal the process through which the separate phrases combined to produce the whole and thereby "explain" that the two interlude segments were actually a continuous music that had been interrupted. Had Debussy simply arranged the three *Bilitis* segments end to end, the result would have been two consecutive statements of the same melody, with the second more elaborately accompanied.

An important analogy may be found in *Syrinx*, the posthumously published unaccompanied flute piece that Debussy composed in November 1913 (under the title, "La Flûte de Pan") as incidental music for a performance of Gabriel Mourey's play *Psyché*.[67] Although Debussy's autograph is lost, a manuscript copy reveals the music's dramatic context.[68] Mourey described the music as representing "the last melody that Pan plays before his death," but that characterization has no bearing on its position in the drama. The manuscript indicates that the music belongs to Act 3, scene 1, in the course of dialogue between an oread (mountain nymph) and a naiad. The oread is trying to allay the naiad's fear of Pan and suddenly indicates that an invisible Pan is about to play again: "Mais voici que Pan de sa flûte recommence à jouer . . ." This is the cue for the first eight measures of *Syrinx*. The naiad is in raptures for eleven lines of verse, but the oread asks her to contain her joy and listen: "Tais-toi, contiens ta joie, écoute." The remainder of *Syrinx* then follows, beginning with measure 9, after which the naiad resumes in her delirium. That, at least, is one way of realizing the textual cues. It is also possible that the naiad's two speeches are simultaneous with the music. Such might be inferred from the stage direction following the naiad's second speech: "Cependant la musique enchanteresse s'est tue. . . ." (In the meantime, the captivating music has died out). On the other hand, the stage direction at the beginning of the scene indicates that "at times" the nymphs "all cease their activities and listen in amazement to the syrinx of the invisible Pan, moved by the melody that escapes from the hollow reeds."[69] This implies that action (and speech) cease whenever Pan plays. Furthermore, Debussy's *Syrinx* is of a complexity that makes it ill-suited to serve as background music for recitation, in contrast to certain parts of *Le Martyre de Saint Sébastien*, where that effect was clearly intended. One thing is certain: In the manuscript score there is an empty bar marked with a fermata between measures 8 and 9, and over that bar, the sentence-long textual cue quoted above. Thus, although we have always heard *Syrinx* as a continuous piece, in its dramatic context it was intended to be performed in two parts, separated by text, whether just a single line or a longer speech. Like the third *Épigraphe antique*, *Syrinx* the concert piece was forged through the melding of "fragments" of incidental music.[70]

The trail of panpipes finally brings us to the *Prélude à l'après-midi d'un faune*, which had its première in December 1894, the same month that saw the publication of Louÿs's *Chansons de Bilitis*. This orchestral work also had its origins in incidental music: a projected performance of the Mallarmé poem with music by Debussy that was announced for February 27, 1891, by Paul Fort's Théâtre d'Art.[71] Debussy would have had less than three months to compose the score since Mallarmé was still working on a new theatrical version of the poem in late November 1890. Just two weeks before the scheduled performance, the poet requested a postponement, but when the program was rescheduled, for March 19 and 20, the "Faune" was replaced by another Mallarmé poem. We do not know what version of the poem Debussy had at his disposal, what music he wrote for the canceled performance, or what relationship these 1890–1891 drafts might have had to the "definitive" score. The autograph of that score is dated 1892 on the title page and September 1894 at the end, apparently delimiting the period of composition and thereby disavowing any connection to the Théâtre d'Art production. But in the spring of 1893, Debussy betrayed the work's theatrical origin when he gave it the provisional title *Prélude, interludes et Paraphrase finale pour 'l'après-midi d'un faune,'* a designation that suggests a manner of performance similar to that of the *Chansons de Bilitis*, but without the recitation and with a concluding paraphrase in lieu of a *tableau vivant*. This evidence and the examples of *Bilitis* and *Syrinx* suggest that the familiar *Prélude à l'après-midi d'un faune* may also have resulted from welding together a series of musical segments that were originally separated by recited verse.[72] It would be an interesting experiment to undo the joins, insert the text, and venture a theatrical performance of the "Faune" as it might have been envisioned in 1891. At the very least, the exercise might enrich our understanding of Debussy's theatrical endeavors and yield insight into his often elusive compositional procedures.

NOTES

1. For details concerning the genesis of the *Chansons de Bilitis* and its various editions, see the critical edition: Pierre Louÿs, *Les Chansons de Bilitis, Pervigilium Mortis: avec divers textes inédits*, ed. Jean-Paul Goujon (Paris: Gallimard, 1990).

2. H[erbert]. P[eter]. Clive, *Pierre Louÿs (1870–1925): A Biography* (Oxford: Clarendon Press, 1978), p. 110.

3. Bailly published a piano-vocal reduction of Debussy's *La Damoiselle élue* in 1893. Earlier, in 1890, Debussy's *Cinq Poèmes de Baudelaire* was available for purchase at his Librairie de l'art indépendant, although the edition itself was subsidized through subscription sales.

4. "Ce sont des pièces qui sont nécessaires à la composition du volume et qui s'ajouteront à lui dès que nous aurons obtenu du legislateur français la liberté morale pour laquelle je fais campagne." Louÿs, *Les Chansons de Bilitis*, ed. Goujon, p. 319.

5. After his death he was found to have produced almost 900 pounds of erotica, and an anthology of these writings, *Pierre Louÿs: L'Œuvre érotique*, ed. Jean-Paul Goujon (Paris: Sortilèges, 1994), contains more than a thousand pages. John Phillips, *Forbidden Fictions: Pornography and Censorship in Twentieth Century French Literature* (London and Sterling, Va.: Pluto Press, 1999), p. 201.

6. Louÿs, *Les Chansons*. p. 258.

7. Jonathan Fryer, *André and Oscar: The Literary Friendship of André Gide and Oscar Wilde* (New York: St. Martin's Press, 1998), p. 74.

8. "Meryem-bent-Ali . . . a été cause que j'ai recommencé entièrement Bilitis d'après elle, à partir du jour où je l'ai vue. . . . Elle était une merveille de grâce, de délicatesse et de poësie antique." Louÿs, *Les Chansons*, pp. 258 and 309–10.

9. Ibid., pp. 258–59; Clive, *Pierre Louÿs*, p. 106.

10. "Nous avons trouvé là-bas une jeune personne de seize ans qui a les moeurs les plus dépravées et qui s'appelle comme un petit oiseau: Meryem-bent-Ali. . . . [N]éanmoins elle sait si bien le français que, dans un moment que je ne puis préciser décemment, elle a laissé exhaler cette constatation: 'Tarrarraboum!! ça y est' . . . [. . .] Il fait chaud, la lumière est épatante, les femmes ressemblent toutes à Bilitis, du moins les petites filles. . ." Louÿs, *Les Chansons*, p. 259.

11. Ibid., p. 251.

12. Clive, *Pierre Louÿs*, p. 106.

13. Louÿs, *Les Chansons* , p. 310.

14. Fryer, *Andre and Oscar,* p. 74.

15. "Nous sommes collés comme deux chiens dans la rue. . . . Et puis, tu ne peux pas imaginer comme elle est brune, vois-tu; et c'est joli, sur les draps blancs, un corps de femme en chocolat." Jean-Paul Goujon, *Pierre Louÿs: Une vie secrète (1870–1925)* (Paris: Seghers/Jean-Jacques Pauvert, 1988), p. 191.

16. One of these photos is reproduced in Robert Fleury, *Pierre Louÿs et Gilbert de Voisins: Une curieuse amitié* (Paris: Editions Tête de Feuilles, 1973), between pp. 224 and 225. Louÿs wrote to his brother on 20 April 1897 that he had taken more than 100 photos of Zohra. Goujon, *Pierre Louÿs*, p. 193.

17. Several of these nude photographs are reproduced in Robert Fleury, *Le Mariage de Pausole* (Paris: Christian Bourgois Éditeur, 1999), between pp. 106 and 107.

18. "Pour mieux taire le nom, je ne dis pas la date. Tout est vrai jusqu'aux moindres détails." "La Chevelure" was one of eight Bilitis songs printed in *Mercure de France*

(August 1897). Four of the "new songs" had appeared earlier, in the December 1895 issue of *Pan*. Louÿs, *Les Chansons*, pp. 248 and 270.

19. "Aux jeunes filles de notre époque et à l'une d'elles en particulier." "Ce petit livre d'amour antique est respectueusement dédié aux jeunes filles de la société future." Goujon, *Pierre Louÿs*, p. 197.

20. Louÿs was certainly aware of his lesbian following in response to the *Chansons de Bilitis*. The lesbian writer Natalie Clifford Barney echoed the dedication of *Bilitis* when she dedicated her *Cinq petits dialogues grecs* (1902) to him: "Dédié à Monsieur Pierre Louÿs par 'une jeune fille de la Société future'." See Pierre Louÿs, Natalie Clifford-Barney, and Renée Vivien, *Correspondances croisées, suivies de deux lettres inédites de Renée Vivien à Natalie Barney et divers documents*, ed. Jean-Paul Goujon (Muizon: A l'Ecart, 1983) opp. p. 54.

21. Henri Borgeaud, ed., *Correspondance de Claude Debussy et Pierre Louÿs (1893–1904)* (Paris: Librairie José Corti, 1945), p. 94. "La Flûte de Pan" is actually Debussy's title. Louÿs titled the poem "La Syrinx" in the first edition and "La Flûte" in the second. Louÿs, *Les Chansons*, p. 269.

22. This version of the poem, whose layout shows that Louÿs originally conceived it in free verse, is reproduced in Louÿs, *Les Chansons*, p. 270.

23. Borgeaud, *Correspondance*, p. 97.

24. "Ce que tu as fait sur mes *Bilitis* est adorablement bien; tu ne peux pas sentir le plaisir que j'en ai." Ibid.

25. During their affair the lovers communicated with one another through "anonymous" messages printed in the "petites annonces" of *L'Écho de Paris*, flagging them with the initials HML, drawn from the first names of Marie and her two sisters, Hélène and Louise de Heredia. Fleury, *Le Mariage*, p. 42.

26. See Debussy's letters to Louÿs of 24 December 1897 and 27 March 1898, in Borgeaud, *Correspondance*, pp. 105 and 109.

27. "Je te demande cela, parce que, *à ta place je le ferais*; et je suis convaincu que tu peux écrire ainsi des pages 'absolument de toi' tout en entretenant le public des Variétés dans l'espèce d'agitation qui lui est nécessaire. — Et puis, ça t'empêcherait de penser au terme de janvier, mon vieux." Ibid., pp. 150–51.

28. Ibid., pp. 100–102.

29. Ibid., p. 152.

30. François Lesure has suggested that Debussy's scoring was inspired in part by that of Chausson's music for a puppet-theater production of Shakespeare's *La Tempête* (in Maurice Bouchor's translation), presented in December 1888 at the Petit Théâtre des Marionettes in the Galerie Vivienne. The five numbers that Chausson extracted for publication as his Op. 18 are scored for flute, violin(s), harp, celesta, and voices. See François Lesure, *Claude Debussy: Biographie critique* (Paris: Klinksieck, 1994), p. 428; and Ralph Scott Grover, *Ernest Chausson: The Man and His Music* (Lewisburg, Penn.: Bucknell University Press, and London: Associated University Presses, 1980), pp. 166–68.

31. Paris, Bibliothèque nationale, Ms. 16280. Léon Vallas acquired the parts from Lilly Debussy and had a score made from them. In this manuscript score, which shares the same call number as the original parts, Pierre Boulez entered the celesta part that he wrote for a concert of the Domaine musical (at that time called the Petit-Marigny concerts) at the Grand-Marigny on April 10, 1954, with recitation by Madeleine Renaud. The program is given in Dominique Jameux, *Pierre Boulez*, trans. Susan Bradshaw (London: Faber and Faber, 1991), p. 72. In 1971 Jobert published a score, with a celesta part by Arthur Hoérée. A critique of the Hoérée and Boulez versions (plus another by Rudolf Escher) is part of a broader discussion of the *Chansons de Bilitis* in Dirk Jacob Hamoen, "The *Chansons de Bilitis*: Fiction, Facts, and a New Face," *Key Notes*, no. 21 (June

1985): 18–24.

32. Borgeaud, *Correspondance,* pp. 157–58.

33. In addition to No. 11, Debussy added some dynamic and tempo markings and made some corrections throughout the parts, but in the second harp part he also entered the music for No. 3, No. 4 (the final section, following the recitation), No. 6 (measures 1–4 and corrections to the first beat of both measures 5 and 6), No. 10, and No. 12 (with the exception of the final four measures).

34. "En particulier, je crois que la *seconde* partie semblera très nouvelle. Jusqu'ici, les lesbiennes étaient toujours représentées comme des femmes fatales, (Balzac, Musset, Baudelaire, Rops) ou vicieuses (Zola, Mendès, et auprès d'eux cent autres moindres). Même Mlle de Maupin, qui n'a rien de satanique, n'est pourtant pas une femme ordinaire. 'C'est la première fois' (je parle comme Landouzy) qu'on écrit *une idylle* sur ce sujet-là." Landouzy was the Louÿs family doctor. Louÿs, *Les Chansons,* p. 317.

35. ". . . le sentiment que Bilitis a pour Mnasidika est une déformation, non pas de l'amour, mais de l'instinct maternel. *Toujours* l'une des deux a pour l'autre (dans ces sortes de ménages) une attitude de *protection* et de pitié infinies. La plus faible est considérée comme un petit enfant qu'il faut préserver et soigner." Louÿs, *Les Chansons,* p. 312.

36. On the relationship between the theatrical tableau and *tableau vivant,* see Martin Meisel, *Realizations: Narrative, Pictorial, and Theatrical Arts in Nineteenth-Century England* (Princeton: Princeton University Press, 1983), pp. 45–49. On *tableaux vivants,* see also Richard D. Altick, *The Shows of London* (Cambridge, Mass., and London: Harvard University Press, 1978), pp. 342–49; and Jack W. McCullough, *Living Pictures on the New York Stage* (Ann Arbor, Mich.: UMI Research Press, 1983).

37. The Jobert edition departs from the manuscript parts in No. 4, in which the interlude should come after the words, "Plaine, où est allée ma maîtresse? —Elle a suivi les bords du fleuve."

38. This pattern of alternating poetry with short musical responses may be seen in Camille Benoît's "Les Bords du Jourdain," as printed in *Revue illustré* 8 (December 1889): 396–99. Here, instead of *tableaux vivants,* illustrations by Ary Renan intermingle with text and piano music (a reduction of the original, which was for string quartet, flute, and solo violin).

39. In the Jobert edition, the "Céder" marking in meas. 12 is editorial.

40. "Dans une soirée privée, qui a reuni une assistance d'élite, hier soir, avait lieu au 'Journal,' dans sa Salle des Fêtes, l'audition des 'Chansons de Bilitis,' de notre brillant collaborator Pierre Louÿs; et disons tout de suite que ce fut un des spectacles les plus artistiques qu'il ait été donné de voir.

"Les 'Chansons de Bilitis,' accompagnées de tableaux vivants dont la mise au point avait été minutieusement surveillée par Pierre Louÿs lui-même, et d'une musique captivante de M. de Bussy, ont obtenu un succès d'enthousiasme.

"Pierre Louÿs n'est plus de ceux qu'on présente au monde littéraire. Son 'Aphrodite' l'a, du premier coup, classé parmi les Maîtres. Ceux qui ont lu ensuite ses chansons ont eu hier l'agrément de les savourer, dites, merveilleusement dites par Mlle Milton. Une musique gracieuse, ingénieusement archaïque, composée par M. de Bussy, prix de Rome, accompagnait la voix de Mlle Milton et formait avec elle un rythme berceur, dont le charme s'ajoutait aux beautés antiques du poème.

"Les vers, la musique, qui eussent suffi pour nous retenir sous le charme, s'augmentaient encore de tableaux vivants les plus artistiques qu'il nous ait jamais été donné d'applaudir. Le sujet était naturellement emprunté aux chansons de Bilitis.

C'étaient le 'Chant Pastoral,' les 'Comparaisons,' les 'Contes,' la 'Partie d'Osselets,' 'Bilitis,' le 'Tombeau sans nom,' l''Eau pure du Bassin,' les 'Courtisanes égyptiennes,' la 'Danseuse aux crotales,' la 'Pluie au matin.'

"Pour la composition de ces divers tableaux, Mlles Loulii, Marcel, Darcy, Marie Chaves, Lucienne Delbeau, etc., ont apporté le précieux appoint de leurs formes impeccables, et un grand effort vers l'idéal rêvé par le poète. A contempler ces merveilleuses académies, tantôt grêles, tantôt puissantes, toujours pures et drapées avec art, les spectateurs purent se croire transportés aux grandes époques de la nudité pure."

41. "Je passe cette semaine toutes mes après-midi avec des femmes nues. C'est du joli. Il s'agit de modèles qui vont représenter onze *Chansons de Bilitis* sur la scène du *Journal*, tantôt avec des voiles drapés, tantôt en robes de kôs, tantôt sans rien du tout que leurs deux mains ou leur position, de 3/4 en arrière." Clive, *Pierre Louÿs*, p. 170; Borgeaud, *Correspondance*, p. 157. The Greek island of Kos (or Cos) was renowned for its sheer purple fabrics.

42. "A part un fond de peluche bleue, assez fâcheux, qui donne aux chairs un aspect tristement Carolus Duran, tout le reste est louable: costumes propres, accessoires exacts, une gaze de fer pleine de bonnes intentions, poses sans pose (sans lever le 5e doigt, tu vois ça) et enfin trois femmes bien sur cinq. Au total une puissante impression d'art." Borgeaud, *Correspondance*, p. 157.

43. ". . . si doux et si fragile qu'au moment où on l'effleura, il se confondit en poussière." Louÿs, *Les Chansons*, p. 37.

44. Borgeaud, *Correspondance*, p. 157.

45. Ibid.

46. Goujon, *Pierre Louÿs*, p. 194.

47. Patrick Waldberg, *Eros in La Belle Epoque*, trans. Helen R. Lane (New York: Grove Press, 1969), pp. 91–92.

48. "Avant le baisser du rideau, Mlle Loulii nous est réapparue en 'Tanagra,' d'après la statue de Gérôme, ce pendant que Mlle Milton nous disait des vers de M. Paul Bilhaud, qui ont captivé l'auditoire.

"Au début de la soirée, nous avons applaudi Mlle Arlette Dorgère, chantant merveilleusement une élégie de Massenet, avec accompagnement du délicat artiste qu'est M. Petitjean; puis Mlle Luz Chavita, dans le piment de ses danses espagnoles, des danses qui feraient se damner saint Antoine lui-même. . . . "

49. Lucy Broido, *The Posters of Jules Chéret* (New York: Dover, 1980), p. 11 and fig. 51a on p. 15. A larger, color reproduction of the poster with the full-length portrait is in François Caradec and Alain Weill, *Le Café-concert* (Paris: Atelier Hachette/Massin, 1980), p. 165.

50. The postcard is reproduced in Peter Leslie, *A Hard Act to Follow: A Music Hall Review* (New York and London: Paddington Press, 1978), p. 154.

51. André Sallée and Philippe Chauveau, *Music-hall et café-concert* (Paris: Bordas, 1985), pp. 138 and 181.

52. Legrand-Chabrier, "Le Music-hall," in *Les Spectacles à travers les âges: théâtre, cirque, music-hall, café-concerts, cabarets artistiques* (Paris: Éditions du Cygne, 1931), pp. 280–81. On "images of race, class, and gender in nineteenth-century France," see Susan McClary, *Georges Bizet: "Carmen"* (Cambridge, Eng.: Cambridge University Press, 1992), pp. 29–43.

53. Stéphane Wolff, *Un demi-siècle d'Opéra-Comique* (Paris: André Bonne, 1953), p. 327.

54. Reynold Higgins, *Tanagra and the Figurines* (Princeton: Princeton University Press, 1986), pp. 163–66.

55. On nineteenth-century polychrome sculpture, see Andreas Blühm, ed., *The Colour of Sculpture: 1840–1910* (Amsterdam: Van Gogh Museum; Zwolle: Waanders Uitgevers, 1996).

56. Gerald M. Ackerman, *The Life and Work of Jean-Léon Gérôme, with a Catalogue Raisonné* (London and New York: Sotheby's Publications, 1986), pp. 136 and 314. The sculpture is S.17 in the *catalogue raisonné* (p. 314) and reproduced on p. 315.

57. Ibid., p. 316. It is S. 21 in the *catalogue raisonné* and reproduced on p. 317.

58. Gérôme himself mass-produced bronzes of the *Hoop Dancer.* Ibid., p. 316.

59. Ibid., pp. 272 and 274. The three paintings are nos. 411, 412, and 419, respectively, in the *catalogue raisonné* and are reproduced on pp. 273 and 275. A color reproduction of *The Artist's Model* is on p. 129.

60. Gérôme depicted this subject in four paintings and one sculpture. Ibid., pp. 268–69 and 318–19. On the fantasy of the statue that comes to life, see Kenneth Gross, *The Dream of the Moving Statue* (Ithaca and London: Cornell University Press, 1992).

61. The relationship of polychromed sculpture to waxworks, ethnographical figures, anatomical models, funeral effigies, death masks, votive sculptures, and *tableaux vivants* is explored in Alison Yarrington, "Under the spell of Madame Tussaud: Aspects of 'high' and 'low' in 19th-century polychromed sculpture," in Blühm, *Colour of Sculpture*, pp. 83–92.

62. This distinction was drawn by Meisel, *Realizations,* p. 47: "Both [the dramatic tableau and the *tableau vivant*] present a readable, picturesque, frozen arrangement of living figures; but the dramatic tableau arrested motion, while the *tableau vivant* brought stillness to life."

63. "Musique de Debussy, conférence de Vanor, récitation par Mlles Moreno ou de Sivry." Borgeaud, *Correspondance,* p. 158.

64. "Le manuscrit mince et rapide de la musique des *Chansons de Bilitis* t'appartient désormais." Ibid., p. 159.

65. Ibid., p. 158.

66. See Robert Orledge, *Debussy and the Theatre* (Cambridge, Eng.: Cambridge University Press, 1982), pp. 248–49, for an account of the musical relationship between the *Chansons de Bilitis* and the *Épigraphes antiques.*

67. For a discussion of this project, see ibid., pp. 253–56. The flutist Marcel Moÿse gave a different account of the work's genesis in *Woodwind Magazine* 2, no. 5 (January 1950): 12.

68. This manuscript copy is published in facsimile: Claude Debussy, *La Flûte de Pan ou Syrinx pour flûte seule (1913),* ed. Anders Ljungar-Chapelon (Stockholm: Autographus Musicus, 1991). The editor's preface includes commentary on the work and its position in the drama, an edition of the music, and the complete text of the scene to which it belongs.

69. "Par moments elles s'arrêtent toutes, émerveillées, écoutant la syrinx de Pan invisible, émues par le chant qui s'échappe des roseaux creux."

70. A further editorial problem pertaining to *Syrinx* is that the short excerpt from the work that Louis Fleury included in his article, "The Flute and its Powers of Expression," *Music and Letters* 3 (1922): 388, is dramatically different from both the manuscript and published versions. Fleury played the flute at the première of *Psyché,* on 1 December 1913, and owned the autograph manuscript.

71. On the genesis of Debussy's *Prélude à l'après-midi d'un faune,* see Jean-Michel Nectoux, *Mallarmé, un clair regard dans les ténèbres: peinture, musique, poésie* (Paris: Adam Biro, 1998), pp. 164–73. The entire program was announced in *L'Echo de Paris* on 30 January 1891, and is given in Stéphane Mallarmé, *Correspondance, L'Écho* vol. 4, bk. 1, ed.

Henri Mondor and Lloyd James Austin (Paris: Gallimard, 1973), 188. The "Faune" was to have been preceded by "Dans les vignes," a sketch by M. Th. Maurer, and *Les Veilleuses*, a play in one act (in prose) by M. Paul Gabillard. It would then have been followed by *La Fille aux mains coupées*, a mystery play in two tableaux (in verse) by M. Pierre Quillard; *Madame la Mort*, a "cerebral" drama in three tableaux (in prose) by Mme Rachilde; and *Prostituée!*, a naturalistic scene in two tableaux by M. de Chirac.

72. This suggestion has been made by others, including Mary Lewis Shaw, *Performance in the Texts of Mallarmé: The Passage from Art to Ritual* (University Park, Penn.: Pennsylvania State University Press, 1993), p. 127. Nectoux, *Mallarmé, un clair*, pp. 171–72, proposed a structural analysis of the Prélude based on this model.

Beyond the Illusions of Realism: Painting and Debussy's Break with Tradition

Leon Botstein

Despite repeated attempts to locate the origins of Claude Debussy's striking originality within the conventional framework of music history, the results have been less than satisfactory. Debussy's debts to Wagner, to Russian composers including Musorgsky, the influence of Javanese and other exotic musical traditions (particularly Spanish), and the early influences of Massenet and even Franck, (as well as that of Schumann and Chopin) have all been scrutinized. But the sources for Debussy's remarkable leap away from tradition, particularly after 1893, remain vague and ill-defined. His originality, clearly acknowledged after the 1894 première of *Prelude à l'apres midi d'un faune,* seems not to connect neatly to a musical past.[1] Not surprisingly, therefore, critics and scholars have sought clues to Debussy's remarkable evolution as a composer elsewhere, particularly in the possible influences exerted by developments in painting and literature. This essay pursues this line of inquiry in search of a speculative and perhaps provocative account of the affinities between the composer's music and innovations in painting in Debussy's lifetime. As Ezra Pound observed on the occasion of the composer's death in 1918, Debussy's "music is like that of no one else . . . it is full of fantastic colour-suggestion, as no other music."[2]

The arguments here are only partly biographical in the narrow methodological sense.[3] The purpose of this foray outside of music history into sources from art history is to suggest, as others have sought to do, that Debussy's project as a composer can be understood by thinking about the painting with which one can legitimately link not only Debussy personally, but his immediate contemporaries. The question is therefore not merely a narrow one of historical linkages. For example, despite the extensive social intercourse between Ernest Chausson and many of the great French painters of the era, there is far less to talk about in terms of the relationship of contemporary painting to the score of *Le Roi Arthus* than there is in the case of *Pelléas*. Chausson's music, in no sense inferior in terms of quality, refinement, dramatic power, and beauty to Debussy's *Pelléas*, emerges audibly from Wagner.[4] The symbolist elements in Chausson's opera, highlighted by Fernand Khnopff's sets for the 1903 première in Brussels, were not so to speak translated by the composer into a radically new musical language.

This is not so for Debussy. As some contemporary observers noted, the newness in Debussy came either from nowhere, or from outside a discourse about music. Why in Debussy's case do the self-referential patterns of music historical explanation fail to suffice? Why does the very distinction between musical and extra-musical influence seem to collapse? There is no shortage of composers who were engaged with the visual arts, but with Debussy one can go well beyond generalizations about the common ground shared by composers and painters in any historical period. At issue are precise aesthetic strategies transposed from painting. Was the way out of the past shown to Debussy by the manner in which traditions and viewer expectations in painting had been challenged successfully by contemporaries? Debussy needs only to have looked closely at developments in modern art for inspiration, which he clearly did.[5]

Among those composers identified as path breaking in terms of early twentieth century modernism, Debussy had the most rapid success with the public. Perhaps Debussy's transformation of painterly notions and procedures permitted him to write music that struck a chord, so to speak, with an audience that had, after some hesitation, embraced a way of seeing impressionism, neo-impressionism, and the symbolist painting in the decades between the first impressionist exhibition of 1874 and the outbreak of World War I. Debussy's music may have invited a way of hearing already prepared by changes in art. Debussy's possible appropriation of the painterly stands in stark contrast to Schoenberg. Although Schoenberg was an accomplished painter himself, he defined his challenges to musical form and structure from within a close critical engagement with the compositional procedures of preceding composers, therefore from within the autopoetic frame of music history.

From the start, Debussy's music was received and understood frequently in terms of painting. But even among Debussy's earliest critics and biographers the conclusions have been contradictory. E. Robert Schmitz felt compelled to debunk the idea that painting played much of a role. Robert Godet, a close friend, asserted that Debussy "never mentioned a word about such things." Yet as Paul Dukas observed,

"Impressionism, Symbolism and poetic realism, were united in one great contest of enthusiasm, curiosity, and intellectual emotion." Debussy could not have been immune, even though according to Dukas "the most powerful influence on Debussy was that of writers, not of composers." For Louis Laloy, both painting and poetry were essential to understanding Debussy.[6]

An important fact is that a striking preponderance of the rhetoric in Debussy's own self-defense and description, particularly in his letters, is visual. His comments on the nature of music return again and again to visual metaphors and analogies appropriated from the contemporary discourse on developments in modern art. Léon Vallas strongly suggested that Debussy harbored aspirations to become a painter, and recent scholarship has confirmed that Debussy's acquaintance with the aesthetics and practices of the painters of his day was acute, whether he mentioned them or not.[7] There is general agreement that Debussy sought to compensate for his lack of formal education. This led him to be interested in the literary—as is evident from his own efforts at poetry—and the visual arts. The one artist Godet was sure Debussy never met but was fascinated by, was Edgar Degas.

Indeed, few assertions about the music of Claude Debussy have remained as commonplace as the notion that his music can be understood as being in some sense impressionist. The widespread idea that Debussy was "a landmark of musical impressionism" infuriated Schmitz.[8] It seemed to detract from a post-World-War-I modernist prejudice that favored an anti-romantic renewal of the pure "art of sounds." Rollo Myers felt compelled to assert "there is in Debussy's music . . . of impressionism very little."[9] The emergence of a "Debussyism" in France, and to a lesser extent in the rest of Europe (after the fame of *Pelléas* spread abroad) was a source of ambivalence for Debussy. More annoying still was the journalistic assessment of his music as comparable in style and character to the paintings of the French impressionists. Debussy was keenly aware that impressionism had been characterized in more than one way after its initial appearance in 1874. Writing to his publisher Jacques Durand in 1908, Debussy chastised those who applied the term "impressionism" to the late paintings of Turner, an artist for whom he had unqualified admiration as the author of "mystery."[10] Nevertheless, his oft repeated sarcastic aside from 1901 referring to impressionism and symbolism as "terms of which kind are to be despised" is rhetorical (reflecting a general distaste for a certain type of pseudo-intellectual writing about music and art), and insufficient as a basis for rejecting painting as a key source for how Debussy shook "off the dust of tradition."[11]

Can the link between impressionism and Debussy be entirely dismissed? One of the most subtle characterizations of the impressionist element in Debussy can be found in Ernest Ansermet's monumental opus on music and human consciousness. Although he grants that there are impressionist tendencies in Debussy's music, particularly early on, and even in the 1894 *Faune*, he maintains that what characterized Debussy was his rapid trajectory from the rejection of naturalism to an incipient neo-classicism more characteristic of the advances of the neo-impressionists and more specifically Cézanne.[12] Ansermet's views correspond to those of Myers, for whom impressionism existed at best as a transition and only in the *Nocturnes,* as the composer followed a path towards classicism. In his last years Debussy began to write "abstract" music without "literary or extra-musical content."[13] Debussy's most recent biographers, however—Edward Lockspeiser, François Lesure, and Roger Nichols—do not dismiss the link between impressionism and Debussy.[14] The shift in Debussy's music marked by *La Mer* (1905) that dismayed Pierre Lalo suggests a closer link to impressionism.[15] Still, these scholars retain a cautionary revisionist point of view directed at the ongoing conflation of Debussy with impressionism, particularly among art historians.

In his fine book on impressionism, James H. Rubin (despite a keen awareness of Debussy's affinity for Whistler and symbolism) concludes that in the music of Debussy "Impressionism had its most successful after-life." He cites the fact that Debussy's *Printemps* from 1887 was derided by critics as "vague Impressionism."[16] The explanation for this, however, may not be anything more than the fact that *Printemps* was submitted just shortly after the last and eighth Impressionist Exhibition of 1886 that featured works not only by "classic" impressionists, particularly Pissarro, but also works by Seurat and the symbolists Redon and Rouart.[17] Impressionism in painting had still not receded from its status as novel and revolutionary. The application of the term by contemporary critics may have been more as an epithet of reflexive conservative condemnation than a considered argument about connections between compositional strategies and the techniques of impressionism. As Debussy would later observe, a listener, particularly a smug self-consciously well-schooled one, usually approached a new piece of music with a closed set of formal expectations regarding the shape of musical time. The failure to hear anticipated events of structural demarcation led to the dismissal of music as "vague" and "indistinct"—echoes of the vocabulary of art critics who considered the impressionists as "enemies of art."

Debussy's admiration for the Hokusai woodcut *The Wave* (which graced the cover of *La Mer*) was shared by many late-nineteenth-century painters. It does not locate a useful link between Debussy and impressionism, as it seems to for Rubin. The enthusiasm for Japanese art consumed both Whistler and Manet, whose relationship to impressionism is at best ambiguous and contested. Furthermore, the linearity of Hokusai, the decorative detail, and the realization of curves and forms in Japanese art were equally influential on the symbolists, particularly Maurice Denis, whom Debussy knew, and Odilon Redon, with whom Debussy corresponded and who admired Debussy enough to send him a work of his own. Neo-impressionism (with which Debussy is also often linked) went not only in the direction of Seurat (who exploited the pseudo-scientific dissection of color and optical function as a route to the application of paint and pigment). Around the time *La Mer* was written, neo-impressionism also reintroduced a divergent post-impressionist emphasis on shape and line, much in the spirit of Japanese woodcuts. The Parisian cult philosopher, the Polish emigré Mecislas Golberg, published his influential tract *La morale des lignes* in 1908, a work that had a decided impact on not only symbolists and expressionist sculptors but on a new generation of artists inspired by a neo-classicism with which Ansermet, Schmitz, and Myers sought to link Debussy.[18]

However, not all the claims that Debussy's music represents the successful transposition of painterly impressionism into music can be dismissed so easily. Alfredo Casella, an astute and sympathetic observer, assumed that Debussy's music was impressionistic in the visual sense.[19] This conviction was most confidently held by German critics. The characterization of impressionism was used in Germany for both disdain and praise. A prejudice about the revolution in form seemingly brought about by a coloristic impressionism suffuses Julius Korngold's critique of *Pelléas* after its Vienna première in 1911, even though Korngold was keenly aware, as were his Viennese contemporaries, that Maeterlinck's libretto needed to be characterized as symbolist.[20] Walter Niemann, in his survey of contemporary music, published in several editions during Debussy's lifetime, devoted an entire chapter to Debussy's "musical impressionism," and asserted that Debussy transposed a painterly strategy to the writing of music.[21]

A less subtle and more nasty version of this German pattern of reception was penned by Karl Storck, who chastised German composers for being seduced by Debussy and his followers. To Storck, Debussy had been influenced by neo-impressionism. Storck conceded that it might be proper for German painters to follow in the path of French painters, since the French dominated the field. But it was a tragedy that young German composers were inclined to abandon the indisputable field of German cultural preeminence—music—with its unique materials, traditions, procedures, and means of expression. Storck complained that they were seduced by a new music imitative of painting. Inspired by post-impressionist French painting, they rejected the traditional handling of the materials of music.[22] The danger Storck alluded to can be inferred from Richard Strauss's remarkable reaction to *Pelléas* in which he claimed that there was, in the main, "no music" to be heard.[23]

Storck's reductive account of cultural nationalism, despite its uncomfortable hostility to cross-cultural influences, nonetheless offers a clue as to how the relationship between impressionism and Debussy might be clarified. Four years after the first impressionist exhibition Edgar Degas made an impressionistic copy of one of the greatest late-nineteenth-century German paintings, Adolf Menzel's *Ballsouper,* painted in Berlin in 1878. Menzel (who was admired by Brahms) was the greatest German realist of his day.[24] Storck's critique of Debussy rested on a recognition of the connection between impressionism and the practices of nineteenth-century realism suggested by Degas's copy. This connection has caused confusion about Debussy's relationship to the impressionist movement. It is at the heart of Debussy's objection to the confusion created by the use of impressionism to describe his music. The undisciplined use of the term obscured the distinction between what he thought he was doing and what he regarded impressionism as having accomplished.

By the mid-1880s late romanticism in music, particularly of German origin and culminating in Wagner, was understood in contradictory ways. Debussy would ultimately side with those who accused Wagner and late romanticism of encouraging facile analogies between realism (and particularly naturalism in the visual arts) and formal strategies and harmonic practices in music. Here one detects key divergences between French and German critical traditions. The first generation of French Wagner enthusiasts, including Baudelaire, located in Wagner a path away from naturalism and realism, terms that admittedly never achieved stable connotations in contemporary critical discourse. Wagnerism became allied with a turn away from the mundane and even the coherently philosophical. Wagner inspired the end of aesthetic representationalism and crass emotionalism. He helped open up new possibilities for a unique poetic discourse and an aesthetics of transfiguration. Hence the link between Wagnerism in France and the Parnassian poets and later the literary symbolism of Mallarmé. However, their successors in France, particularly the composers Gustave Charpentier and Alfred Bruneau (for whom Debussy had little regard), pursued an opposite track. They saw in Wagner techniques that could serve a radical aesthetic naturalism of the sort realized by Emile Zola in literature.[25]

In Germany, however, those critical of Wagner from the 1850s on identified the roots of Wagner's popularity in the debasement of the autonomy of music. Music, through the use of repetition and harmonic and orchestral color, became narrative and illustrative—a kind of musical prose that rejected the self-referential formal traditions of musical logic and composition. Wagner's overt subject matter may have been mythical, but the strategy and impact of the music were representational, descriptive, and emotionally manipulative in a manner more closely allied with the realist illusionism in literature characteristic of the novel. The abstract in music had been subordinated to the real, defined linguistically. This made Wagner's music seductive and easy to grasp. Even Wagner's ardent German defenders found in his work not only musical innovation per se, but philosophic content and an emotionally compelling nationalist ideology cloaked only superficially in legend and myth. His work offered a new type of realism, mediated by music.[26] Wagner's own taste in the visual arts (as typified by the set designs from Bayreuth before 1883) only confirms this suspicion. Wagner admired the grandiose historical painting of Hans Makart, painters of the German-Roman movement such as Anselm Feuerbach and Arnold Böcklin, the landscape painter Josef Hoffmann, as well as Menzel. Like Liszt, he was more influenced than he was willing to admit by the Munich historical painter Wilhelm von Kaulbach.[27]

Degas's copy of Menzel underlines the close link between realism and impressionism in the visual arts. It also helps clarify the way the impressionists understood Wagner. Through the theory and practice of Wagner they found inspiration for painterly ways of finding new paths to penetrate beyond a superficial construct of reality. They did not reject the premise of realism in art. Storck, an accomplished student not only of music but of art as well, shared this view of Wagner and impressionism. For him Wagner's achievement and success with the public rested less on the purely musical than on his genius of employing music as a didactic art. His work generated a worldview and gave concrete shape to ideas. Debussy, he realized, had gone well beyond both Wagner and impressionism.[28]

The weakness in the connection between Debussy and impressionism lies in the fact that Debussy sought to set aside the inherited strategies of naturalist or pseudo-realist musical practices of the sort advocated by Massenet (in both his Wagnerian and non-Wagnerian works) and Charpentier; this involved, for Debussy, a rejection of Wagner. In Debussy's view, music had to move away from descriptive naturalism, the subordination of music to a narrative and a linguistically evident didactic purpose. Debussy traveled further in the direction charted first by Baudelaire's view of Wagner. Most impressionists, however, with their far more intense engagement with realism and despite their painterly innovations, understood Wagner in a manner more comparable to Charpentier and Bruneau.

There is little dispute that Debussy admired the virtuosic and brilliant French symbolist poet and essayist Jules Laforgue, who died in 1887 at the age of twenty-seven.[29] Laforgue, like Maurice Denis, was an admirer of Seurat and the neo-impressionists. And like Seurat Laforgue was a devotee of the French scientist Charles Henry, whose ideas on art and optics influenced a generation of French painters. Laforgue, admired by Debussy as a symbolist, wrote an appreciation of impressionism for an exhibition held in Berlin in 1883.[30] In Laforgue's analysis of impressionism one can find a source for Debussy's view of impressionism, and insight into why the thoughtless application of the term impressionist to Debussy's music is indeed misleading. Laforgue's symbolist affinities led him to conclusions about the relationship between art and nature quite similar to those articulated by James McNeill Whistler in his famous "Ten O'Clock" lecture held two years later. In Laforgue's view, impressionism was a radical advance on realism, not a contradiction of it. With impressionism, realist painting had shifted its focus from a diminished and artificial account of external reality to a more advanced realism that took into account the science of seeing. "The Impressionist eye is in short the most advanced eye in human evolution, the one that has succeeded in grasping and rendering the most complicated combination of nuances known." Laforgue, as a symbolist poet, recognized all too well the gulf between the strategies of impressionism and the aesthetics of symbolism. Impressionism was lauded for its capacity to create a scientifically defensible presentation of reality as a totality. What Monet and Pissarro are able to do is to abandon mere "melody" and create a true "symphony of life."[31] The account given of the external world before impressionism turns out to have been fragmentary. The impressionist painter transcends the limitations of the flat canvas by recording the complexity of visible reality. Impressionism explodes the illusionism of painterly traditions characterized as naturalist or realist. Impressionism offers an aesthetic equivalent to the progress in science made by atomic and electromagnetic theory.

The version of what one sees in a classical realist painting is therefore only superficially real. It turns out not to be what "is." The claim to truth is artificial. A unitary single color is actually an assemblage of gradations and tones. The tradition of naturalist painting, far from bequeathing formal conventions that do justice to nature, in fact trivializes it, just as medieval science or alchemy falsely represented the nature of things.

Although critics of impressionism consider impressionist painters as having abandoned normative standards of nature and truth and the epistemological legacy of empiricism, it turns out that impressionists are utilizing nothing less than an advanced form of empiricism. Impressionism contains no anti-positivist undercurrent, as does symbolism. To the conventionally educated beholder, impressionist paintings may seem unreal, vague, and unfinished. But in Laforgue's view this educated viewer was no nearer the truth about reality than an individual who asserted that water was a fundamental element of nature. That person was at best only superficially educated. Water can be more accurately said to be a combination of elements, just as a straight line, on close inspection, is an accumulation of irregularities.[32]

Laforgue defended the plein-air procedure and speed of painting among the impressionists. This enabled them to record correctly the results of "three retinal fibrils" that compete with one another. In fifteen minutes, the painter can record the variations and oppositions that actually occur as the eye and the brain encounter a dynamic external reality—in particular the instability of light. What is clearly exploded here is the notion that there is anything called "absolute, objective beauty." The rules of realist painting were not only not normative, but obsolete. Laforgue observed that impressionism also rejected the romantic conceit of subjectivity. "The subjective taste of absolute man" is replaced by an objective defense of visual variation. The result is that "today we have a more exact idea of life within and outside of ourselves." Citing Gustav Fechner, nature and the exterior world become "a perpetually changing symphony." Rejecting both nihilism and dilletantism, Laforgue concluded that each individual can record reality differently, because reality is no longer reductively understood. The absolute definitions of color, beauty, perspective, harmony, and proportion become "pipe dreams." Impressionism records "living beings and objects within their own specific atmospheres," achieved by pairs of eyes in moments of time that are never identical.[33]

What recommends Laforgue's account of impressionism is more than Debussy's admiration of him. Rather, Laforgue stresses the temporal dimension of the new painting. Time is no longer written into the narrative of a canvas or distilled by the canvas as either timeless, or as a moment frozen in time. Time in painting ceases to be arbitrarily conflated, but is enlarged. The canvas records the act of seeing over time. And it permits the viewer to sense the passage of time as recorded by infinite variations in color and light. It represents reality as dynamic, as the accumulation of a particular sequence of variations in light and color. This notion comes quite close to the view, held by Debussy and his defenders, that Debussy emancipated pitch and rhythm as well as harmonies from relationships defined by tradition and rules. As in the fifteen minutes of painting, in each piece of music the sequence of sounds is suggested by their gradual unfolding, one from the next, permitting new and unexpected sounds and colors to emerge from the actual (if not natural) and non-artificial character of sound. The true nature of music, in Debussy's mature view (conceived in terms both of single elements—notes—and the totality of musical experience within a period of elapsed time), could make it "more true to life." Music was for the thirty-three-year-old composer a species of reality: "not even the expression of feeling, it's the feeling itself."[34]

Impressionism brings painting closer to music. It is realism over elapsed time, recorded by seeing; but it captures—realistically—the dynamism of the moment in time in a way that suggests an ongoing continuum. The beholder becomes part of that continuum as he or she observes the canvas. In Laforgue's essay, as in many other contemporary defenses of impressionism, the influence of musical metaphors mediated by the intense engagement with Wagner is palpable. The result in Laforgue, however, is that painting becomes precisely musical in its role as the visual representation of the passage of time, since the object of impressionism is the specific and particular realist account of the act of seeing in nature. Laforgue's defense explains Debussy's phrase in the aforementioned letter to Durand that in *Images* he is doing what "imbeciles call 'impressionism,' a term employed with the utmost inaccuracy." Debussy understood, as many did not, impressionism's recasting of realism. As Debussy wrote, he was "trying to write 'something else'—*realities*, in a manner of speaking."[35] In 1885, at the age of twenty-three, Debussy defined a key aspect of those 'realities' with prescience: "I don't think I'll ever be able to cast my music in a rigid mould. . . . I'm not talking about musical form, merely from the literary point of view. I would always rather deal with something where the passage of events is to some extent subordinated to a thorough and extended portrayal of human feelings."[36] The kind of false realism of the sort he once imitated successfully in *L'Enfant prodigue* (using the model of Massenet) needed to be supplanted by a compositional procedure that gave full expression to possibilities of feeling. In his 1902 defense of *Pelléas* Debussy wrote "I also tried to obey a law of beauty that seems notably ignored when it comes to dramatic music: the characters of this opera try to sing like real people, and not in an arbitrary language made up of worn-out clichés."[37] When Debussy described his *Faune* to Gauthier-Villars, he said it was "a general impression of the poem. . . . It also demonstrates a disdain for the 'constructional knowhow'" and is "in a mode which is intended to contain all the nuances" of tonality adequate to the poem.[38]

There are uncanny correspondences between Laforgue's account of impressionism, Debussy's ideas, and the view of James McNeill Whistler on art and nature.[39] The language in Debussy's letters makes it clear that he read Whistler and not only admired his paintings; Whistler's influence on Debussy extended to the way he thought about art. Whistler closes his famous "Ten O'Clock" lecture with a paean to Hokusai.[40] Perhaps it was Whistler who gave Debussy the idea of identifying his own music criticisms, published under the nom de plume Monsieur Croche, as the work of the "anti-dilettante."[41] Whistler and Debussy participated in and helped promote if not codify the formulae appropriated by fin-de-siècle musical modernists, particularly Schoenberg, in their self-defense. Debussy's ire is consistently directed not at an ignorant public, but at a pseudo-educated one whose capacity for music appreciation had been destroyed by schooling. He thought that "trying to familiarize one's contemporaries with the sublime is a fool's game." The audience consisted "for the most part" of "idiots."[42]

By the 1880s a palpable tension existed throughout Europe between the artistic conceits of these so-called "idiots"—the cultured public—and a rising new generation of artists. The tension must be understood as having less to do with content and style than with the socio-psychological valence that education in the arts possessed among the reading, concert-going and art-beholding public, particularly within the wide range of middle-class city dwellers. By the time Debussy won his Prix de Rome, the major capitals of Europe and America boasted vast and daunting publics who identified their social advancement with the successful appropriation of earmarks of sophistication from the cultural arena once reserved for the landed aristocracy. We now associate aristocrats of birth with non-intellectual habits (sports and hunting), society pages, and an overall anti-intellectualism. But the middle-class protagonists in the Paris of Balzac and Flaubert, the Berlin of Fontane, the Vienna of Schnitzler, and the Boston and New York of Henry James knew better. The great traditions of culture in music and painting were the legacy of a pre-industrial, pre-liberal Europe. Patronage and connoisseurship, once the province of the aristocracy, had become, through education, the acquired conceits of newcomers. These newcomers, however, internalized a lingering self-doubt. Were they merely arrivistes and parvenues? Bourgeois achievement in the cultivation of taste came at the price of deep insecurity about the authenticity of the acculturation made possible by material and economic success.

Wagner exploited this new public. His music of the future was based on musical innovations that helped make his work accessible. Yet once

Wagnerism had taken full root within this modern public, innovation or rebellion in artmaking triggered an intense and reflexive negativity from the audience. Although Wagner's initial influence among artists and composers had been as an innovator who sparked a break with past practice, after his death in 1883 he became for many, including Debussy, the last great exponent of an outdated but popular late romantic legacy. From the public's perspective, any fundamental post-Wagnerian innovation (as audible for example in Mahler), directly attacked the hard won expertise of the audience. It challenged the authority of the institutions and academies created to inculcate art and taste.

The hostility that greeted Debussy and later Schoenberg (and even the painters who quickly found success), revealed not so much the public's disdain as its terror. The critics of the daily press—the favorite medium of the new educated classes—mirrored and articulated this insecurity and rage, even if critics masked these sensibilities with arrogance and the jargon of expertise. Debussy's contempt for the Conservatoire and the impressionists' conflict with the official Salon revealed the conviction among young artists that the academic canons of artistic quality were not only corrupt but defensive. The officialdom in the arts was supported by and dependent on a public that had learned how to hear and look as consumers and dilletantes. The public lacked the confidence to go beyond that which they already knew and found familiar. Rigidity in taste and the tendency to pit so-called tradition as healthy and beautiful against the new as degenerate or formless seemed a consequence of the modern commerce of music, which depended on high circulation newspapers and a powerful cadre of publishers, professionals and teachers who lived off the business of art. These individuals in turn had a vested interest in trying to guide the taste of an urban public uncertain of its own powers of judgment.

Debussy's call for the restoration of the status of Rameau is reminiscent of Whistler's evocation of the Renaissance. They both pursued the line of thought advocated by the pre-Raphaelites in England and the mid-nineteenth-century German-Roman movement among German painters. The art and music of the past had either been misunderstood or ignored by the philistine modern critic and consumer. Nineteenth-century romantic music and realist painting tied to claims of narrative truth and naturalism not only dominated bourgeois taste but distorted the historical legacy. From Whistler's, Debussy's, and Mallarmé's point of view, the appeal to tradition and canons of beauty misrepresented the qualities of the past by inventing a palatable canon of history and construct of aesthetics.[43] Despite evident differences, Debussy never lost his respect for Vincent d'Indy, in part because d'Indy established the Schola

Cantorum and challenged not only the monopoly but the mediocrity of the musical training at the Conservatoire. Like Debussy, d'Indy tirelessly advocated a return to a French pre-classical tradition of music.[44]

Through the post-Napoleonic network of cultural institutions, the state collaborated with the new mass of museumgoers, listeners, amateurs, and journalists. The academies and conservatories that legitimated established practices actually came to represent the new public. Laforgue put it succinctly: ". . . the State [should] cease to concern itself with art. The School of Rome . . . should be sold, the Institute should be closed; let there be no more medals or other honors. . . . No more official designation of beauty."[45] Yet, true to their conviction that new art possessed a deeper connection to reality and truth, both Laforgue and Debussy (at least for some of the time) still held faith with the possibility of reaching a larger public. Unlike the Parnassian poets and many of the symbolists, as well as pre-Raphaelites, Debussy and the impressionists wavered between a belief in the exclusivity of a genuine aesthetic sensibility and the more open idea that a large appreciative contemporary audience was not out of the realm of possibility.[46] In contrast to Schoenberg, Debussy's writing, particularly later in life, holds out the hope that if a successful revolution took place, the very same public for which he had once had contempt could respond to the work of modern artists and musicians. Debussy, like his contemporaries in painting, attempted to get the audience to break both its habits (deepened in the case of music by the embrace of Wagner), and the artificial barriers erected by education.[47]

To return to Whistler: it was he who in 1885 harked back for the time when "the amateur was unknown and the dilettante undreamed of." More than Laforgue, but much like Debussy, he hammered away at the toll taken on art by modern industrial civilization. A clue to the connection between Whistler, impressionism, and Debussy is Whistler's use of the musical to explain what art really does. Without any reference to scientific rhetoric about optics or evolution, Whistler comes to conclusions more akin to Laforgue's symbolism than Laforgue's 1883 defense of impressionism. Nature merely contains the elements of art in color and form, just as a keyboard contains the notes of music. As Whistler noted: ". . . the artist is born to pick, and choose, and group with science, these elements, that the result may be beautiful—as the musician gathers his notes, and forms his chords, until he brings forth from chaos glorious harmony. To say to the painter, that Nature is to be taken as she is, is to say to the player, that he may sit on the piano."[48]

The key difference between Laforgue and Whistler is that Whistler remained more indebted to the romantic privileging of the subjective genius of the artist. Amid the infinite possibilities that nature puts at the foot of the artist, the artist creates masterpieces through his own agency. The truth in nature that the academic schools and the strategy of pictorial realism was supposed to honor was not so much inadequate as fundamentally misunderstood. In Whistler art is defined by the subjective vision of man inspired by his encounter with nature. The radical point: the entire bulwark of moralizing about aesthetic truth, beauty, and morality in relation to any subject–object correspondence is ludicrous, since nature never produces a picture, only the artist does. Whistler is closer to Nietzsche's Zarathustra, who inverts the traditional relationship between man and nature by telling the sun that it should be grateful to have man to shine upon. The artist, in Whistler's view, makes Nature "his resource"; it is always "at his service."

Whistler, unlike Laforgue and Debussy, highlighted a particularly pernicious symptom of the superficiality of judgment within the new educated classes: the widespread belief that the present was a time of material progress, but of spiritual and artistic decay. For Whistler, cultural pessimism of the type argued by Matthew Arnold clinched the argument that the cultured public had been led totally astray about art. By abstracting elements from the traditions of the past and rendering them normative, it became possible to confound a taste for art with the acquisition of a teachable fixed system of values. But doing so also meant foregoing the individual artist's only claim to legitimacy—the creation of truths through the realization of the subjective through art. Whistler does not entirely resolve the tension between a residual allegiance to static normative criteria and a progressive historicist plea on behalf of the changing cultural and historical context of the artist. The normative survives in the artist's devotion to the primacy of an authentic aesthetic motivation. As Debussy never tired of asserting, the artist was not beholden to rules defended by some appeal to reality and truth. In fact, for Whistler the act of making art "surpasses in perfection all . . . what is called Nature; and the Gods stand by and marvel, and perceive how far away more beautiful is the Venus of Milo than was their own Eve."[49] Art is not divine, but the exclusive province of the genius of the human imagination. God's creation—nature—is merely the artist's most fruitful field of prey.

Therefore Whistler, whose paintings, particularly the *Nocturnes*, deeply impressed Debussy, differs substantially from the impressionists in his philosophical and painterly strategies. The paint is thinly applied. In paintings with a human figure as the subject, there is an intentional subordination of the visible specificity of the object to an independent aesthetic treatment. That is why Whistler's portraits were so often assumed

James McNeill Whistler, *Nocturne in Blue and Silver.* c.1871

to have symbolic meaning that had nothing to do with psychological realism, narration, or the depiction of real events in time. The intervention of the painter was designed to interrupt an implied correspondence between the visual and the linguistic. If one of the primary functions of language is to locate ourselves in the world (to the extent of defining an external reality), then naming is one of language's most powerful tools. Realism as a painterly objective offered a visual equivalent to naming. The still life, the chair, the railway station, or the subject of a portrait are never, so to speak, really as they are. Yet in nineteenth-century realism the artist exploited conventions and a vantage point from which an illusion of reality was achieved for the viewer. This was accomplished by a shrewd but deceptive aesthetic strategy. Believability, plausibility, and recognition—even moral argument and documentation—were achieved from the standpoint of the beholder through a correspondence between linguistic naming, description, and visual representation. Illustration was clearly the minimal achievement not only in painting but, within so called program music even in instrumental music.

Since the eighteenth century music as a medium had been accorded special status precisely because it seemed entirely abstract and incapable of illustration. Efforts at tone painting (e.g., in Haydn), narration, and illustration—even in Wagner and later in Strauss—repeatedly came under fire as a trivialization of music's unique power as an art. Whistler's reliance on musical analogy revealed his recognition of music's failure to inherently possess obvious correspondences with the external world. He argued that in genre painting, historical painting, or painting where there is either a theatrical composition or a narrative (whether in a large tableau or a smaller fragment), the minimal expectation of realism was the achievement of an inadequate correspondence to which music had no access.

Whistler sought to go beyond the achievements of the great realist painters of the generation of Courbet. He pressed beyond the work of painters from the German romantic tradition of the German-Romans (Feuerbach and later Böcklin). They had gone beyond conventional correspondences, seizing the ample room within the traditions of realism to generate, through implied narrative, sensibilities not ordinarily associated with the everyday experience. Myth, the grotesque, and the ideal took on realist contours. Debussy understood this well, as his uncanny and perceptive 1912 comparison of Richard Strauss and Böcklin reveals.[50] Whistler deviated from this trajectory by using the painted canvas to deliberately undercut any manipulation of correspondence. He cast the link between word and image into doubt, and derailed it. His strategy vis-à-vis tradition was subversive, which is partly why it appealed to Debussy. Whistler produced an ethereal and to some an unfinished veneer of paint on the surface. He organized the canvas through an emphasis on a single overriding tonality, unifying color, and a palette entirely the invention of the artist.

Consequently the correspondence strategy we associate with naming, particularly beyond the general (e.g., man, woman) and toward the specific, (e.g., Whistler's mother), suddenly is overwhelmed by the conflating of background and foreground and the striking preponderance of, to use a musical metaphor, a single composition of color and tone. The "real" subject diminishes in importance and an aesthetic intent emerges. Whistler was precise in naming his own paintings: *Symphony in White, No. 3* (1865–67), *Symphony in Blue and Pink* (c.1868), *Harmony in Blue and Silver: Trouville* (1865), and most famously, *Arrangement in Gray and Black: Portrait of the Painter's Mother* (1871). The *Nocturnes* from 1870s that are most closely linked to Debussy's music with the same title are strikingly transparent and detailed. But a consistent surface and tone permeate the whole of the canvas.[51] As Debussy put it himself, describing the *Nocturnes* (Debussy's) to Ysaÿe, "It's an experiment, in fact, in finding the different combinations possible inside a single colour, as a painter might make a study in grey, for example."[52] For Whistler the essence of music and therefore the idea in painting lay in harmony, in an overall composite sound and visual effect. Not surprisingly, when d'Indy criticized Debussy in his textbook, *Cours de Composition*, it was for his excessive reliance on harmony.[53]

Whistler's frequent use of the words symphony and harmony for his paintings was not lost on Debussy, even if "symphony" often meant something pejorative to Debussy. He thought it suggested an artificial adherence to formal conventions that privileged particular relationships between sound over time as in the music which Saint-Saëns excelled in writing. Indeed for Debussy, as he and his apologists would never tire of asserting, notions of variation, repetition, and thematic development derived from the classical era and expanded by romanticism had assumed a false status as normative. This was analogous to the way academic realist techniques and expectations in painting had become confused with beauty and truth in art. But in Whistler the naming of paintings in terms of color relationships and musical forms was designed to assert the primacy of an autonomous aesthetic and the unity of the field of vision. Discrete elements of color and tone were placed in the foreground as the magical and powerful elements of the painter's vision. They made it possible to penetrate the limits of language, particularly its dominance as the instrument of description and representation of experience, time, and space.

Purely aesthetic variables detached from external reality made their point using mundane subject matter by transfiguring it, offering the viewer something that could not be imagined or experienced except through the medium of painting. What nature gave the painter was the opportunity to do what the elements of music made simple: the opportunity not to abstract, but to perceive without reference to linguistically-based notions of accuracy in narrative and identity. There was an irony in Whistler's rejection of the gilded frame and his habit of painting the frame to specifically fit the picture (a practice employed also by the pre-Raphaelites, Seurat, and some symbolists). The apparent unreality of the painter's vision did not deserve to be artificially framed. Whistler's art was, in its own way, far less contrived. It is as if one removed the proscenium arch that in naturalist drama enhanced the illusion of realism. Now that the pretense was abandoned, the frame became part of the composition itself.

What also recommended Whistler to Debussy was his enthusiasm for Japanese art, Chinese porcelain, and ornamental design. Ornament was not conceived of as supplementary. Rather it could make the visual experience unified and continuous. Freed from narrative and representational objectives, a visual tapestry could be realized that lacked the ritual demarcations associated with realism. The presumed opposition and contrast among and between several compositional categories (e.g., form and ornament, line and color) were reconciled through the integration of large forms and details. The emphasis was on the continuity and simplicity of design. Louis Laloy, Debussy's friend and first biographer, pointed out (directly echoing Debussy's own self-representation) that the essence of Debussy's achievement was a radically economical abandonment of artificial demarcations within musical time. Expectations regarding scale structure, cadences, and a demand for contrast and modulation are set aside, so that "nothing is done to order."[54] Here one can locate the impact of Whistler. What within the realist strategy were sharp, conventional, and perhaps reductive distinctions were abandoned to a form of vision that favored an all-encompassing, grand, and unifying continuity.

The disturbing perceptibility of subject matter within Whistler created the awareness of this continuity in the viewer. Whistler generated a tension between a path-breaking manner of painting and the presence of a recognizable and named subject. Whistler opened himself up to symbolist readings because of this apparent tension between the act of representation—the presence of an image—and the distinctive painterly transformation that robbed the image of its comfortable correspondence to the external world. However, the assertive aestheticism of Whistler, despite his penchant for subdued tonalities, predominates over any latent mystical, fantastic, or encoded meaning. When Debussy cautioned Chausson to focus on a "central idea" he was evoking the influence of Whistler on himself: ". . . too often we're concerned with the frame before we've got the picture; it was our friend Richard Wagner, I think, who got us into this fix. Sometimes the frame is so ornate, we don't realize the poverty of the central idea. . . . It would be more profitable, I feel, to go about things the other way round, that's to say, find the perfect expression for an idea and add only as much decoration as is absolutely necessary."[55]

Debussy's biographers have properly stressed the direct connection between Whistler and Debussy as more significant than the influence of the impressionists on the composer. Indeed, what distinguishes Whistler from the impressionists is his abandonment of the effort to redefine realism. Yet he had no desire to supplant realism entirely. He used its basic strategy—working from the external world—merely to deny its priority in art, which is why the paintings often have two titles. An aesthetic composition is described and then followed by a naming of the "real" subject. The impressionists redeemed realism by asking the beholder to rethink how one understands, sees, and experiences light and color. The ease with which the first generation of impression-ists, particularly Renoir, became the favorite objects of acquisition by the very bourgeois elite derided by Whistler and Debussy points to this fact. Their project was not as radical as it seemed —as Degas's copy of Menzel and the endorsement of Zola (not one of Debussy's heroes) suggest. Furthermore, the impressionists and neo-impressionists did not stress a unifying tonality and unmodulated surface in their painterly strategies. Roughness of surface, thickness of texture, and variation in color and tone applied with rapid brushwork, intensively applied in the experi-ence of the outdoors, were accumulated on the canvas. From a distance, particularly in Monet, beholders could recognize a spontaneous visual experience that they themselves might have perceived. A defining aestheticism and eerie unreality dominate Whistler's canvases that sug-gest an artificiality not present in the plein-air paintings of the early impressionists. One finds this however in Seurat.

In terms of Debussy's evolution therefore, impressionism seems not to have been the decisive source of inspiration. The compatibility between Whistler and symbolism and Debussy's attraction to the dream-like mystery in Turner and pre-Raphaelite painting more precisely locate the overriding influence of the visual in his music. There is nonetheless a justifiable link to impressionism, as Laloy's seminal 1910 essay on Debussy suggests. In the essay Laloy tried to explain in what way Debussy was indeed an impressionist.[56] By 1910 it was clear that the notion that Debussy was a musical impressionist was widespread. Given the popu-larity and fame of the impressionist painters, that association was a useful and positive way to highlight Debussy's achievement. Laloy himself (perhaps through Debussy) was aware of the inconsistencies and uneasy fit between impressionism and Debussy. For Laloy the impressionist painters had declared war "on abstract reason." They celebrated a normative sense of art that, according to Laloy, centered on sensation.

Laloy characterizes the prior traditions of art as being excessively rational. But he fails to understand the enormous implicit rationalism in impressionism articulated by Laforgue: the conceit that the impres-sionist eye is scientifically the more rational, making the painter's documented impression a legitimate act of truth-telling. Laloy attributes to the impressionists an aestheticism more appropriate to Whistler. Impressionism becomes the "apotheosis of sensation" in a manner that suggests either aestheticism or non-objectivity. From this conclusion Laloy proceeds to say that Debussy learned from the impressionists that sound has neither meaning nor the capacity to represent. Debussy has produced "a purely auditory music, just as Impressionist painting is entirely visual."[57]

However this turns out not to be the link between Debussy and impressionism. It is as if Debussy had redeemed Hanslick's absolutist aesthetics, but without any reference to the formalist baggage that Hanslick believed was inherent in the Western system of music, particularly functional tonal harmony. For Laloy, in Debussy's music "note attracts note directly, without the justification of a scale; similarly chord attracts chord without a cadence; idea attracts idea with no need for contrast or modulation."[58] This accurate description speaks as much to Whistler as it does to the impressionists' technique of recording visual sensation. In an overwhelming number of Debussy's instrumental compositions and works for piano without text there is a reality at the core of the musical experience, as the composer himself asserted.[59] That reality is not the direct object of music. But real emotion and feeling in the world (in contrast to Hanslick's notions of the autonomy of music) were the goals in Debussy's musical project until very late in his career. He was impressionistic in Laforgue's sense, not in Laloy's, even though Laloy understood Debussy's critique of the limits of musical romanticism. The most impressionist work is not surprisingly *La Mer*, (not the *Nocturnes*) which a few adherents, notably Pierre Lalo, considered an unfortunate departure from *Pelléas*.[60] *La Mer* uses sound not to illustrate or narrate by artificially engaging in a correspondence between sight and music, yet it is a musical evocation of a specific open-air experience of the sea over elapsed time.

What distinguishes the music in Debussy is the belief that music "by its very essence . . . consists of colours and rhythmicized time."[61] Traditional forms are rejected not because they aspire to a musical language of realism, but because they obscure the particular power of music to express the real experience of life. Music is more than "purely auditory." Commenting on the lamentable state of contemporary music in a letter to Paul Dukas in 1901 Debussy wrote, "music is devoid of emotional impact." Music needs to make people "*listen* despite themselves and despite their petty, mundane troubles." Music remains for Debussy, "for all time the finest means of expression we have."[62] This is not music as mere sensation. For Debussy, particularly in *La Mer*, music is an act of expression responding to the human being in life, creating consciousness through sound in response to the external world. In *La Mer* Debussy sustains the early nineteenth-century romantic conceit about the special power of music to reach to a reality beyond the grasp of the visual and the linguistic. Rhythmicized time and the color of sound can make the experience of life transcend a reductive notion of the external world (e.g. the sea) inscribed by convention, tradition, and modern everyday existence.

Debussy's most impressionistic assertions therefore appear around the period of *La Mer*. In his 1906 letter to Raoul Bardac, his pupil and stepson, Debussy wrote: "Collect impressions . . . that's something music can do better than painting: it can centralize variations of colour and light within a single picture—a truth generally ignored."[63] In contrast to Whistler and the *Nocturnes* of the 1890s, the centralization doesn't always imply a dominant sense of unity; it can tend towards the impressionistic. The advice he gives to Bardac is consistent with the admonition he gave to Charles Levade in 1903 (the year in which he began to compose *La Mer*). Debussy writes, "To be honest, you learn orchestration far better by listening to the sound of leaves rustling in the wind than by consulting handbooks."[64] Musical apperception, freed from constraint, in response to nature, creates an expressive and emotional possibility defined by color, texture, and rhythmicized time.[65]

At the same time music's special mode of response to nature created for Debussy, as for Whistler, a mystery. That attraction to the unreal and mysterious, seemingly absent in impressionism, is where Debussy's engagement with Turner, the pre-Raphaelites, and symbolism is most suggestive. However, before turning to Debussy and these painters, a word needs to be said about the influence of Manet.[66] Manet produced masterpieces in the 1860s before the onset of impressionism. He has, as Michael Fried has brilliantly argued, become too linked to impressionism.

It is clear from various accounts that Debussy took an interest in Manet and made a special effort to see a Manet exhibition. Debussy's acquaintance with French painters and poets was in part the result of his ultimately aborted friendship with Ernest Chausson and his contact with Stéphane Mallarmé's circle. The friendship between Chausson and the painters was indisputably close. Redon was perhaps the most famous of the many artists who painted Chausson and members of his family. The collection owned by Chausson was extensive and included many works by Degas, Delacroix, and an enormous collection of Japanese graphic art. Chausson also owned one Manet canvas, as well as works by Courbet, Redon, Bonnard, Gauguin, and Puvis de Chavannes.[67] One central innovation in Manet's canvases was their directness and immediacy. Manet's radical reorientation of the relationship between viewer and canvas utilized the heritage of realism but abandoned the seemingly artificial barriers created by traditional formal procedures that placed the painter as an intermediary, observer, and commentator.

Two of Manet's most famous paintings from the 1860s, *Olympia* and *Luncheon on the Grass*, possess an arresting quality in that they reject the idea that the frame of the canvas contains a self-conscious narrative and an object of contemplation. There is neither a theatrical narrative nor the implication that the painter is an implied witness of a scene made available to the viewer, who becomes an indirect onlooker. Rather, in a manner not entirely dissimilar from Whistler's transformation of realism with color, design, and tone, the figures in Manet's canvas look out and confront the viewer directly, using a more flattened pictorialism and an inconsistent use of finish. The painter's role is signaled by intentional marks of painterly incompleteness (measured in traditional technical terms), if not spontaneity, and not by a theatrical narrative superimposed upon the aesthetic elements. The paintings achieve an almost aggressive confrontational presence. Manet's defenders, particularly Zola, argued that Manet was committed to an aesthetic naturalism (something not favored by Debussy). Yet the comparative neutrality and calm with which the subject matter is placed within the canvas heightens the intense emotional impact of the paintings. In his appropriation of models from art history. Manet pays homage to the great historical tradition of painting in a way not evident in the impressionists. But Manet uses a painterly tradition against itself.

The young Debussy's conviction that the traditional rules of musical procedure involved anti-aesthetic impositions that eviscerated the power of music can be compared to Manet's strategy in the 1860s. In music Debussy thought that Wagner and his emulators had created a double barrier—one erected by the composer and one assented to by the listener—both designed to impose on music a sense of drama and meaning. His observation of the controversy and success of Manet in electrifying the public could only have confirmed this suspicion. Manet removed a level of artificiality. By using the calm directness afforded the painter Manet engendered a direct emotionalism in seeming contrast to the controlled and elegantly economical visual surface. Debussy sought to do the same.

Manet's relationship to tradition can be perhaps compared to Debussy's lifelong, albeit transformed, debt to the Wagnerian sound world of *Parsifal,* if not to Wagner's conception of music as a medium of emotion. Following the example of Manet, Debussy sought to reorient the listener using sound elements and strategies borrowed from Wagner—but without the romantic and naturalist superstructure of musical events. In this comparison, however, the differences between music history and the history of painting are instructive. Debussy's rejection of historic expectations of musical form and procedure was not so much inconsistent as it was ambivalent. The sentimental superficialities of Massenet and the charm of Gounod did not evoke his ire as much as the vulgar and pretentious aspirations of Charpentier and the verismo composers Mascagni and Puccini.[68] It was not mere nationalism

Edouard Manet, *The Old Musician,* 1862

that led him away from Beethoven, made him dismiss Brahms, and remain unimpressed by Mahler.[69] Just as he reserved admiration for the orchestral sound of Wagner and the sustained integration of text and music, he was not unappreciative of the skill and power of Richard Strauss.[70] Liszt, Schumann, and Chopin Debussy held in high regard for their use of musical time and the nearly improvisatory freedom audible in their work. Like Manet, he had a keen sense for the craftsmanship of these past masters. Musical beauty was more than spontaneity. Writing to Laloy in 1906, he made clear that what he hated most was the subordination of music to other agendas, such as "Gluck's deceitful grandiloquence, Wagner's bombastic metaphysics," and César Franck's "false mysticism." Charpentier (a favorite of Zola's) exemplified how contemporary music had become mired in a "cosmopolitan stew." The reason Rameau was worth paying attention to was that he showed "perfect taste and strict elegance," a combination which accounted for the "consummate beauty" of his work.[71] This construct of an ideal of musical beauty was close to Manet's penetrating and elegant directness, and the radical painterly beauty of the surface that made the art more powerful. As Fried observed, Manet's canvas "seeks by its conspicuous lack of narrative or dramatic coherence as well as by various 'formal' devices . . . to compel the beholder to take it in as a whole, a single intense facing object of vision—a single *striking* object of vision."[72] Debussy's music aspired to this effect.

Insofar as Manet's example suggests a dynamic in art history between tradition and innovation, it becomes useful to compare Debussy and his relationship to music history with his contemporary and polar opposite, Vincent d'Indy. Debussy's respect for d'Indy's thinking was genuine, despite his dismissal of d'Indy's music itself, with the possible exception of passages from *Fervaal*. D'Indy and Debussy were not the arch-rivals that some contemporaries would like to have made them, even though they had little in common, particularly on the question of César Franck. There are elements in d'Indy's initial premises in his philosophy of art and music with which Debussy might have agreed. The difference was located in d'Indy's highly moralizing apparatus regarding the purpose of music and his ambition to construct a system that could sustain it. D'Indy wished to perpetuate a relationship between composer and the elements of music that in the end required of the listener an acceptance of the composer as sustaining a stable structural context in which music assumed a larger meaning.

But it was precisely d'Indy's effort to construct both an analytic and synthetic system of musical composition that troubled Debussy. D'Indy sought to connect music to general metaphysical categories such as passion, charity, hope, and love. When Debussy spoke of rhythmicized time he had something quite different in mind from d'Indy's conception of rhythm as the creation of order and proportion in time and space.[73] D'Indy was reasserting the limited realist fallacy in a spiritual fashion. By so doing he robbed music of the freedom to respond to the particularity of experience in ways that liberated music's power to transport the listener by music. Furthermore, despite their shared affection for a pre-classical tradition of music-making, d'Indy's subordination of harmony to melody was not merely didactically rigid, but implausible. Harmony was not, for Debussy, merely an outcome of the linear aspect of music defined by rhythm and melody. Debussy admired Palestrina's "melodic arabesques" and the capacity to form harmony "out of melodies."[74] But Debussy had no sympathy for a musical system whose results and logic placed the symphony at the apex of musical achievement. Even Camille Saint-Saëns found d'Indy's ideas all too German and too indebted to Hugo Riemann.[75]

In the brief span of eight years from 1894 to 1902, Debussy's music became widely known for its striking novelty. This novelty, dubbed Debussyism, owed its success to the fact that the music—from *Faune* to *Pelléas*—seemed magical and spontaneous: without a prehistory. As

Laloy put it, Debussy, the "saviour," came "at the appointed time." Movements tend to fashion their own genealogies and founding myths. Laloy's emphasis was not only on Debussy's messianic power, but on his capacity to achieve a revolution without controversy. Debussy's "deliverance . . . was sudden and effortless; as if touched by a magic wand, the ramparts vanished instantly into thin air, and nature was opened up, quivering, rustling, radiant and unlimited." Putting aside the religious and faintly erotic rhetoric, one sees that Laloy is making an unusual point: that Debussy "destroyed nothing." He brought "peace and not war" and painlessly found the way for composers and listeners to substitute pleasure "for duty." This miraculously non-aggressive and non-violent revolution was achieved, according to Laloy, because Debussy "had contemplated the example of the sister arts, and above all because he had listened to the voices of nature."[76]

The sister arts that Laloy had in mind are not only painting, but poetry. As Myers, Lesure, and Jarocínski[77] have argued, it was symbolism, first in poetry and then in painting, that was more influential than impressionism. Symbolism in poetry sought to emancipate language from its ordinary usages and meanings.[78] Using the linguistic, an aspect of mundane life, one could, through art, enter a realm of meaning and correspondences that eschewed the criteria of realism and naturalism. Because of its essential artificiality, music gained a particular prestige among symbolists, particularly Mallarmé. Debussy's symbolist leanings can be gleaned from his musings about the relationship between music and memory and dreams. In 1893 letters to Poniatowski and Chausson Debussy spoke of "music's wonderful symbols" and defined music as "as dream from which the veils have been lifted. . . . " "Music really ought to have been a hermetical science, enshrined in texts so hard and laborious to decipher as to discourage the herd of people who treat it as casually as they do a handkerchief." Writing in 1898, Debussy noted that "memory is a superior faculty, because you can pick from it the emotions you need." In 1910 Debussy observed, "an artist is by definition a man accustomed to dreams and living among apparitions. . . . " To Chausson the model for the composer might be found in "the attenuation of symbol at the center of some of Mallarmé's last sonnets." Symbolism, from the formalist point of view, provided a means to focus a work of art so that its "central idea" did not force a conflict between "inner parts" and "the principal line" of a piece of music.[79]

The connection between Debussy's instinct about the formal advantages of symbolism combined with his notion of music as an art form capable of communicating the sensibility of dreams. Apart from the literary sources for the connection of symbolism and music, it is the late canvases of Turner that provide the first link between painting and Debussy's obsession with music's capacity to transcend romanticism and its conventions, particularly its links to narrative realism and the mundane. Turner created a visual spectacle of enormous intensity. Turner transfigured through painterly means not only a moment in time, but he communicated actual movement, not, as in impressionism, the accumulated sense of movement. Unlike the impressionists, he did not seek to represent the sensation of reality. But like the pre-Raphaelites and symbolists (who did so quite differently), he manipulated traditional expectations of realism. The temporal turned into fantasy and evoked, as many observers have noted, a dreamlike act of the imagination, not unlike memory, that forced the viewer to lose a connection with the depicted subject matter.

In Turner's paintings, the viewer could sense a heightening of the imagination away from the subject and real time, and not as with the impressionists, a deepening of perception into the subject. Hence the canvases have a kinetic energy; they can easily be seen as sounded music visually represented. Turner's paintings have none of the restrained surface of Whistler or the suggestion of control. The visionary dimension in Turner—the mystery—is particularly evident in the obsession he shared with Debussy about water, the sea, and the sky and in his treatment of them. The paintings' instability of imagery, their brilliant colors, their sense of motion, all invite a comparison to dreaming.[80] The painter renders the sense of the mysterious concrete.

Dreams and visions, however spectacular, are in Turner still contingent on the linguistic and visual apparatus that defines a sense of the real. Yet his canvases detached the viewer from realism. The allure of symbolism and above all music is that the distortion and extension of experience into the realms of the imaginary can be best assured by a medium that has a tenuous connection with the real. Turner's use of paint and color was musical because of its sense of motion. For Debussy music was the most powerful of the arts because, as in a dream, music reorients the sense of time and duration. It is true that dreams, visions, and the supernatural still can demand language—but in them the correspondences between images and words and presumed objects take on meanings contingent only on the narrow context of the dream itself. This is why music might itself be a dream—one whose essential meaning—"feeling itself" has become clear (i.e. with its veil lifted, as Debussy puts it). Turner seemed to paint feelings, not impressions.

Debussy recognized that music could go beyond painting and poetry, beyond even Whistler's aestheticism. The making of art could be emancipated from a mundane reliance on description, narration,

J. M. W. Turner, *The Burning of the Houses of Lords and Commons, October 16, 1834*

illustration, explanation, and identification. Music derived a benefit from following on the achievements of painters and poets—Turner, Whistler, Manet, Mallarmé, and Poe. They had emancipated the word and image as rigidly interdependent instruments of aesthetic expression. They made it possible to render music a symbolic medium by generating novel correspondences with words and images. The distinction between Debussy's concept and Wagner's librettos (or Chausson's for *Arthus*) was that the music created by Wagner and Chausson was still closely tied to generating recognizable correspondences with language's everyday function. The advantage of symbolism in literature was its success in detaching language from its ordinary usages and meaning. Music would remain tied to a pseudo-naturalist or realist function unless word and image took the first step away. This is what Turner and Whistler had done in painting. The next step was for music to realize the essence of the imagination and an unmediated freedom of feeling. Turner created mystery using a temporal event in real space in time as in *The Burning of the Houses of Lords and Commons* (1834 and 1835) or *Snowstorm* (1842).[81] The composer could go even further, by triggering within the listener's real time an even stronger feeling based on an expression of the imaginary, dreamlike, and supernatural. Music possessed duration and sound well beyond Turner's evocation of it. It could even reconfigure the experience of silence, as Debussy did in *Pelléas*.[82]

Debussy's formulation of the role of music in the transfiguration of reality and the emancipation of art from the mundane was shaped by his encounter with the art of the pre-Raphaelites, Edgar Allan Poe, and symbolist poetry. The Mallarmé and Poe connections have been well explored. Debussy shared Baudelaire and Mallarmé's understandable obsession and admiration for Poe. One speculative thought, however, is in order. The relation between the use of language and overall form and effect in Poe was never lost on Debussy. One can explain his failure to set successfully the texts of Poe on which he worked for years by the fact that Poe was uniquely successful in seducing the reader into forgetting entirely the artifice of his narrative technique. Poe swept the reader away in a manner that was extremely difficult to dissect into constituent units sufficient to weave a continuous musical tapestry.[83] The words were in effect their own music, despite the surface of imaginary and supernatural narrative tale-telling. Debussy's frustration may be compared to Schumann's decision in his setting of Byron's *Manfred* to leave huge sections of the text alone merely to be spoken aloud. Reading can make the individual forget or distort the passage of time. When reading Poe, one may become oblivious to time. Although music, like a dream, distorts time, the listener can never become totally unaware of how time is being manipulated. Even though one may be transported in the temporal space occupied by music, one is always conscious of the accumulation of sequential events, cognizant that time is indeed passing, even though the sense of duration may be skewed.

Debussy's failure with two major Poe projects must be juxtaposed with his early success involving Gabriel Dante Rossetti's *The Blessed Damozel*. Twenty years ago Richard Langham Smith observed that Debussy's affinity for the pre-Raphaelites was more than a youthful fancy.[84] It left its distinct residue in *Pelléas*. Pre-Raphaelite painting, more than impressionism, was the visual sister art that permitted Debussy to realize his painless revolution. The pre-Raphaelites placed themselves in explicit opposition to naturalism. They did not offer an unmediated celebration of modernity or a high-minded moralist social critique parallel to the novels of Zola and Tolstoy (one of d'Indy's heroes). They created a brotherhood not dissimilar to the society for musical esotericism that Debussy yearned for in his 1893 letter to Chausson. Although their project has often been seen as anti-modern and regressive, the painterly realizations of the pre-Raphaelites are in fact not reactionary, but radically discontinuous with the past. They point forward and not backward.[85] The canvases are richly detailed, with a myriad of ornamental color that anticipates the brilliance of many impressionist and neo-impressionist canvases. The technical illusion of realism is so exaggerated that it becomes fantastic and destroys conventional correspondences and meanings. There is an enormous attenuation of detail similar to the attenuation of symbol Debussy noted in Mallarmé. In a way quite distinct from Turner, the pre-Raphaelite paintings suggest a remoteness in terms of ordinary time. Here the aspect of the dreamlike or supernatural is achieved not by the blurring of outlines and the explosion of color and light but by the very opposite. If Turner suggests motion, the pre-Raphaelites evoke stillness. There is an eerie manipulation of the visual depiction of arrested real time. The objects in the paintings appear more two-dimensionally defined than in life itself, as if within a dream. The boundary between reality and fantasy is not only blurred but convincingly eliminated. This is achieved by the integration of background and foreground. One encounters the flattening of perspective, the intensity of color, and, in contrast to Whistler, the avoidance of a muted surface. There is in these paintings the integration of principal line and ornament that Debussy identified as audible in the music of Bach. A patterning defines the entire composition. Even the paintings' narratives suggest a remoteness in time and silence. Depicted action is placed at an unreachable distance. The spiritual interior of the viewer becomes the subject of the image, as in a dream. Meanings and identities are displaced in a vivid hyperrealism.[86]

The pre-Raphaelites evoked a visionary mysticism quite different from that of Poe. Even in Hunt's overwrought 1905 depiction of the *Lady of Shallot*, there is little of the grotesque or monstrous. Further, the silence and stillness evoked by these paintings (as in Millais' *Ophelia*), invite a symbolist reading in a way quite different than does Whistler. Whistler's subject matter is presented as contemporary and not temporally distant. The underlying realism is not artificial; instead of stillness and silence there is muted and quiet subtlety. Many of the pre-Raphaelite paintings sport a controlled, often garish, but always brilliant tone (even when dark colors are used), without the spontaneous admixtures or rough surface of Turner. There is in many pre-Raphaelite paintings a kind of visionary fatalism. The subject of death is frequent, as it is in the dream world. When the viewer's eye passes from the canvas there is a sense of loss, much as there might be at the end of a musical experience.

The intent and effect of the pre-Raphaelite painters can be encapsulated by their setting of text. Consider their affection for Tennyson's *The Lady of Shallot*. The painters Hunt, Waterhouse, Meteyard, Thomson, and Siddall all took the poem as a subject.[87] Much like an artist, Tennyson's Lady can only observe and record life not by looking directly at reality, but in a mirror, by gazing at the distorted, detailed reversal of the external. When she turns around, mesmerized by real erotic desire, she dies—but not before parading herself much like a picture, with her own name as a title, decked out, lying flat in a boat (a metaphorical picture frame), decorated every inch by patterns created by nature. Like the artist, she cannot survive the direct engagement with life and reality. True to her art, in death she becomes her own work of art. After all, what is left of her life, as Lancelot observes in the poem's final lines, is only the beauty communicated by the aesthetic tableau of her own creation.[88]

The residues of these pre-Raphaelite convictions, as Smith observes, are evident in *Pelléas*. They also illuminate Debussy's control of sound color and his technique of orchestration. Orchestral color in Debussy derives not only from his response to nature, and to Whistler's subtle differentiations within a muted fabric, but also to the brilliance and vividness of pre-Raphaelite color and detail. Pre-Raphaelite painting inspired in Debussy a different kind of transparency: a dense but nearly seamless visual tapestry, what Laloy describes as "a coherent thread . . . woven around *Pelléas*, clearly expressing the fatal progression of the emotions." That fatalism is akin to the pre-Raphaelites, and reflected particularly in Debussy's "spontaneous use of silence" as the "way to give the emotion of a phrase its full value."[89]

The Symbolist painters Maurice Denis and Odilon Redon illustrate the links between pre-Raphaelite and symbolist painting, with which Debussy had many direct connections.[90] The composer knew Henry de Groux and the work of Puvis de Chavannes.[91] He was also acquainted with Georges Vanor, who wrote the first book on symbolist art in 1889. Vanor introduced Debussy to Denis. Vanor's definition of symbolism reads as follows: "Art is the method by which a dogma is cloaked in a human symbol and by which it is developed in constantly changing harmonies."[92] This followed Mallarmé's earlier reversal of Wagner's conception of the link between word and music. Within the fusion of art forms, music was used to provide the rhythm of the idea; it was not, as in Wagner, a tool of illustration or of the augmentation of meaning.[93]

Solitary contemplation and silent reading, particularly of poetry, helped stress the autonomy of words and the end of linguistic functionalism. A new possibility of meaning and correspondence could emerge. Mallarmé, like the pre-Raphaelites, glorified the pre-modern and expressed a hostility to modern society, and used those sentiments to call for a dissolution of the perception of form so that the mysterious and inexpressible could flourish.[94] For him, art had to "evoke in a

Maurice Denis, *Yvonne Lerolle in Three Poses,* 1897

deliberate shadow the object which is silenced, the elusive and never direct." The purpose of art was "the expression of the mysterious meaning of the various aspects of our existence." Although the German romantic poets, including Novalis, anticipated the notion that poetry should aspire to the status of music, in Mallarmé there is the belief in new levels of meaning that words take on as autonomous elements in the framework of a particular work of art. So too are visual elements detached from reality. Music spurs word and image beyond themselves and beyond music itself, whose limitations Mallarmé highlighted. The gaze of the artist "isolates . . . the day's luminosity."[95] A major distinction between symbolism and Debussy must however also be remembered. With the exception of *Le Martyre de Saint Sébastien* (whose origin and place in the canon of his works are sources of dispute), Debussy showed little in the way of either the Catholic enthusiasm of Denis or the spiritual mysticism and occultism of many symbolist and pre-Raphaelite artists.

But a Debussy-like elegance, refined distance, and completely dreamlike mystery can be seen in Maurice Denis's portrait, *Yvonne Lerolle in Three Poses* from 1897, as well as his 1892 painting *April*.[96] Here a Whistler-like tonality is combined with simplified color, a linearity, and a compositional strategy derived from the pre-Raphaelites. The images, particularly the portrait, are decidedly dreamlike. In symbolism, the appearance of reality is totally subversive, since meaning derives not from the recognizable, but from the vision of the artist. The sense of correspondence between image and word is rendered complicated by a post-Whistler and post-Manet surface clarity, flatness, and simplicity. This visual directness is at odds with the fact that the meanings are obscure, depending on coded, implied, unreal, and often spiritual narratives well beyond the pre-Raphaelites.

Critics could easily link Debussy's symbolism to the paintings of Fernand Khnopff, partly because he, like Maeterlinck, was Belgian. Khnopff's most famous painting (and one of the most famous of all symbolist works) was *I Lock Myself In* (1891) which reminded viewers of Melisande. The link between symbolism and the pre-Raphaelites is particularly evident in Khnopff's 1889 painting *Memories*, whose dreamlike narrative unreality was created by the artist photographing his wife in six different poses and then theatrically reorganizing them for the painting.[97]

Khnopff's painting shares with Denis a Whistler-like tonality combined with a pre-Raphaelite flatness and detailed clarity of line. In a statement reminiscent of Debussy, Denis wrote that "from our Symbolist point of view . . . the work of art is a general translation of individual emotions . . . art does not have superior value unless it corresponds to the noblest and most mysterious characteristics of the human soul."[98] Denis's expression of the new credo of correspondences generated by symbolism in painting is germane to Debussy. Denis affirms that "the emotions or states of the soul provoked by some spectacle create in the artistic imagination signs or plastic equivalents capable of reproducing these emotions or states of the soul without the need to create a *copy* of the initial spectacle."[99] In this act of reproduction an objective harmony within a work must be achieved so that the translation into emotion and "states of the soul" becomes possible.

The radical modernism of symbolist painting in its execution was strikingly similar to the break with the past that Debussy sought to achieve in his career. It combined a pre-Raphaelite strategy towards imagery with modernist painterly means. It paved the way to abstraction and formed the bridge to Debussy's last works as it did to the pictorial abstraction and non-objective painting we associate with modernism. As Denis put it, using the "fresh resources of modern art" the artist had to organize "our realities in such a way as to allow us to reconcile the example of the masters and the demands of our sensibility." Like the Parnassian poets before them, Debussy and the symbolists did not reject the true example of a great past, but rather the arid codification and reformulation of the past's achievements supported by a corrupt modern taste. The attempts to represent or render aesthetically or to comment directly on ordinary life were abandoned.

Indeed the paintings of Odilon Redon are the most strikingly Debussy-like.[100] In the works from the 1890s, dreamlike imagery with arresting colors and a sense of the ethereal prevail in integrated, organic compositions in which the elements of color, line, tone, and image relate as unstable elements to one another in a manner defined purely in terms of the specific work. There is more of a Turner-like kinetic and coloristic intensity in Redon than in Denis. But the elements of painting are neither abstract nor realistic. They become imaginary and aesthetically rendered with a sensual immediacy, even in the well-known flower paintings. Redon's symbolism initially seemed as bizarre as Debussy's new music once did. In Khnopff and Denis, as in Whistler, both the illusion and presence of the visible and real remain far more present. But it is Redon who most profoundly succeeds in achieving Debussy's goal of "a school of Neomusicians where care would be taken to keep music's wonderful symbols intact and to bring back respect for an art which so many outsiders have dragged in the mud."[101] It was no coincidence that Redon had admiration for Debussy.

Debussy composed with the contemporary ferment in painting in view. By cultivating a way of seeing, Debussy achieved a translucent, suggestive, and complex musical language of feeling whose novel character may have derived from visual models. This language's most elaborated form can be heard in the ballet *Jeux* and in *En blanc et noir*. In the end what distinguishes Debussy's modernism is his insistence that music has as its objective the achievement of something more than art for art's sake, or a rarefied construct of beauty. As he wrote, "textures and colors are no more than illusory disguises." If music was capable of evoking the interior life of the soul, as the symbolists thought, then the logic of music had to conform accordingly. It need not follow the traditions of realism or naturalism, or to subscribe to the compact between late romantic style and the tastes of the modern urban audience. Symbolism in this sense provided a model. "[I]ntentional disorder whose aim is merely to deceive the ear" or "bizarre, intriguing harmonies which are no more than parlour games" were as worthy of contempt as slavish imitation of late romanticism in search of commercial success. "How much has first to be discovered, then suppressed, before one can reach the naked flesh of emotion," he wrote. Debussy's process of discovery and suppression was facilitated by his encounter with the painting and painters of his world.[102]

NOTES

1. See for example the musical genealogy in E. Robert Schmitz's *The Piano Works of Claude Debussy* (New York, 1966), pp. 15–19. See the early biographies by Rollo H. Myers, *Debussy* (1949; repr., Westport, Conn., 1979) and Léon Vallas, *Claude Debussy. His Life and Works*, trans. Maire and Grace O'Brien (London, 1933).

2. R. Murray Schafer, ed., *Ezra Pound and Music. The Complete Criticism* (London, 1978), p. 96.

3. The strategy here is different from that taken by Jean-Michel Nectoux in his fine 1997 essay, "Portrait of the Artist as Roderick Usher," in *Debussy Studies*, ed. Richard Langham Smith (Cambridge, Eng., 1997), pp. 108–38.

4. As the correspondence between Chausson and Debussy indicates, both composers worked simultaneously on their respective operas through the 1890s. They were keenly aware, if only as a matter of envy, of how the other was or was not progressing. Chausson in particular sensed the incipient originality and daring of Debussy as a composer and Debussy in turn understood Chausson's struggle with the lure of Wagner. It is curious that after years of friendly rivalry neither composer ever heard the other's work. Chausson died in 1899 after breaking with Debussy and before the première of his own opera in Brussels in 1903 or the première of *Pelléas* in 1902. And Debussy did not go to Brussels to hear *Le Roi Arthus*. A recent (2001) successful concert revival of *Le Roi Arthus* in New York and the reissue of Armin Jordan's recording from the 1980s make clear that the Chausson is a great work, fully deserving of a permanent place in the repertory alongside *Pelléas*. See Jean Gallois, *Ernest Chausson* (Paris, 1994), pp. 299–371; François Lesure and Roger Nichols, eds., *Debussy Letters*, trans. Roger Nichols (London, 1987), pp. 45–65;

and Lesure, ed., *Claude Debussy. Lettres 1884–1918* (Paris, 1980), pp. 25, 42–47, 51–60, 63–66.

5. See François Lesure, *Claude Debussy avant Pelléas ou les années symbolistes* (Paris, 1992), pp. 93–124, 203–10.

6. It is clear from Debussy's friendship with Pierre Louÿs, and his frequent references to being around Stéphane Mallarmé, that his contact with writers was far closer than with painters. No important painters were comparable intimates. See Roger Nichols, *Debussy Remembered* (Portland, Or., 1992), pp. 36 and 98; and Vallas, *Claude Debussy*, pp. 52f.

7. See Nectoux, "Portrait of the Artist," pp. 110–16; and Nectoux, "Musique, Symbolisme et Art Nouveau. Notes pour une esthétique de la musique française fin de siècle," in *Art Nouveau. Jugendstil und Musik*, ed. Jürg Stenzl (Zurich, 1980), pp. 13–30.

8. This phrase is from the contemporary critic Emile Vuillermoz, quoted in Nectoux, "Portrait of the Artist," p. 108.

9. Myers, *Debussy*, p. 84.

10. Lesure and Nichols, *Debussy Letters*, p. 188.

11. I am using Nectoux's translation in "Portrait of the Artist," p. 108. He quotes the French text. See Richard Langham Smith's version in *Debussy on Music*, ed. and trans. Richard Langham Smith (New York, 1977), p. 48. As far as protecting the "sovereignty" of art, Debussy had observed already in 1893 that writers and poets "have been the most successful in guarding" it.

12. Ernest Ansermet, *Die Grundlagen der Musik im menschlichen Bewußtsein* (Munich, 1985), pp. 434–39. (The German translation was supervised by Ansermet.)

13. Myers, *Debussy*, p. 109.

14. See Edward Lockspeiser, *Debussy. His Life and Mind*, 2 vols. (Cambridge, 1978); François Lesure, *Claude Debussy. Biographie critique* (Paris, 1994); and Roger Nichols, *The Life of Debussy* (Cambridge, Eng., 1998).

15. See Vallas, *Claude Debussy*, p. 172.

16. James H. Rubin, *Impressionism* (London, 1999), p. 407. See the collected criticism in *The New Painting: Impressionism 1874–1886*, vol. 1: *Reviews*, ed. Ruth Berson (San Francisco, 1996).

17. See *The New Painting: Impressionism 1874–1886*, vol. 2: *Exhibited Works*, pp. 239–79.

18. See Mecislas Golberg, *La morale des lignes* (Paris, 1908). It is curious to note that much of the criticism on Debussy written by those who participated in the heyday of modernism—the inter-war years—was particularly keen on debunking the notion of a serious link between the visual and musical arts, particularly impressionism and Debussy.

19. See Alfredo Casella, *Music in My Time*, ed. and trans. Spencer Norton (Norman, Okla., 1955), p. 87.

20. See Julius Korngold, *Die romanische Oper der Gegenwart* (Vienna, 1922), pp. 188–95.

21. See Walter Niemann, *Die Musik der Gegenwart*, 8th ed. (Berlin, 1913), pp. 229–39. This view was reiterated a half century later by H. H. Stuckenschmidt in his *Musik des 20. Jahrhunderts* (Munich, 1969), p. 24, although the connection to neo-impressionism is also discussed.

22. See Karl Storck, *Die Musik der Gegenwart* (Stuttgart, 1919), p. 180. It is significant that these national stereotypes—the German as preeminent in music and the French as the leader in painting—may have led Debussy to reject the efforts to connect his work to French painters. He wanted in the end to redeem the quality and significance of French music. The desire to locate his greatness in terms of German musicians (e.g., Wagner)

and French painters only too thinly hid a nasty prejudice about French music and its history.

23. See Richard Strauss and Romain Rolland, *Correspondence*, ed. Rollo H. Myers (Berkeley, 1968), pp. 151–52.

24. See Gisold Lammel, *Adolph Menzel. Bildwelt und Bildregie* (Dresden, 1993), plate 12. For the Degas copy, see *Adolph Menzel 1815–1905: Between Romanticism and Impressionism*, ed. Claude Keisch and Marie U. Riemann-Reyher (New Haven and London, 1996), p. 400.

25. Lesure and Nichols, *Debussy Letters*, p. 90.

26. I want to thank Jane Fulcher for her comments on this discussion of Wagnerism. See Jane F. Fulcher, *French Politics and Music* (New York, 1999), pp. 81–83 and 170–77; Gerald D. Turbow, "Art and Politics: Wagnerism in France," in David C. Large and William Weber, eds., *Wagnerism in European Culture and Politics* (Ithaca, 1984), pp.134–66; and Leon Botstein, "Wagner in Our Century," in Joseph Kerman, ed., *Music at the Turn of the Century* (Berkeley, 1990) pp. 167–80.

27. See Günter Metken, "Wagner and the Visual Arts," in *The Wagner Handbook*, ed. Ulrich Müller and Peter Wapniewski, trans. John Deathridge (Cambridge, Mass., 1992), pp. 354–55.

28. Storck, *Die Musik*, pp. 6–7. Storck (1873–1920) wrote extensively on literature and art as well as music.

29. See Lockspeiser, *Debussy*, vol. 1, p. 130; and Lesure, *Biographie*, pp. 419 and 430.

30. The text, "Impressionist Art," by Jules Laforgue, is reprinted in Richard R. Brettell, *Impression. Painting Quickly in France, 1860–1890* (New Haven and London, 2000), pp. 233–35.

31. Ibid., p. 234.

32. See Wofgang Kemp, *Der Anteil des Betrachters. Rezeptsionsästhetische Studien zur Malerei des 19. Jahrhunderts* (Munich, 1983), esp. chapters 4–6.

33. See ibid., pp. 234f.

34. Lesure and Nichols, *Debussy Letters*, p. 41.

35. Ibid., p. 188.

36. Ibid., p. 8.

37. R. L. Smith, *Debussy on Music*, p. 75.

38. Lesure and Nichols, *Debussy Letters*, pp. 84f.

39. In addition to Lockspeiser, *Debussy*, see Kurt von Fischer's essay "Claude Debussy und das Klima des Art Nouveau. Bemerkungen zur Ästhetik Debussys und James McNeill Whistlers," in *Art Nouveau. Jugendstil und Musik*, pp. 31–46.

40. See James Abbott McNeill Whistler, "Ten O'Clock," in Whistler, *The Gentle Art of Making Enemies* (New York, 1967), pp. 131–59. It is important to note that the lecture was translated by Mallarmé and published in 1888 in the May issue of the *Revue Independente*.

41. Uncannily, many points of comparison exist between Debussy and Schumann, including their engagement with literature and of course their foray into criticism. Even Schumann's notion of philistinism can be compared with Debussy's later tirades against contemporary taste. The key difference is that Schumann's criticism was not an act driven by the need for money. It was not cynical and calculated. In contrast, it is hard to read Debussy's criticism as an entirely reliable guide to what he thought. The letters, however, are indispensable for a closer account of his views.

42. Lesure and Nichols, *Debussy Letters*, p. 228.

43. Wagner's influence on the character and dissemination of a reigning construct of music history and aesthetics was great. This fueled the attitude of those in the 1880s who began to see Wagner as the last great exponent of an unusable romantic past.

44. This precise point was made by Richard Langham Smith in *Debussy on Music*, pp. 69f; see also Andrew Thomson, *Vincent d'Indy and His World* (Oxford, 1996), pp. 96f. and 147f.; and Norman Demuth, *Vincent d'Indy 1851–1931, Champion of Classicism* (London, 1951), pp. 21–22, 39–40, and 92.

45. Laforgue, "Impressionist Art," p. 235.

46. See Lesure and Nichols, *Debussy Letters*, pp. 52, 189, 195.

47. See in particular the 1914 interview with M. M. D. Calvocoressi in *The Etude*, reprinted in R. L. Smith, *Debussy on Music*, pp. 317–21.

48. Whistler, "Ten O'Clock," p. 143.

49. Ibid., p. 146.

50. See R. L. Smith, *Debussy on Music*, pp. 270f.

51. See the paintings in *Whistler. A Retrospective*, ed. Robin Spencer (New York, 1989), pp. 90, 92, 93, 111.

52. Lesure and Nichols, *Debussy Letters*, p. 75.

53. The subject was *Pelléas*. Ironically one of Debussy's least favorite composers, Saint-Saëns criticized d'Indy for subordinating harmony to melody in his textbook. But Saint-Saëns's view was based on the truth value of tonality as the guiding principle of melodic construction, a view not shared by Debussy who, as Laloy pointed out, emancipated tones from their supposed fixed relationships with other tones according to conventional scales. Hence Debussy's attraction to other patterns, including pentatonic scales that suggested different note relationships. See R. L. Smith, *Debussy on Music*, p. 69; Vincent d'Indy, *Cours de composition musicale*, vol. 1 (Paris, 1912), pp. 7–21; and Camille Saint-Saëns, *Outspoken Essays on Music*, trans. Fred Rothwell (London, 1922), pp. 1–51.

54. *Louis Laloy (1874–1944) on Debussy, Ravel and Stravinsky*, ed. and trans. Deborah Priest (Aldershot, Eng., 1999), pp. 90–91.

55. Lesure and Nichols, *Debussy Letters*, p. 58.

56. Laloy, "Claude Debussy and Debussyism," in *Louis Laloy*, pp. 85–98.

57. Ibid., p. 91.

58. Ibid., p. 90.

59. As Debussy wrote in 1911 to Godet, "textures and colours are no more than illusory disguises." Lesure and Nichols, *Debussy Letters*, p. 250.

60. See Vallas, *Claude Debussy*, pp. 171–72, and Myers, *Debussy*, p.79.

61. Lesure and Nichols, *Debussy Letters*, p. 184.

62. Ibid., p. 118.

63. Ibid., p. 166.

64. Ibid., p. 140. Levade was the 1899 Prix de Rome winner.

65. See François Delalande, "The Construction of Musical Form by the Listener in Debussy's *La Terasse des Audiences du Claire de Lune*" in *Der Hörer als Interpret*, ed. Helga de la Motte-Haber and Renhard Kopiez (Frankfurt, 1995), pp. 149–67.

66. I follow Michael Fried's discussion in his *Manet's Modernism or, The Face of Painting in the 1860s* (Chicago, 1996).

67. Lockspeiser, *Debussy*, vol. 2, pp. 18 and 140. See also Vallas, *Claude Debussy*, p. 53, and Gallois, *Chausson*, pp. 574–79.

68. See R. L. Smith, *Debussy on Music*, pp. 120 and 223–25; also Lesure and Nichols, *Debussy Letters*, pp. 14, 41, and 110f.

69. See for example, *Debussy on Music*, p. 146; *Debussy Letters*, pp. 77, 89, and 216. For Mahler, see Lockspeiser's chapter on Strauss and Mahler in *Debussy*, vol. 2, pp.

96–111. To Mahler's credit, he chose to conduct Debussy relatively often when he was in New York. See Knud Martner, *Gustav Mahler im Konzertsaal* (Copenhagen, 1985) pp. 158–59.

70. See Lockspeiser, *Debussy*, vol. 2, pp. 96–111; R. L. Smith, *Debussy on Music*, pp. 101, 159–61, and 270f.; and Lesure and Nichols, *Debussy Letters*, pp. 111 and 179.

71. Lesure and Nichols, *Debussy Letters*, p. 172.

72. Fried, *Manet's Modernism*, p. 289. The painting Fried describes is *The Old Musician* from 1862.

73. In addition to the pages cited above, see d'Indy, *Cours de composition*, pp. 23–46.

74. Lesure and Nichols, *Debussy Letters*, p. 42.

75. After all, one of the few things Saint-Saëns could say positively about Debussy was that he rejected the German example, even Wagner, with the exception of Debussy's Wagnerian emphasis on the orchestra in *Pelléas*. See Saint-Saëns, *Outspoken Essays*, p. 40.

76. Laloy, "Debussy's Compositional Style," in *Louis Laloy*, pp. 81–84. The final phrase suggests Laloy's linkage of Debussy to impressionism (p. 83).

77. See Stefan Jarocínski, *Debussy, impressionnisme et symbolisme* (Warsaw, 1966; French trans., Paris, 1970).

78. See Claude Abravanel, "Symbolism and Performance," in *Debussy in Performance*, ed. James R. Briscoe (New Haven, 1999), pp. 29–34.

79. Lesure and Nichols, *Debussy Letters*, p. 41, 52, 58, 94, and 220.

80. See the excellent discussion of Turner in Lawrence Gowing, *Turner: Imagination and Reality* (New York, 1966).

81. See reproductions in Gowing, *Turner*, pp. 14 , 33, 44.

82. See Lesure and Nichols, *Debussy Letters*, p. 87.

83. See the three letters in which Debussy describes his difficulties (two letters to Godet in 1911, and one to Caplet in the same year). Ibid., pp. 235, 250, and 252. See also Edward Lockspeiser, *Debussy et Edgar Poe: manuscrits et documents inédits* (Monaco, 1962).

84. See Richard Langham Smith, "Debussy and the Pre-Raphaelites," *Nineteenth-Century Music* 5, no. 2 (fall 1981): 95–109.

85. I am indebted to the fine monograph by Elizabeth Prettejohn, *The Art of the Pre-Raphaelites* (Princeton, 2000). See also Timothy Hinton, *The Pre-Raphaelites* (London, 1970).

86. The reader is referred to the paintings *The Blessed Damozel* (c.1856–1861) and *The Beguiling of Merlin* (1870–1874) by Edward Coley Burne-Jones; *Paolo and Francesca da Rimini* (1855), *Dantis Amor* (1859), *Before the Battle* (1858, retouched 1862), *The Blue Closet* (1856–1857), and *The Blessed Damozel* by Dante Gabriel Rossetti; *Ophelia* (1851–1852) by John Everett Millais; and *The Lady of Shalott* (1886–1905) by William Holman Hunt. Reproductions of all paintings listed are to be found in Prettejohn, *Pre-Raphaelites*.

87. The various depictions of the "Lady of Shallot" can also be found in Prettejohn, *Pre-Raphaelites*.

88. "He said, 'She has a lovely face;/ God in his mercy lend her grace,/ the Lady of Shallot.'"

89. Laloy, p. 78; also pp. 57–60.

90. For Redon, see Jean Vialla, *La Vie et l'œuvre d'Odilon Redon* (Paris, 1988); and *Odilon Redon. Prince of Dreams, 1840–1916*, ed. Douglas W. Druick et. al. (Chicago, 1994); for Maurice Denis, see Robert L. Delevoy, *Symbolists and Symbolism* (New York, 1983); Michael Gibson, *Symbolism* (Cologne, 1995); Philippe Jullian, *The Symbolists* (London, 1973); and Russell T. Clement, *Four French Symbolists. A Sourcebook* (Westport, Conn., 1996).

91. Lesure and Nichols, *Debussy Letters,* p. 249; Nectoux, "Musique, Symbolisme et Art Nouveau"; see also Delevoy, *Symbolists and Symbolism.* For a general discussion of symbolism, see Delevoy, Gibson, and Jullian, among others.

92. See Jullian, *Symbolists*, p. 35.

93. See Mallarmé's 1885 "Richard Wagner. Rêverie d'un poëte français," in *Œuvres complètes,* ed. Henri Mondor and G. Jean Aubry (Paris, 1945), pp. 541–46.

94. See in particular the lecture fragments from 1894 given at Oxford and Cambridge by Mallarmé, published as "La Musique et les lettres," in *Œuvres complètes,* pp. 642–54, particularly 647–50.

95. See the discussion of Mallarmé in René Wellek, *A History of Modern Criticism,* vol. 4 (New Haven and London, 1965), pp. 452–63.

96. On Debussy's relationship to Yvonne Lerolle, see Nectoux, "Musique, Symbolisme et Art Nouveau," pp. 114f.

97. See Gibson, Symbolism, p. 91.

98. Maurice Denis, "Cézanne," in *Art in Theory, 1900–1990: An Anthology of Changing Ideas,* ed. Charles Harrison and Paul Wood (Oxford, 1993), pp. 41–53. For paintings by Denis, see Jullian, *Symbolists.*

99. Denis, "From Gaugin and Van Gogh to Neoclassicism," in *Art on Thery,* p. 50.

100. See for example, *Spring* (1883), *Saint John* (1892), *Mystical Conversations* (c.1896), *The Boat* (c.1897), *Sita* (c.1893), *Oannes* (c.1910), and *The Cyclops* (c.1914). Reproduced in Druick et al., *Prince of Dreams.*

101. Lesure and Nichols, *Debussy Letters,* p. 56.

102. Ibid., p. 250.

The Symphony in Debussy's World

A Context for His Views on the Genre and

Early Interpretations of *La Mer*

B RIAN H ART

The history of the symphony in France is quickly told, for there
are remarkably few notable symphonies by Frenchmen. [. . .]
French composers who did write symphonies were either too heavily influenced by models from across the Rhine or simply lacked
the essential qualities for the task. This certainly applies to
Chausson, Dukas, Lalo and Saint-Saëns, to the young Bizet and,
in a lesser degree, to Franck and d'Indy.
> —*John Manduell, "Albert Roussel," in* The Symphony

There is but one true music, and it carries within itself the right to
exist, whether it borrows the rhythm of a waltz (even one from the
café-concert) or the imposing frame of a symphony. And why not
admit that of the two, good taste will often be on the side of the
waltz, while the symphony will scarcely hide the pompous heap of
its mediocrity!
> —*Claude Debussy, "Du Goût"*

The French symphony finds as little favor among many contemporary
scholars as it did with Debussy, a famous antagonist of the genre. The
subject has received little study, and writers who discuss French symphonies and their composers often use terms similar to those of Debussy,
especially when they speak of symphonies composed between 1885 and
1920, ironically the most vital period for the genre in France.[1] To blithely
stereotype all French symphonists of this time as incompetent creators

of sterile works, however, does an injustice to a whole body of symphonies (some of which hold secure places in the standard repertory) and misrepresents the central position the genre occupied in turn-of-the-century France. In the years around 1900 and throughout the age of *debussysme*, the symphony found acceptance at the highest levels of the musical establishment; for the first time in France, composers were actively encouraged to write symphonies. The types of symphonies they wrote, and the purposes for which they composed them, varied widely, but their activity indicates a renewed vitality for the genre. Several composers from César Franck's circle pioneered a new kind of symphony in which they attempted to express aesthetic, philosophical, spiritual, or political ideas through the work. A proper appreciation of this uniquely French composition—the "message-symphony," as I will call it—is central not only for recognizing the importance of native symphonists in Debussy's time but, as we will see, for understanding his own critical and compositional responses to the genre.

By considering what the genre meant to French composers of the prewar era and examining the kinds of symphonies they wrote, we will gain a clearer picture of Debussy's attitude toward the symphony than we have had to this point. Most discussions of the composer's aesthetics make at least passing mention of his hostility, but none of these adequately explains the rationale behind his antagonism because they do not sufficiently examine the genre as it existed in his day, nor do they observe that his responses to it changed over time. For example, writers cite the composer's assertions that the symphony is obsolete, dependent on "rules," and of Germanic origin, but not his charge that modern French symphonies were presuming to express "profound" thoughts and abstract ideas—a direct response to the message-symphony.

To study the French symphony also provides insight into one of the most authoritative early reviews of *La Mer*. Debussy's close friend Louis Laloy described the composer's self-proclaimed *trois esquisses symphoniques* ("three symphonic sketches") as a symphonic poem whose movements had "the role and form" of a symphony. Other critics supported Laloy's interpretation and Debussy did not object. As Laloy suggests, the work appropriates certain technical elements associated with the symphony, such as cyclic organization, and manipulates others freely. Significantly, the type of symphony that *La Mer* most closely approaches stylistically is the polemic "message-symphony," the French symphony most popular in his time—though, as one would expect, Debussy assiduously avoids those aspects of the symphony that deal with expressive or metaphorical communication. *La Mer* freely salvages and reinterprets selected technical processes of the message-symphony but rejects its essence.

The Symphony in Debussy's France

Nineteenth-century French composers who aspired to write symphonies received little support from the musical establishment. Vincent d'Indy, the director of the newly founded Schola Cantorum, determined to rectify the official neglect of the symphony. In 1900 he initiated a composition program at the Schola designed to rival the Conservatoire's. Whereas the latter valued dramatic music, the Schola favored symphonies and other forms of instrumental music.[2] Within a few years, the success of the Schola's program impelled the Conservatoire to follow suit and add the symphony to its own curriculum. The two schools became engaged in a highly publicized "war" (their term) in which, among other things, they developed opposing pedagogical models for the symphony—the Schola's strict, the Conservatoire's relatively liberal—and claimed that only theirs represented the viable paradigm for French symphonists.[3]

Partially as a result of the *guerre des écoles*, supporters of the symphony split into two mutually hostile factions; one included d'Indy, musicians associated with the Schola, and former pupils of Franck; the other consisted of composers from the Conservatoire. Not only did these camps differ in the symphonic models they followed but, even more importantly, they composed their symphonies for sharply divergent purposes. The Schola-based faction believed that one could convey feelings, experiences, and even ideas in a symphony without compromising its integrity. On the other hand, symphonists allied with the Conservatoire valued the genre for the dispassionate expression of clear form and logical flow; intense feelings might motivate the work but the composer tempered their heat in the "cool" jar of rationally conceived symphonic structures. While the *scholiste* symphony challenged the listener to ponder messages symbolically conveyed by the music, the *conservatoiriste* symphony invited the same to derive intellectual stimulation and pleasure from following the composer's manipulations of the musical argument. Paul-Marie Masson aptly described the difference between the two groups when he wrote that d'Indy's faction sought to create a *musique-discours*, while his opponents cultivated a *musique-contemplation*.[4]

Let us look more closely at the scholiste message-symphony, since this is the type of native symphony most relevant to our consideration of Debussy. D'Indy and his camp believed strongly in the power of a symphony to convey ideas. As Guy Ropartz wrote, speaking of Franck's symphony, "As it is childish to try to paint objects of the outside world through sounds, so it is rational to choose the immaterial language of music to translate sensations, sentiments, the ideas of a lofty philosophy.

One can think in music the same as one can think in prose and in verse."[5] Symphonists in this camp thought of nineteenth-century symphonies in terms of a progression from states of darkness to light or doubt to faith, the meanings they associated with Beethoven's Fifth and Franck's symphony respectively; and indeed many of their own works follow the same implied program but are otherwise abstract. But sometimes they gave more specific identities to the "darkness" and "light" with reference to the artistic and political debates going on around them, and such topical symphonies represented not just works of art but vehicles for communicating the composer's ideological and moral convictions to an audience. The beginning of the century, therefore, saw the emergence of the message-symphony, designed to express a clearly defined and frequently controversial extramusical idea, which the composer considered an immanent part of the work.[6]

Since an idea or message in a symphony could not speak for itself without verbal mediation, the composer explained it to the audience by means of a printed exegesis, a text set in the work, or the quotation of familiar melodies. Message-symphonies were not designed for casual listening: composers expected audiences to follow the abstract musical argument and apply whatever commentary was provided in order to interpret the message correctly. To communicate the message aurally the composer employed conventions drawn both from the realms of program and absolute music. Cyclism unified the piece and kept it "on topic"; thematic transformation depicted the metamorphosis of the "dark" element into "light"; and a closing peroration, usually symbolized by an affirmative chorale, announced the final defeat of the dark element.[7] All of these elements can exist to some degree in *franckiste* symphonies that lack messages, but they are especially prominent in the message-symphony.

French message-symphonies are not the first to convey explicit ideas, of course: Beethoven's Ninth did so long before, and many non-French musicians contemporaneous with d'Indy did the same: Mahler, Tchaikovsky, Ives, Nielsen, and others. What distinguishes message-symphonies from these non-French compositions is the intentionally *polemic* nature of many of its ideas. Symphonies created in part as musical pamphlets—the composer's personal salvo into the cultural battles and ideological quarrels of the day—epitomized Masson's *musique-discours*; although such works could be appreciated without knowledge of their message, they made no pretense to be simply and exclusively a meditative aesthetic experience (*musique-contemplation*).

The messages took many forms. D'Indy's Second Symphony in B-flat (1902–1903) and Ropartz's Third Symphony in E Major (1905–

1906) are the most celebrated examples of the message-symphony but differ strikingly in their ideas as well as in the means used to convey them.[8] D'Indy based his symphony on the interplay of two motives heard at the beginning: throughout its four movements these motives struggle for priority, both in their original form and as proxy themes they create. The finale culminates in a large peroration in which the second motive (as a chorale) triumphs decisively over the first. The composer declined to explain the implied "narrative," but soon after the premiere in 1904 his pupil René de Castéra published an extended analysis that assigned concrete and provocative identities to the dueling motives: the vanquished motive "in the composer's mind vaguely symbolizes the modern element of bad influence," while the victorious one "is the element of tradition, of good influence."[9] Castéra's interpretation portrayed d'Indy's symphony as an allegorical contest between the forces of traditional and modern (i.e., Debussyist) musics, in which "tradition" (the art of Beethoven, Wagner, and Franck) emerged triumphant. The composer himself remained silent about his intentions, saying only that the thematic struggle represented a fight between good and evil;[10] yet he clearly sanctioned or at least accepted the distribution of Castéra's analysis, for scholistes and informed critics reprinted it in reviews as well as concert notes for subsequent performances.

Few critics engaged the message of this symphony in their reviews, even after becoming aware of it; they praised or rebuked d'Indy's work (usually the former) almost solely on musical grounds. They did not hold their peace in 1906, however, when they encountered a much more direct and divisive message in Guy Ropartz's Third Symphony. Rather than relying on music alone to carry the argument, as d'Indy did, Ropartz's symphony sets a poem of his own creation. The text considers the contrast between the radiance of nature and the misery of humanity. As a solution to the mortal condition, the composer encourages his listeners to love one another and boldly commit themselves to seeking after Truth and Justice:

> Let us love one another! Transformed humanity rises toward the city of joy and ideal liberty where kings are no more, neither masters, where the single law of love has replaced all the henceforth useless laws! [. . .] And you, Sun, arise radiantly! Unite your dazzling light to the fires of the ideal sun of Truth, Justice, and Love![11]

This time the message was unambiguous and aroused consternation among the critics. Some interpreted the work as a socialist tract and responded accordingly.[12] Indeed, as the above passage suggests, the poem abounds with incendiary rhetoric certain to appeal to the Left and inflame the Center and the Right, with its references to internationalism and antimonarchism and the valuation of Truth, Justice, and Love above duty, honor, and authority. The symphony is scored for four soloists, chorus, and orchestra. Leitmotifs represent "joy," "human suffering," and "love." At the climax of the finale, Ropartz transforms the "suffering" motive into the "joy" theme to demonstrate the ultimate victory of the human spirit when love reigns.

Other composers followed the lead of d'Indy and Ropartz in writing message-symphonies. Franck's pupil Charles Tournemire wrote five between 1913 and 1924, each accompanied with a detailed poetic exegesis. While the messages of d'Indy and Ropartz took opposing sides in artistic and sociopolitical disputes, Tournemire's symphonies proclaimed faith in overt and increasingly mystical terms.[13] Even composers at the Conservatoire occasionally tried their hands at the genre, with messages slanted to reflect Republican sympathies. Théodore Dubois's *Symphonie française* (1908) featured a rendition of the *Marseillaise* at the climax, leading many critics to interpret this work as a patriotic declaration of moral victory of the modern Republic over Germany; and Charles-Marie Widor described his *Symphonie antique* (1911) as a dramatization of the musical evolution of the *Te Deum* melody from its origins as a Greek war hymn to a Gregorian chant, the intent apparently being to assert an equality between pagan and Christian worlds.[14]

The symphony, then, flourished in Debussy's Paris—a world in which it was embraced by numerous composers, critics, administrators, and polemicists, each of whom developed their own agendas for the genre. Composers responded with vibrant new works which, contrary to their current reputation, were neither Teutonic epigones nor pedantry incarnate. Three kinds of symphonies emerged: Conservatoire-sponsored works that made no claims to having any extramusical meaning; franckiste symphonies that expressed a general emotional state or idea, such as doubt emerging to faith; and the much more explicit "message-symphony" designed to assert specific and topical philosophical convictions.[15] By the war the message-symphony had become the dominant form—a uniquely French representative of a litigious age in which musicians openly participated in sociopolitical debates. The influence of this symphony was such that many writers regarded all new symphonies as works purporting to relate ideas—a significant point when considering Debussy's relationship to the genre.

Debussy's Opposition to the Symphony

Throughout his brief tenure as a music critic, Debussy condemned the symphony relentlessly—literally from his first to last articles.[16] One finds interesting aberrations: for instance, he always seems to have spoken of Franck's Symphony in D Minor with respect.[17] Most other post-Beethoven symphonies he sharply criticized or flippantly dismissed.[18] The *reasons* Debussy gave for his antipathy changed over time, however, and one can trace three distinct phases in his writings. The early articles (1901–1903) emphasized technical and aesthetic deficiencies in the symphony, and these are the ones that commentators quote almost exclusively. In succeeding years Debussy changed his focus to condemn the goal behind the writing of many symphonies of the day, i.e., to express ideas and ideologies—a direct response, presumably, to the message-symphony. Finally, in his late articles, written on the eve of the war, Debussy's attacks took on a nationalistic cast and, while not disavowing any of his earlier criticisms, he now denounced the symphony primarily for its Germanic origins.

Debussy wrote his first set of reviews for the journal *La Revue blanche* (April–December 1901). The opening article contains his most famous and extensive commentary on the symphony, a review of the Symphony No. 1 (1900) by d'Indy's pupil Georges-Martin Witkowski. In it he reiterates the familiar charge that the genre was obsolete and continued to exist merely out of a misplaced respect for the past.

> It seemed to me that [Witkowski's symphony] proved the uselessness of the symphony since Beethoven. As early as Schumann and Mendelssohn the symphony is but a deferential repetition of the same forms, already with less authority. [. . .] [T]he few inspired successes in this genre poorly excuse the studious and stiff exercises one habitually calls symphonies. [. . .] Must we conclude that despite so many attempts at transformation, the symphony belongs to the past, in all its rectangular elegance, ceremonious order [and] philosophical and rouged public? Really, haven't we only placed the disobliging copper of modern instrumentation upon its old frame of faded gold?[19]

Since Beethoven achieved the fullest possible expression in the symphony, Debussy argued that theorists thereafter converted his personal style into immutable principles. To write an acceptable symphony today, one must write it "correctly." Before composing a note, the symphonist knew to parse his work into three or four movements; set the first in sonata-allegro form and make the primary and secondary themes oppose each other in character and key; develop and recapitulate the themes; and transform the principal theme into a victory chorale or something similar at the end of the composition—all done in a way to astonish the *Kenner* and excite the *Liebhaber*.[20] Like the Conservatoire professors of his youth, Debussy therefore regarded virtually any new symphony, scholiste or conservatoiriste, as an academic exercise (a *symphonie d'école*). He concluded his critique with the observation that Witkowski "listens to the voices that are certainly 'authorized': it seems to me that they hinder him from hearing a more personal voice."[21]

Debussy resumed his commentary about the symphony in a cycle of reviews for the daily *Gil Blas* in 1903. Here he concentrated less on the "rules" of the genre than on the heavy burden its lofty reputation laid on composers. The contemporary symphonist's effort-filled attempts to write works worthy of that legacy always led, in Debussy's view, to unfortunate results, as in Ropartz's First Symphony (1894–1895). Like Witkowski's, the work centered around a Breton tune. Debussy deplored this practice: to subject liturgical melodies or folk songs to symphonic developmental procedures ruined the tune and did nothing for the symphony.[22] But he had a more fundamental complaint. Although Ropartz tried to make the "authorized" forms speak with "a more personal voice," the cumbersome legacy of "symphonic tradition" ultimately defeated him.

> The [First Symphony] has many of the qualities that make Guy Ropartz an energetic and productive man. Why does he sometimes seem thwarted and even a bit paralyzed here? Would it not be because of this kind of fascination that the word "symphony" holds for today's musicians, where the concern for form prevails over freedom of ideas?
>
> By alternating fast and slow passages Guy Ropartz has tried to shake off the heavy block of marble that a symphony represents; but right away this harms the unity of the composition—the first movement can take the place of the last and vice-versa, nothing distinguishing them very clearly.[23]

Instead of grappling fruitlessly with traditional expectations, Debussy concluded, the post-Beethoven symphony would do better to eject them completely; thus he praised *Antar* as "a pure masterpiece" that "[renewed] the symphony by sending the customary form packing."[24]

Soon thereafter, Debussy reviewed the Third Symphony of Franck's pupil Paul de Wailly, and concluded that contemporary symphonists, striving to create sufficient "profundity" and "grandeur" in their "heavy blocks of marble," smothered themselves:

> This little party began with a symphony by P. de Wailly. [. . .] In it I found not his usual tenderness of ideas but a concern with being robust to the point of breathlessness. And not that he doesn't show serious qualities, but I decidedly believe this title of "symphony" has such a serious air that it intimidates whoever has the audacity to assume responsibility for it.[25]

Debussy retired from music criticism between 1904 and 1912, the period in which the message-symphony arose. In letters and interviews from the period, however, he continued to criticize the symphony. Now, his concerns moved from the "suffocating" content of the symphony to its goal, the attempt to convey ideas and messages through music. He never mentions the message-symphony by name, much less specific examples, but given the attention that the works of d'Indy, Ropartz, and Dubois received in the concert hall and in print at this time, it is reasonable to suppose that he had such works in mind.

As early as 1901, Debussy complained to Paul Dukas that their contemporaries were writing music for the wrong motives:

> There's no need [. . .] for music to make people think! [. . .] It would be enough if music could make people listen, despite themselves and despite their petty, mundane troubles [. . .] It would be enough if they could no longer recognize their own grey, dull faces, if they felt that for a moment they had been dreaming of an imaginary country, that's to say one that can't be found on the map.[26]

By 1909, in the face of the popularity of the message-symphony, even within some pockets of the Conservatoire, Debussy took his grievance public, decrying attempts to compose musical sermons instead of works that inspired and expressed feelings:

> We attach too much importance to the writing of music, to formula and to craft! We seek ideas within ourselves when we should seek them outside ourselves. We combine, we construct, we imagine themes that seek to express ideas; we develop them, we modify them when encountering other themes that represent other ideas. We are making metaphysics, but we are not making music. Music

should be recorded spontaneously by the listener's ear; it should not be necessary for him to have to try to decipher abstract ideas in the meanderings of a complicated development.[27]

To dream, to let the imagination soar, to engage in "the sentimental transposition of the *invisible* aspects of Nature"—this for Debussy was the true purpose of music.[28] He protested against the common practice of accompanying performances of modern symphonies with concert notes that contained detailed analyses, theme sheets, and/or written interpretations to help the audience "understand" the work. Such guides encouraged listeners to rely on the notes instead of their own ears to hear and judge a work, seduced them into thinking that anyone could write a symphony by following the proper "recipe" ("it is to encourage the symphony in all its horrors"), or simply mystified them.[29] True music needed neither interpretive aids nor repeated hearings for comprehension, and any composition that required either—such as a message-symphony—was "metaphysics" rather than art.

Debussy once more became a professional critic when he agreed in 1912 to serve as co-reviewer with d'Indy for the progressive journal of the Sociéte Internationale de Musique (the *Revue musicale S.I.M.*). The state of French music at this time gave Debussy no joy. As relations between France and Germany deteriorated, he became increasingly distressed about the degree of Teutonic influence on French composers. Debussy repeatedly exhorted his fellow musicians to stop tilling their neighbor's garden and attend to their own, which was dying of neglect.[30] They should "decongest" their music and not "stifle emotion under a mass of motives and superimposed designs."[31] Debussy's attacks on the symphony accordingly adopted an overtly patriotic tone: now, instead of citing technical or aesthetic deficiencies in the genre, he focused on its provenance. For the symphony to be Germanic in origin was motive enough for French composers to avoid it.

[W]here does the symphonic music of our land come from? What is the heredity that guides us toward this mode of expression? . . . With great docility our musicians take their inspiration first from the poems of Liszt and then from those of Richard Strauss. Take note, moreover, that all their attempts at emancipation were severely put down. Each time they wanted to free themselves from this tradition, they were called back to order. They were crushed under the weight of sublime examples. [. . .] Beethoven was called to the rescue.[32]

In his final public statement, Debussy wrote, "Let us rediscover our liberty, our forms [. . .] Let us no longer smother ourselves writing symphonies, for which we strain our muscles without very appreciable results. If needed, let us prefer operetta to them."[33]

Throughout his career as a critic and public spokesman for French music, Debussy amassed a list of grievances against the symphony; his hostility never abated, though the reasons for it evolved. At first he concentrated on technical and aesthetic issues, especially the notion that to swear fealty to "rules" of symphonic composition was to abdicate authorial responsibility. The perceived obligation to remain worthy of Beethoven might signify seriousness of purpose to symphonists, but Debussy saw it as an invitation to grandiloquence and inspirational sterility. After the rise of the message-symphony, Debussy began to censure composers for making music a conduit for ideas rather than feelings. Finally, as war approached Debussy added the charge that French symphonists worked with a genre whose conventions and rhetorical style belonged ultimately to a hostile outsider. His concerns therefore moved from mechanical issues involved in composing symphonies to considering what the genre *meant* in his day.

Louis Laloy's Interpretation of *La Mer*

Recognizing the prominence of the symphony—especially the message-symphony—also allows us to place an important early interpretation of *La Mer* into context. Reviewing the premiere in 1905, Louis Laloy remarked that Debussy's new composition was more large-scale and developed than his previous works but no less evocative.[34] Upon the second performance three years later, Laloy offered a more detailed analysis based on the following premise:

[T]he three movements of the work have the role and form of a first movement, scherzo, and finale of a symphony. You will respond that the laws of symphonic composition are not those of the symphonic poem. This is true if one thinks of certain particular laws, such as the obligatory modulation for the second idea; it is false, however, if one means to speak only of the general laws of equilibrium, which are the necessary condition for art. [. . .] The music of *La Mer* can, strictly speaking, be explained by itself; this fact in no way diminishes the descriptive power of the music, in fact quite the contrary.[35]

Laloy was one of Debussy's closest confidantes, and he could write of the composer's intentions with authority. Debussy warmly praised his friend's 1905 review, and although Laloy raised the specter of the symphony only later, one doubts that he would have done so at all without the composer's indulgence, and Debussy apparently never challenged Laloy's reading.[36] One can only speculate whether the composer himself thought of *La Mer* as a disguised symphony, but we know he considered it a unified entity. In 1907 he declined Gabriel Pierné's offer to conduct "Jeux de vagues" by itself (at a time when *La Mer* had been played only once in a poor performance and opportunities to rehear the whole had not yet materialized), while by contrast he regularly agreed to partial performances of *Nocturnes*.[37] In a 1910 interview, Debussy referred to *La Mer* as "ma symphonie"; whether he meant "symphony" or "symphonic work" is not clear (*symphonie* can signify either), but he definitely did not say "mes esquisses symphoniques."[38]

How, by the criteria of Laloy's day, did the sections of *La Mer* "have the role and form of a first movement, scherzo, and finale of a symphony"? According to composers, theorists, and critics from both camps, the most important attribute of a modern symphony was that it possessed some means of organic unification by which the disparate movements bonded into an indissoluble whole. Some writers insisted that the unity be audibly demonstrated through thematic interconnections while others argued for a more intuitive singularity of style and character.[39] *La Mer* possesses both kinds of unity: two themes introduced in the first movement return in the last, whereas most French symphonies confine themselves to one cyclic motive. More important, the work has that oneness of style and character that most critics valued above thematic recall. Debussy reveals this deeper homogeneity through subtle interconnections among themes, rhythms, harmonies, and methods of growth.[40] Further, although he characteristically keeps tonal areas vaguely defined, the larger trajectory suggests a plan similar to those of many nineteenth-century symphonies: the first and last movements are rooted around the same center (D-flat, the first tenuously so), and the middle occupies a third-related key (E Major, the flattened mediant).

Theorists expected a symphony to observe at least the basic outline of sonata-cycle structure—first movement in sonata-allegro form, interior movements as slow and/or scherzo passages, finale a summation. They did not, however, oblige a symphonist to follow the cycle blindly: they welcomed experimentation as long as the results justified the innovations.[41] That *La Mer* has only three movements places it firmly in the French symphonic tradition, for many of these works (especially those by franckistes) follow a tripartite division. Although highly elusive, the forms of the movements arguably bear enough superficial resemblances to the traditional structures that many analysts cite them as a frame of reference. Some interpret "De l'aube à midi sur la mer," for example, as an irregular sonata without a recapitulation, though others dispense with the sonata paradigm entirely in favor of a sectional form.[42] Whatever the case, "De l'aube à midi" satisfies the principal function of a first movement by introducing the cyclic themes and setting out the terms for subsequent movements. "Jeux de vagues" clearly functions as a scherzo (and as an interlude between the related action of the outer movements), although it does not adhere to any conventional scherzo form.[43] "Dialogue du vent et de la mer" has at first glance the most traditional design: to many it suggests a rondo built upon the alternation of material representing wind and sea, though others see it as another sectional structure.[44] More important, "Dialogues" alludes to the rhetorical features of a nineteenth-century symphonic finale: the reprise of its principal theme leads to the dynamic and textural climax of the composition, followed by a chorale peroration;[45] and, unlike the preceding movements, it ends with a firm tonic cadence. Like most post-Beethoven symphonies, *La Mer* places its primary weight on the finale: one senses a steady progression from first movement to last.[46]

As Debussy caustically suggested, the symphony aroused expectations of solemn musical statements. All the more telling, then, that to many listeners *La Mer* carried a "serious" ambiance, at least compared to his earlier works: his evocation of the sea was not merely picturesque music for pleasure. Debussy's vision in fact struck some critics as so earnest that they deplored the supposed loss of spontaneity and poetic sentiment.[47] Debussy wrote *La Mer* at a time of considerable turbulence in his personal life: his abandonment of his wife Lily Texier and her attempted suicide, his liaison with Emma Bardac, and the resultant estrangement of the composer from many of his friends all took place within the two years that he wrote and premiered this work. Simon Trezise hypothesizes that these events inform the agitated mood of the finale: consciously or not, the seastorm mirrored the tempest in Debussy's own life.[48] Nineteenth-century composers valued the symphony in part because of its reputation as a medium for musical catharsis; might Debussy have approached *La Mer* in a similar light, done in his own way? In any case, his contemporaries heard a new voice in *La Mer*, one which they interpreted as that of a newfound sobriety.

Many of the preceding correlations between *La Mer* and the symphony have been enumerated by others and allow us to conclude with Trezise that "*La Mer* comes surprisingly close to the rhetorical and generic characteristics of the nineteenth-century symphony."[49] In terms of codes and stylistic signs, *La Mer* comes especially close to the franckiste cyclic symphony and is in fact more integrated than most such works. But another symphony *does* enjoy the same kind of tight organization and unity of *La Mer*: the message-symphony. Unity in such symphonies as d'Indy's Second and Ropartz's Third typically existed at a deeper level than in works like Witkowski's, which simply recalled themes; the composer used thematic transformation and thematic interconnections to guide the progress of the discourse and the metamorphoses of the ideas. Similarly, last-movement conventions like the summation of themes and the culminating peroration served a much more central function because they were so invested with extramusical meaning. The message-symphony was in its infancy when Debussy unveiled *La Mer*: d'Indy's symphony had premiered the previous year. By 1908 the genre had reached full bloom: Ropartz's symphony had appeared and other composers like Dubois were about to release theirs. On a strictly musical level, then, Debussy seems to be making a rapprochement not only with the symphony in general or even the franckiste symphony in particular but specifically with the kind most opposed to his personal aesthetics—the kind most dependent upon the rhetorical conventions Debussy despised (development, recapitulation, peroration) and more dedicated than any other to the expression of "profound" ideas.

Nevertheless, although analysts today routinely describe *La Mer* as a symphony, even as the greatest French symphony (usually to the detriment of more traditional works), those of Debussy's time would most likely have categorized the work as a *voisin-symphonie* or pseudosymphony—Conservatoire theorist Albert Lavignac's term for a work that strayed too far from structural and stylistic norms.[50] None of the movements adhere to traditional symphonic structures in any orthodox way, however much they might allude to those forms. Further, the thematic material of *La Mer* is not what one would expect in a composition of "serious" character: it has few extended themes, and none yield to fragmentation or motivic development; the work mostly consists of short motives and arabesques that constantly evolve into other motives. As for the message-symphony, the most obvious difference between it and *La Mer* is that Debussy's work makes no attempt to express personal thoughts, metaphysical ideas, polemic positions, or anything other than feelings and the aquatic images that inspire them. *La Mer* may assume some of the outer trappings and inner processes of the message-symphony but it rejects the essential element of that genre—its purpose.

To acknowledge the heterodoxies in *La Mer* yet allow the analogy with the symphony to stand, Laloy declared that *La Mer* united the symphony and the symphonic poem by encasing picturesque and programatic elements within a structure of "rigorous logic."[51] One could thus listen to this symphonic poem as if it were an abstract symphony: "reason is satisfied at the same time nature is observed."[52] Theorists described a symphonic poem as a work in which content determined the form, thus permitting the composer to omit recapitulations, create ambiguous forms, base the work on "unsymphonic" themes, and avoid traditional development with impunity. Conversely, the blending of symphony and symphonic poem permitted Debussy to use selected symphonic procedures for specifically programatic purposes. In each movement the conventional form, to the extent that it appears, serves to *illustrate* the title (the "content"), which in turn is inspired by Debussy's contemplations of the sea. However one views the form of "De l'aube à midi," it proceeds by continual growth toward the climax, mirroring the progression from dawn to noon on the sea. The fast, continuous and unpredictable evolutions of motives in "Jeux de vagues" suggests the overlapping of the billows and the constant mutations of the watery surface; and a scherzo of course is an appropriate choice for a piece about the *play* of waves. In the last movement, a rondolike alternation of two thematic blocks makes the "dialogue" of wind and sea musically apparent.

Debussy's subtitle "trois esquisses symphoniques" elicited considerable comment, as many critics found the movements too developed to merit that designation. Even Laloy's 1908 reviews concentrated on the "symphonic" aspects of *La Mer* and ignored the "sketches." Presumably Debussy chose this subtitle (one associated with more traditional evocations of the sea[53]) as a ruse to situate *La Mer* in a middle ground between symphony and symphonic poem—sketches rather than a symphony, symphonic rather than programatic or even Impressionistic.[54] He thereby avoided indenturing himself to symphonic "tradition" and the responsibility to do right by it, and bypassed unpleasant ideological associations that the symphony evoked for him and others—personal confession, messages, alliance with the Schola Cantorum, Germanic loyalty. Furthermore, he escaped the embarrassment of seeming to embrace a genre he had publically repudiated.

But the label did not just serve a negative purpose. Charles Malherbe argued that it reflected the composer's free approach. "This term [. . .] is not used here without reason, because it really is a matter of pictures or rather studies made from nature. [. . .] [O]ne must not seek the classical allegro or the moving adagio or the traditional finale. One will hardly find the development of themes in the technical and academic sense of the word. There is more independence in the thought and more suppleness in the realization; here imagination has priority over rules."[55] One might describe *La Mer* as a "sketch" of a message-symphony—Debussy traces its outer lines, hints at the form, and offers glimpses of its processes, but does not give us its essence. As the message-symphony (as well as many abstract symphonies) used constitutive procedures from the symphonic poem without borrowing the programatic substance, *La Mer* similarly employed conventions of the message-symphony but cast the "content"—the message—aside.[56] In addition, by applying these symphonic conventions for programatic purposes, *La Mer* avoids the complete musical abstraction desired for the conservatoiriste symphony and thus evades too close an identification with either camp of symphony then being practiced in France. At the same time, Debussy offers individual "sketches" (momentary glimpses, not a whole picture) of various aspects of the unchanging yet ever-changing sea and the emotions they stir within him.[57]

*   *   *   *

This essay has attempted to demonstrate that by understanding the true nature of the symphony in Debussy's time, especially the rise of the message-symphony, we can view his relationship to the genre in a more nuanced manner. His criticisms of the symphony reflected the dominance of this uniquely French genre, for he objected to it not only because of its formal traditions, legacy, and origins but also because of its perceived goals. By tracing the chronology of his attacks on the symphony, we can see how his ideas evolved in response to the various ways in which the symphony was practiced during his time. Knowing the message-symphony also gives us insight into Louis Laloy's significant, and perhaps authorized, description of *La Mer* as a quasi-symphony, and tells us more than we have known before about the ways in which Debussy's composition relates to the older genre; for it is the message-symphony to which *La Mer* comes nearest. While Debussy censured the goal behind this genre, he found some of its processes, suitably transformed, useful for conveying the musical argument and programmatic content of his own composition. In many ways, this truculently anti-symphonic symphony demonstrates the continuing viability of the genre in Debussy's day.

NOTES

The Manduell and Debussy epigraphs can be found in *The Symphony*, vol.2, *Elgar to the Present Day*, ed. Robert Simpson (London, 1967), p. 104; and in "Du goût," *S.I.M.* 9 (15 February 1913): 48; rpt. in *Monsieur Croche et autres écrits*, ed. François Lesure (Paris, 1987), p. 230.

1. The best overview is Ralph P. Locke, "The French Symphony" in *The Nineteenth-Century Symphony*, ed. D. Kern Holoman (New York, 1997), pp. 163–94; it covers the period ca. 1850–1914. The present author has prepared a comprehensive analytical study covering the same period for *The Symphonic Repertoire*, vol. 3: *The European Symphony from 1800 to 1930*, ed. A. Peter Brown (Bloomington, Ind., forthcoming). Detailed—and respectful—analyses of individual works are similarly rare, except for Daniel M. Fallon's "The Symphonies and Symphonic Poems of Camille Saint-Saëns" (Ph.D. diss., Yale University, 1973). For a discussion of early twentieth-century symphonies, see Brian J. Hart, "The Symphony in Theory and Practice in France, 1900–1914" (Ph.D. diss., Indiana University, 1994).

2. D'Indy's lessons on the symphony are summarized in "La *symphonie* proprement dite" in his *Cours de composition musicale, IIe livre, 2e partie*, ed. Auguste Sérieyx (Paris, 1933), pp. 99–177.

3. For more on these models, see Chapter 2 of Hart, "Symphony," pp. 67–128. The *guerre des écoles* became a proxy battle between the political forces of Socialists and center-left Republicans who controlled the government on the one hand and the opponents of the republic from the Right on the other. The state subsidized the Conservatoire and the Schola sided with the Right. D'Indy and other composers from both sides participated actively in the sociopolitical debates and believed in using the symphony as a tool for declaring and advancing their positions. For a recent study of the political background between 1894 and 1914 and the influence of its ideological and aesthetic disputes on French music, see Jane F. Fulcher, *French Cultural Politics and Music from the Dreyfus Affair to the First World War* (New York, 1999).

4. Paul-Marie Masson, preface to *Rapport sur la musique française contemporaine* (Rome, 1913), pp. 10–14.

5. Guy Ropartz, "A propos de quelques symphonies modernes," in *Notations artistiques* (Paris, 1891), p. 190.

6. Charles Tournemire wrote the following as he began his Symphony No. 7: "The themes exist, the plan is established, the philosophical substance, the emotive side have left my brain and heart, *volcanically*." For Tournemire, the "philosophical substance" of this symphony was not an afterthought but an essential element of the composition. Letter to Pierre Garanger, 28 September 1918; quoted in Raymond Petit, "Introduction à l'étude de l'œuvre de Charles Tournemire," *L'Orgue* 115 (July–August–September 1965): 116.

7. Despite the appeal to processes of the Lisztian symphonic poem—thematic transformation, philosophical programs, and written exegeses—composers of message-symphonies did not consider their works programatic. To use Ropartz's terms, to "translate" metaphysical or philosophical concepts into music was not the same as "childishly" attempting to paint a scene or tell a story.

8. A detailed analysis of these works can be found in Hart, "Symphony," pp. 100–101, 156–62, and 211–41, as well as the same author's "Wagner and the *franckiste* 'Message-Symphony' in Early Twentieth-Century France," in *Von Wagner zum Wagnérisme: Musik, Literatur, Kunst, Politik* (Leipzig, 1999), pp. 315–38.

9. René de Castéra, "La Symphonie en *si bémol* de M. Vincent d'Indy," *L'Occident* (April 1904): 174.

10. D'Indy made this comment privately to Michel-Dmitri Calvocoressi, who recounts it in his *Musicians Gallery: Music and Ballet in Paris and London* (London, 1933), pp. 114–15.

11. For a full version of the text and translation see Hart, "Symphony," pp. 228–30.

12. Alfred Bruneau, the chief Dreyfusard among musicians, praised the work as "the glorification of truth, justice, goodness, peace, and love," while Pierre Lalo, whose paper represented centrist Republicans, condemned the naturalist style of the poem as "utopian frankness, false dignity and superficial banality." Alfred Bruneau, "Les concerts," *Le Matin*, 12 November 1906; and Pierre Lalo, "Concours Cressent—M. Guy Ropartz," *Le Temps*, 10 February 1907.

13. Tournemire's "programs" are reprinted in Joël-Marie Fauquet, *Catalogue de l'œuvre de Charles Tournemire* (Geneva, 1979), pp. 68–72.

14. Gaston Carraud provides a review and interpretation of Dubois's symphony in "Les concerts," *La liberté*, 8 March 1910. The program of Widor's work is found in Anonymous, "*Symphonie antique*, Ch.-M. Widor," *Le guide du concert* 3 (23 December 1911): 189.

15. Even composers resolutely opposed to the idea of expressing messages in music could not entirely escape its allure. André Gedalge, a respected counterpoint professor at the Conservatoire, placed the following rubric at the head of the score of his Third Symphony (1910): "Neither literature nor painting." The concert notes explained that through this symphony Gedalge wished to demonstrate the conservatoiriste position that music could not and need not express ideas. But by accompanying the music with a combative proclamation, to which he called as much attention as to the music itself, Gedalge gave his work a de facto message directed against the d'Indyist message-symphony. Whatever his contention that music existed only to give enjoyment, Gedalge proved no less adept than d'Indy at using his symphonies to prove a point.

16. As has often been noted, one must interpret Debussy's writings with caution. His prose contains many enigmatic and ironic passages, sometimes humorous, sometimes malignant. A case in point is his terse and apparently innocuous review of Gedalge's "robust" and "fearless and irreproachable" Third Symphony. Are the modifiers meant positively or—more likely—as a sly reference to the qualities Debussy detests ("fearless" in its "robust" demeanor, "irreproachable" in its deference to tradition)? Debussy almost always uses "robust" as a term of contempt with regard to the symphony. "Pour la musique," *S.I.M.* 10 (1 March 1914): 51; *Croche*, p. 264.

17. He once said to Ernest Guiraud, "The symphony of Franck is amazing. I could do with less four-bar phrases. But what splendid ideas!" Edward Lockspeiser, *Debussy: His Life and Mind*, Vol. 1, App. B (New York, 1962), p. 208. In 1903 he described the work, apparently without irony, as a "fine work" of "innumerable beauties." *Gil Blas*, 6 April 1903; *Croche*, p. 145.

18. Debussy reviewed various symphonies by Haydn, Mozart, Beethoven, Schubert, Mendelssohn, Rimsky-Korsakov, Sigismond Stojowski, Berlioz, and Franck. Contemporary French symphonies included works by Georges-Martin Witkowski, Ropartz, Paul de Wailly, Dubois, and Gedalge. Parisian audiences could also regularly hear symphonies by Schumann, Brahms, Tchaikovsky, Saint-Saëns, d'Indy, Lalo, and Chausson.

19. "Musique: A la société nationale," *La Revue blanche* (1 April 1901): 550–51; *Croche*, pp. 25–27.

20. "M. Witkowski's symphony is constructed upon a Breton song. The first [movement] is the customary presentation of the 'theme' on which the composer is going to work; then comes the obligatory dismemberment. [. . .] The third [movement] cheers up a bit with a gaiety that is totally Breton, interspersed with phrases of strong feeling; during these latter passages, the Breton song retreats—this is more seemly—but it reappears and the dismemberment continues, which visibly interests the specialists; they wipe their brows and the audience calls for the composer . . ." "A la société nationale":551; *Croche*, pp. 26–27.

21. "A la société nationale": 551; *Croche*, p. 27.

22. "A la société nationale": 550; *Croche*, p. 26.

23. "Au Concerts Lamoureux," *Gil Blas*, 23 February 1903; *Croche*, p. 105. Debussy's remark that Ropartz's movements sound interchangeable presumably means that the work lacks a sense of inevitable progression and growth.

24. "Au Concerts Lamoureux"; *Croche*, p. 127.

25. "A la société nationale," *Gil Blas*, 9 March 1903; *Croche*, p. 119.

26. Letter to Paul Dukas, 11 February 1901; reprinted in *Debussy Letters*, ed. by François Lesure and Roger Nichols, trans. by Roger Nichols (Cambridge, 1987), p. 118.

27. From an interview in "La musique d'aujourd'hui et celle de demain," *Comœdia*, 4 November 1909; *Croche*, p. 296.

28. "M. F. Weingartner," *Gil Blas*, 16 February 1903; *Croche*, p. 96.

29. "Aux Concerts Lamoureux," *Gil Blas*, 23 February 1903; *Croche*, pp. 104–105.

30. "Enfin, seuls!" in *L'Intransigeant*, 11 March 1915; *Croche*, pp. 265–66.

31. "Concerts Colonne," *S.I.M.* 9 (1 November 1913):43–44; *Croche*, pp. 247–48.

32. "Concerts Colonne":43; *Croche*, pp. 246–47.

33. Preface to *Pour la musique française: douze causeries* (Paris, 1917), p. vi; *Croche*, p. 268.

34. Louis Laloy, "Concerts Chevillard," *Le Mercure musical* 1 (1 November 1905): 487–89.

35. Laloy, "La nouvelle manière de Claude Debussy," *La Grande Revue* 47 (10 February 1908): 533. He reprinted much of this article in "*La Mer*: trois esquisses symphoniques de Claude Debussy," *Bulletin français de la S.I.M.* 4 (15 February 1908): 209–14. For a recent translation of the former article (with score examples from the latter added), see *Louis Laloy (1874–1944) on Debussy, Ravel, and Stravinsky*, trans. with introduction and notes by Deborah Priest (Brookfield, VT, 1999), pp. 195–204.

36. In his 1909 biography of Debussy, Laloy describes *La Mer* simply as "three symphonic sketches first conceived in 1903." When he published a revised version in 1944, Laloy once more raised the symphonic connection, but this time he explicitly *regretted* its influence on *La Mer*. He alleged that the stress of the Bardac scandal temporarily robbed the composer of his full creative powers and forced him to rely upon traditional developmental procedures as a crutch (*Debussy* [Paris, 1944], pp. 88–89; see also Priest, *Laloy*, pp. 194–95). Did Laloy play the hypocrite when he praised the symphonic scope of *La Mer* in 1908 or did he later change his mind, especially in light of wartime considerations about the symphony and Germanic origins? Either way, he continued to assert a close relationship between *La Mer* and the symphony.

37. Letter of 22 October 1907, Lesure and Nichols, *Debussy Letters*, p. 185.

38. Interview with the Budapest paper *Azest* (6 December 1910), reprinted in *Croche*, p. 310. It may be significant that Debussy made this remark in a foreign publication; perhaps he felt freer in such a venue to express his true thoughts.

39. Jean Marnold argues for cyclic unity in "François Liszt, la Symphonie et quelques symphonies," *Mercure de France* 41 (March 1902): 817–18; for characteristic unity, see Gaston Carraud, "Le mois: Concerts Lamoureux," *S.I.M.* 5 (15 December 1909): 1042.

40. For details see Simon Trezise, *Debussy: La Mer* (Cambridge, 1994), Chapters 6 and 7. In addition to Trezise's comprehensive study, significant analyses of *La Mer* include Marie Rolf, "*La Mer*: A Critical Analysis in the Light of Early Sketches and Editions" (Ph.D. diss., The University of Rochester, 1976); Wolfgang Dömling, *Claude Debussy: La Mer* (Munich, 1976); and Jean Barraqué, "*La Mer* de Debussy, ou la naissance des formes ouvertes," *Analyse musicale* 12 (June 1988): 15–62. Of these, Trezise examines the symphonic relationship most closely, but he does not discuss the variety of symphonies at the time and summarily dismisses franckiste symphonies as "an awful orthodoxy that robbed music of expression and freedom" (p. 46).

41. French symphonies in this period became very innovative in their treatment of symphonic structures. The scherzo of d'Indy's Second Symphony, for instance, combines theme and variation with rondo form (each recurrence of the refrain is a variation of the rondo theme).

42. For an example of the former reading, see Rolf's dissertation on *La Mer*, pp. 217–18; for the latter, see Trezise, p. 54.

43. No two commentators agree on the form. Arthur Wenk compares six different analyses in his *Claude Debussy and Twentieth-Century Music* (Boston, 1983), p. 71. The book predates Barraqué and Trezise, both of whom postulate an "open" sectional form.

44. Rolf suggests a five-section rondo, with introduction and coda (pp. 197–98). Dömling and Barraqué propose sectional forms. Trezise poses a hybrid of rondo and sectional form.

45. In his sketches, Debussy adjusted the final chorale so that it would correspond exactly to the appearance of the motif in the first movement. Rolf, "*La Mer*," p. 199.

46. Trezise reads *La Mer* as a series of tonal, rhythmic, harmonic, and structural "narratives," the principal one being the progression from a radically open structure in the first movement to a much more definite form in the last; Debusy, *La Mer*, pp. 75–76.

47. See, for example, Pierre Lalo's reviews, reprinted in the documents section of this volume.

48. Trezise, *Debussy, La Mer* pp. 1–6. Recall that in his later writings Laloy also linked Debussy's personal life to his compositional choices in *La Mer*.

49. Ibid., pp. 47.

50. Albert Lavignac, *La Musique et les musiciens* (Paris, 1924), p. 408.

51. Laloy, "Concerts Chevillard," *Bulletin français de la S.I.M.* 4 (15 December 1908):1302.

52. Laloy, "Nouvelle manière": 534.

53. The most notable of these was a four-movement program symphony by Belgian composer Paul Gilson entitled *La Mer, esquisses symphoniques* (1890). Parisian audiences knew this work, and, as Trezise writes, "it is surely no coincidence that Debussy adopted Gilson's subtitle" (*Debussy's La Mer*, p. 35).

54. Debussy felt that the symphonic poem, no less than the symphony, subordinated music to an extramusical end; furthermore, he associated it with German music.

55. Charles Malherbe, *Programme des quatre concerts d'orchestre de musique française moderne* (Paris, 1910), pp. 39–40. According to Trezise, Malherbe may have received this explication from the composer himself (p. 39).

56. In its merger of procedures from absolute and program music, the message-symphony fits into what Carl Dahlhaus has termed "the Second Age of the symphony," in which abstract works borrowed conventions of the symphonic poem but dispensed

with the programatic content. Dahlhaus, *Nineteenth-Century Music*, trans. J. Bradford Robinson (Berkeley, 1989), pp. 265–76.

57. Many *fin-de-siècle* French musicians sought to create multimovement alternatives to the symphony. One option was the "symphonic suite," a term coined by Rimsky-Korsakov for *Antar* and *Sheherazade*. Such a genre can be seen as a hybrid between symphony and picturesque orchestral suite: symphonic suites consisted of three or four integrated and non-detachable movements, whereas the *suite d'orchestre* generally eschewed standard symphonic forms and was unified only by suggestive titles. Symphonic suites thus combined the descriptiveness and structural liberty of symphonic poems or suites with the unity and internal logic of a symphony. By this measure, we might consider *La Mer* the finest example of a *suite symphonique*; others include d'Indy's *Jour d'été à la montagne* (1905) and Albert Roussel's *Evocations* (1911). For more on the symphonic suite and *La mer* in particular, see Hart, "Symphony," pp. 358–78.

Speaking the Truth to Power:

The Dialogic Element in Debussy's

Wartime Compositions

JANE F. FULCHER

The essential component in all truly great art was no mystery for Mikhail Bakhtin, the renowned Russian literary critic, whose seminal insights still resonate across multiple disciplines. Greatness remains elusive, Bakhtin maintained, without "inner dialogy," or the ability to think "against oneself" in an ongoing dialogue among possibilities. Dialogy, after all, precludes the formulaic: It ineluctably exposes the inherent limitations of any particular orthodoxy, and above all "the authoritarian discourse of monologic consciousness."[1]

For Bakhtin's French contemporary, Julien Benda, this quality, significantly, was equally central to the definition of a "true" intellectual, as it emerged in his impassioned *La Trahison des clercs*.[2] The intellectual, for Benda, as Edward Said points out, acts as "the conscience of mankind," upholding the "eternal" criteria of truth by exposing reductiveness, stereotypes, and dogma. Inherently marginal, he or she knows when it is crucial to "intervene in language," disrupting its images, halftruths, and justifications using another—that which "speaks the truth to power."[3]

To consider Claude Debussy as an intellectual and artist whose greatness inheres in his critical dialogy, or questioning of "the language of power," may at first seem gratuitously iconoclastic. For it shatters our conventional image of the composer as an aesthete, or immured in his art, and venturing outside it exclusively when compelled by the aesthetic stimuli of either poetry or painting. However, as I shall argue, if we examine the context of French culture during World War I and its attempt to control all language, including that of the arts, Debussy's dialogy, as an intellectual, is unmistakable. For even while upholding much of the monologic discourse of French nationalism in his prose, the composer could not keep the dialogic—the questioning of orthodoxy—from his work, any more than before. His marginal social identity, I contend, as well as his intrepid artistic integrity, here armed him with an inherent resistance to dogma, ideological or aesthetic, in his art.

Accordingly, my aim shall be first to analyze wartime myths, including that of classicism, as they were diffused and enforced through different venues and means throughout the French musical world. From here I shall turn to Debussy's singular inflection of such nationalist doctrine in his prose, both before and during the war, especially his personal definition of French tradition and the canon. Finally, I shall consider his intellectual engagement as it emerges within his compositions, beginning with those that seek musically to "represent" the war, but in a register that exposes stereotypes and clichés. And last, I shall examine Debussy's "inner dialogy" in his abstract compositions, in which he mordantly "thinks against himself," questioning not only his own doctrine, but also his stylistic past.

*   *   *   *

No composer in France could remain unaware of the function that music was intended to serve within the thorough yet subtle, serpentine network of French wartime propaganda. All cultural institutions, including those of music, were to be shaped into being purveyors of national memory and myth thus to instill a unified wartime identity in a still politically and culturally fractured France.[4] For the country remained in the wake of the "cultural war" that had followed the Dreyfus Affair, when the defeated French nationalist Right belligerently posed the question of "essential French values." Leagues like the Action Française had challenged the legitimacy of Republican institutions as incarnations of endemic French identity, true national values, and of "authentic" French culture. Moreover, well before the war, the Action Française had reasserted French culture as classic, although not without resistance to its definition, particularly on the part of the Left.[5]

Now, with the nationalists' triumph and the war, the state's task was to enlist the aid of leaders not only in education, but in religion and the arts, in implementing official wartime doctrine. All areas had to be "mobilized" and consensus regarding French cultural identity achieved, for it was, according to propaganda, not just a war of arms, but a "war of cultures."[6] The combat was thus to be referenced in this myth in order to galvanize energies, and concomitantly to create an emotional bond in a still politically contentious nation.[7] But the myth had to have its roots in history, since in France, as in Great Britain, history became the very core of a national identity—a "legitimator of action" and a "cement of group cohesion."[8]

French history and classicism were inherently bound in the ideology of Charles Maurras, the founder and principal theoretician of the now prestigious Ligue de l'Action Française. Maurras attributed his political perception of the necessity of a return to monarchy to his search for the basic principles of order, which he believed inhered in great art. As a result, he unequivocally supported "absolutist" judgments in art, his model being the world-renowned classicism produced in hierarchical seventeenth-century France.[9] Hence according to Maurras, and to his fellow nationalist, the writer Maurice Barrès, politics and art should be imbued with the same national spirit from which each was originally born. For "the French" comprised not only a language, but a mode of thought and feeling, or common values and traits that bound the community in a political and aesthetic whole. Literature and art, for French nationalists, were thus "the principal model and support of politics," expressive of "the ideal form and fundamental nature of the national community and the people."[10]

Barrès placed consistent emphasis on the tight imbrication of French politics and art, and especially on the role of art in the "mythologizing of the nation." This concept, of course, was to find a particular resonance in wartime France, when Barrès's conviction would become a cornerstone of propaganda, which again centered largely on culture. Barrès's prestige, like that of Maurras, reached its height in the course of the war, and his ideas concerning the "national genius" were widely accepted and deftly vulgarized.[11] Now it was commonly maintained that there was not only a French "style" of thought or philosophy, based on classical lucidity and precision, but of expression, which followed similar principles. As a result of such reasoning, the highest forms of culture were no longer considered to be universal, but rather national: art, like intellect, unequivocally had a *patrie*.

Classicism, however, carried specific connotations within this ideological context, being associated not with Greek universalism, or the fundamental principles of ancient Greek philosophy. Rather, it was tied to "Latinity." In contrast to the "Nordic" romanticism and irrationalism of the "Huns," it stood for the purportedly endemic Latin virtues of purity, proportion, and order. Abjuring the egalitarian universalism of Republican classicism for the orderly, hierarchical model of traditional Catholicism, this conservative classicism emphasized "balance." Hence it was welded to yet another tenet of wartime dogma in France—anti-individualism, the "individual" being associated with both chaos and with German Romanticism.[12] Accordingly, theorists of the Action Française pointed out that the greatest artists did not reject, but harmoniously incorporated the influence of their illustrious national predecessors. By extension, classicism, for them, connoted "discipline, obedience, and self-abnegation"—a "strictly regulated moral and aesthetic now essential to the nation's survival."[13]

As a result of all these conceptions, classicism was linked to the "defense" of French culture, including protection against contamination from elements outside of the "national organism." "Purity" was thus considered essential, and demanded the immediate extirpation of all foreign traits that could be identified as "polluting" any component of the "génie national."[14] In music, this classic dogma was tyrannical, and it was the task of state institutions to impose its tenets, if through the prism of their specific professional concerns, means, and techniques. All French musical institutions were charged with the task of both national and historical education, or with the construction of memory via a canon, the meaning of which was to be fixed. Great French composers of the past had to be constructed or "reconstructed" within this context—the production of meaning in their music controlled to harness it to the service of national myth.

But in music the problem of factions remained: Not all concurred with the dominant classic doctrine, and different institutions and performance societies conceived "French tradition" in varying manners.[15] The task of reconciling these disputes fell on the shoulders of French bureaucrats, or cultural officials, who now established a hegemonic network of control that musicians would find hard to escape. Indeed, the distinction between public and private musical realms was increasingly effaced, for both were now subject to state intervention as well as to incessant, if indirect, pressure. The stealthy new modalities of French state intrusion into a mobilized institutional network created an official dominance in public education and performance, and would eventually impinge on creativity.

With all these techniques of intervention, musicians, as intellectuals, were to face the dilemma, not confronted so baldly since the French Revolution, of ceding to conformity or risking dissent. For the musical culture they confronted comprised a maze of ideological controls applied to lectures, concerts, editions, and the operatic institutions, among others. Here the pianist and teacher, Alfred Cortot, played a central and highly visible role as the "chef du service officiel de la propagande musicale" in the Ministère des Beaux-Arts. Cortot attempted at least a temporary reconciliation among musical factions, and encouraged a fusion of contestatory performance societies to conserve personnel, facilities, and funds.[16]

Despite such forced cooperation, however, dissension remained deeply embedded, manifest in disputes over the sensitive problem of what to exclude from the repertoire in wartime. This principally concerned German music, which in the past had been central to French concert life, particularly with the vast popularity of Wagner in France since the 1890s.[17] Now the principal questions were clearly "Should all German music be peremptorily banned?" Were all German composers now "the enemy," even those of the nation's distant cultural past? Once again, the major concern was with "purity," or how French music should be "protected" from a noxious contamination by foreign music—a concern that would similarly preoccupy Debussy.

It was for this reason that most major French composers either chose to or were pressured to join a new league, which was founded with the official support of the sous-secretariat des Beaux-Arts in 1916. It is, perhaps, this organization, the Ligue pour la Defense de la Musique Française, which most aptly illustrates how official hegemony was subtly realized in the musical world. The formation of the league, as well as its subsequent activities, was made widely known through the propagandistic journal, founded the previous year and which promoted it, *La Musique pendant la guerre*. It was here that the principal instigator of the league, the jingoistic and opportunistic music critic, Charles Tenroc, published the statutes of the league in January 1916.

The league's stated goal was to safeguard the (implicitly classic) "patrimoine artistique nationale," and to foster its development and diffusion, without respect to any particular "school." Its central purpose, nevertheless, was to develop all the possible and necessary means to oust the "enemy" culturally, and to prevent the return of any *infiltrations funestes* (disastrous infiltrations).[18] Hence its first aim was to instigate and implement the prohibition of public performance in France of any contemporary German or Austrian work not in the public domain. In addition, it presumed to pronounce on all questions concerning the still central issue of the future of French music, not only within the country, but also outside of France. The league would therefore help to determine not only what would and would not be encouraged at home, but how French music—and thus France herself—would be represented abroad. Its fundamentally xenophobic intentions were boldly emblazoned on its brochure, intentions that still resonated long after the war: "La Musique de France aux Français."

The president of the league was Charles Tenroc himself, who was clearly positioning himself for power in the postwar French musical world, and would succeed as the influential editor of the *Courrier musical*. However, there were several "Presidents d'Honneurs," among whom were most of the leading figures within French music, drawn from all of the prewar factions.[19] These included Camille Saint-Saëns, Théodore Dubois, Gustave Charpentier, Vincent d'Indy, and the now lesser known Xavier Leroux and Charles Lecoq. Significantly, Debussy, now weakened by cancer and thus increasingly reclusive, was not among them, although, as we shall see, his prose of the period asseverated their assumptions and goals.

The league, in addition, cleverly included two politicians, both deputies and co-presidents of the Groupe Parliamentaire de l'Art, Paul Meunier and Lucien Milleronge. For this group, according to the statutes of the league, intended to act simultaneously on both the musical and political worlds through the following practices and means of action: propaganda, intervention with those in power, demands for reform in specific *cahier des charges* (government contracts) and rules of the state-sponsored schools, as well as through imposing interdictions on and influencing French editors.[20]

The league's list of adherents, probably actively recruited, related closely to the tactics it proposed, for it included the codirectors of the Opéra-comique, the directors of the Odéon and the Trianon-lyrique, and the director of the Maison Pleyel. Among the other members were the musicians Francis Casadesus, Gustave Samazeuilh, and Raoul Bardac, Debussy's pupil and stepson, who did little without Debussy's advice. The league established a tight network of control, one through which French officials and their allies could act upon and influence musical life, even that outside the official domain.

But the league and its journal also "constructed" French music, or a conception of what it should be, through a series of "Festivals de Musique Française," begun in 1916, again with the support of the sous-secretariat des Beaux-Arts.[21] Significantly, Alfred Cortot (a former Wagnerian), again chef du service officiel de la propagande musicale, was a prominent member of the program committee. Although the festivals presented music of the members of the two leading performance societies for new music, the Société Nationale and the Société Musicale Indépendante, composers who refused to join the league, such as Maurice Ravel, were emphatically excluded.[22] In fact, significant if discreet disagreement remained over the questions of where patriotism lay, over "the French tradition" (an enduring issue in France) and interpretations of "the classic"—dissensions in which Debussy could not help but be involved.

*   *   *   *

Even if his health had permitted, it is doubtful that Debussy would have adhered to the Ligue pour la Défense de la Musique Française, given his abiding distaste for factions and "schools" of any kind.[23] Debussy could not tolerate orthodoxies: he had always to consider and define a position for himself, particularly now, given his personal construal of the French tradition and of wartime exigencies. Like others during the war, Debussy needed a myth of "the French" in music to spur creativity, but he insisted on defining his own, which only in certain aspects resembled that of the propaganda. However, unlike his contemporaries, Satie and Ravel (also intellectuals), he would discover creative tensions with this "personal myth," as well as with his stylistic past, while composing his final set of works.

Throughout his career, in both his prose and his music, Debussy unremittingly questioned all doctrine, particularly that concerning French traits in music, as well as the "rules" taught in the schools. Although someone who now firmly believed that "the collective" could ultimately produce individual freedom, he resisted the crass attempts of officials to direct musical style, or to tell the public what to think.[24] This emerges clearly in a preface that Debussy was asked to write for a wartime volume, which was originally a series of lectures delivered in Lyon, in 1916. The lectures were sponsored by one of the many groups that now developed to encourage French music, the Lyonnais "Amis de la musique française," under the leadership of a member of the University of Lyon's Faculty of Law. The presentations were subsequently published in a book that was edited by the *femme de lettres* (woman of letters) Mme. Bach-Sisley, under the title *Pour la musique française. Douze causeries* (For French music. Twelve talks).[25] Typical for such a series, the contributors came from different professional fields, all of which were concerned with instilling ideological orthodoxies with regard to French culture.

Debussy's text, however, immediately reveals his latent tensions with certain key elements of the classic dogma—tensions that would permeate his compositions of the period. As we shall see when examining them, while he agreed with the necessity of "protecting" French culture and of returning French music to a "purified" state, his interpretation of how to do so was defiantly original.

Debussy begins compliantly, remarking that for some time now it has been all too clear that French music has suffered from what he refers to as "importations singulières." He then acutely observes that while France is in the process of sacrificing its very best youth, regardless of social class, one hears strange things about Beethoven and Wagner. Here he is undoubtedly referring to the argument that Beethoven was Flemish in ancestry, and hence acceptable, and to d'Indy's rhetoric concerning the valuable service Wagner rendered by "ennobling" French music. Rejecting such reasoning, he proceeds with arresting violence of imagery to observe: "It is a matter of pulling out the weeds without pity, just as a surgeon cuts off a gangrened leg."[26]

Debussy then addresses the complex and delicate question of how to do this, and again with d'Indy's nationalist Schola Cantorum undoubtedly in mind, he turns to the key issue of form: "Let us recover our liberty, our forms: having invented them for the most part, it is right that we conserve them; there are none more beautiful. Let us no longer exert ourselves in writing symphonies, for which we stretch our muscles without an appreciable result . . . let us prefer the operetta."[27]

Long a critic of the symphony as a genre that was not endemically French, Debussy is here squarely positioning himself against d'Indy, who still taught the Beethoven symphonic model at the Schola. As we shall see when examining his works, unlike d'Indy, who continued to promote and write symphonies, Debussy was rather turning to the sonata, in its earliest, or still amorphous, state. And as opposed to Germanic conceptions, he would here reappropriate the genre as "French" by attempting to utilize French thematic material, and thus redefining an appropriate form.[28]

But Debussy is heterodox on other key points: as opposed to the dominant view of the French being "serious," as well as "master crafts-men" (to rival the Germans), he argues, as before the war, that they are rather distinguished by "fantasy."[29] As a model of this vision of the French, Debussy turns again to his beloved Chabrier, praising his "fan-taisie" in works like the "Marche joyeuse," as well as in his unpretentious songs. And as against the conventional view, Debussy concludes by asserting the senselessness of the French still striving to write "la grande musique" associated with Germanic conceptions and forms. Here he tartly observes that this has led not only to imbecilic journalistic opin-ions, but to the construction of "faux grands maîtres"; paradoxically, he was now subject to both.

Writers in the newspaper *Action française* were currently "construct-ing" Claude Debussy according to their conception of French music, one heavily influenced by the Schola Cantorum. Critics associated with the league had long supported d'Indy's traditionalist teaching, espe-cially his stress on past French masters, although flatly rejecting his argument concerning Wagner. Now, by assimilating Debussy to the Schola's conception of traditional French form and style, they were attempting to ensure his consecration in the canon, which was by no means sure at this point. Hence in 1915 *Action Française* ran a series of two articles on his music, the content of which is revealed by the title: "La Musique française: Claude Debussy."[30]

In both these articles, Jean Darnaudet attempts to accentuate Debussy's later style, thus dissociating the composer from the pernicious "impressionist" influence, which he condemns as follows: "It is the system of art that sacrifices the ensemble to the detail, that makes up for the absent or weak idea by the multiplication and refinement of sensations, that makes up for the weakness and indecision of lines and of the larger form with a prodigality of small touches and nuances."[31]

The "true" French, or authentic classic style, for Darnaudet, rather emphasizes the "collective"—the formal element or the "whole"—as well as a guiding idea throughout, one that is firm and precise. For him, as well as for d'Indy and the Schola, the form and unity of the whole work depend directly on a clearly defined melody and rhythm, which facilitates the development of themes and the "economy" of tonalities. Darnaudet, of course, is quick to assert that Debussy's greatest works — those of his more recent, or traditionalist style—are no longer lacking in the spheres of line or rhythm. He concludes that in the present the values of line, simplicity, and amplitude of form are reclaiming their place in French music, which is returning to its authentic classic heritage.[32]

It was, then, the conservative classic model that Darnaudet and other French critics in wartime projected onto Debussy's later compositions, perceiving them as the fruit of his return to tradition. As we shall shortly see, however, Debussy's compositions in these years pointedly flout this dogma, even if he himself, in wartime, discreetly did not object to such interpretations. For Debussy, who emulated Rameau, had already noted with reference to the Schola, that such a model, now ironically the paradigm of French classicism, was essentially Germanic, and specifically Viennese.[33] However, in two significant points Debussy did concur with the now dominant position: Not only should French culture be defended, or kept "pure," but the enemy could be combatted most effectively through culture. For as he concludes his preface, "there are many ways that one can vanquish the enemy, and it is important, above all, to remember that music is both an admirable and fecund means to do so."[34]

In his other published prose of the period, Debussy reiterated many of his earlier themes concerning the necessity of rediscovering the "authentic" French tradition—but, as he conceived it. Now, however, his concepts of race, blood, and purity engage with the discourse of the Action Française, to which he bore a complex intellectual relation at this point. As we saw in his preface to the collection, *Pour la musique française*, his primary concern was with the extirpation of anything he construed as "unFrench," especially the German classic model. His solution here was to return to "authentic" French forms, abjuring those that he believed were not endemically French. Again he included his old target, the symphony.

In an article of March 11, 1915 in the ardently nationalist *L'Intransigeant*, Debussy states his position on these issues in appropriately bellicose terms: "For many years now I have been saying the same thing: that we have been unfaithful to the musical tradition of our race for more than a century and a half . . . since Rameau we have had no purely French tradition . . . . Today, when the virtues of our race are being exalted, the victory should give our artists a sense of purity and remind them of the nobility of French blood."[35] Here Debussy's argument indeed resembles that of the Action Française, which similarly stressed intellectual purity, or the importance of preserving the purported "French style of thought."

Debussy's letters in this period continue to reiterate the same set of themes, but here with even less circumspection and circumlocution than in print. In a letter to Igor Stravinsky of October 24, 1915, Debussy speaks far less cautiously of the issues of race and the necessity of preserving the "purity" of French culture: "It will be necessary to cleanse the world of this bad seed. It will be necessary to kill the microbe of false grandeur, or organized ugliness, which we have not perceived as simply being a weakness . . . . You are assuredly one of those who could victoriously combat the other gasses that are just as lethal as the other [kind], and against which we had no masks."[36]

Here Debussy treats Stravinsky as an ally—a Russian artist equally hostile to German post-romanticism and to the concomitant noxious legacy of "false grandeur," as disseminated at the Schola. He proceeds to assure Stravinsky that he is indeed a great artist, but then implores him to be, with all his force, above all a great "Russian artist." For, as he puts it, again recalling Barrès's argument concerning "rootedness" in the soil, "It is so beautiful to be of one's country, to be attached to the earth like the humblest peasant."[37] Debussy's real worry here, however, was that Stravinsky was not only a threat to his preeminence, but that he was becoming far too "boche" (Germanic and modernist), an opinion that he had expressed ten days earlier in a letter to Robert Godet.

In the course of this letter Debussy complains about the problem of German "infiltration" in France, and particularly the baleful influence of Wagner, which unfortunately continues to loom. Again, he speaks of "this heavy hold on our thought, our forms," and then goes on to remark, "Here is the grave fault, unforgivable, difficult to repair because it is in us like vitiated blood." This is also the context in which he speaks of the young Russian school as far too German, and observes that "Stravinsky himself is inclining dangerously toward Schoenberg's side."[38] Apparently Debussy's fundamental concern was that Stravinsky would help to further, and perhaps to bring this decidedly pernicious Germanic influence directly into France.

In the rest of his letter to Godet, Debussy reiterates his obsessive concern with the nature of "true" French music and its implications for both the nation's present and future. Here, as before the war, he returns to the theme of the old French "clavecinistes," a group excluded from the national canons of both Republican institutions and the Schola. Omitted because they were not "virile" or "serious," and thus rejected as *infants ingrats* (unattractive children), Debussy pointedly includes them on the basis of their *grace profonde* and their *emotion sans épilepsie*. His canon was singular, although, like others, he included his beloved Rameau; however, he interpreted this illustrious predecessor, and his implications, in a personal manner. Earlier in his letter to Godet, in fact, he speaks of the current shared obsession with Rameau, pointing out that no one will admit that they don't know how to perform him authentically—and they certainly won't learn from d'Indy.[39]

*   *   *   *

Despite all the certitudes of his rhetoric, however, Debussy's music of the period reveals a search for a personal conception of "purity," of French roots, and his place in relation to this past. For here he equivocated with wartime dogma and assertions far more than in his prose, confronting current significations, questioning his own beliefs and past works, and facing these inconsistencies with irony. But it was the macabre and honest irony of someone confronting an imminent death in a traumatic time of war, and hence preoccupied not only with the nation's future, but with his own past and reputation. Debussy's compositions of the war years attempt not only to define French tradition, to explore those aspects of France's past that he construed as "pure," but to unmask all myths, including his own.

One series of Debussy's compositions in this period confronts contemporary propaganda, or "the language of power," through his musical language, and thus with an impunity not possible in other arts. Here Debussy is intractably locating his roots in the work of French Renaissance composers such as Janequin, whose realism previous Republican spokesmen (like Bruneau) had identified with true French tradition.[40] Yet in all of Debussy's wartime works the emphasis, as propaganda demanded, is no longer on asserting his individuality or indulging in the sensual; it is on ideas, and his links to the past.

The first of these boldly realistic compositions, written at a time when both heroism and myth were promoted, was his *Berceuse héroïque* (which belies its title), composed for *King Albert's Book*, in 1914. The latter comprised a series of works assembled by Hall Caine, an English novelist, as a tribute to the King of Belgium and his heroic soldiers. Caine solicited works from prominent artists and intellectuals from the allied countries, including Elgar and Monet, and published them in *The London Daily Telegraph*.[41]

Here Debussy confronts the intellectual problem of honestly "representing" the war, well aware of the limitations of language in capturing the horrific reality of the unprecedented carnage. He was also inescapably aware of the standard images that were being disseminated, which often employed the Christian reference of sacrifice and resurrection, or banalized and commercialized the war in antiseptic icons.[42] These he clearly could not accept, and in the piece he rather expresses his personal anguish, in a manner far less subtle, more direct and linear, than in all his previous compositions.

Although opening in a stately manner, and invoking the rhythms of a slow march, Debussy then introduces harsh dissonances, including, at one point, simultaneous reference to three different tonalities.[43] But he is even more specific in meaning in his inclusion of an identifiable quotation—in this case several bars that, poignantly in the context, are drawn from the Belgian national anthem, yet arrestingly juxtaposed within an almost opposite stylistic context. And the war itself is vividly evoked in his explicit imitation of distant bugle calls; moreover, although the work is obligingly in traditional ternary structure, Debussy, in honest commentary, suggests a funeral procession (Example 1).[44]

The composition was originally for piano, but the now associated Concerts Colonne-Lamoureux performed the *Berceuse héroïque* in a version that Debussy orchestrated for the occasion. But the composer's realism and substitution of the lugubrious style of the funeral march for the "heroic" (despite the title) was apparently too honest for the French public in 1914. What it desired, toward the start of the war, was neither reality nor a statement of anguish, but rather a simple triumphal idiom that Debussy, unlike Saint-Saëns, could not produce.[45] But this was only the first in a series of straightforward, if not popular, compositions in which Debussy, as an intellectual and in the minority, refused to adhere to wartime myth.

Example 1. Debussy, *Berceuse héroïque*

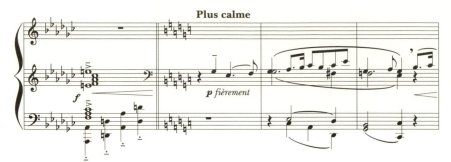

Example 1 continued

Despite cool public response, the following year (1915) Debussy then composed another somber and realistic work, his *En blanc et noir*, for two pianos. Again he would suggest the bald reality of combat, here employing almost expressionistic techniques in even more dissonant composition that, in another composer, he would have decried as "boche." And, in an attempt to make his commentary or intended meaning explicit, Debussy employs several literary inscriptions, thus creating a kind of "hermeneutic window."[46]

The first of the three pieces is prefaced with four lines that are drawn from the libretto of Gounod's *Roméo et Juliette*; hence, although the movement is abstract, the epigram immediately invests it with specific meaning. The lines chosen indicate, if obliquely, Debussy's still ardent sense of personal patriotism:

He who remains in his place
And does not dance,
Of some disgrace
Whispers a confession.[47]

The reference here, although veiled today, was widely understood in the period as being to those who attempted to avoid military service on the false pretext of a medical disability.[48] It is also significant that here Debussy, although again indirectly, rebelliously invokes Gounod, who had long been a part of "his" canon, representing the grace and the charm of the French. Yet this movement, ironically, is more orthodox than before, both in form and in certain stylistic aspects, for it is generally tonal (in C major—the "heroic" key), with a sonatalike thematic recapitulation and coda.[49]

Each of the work's movements creates a mood, or an emotional response to the war: the first, marked simply "avec emportement" (with anger), suggests the bold ardency of a wartime patriot. The second, "Lent et sombre," evokes the emotions felt preceding and during battle, and is similarly prefaced by an epigram, here drawn from a French poet of the past, whose work Debussy had set. He had long admired, and in fact personally identified with, François Villon, a fifteenth-century poet who, like him, often made candid observations from a position of social marginality.[50] Here the lines selected address not the national problems within, as before, but the threat from outside, chosen aptly from Villon's "Ballade contre les, enemies de la France." But poignantly and personally, it is dedicated to one of Debussy's recently deceased associates and friends, Lt. Jacques Charlot, who was killed in battle on March 3, 1915.[51]

Hence, stylistically, the piece includes subtle reference to a traditional genre, the tombeau, a memory or mourning piece for the dead, particularly characteristic of the French Renaissance. Debussy invokes the genre here by employing the effect of a funereal drone, although the harmonies are nonfunctional and, in some cases, highly dissonant. Death is thus represented, but the unspeakably horrific reality of the war is here couched in terms of French tradition, although not the one being promoted by propaganda.

But other Renaissance idioms then follow, for recalling the battle pieces of composers like Janequin (whose works he knew), Debussy evokes the war realistically through suggestions of bugle calls and the rumbling of guns.[52] He even resorts to non-Western pentatonicism, together with clashing seconds, to achieve an almost visceral effect, and to imply that the Germans are not occidental, but oriental, as propaganda demanded. Further buttressing the martial references are the descriptive and simultaneously emotionally explicit markings in the score, such as "alerte," "joyeux," and "sourdement tumultueux" (dully tumultuous). Thus, in a manner still characteristic of the past symbolists, the composer is describing not external events or images in themselves, but rather the emotional response they elicit, as filtered through consciousness. Such a description, less of the war than of its emotional realities, including joy, was indirect enough not to be labeled "defeatist," unlike realistic novels, such as Henri Barbusse's *Le Feu* (of 1916).[53]

However, Debussy is equally explicit yet circumspect in his deployment of musical quotations, a practice he had explored before the war, but here carries to a new degree of almost collagelike abstraction, as opposed to his earlier seamless interpolations or interweavings. In fact, he cites Luther's chorale, "A Mighty Fortress Is Our God," recognizably, to evoke the Germanic, but presented here, as propaganda obliged, transmogrified into ponderous, jarring discords (Example 2). And in order to "cleanse" the atmosphere of these "poisonous fumes," as Debussy put it (recalling his letter to Stravinsky about noxious cultural gasses) he makes a passing reference to the "Marseillaise."[54]

The piece, however, is not without other conciliatory gestures to wartime propaganda, for Debussy attempts to suggest the mythic gaiety of the French, as opposed to the humorless Germans, in battle.[55] However, here he does so not only through reference to the traditionally lighter genre of the scherzo, but through an almost Cubistic juxtaposition of French folk songs (introduced earlier) with military bugle calls. Yet the overall atmosphere still emerges as grim, as Debussy was well aware, for although he attempted to tone it down, his authentic creative response would not permit it.[56]

The third piece, marked "Scherzando," ironically is dedicated to "Mon ami Igor Strawinsky" [sic], and modernistically suggests both the physical atmosphere and emotional mood of the war. This results not only from the unmistakably Stravinskian motor rhythms and ostinati that immediately evoke wartime mechanization, but from the epigram, drawn from Charles d'Orléans, "Yvers, vous, n'êtes qu'un villain" (Winter, you are nothing but ugly). While critical of Stravinsky for his bochelike modernism in his letters, Debussy could not prevent himself creatively from employing these same techniques when they served his artistic, expressive goal. Yet Debussy, characteristically, here explores

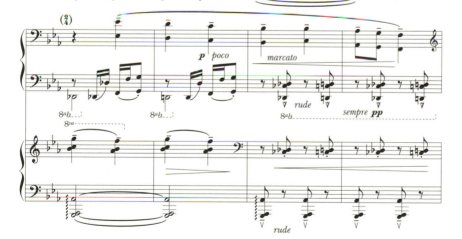

Example 2. *En blanc et noir*

the future of French music without giving up the past, seeking his "French identity" by looking both forward and backward. Indeed, there were never any simple dichotomies of traditionalism or modernism in Debussy's work; poised precariously between the past and the future, he sought the "spirit," not the "letter," of tradition.[57]

Debussy clearly could not remain conciliatory for long, and once more confronted wartime myth in his terrifying last song, the "Noël des enfants qui n'ont plus de maison," which he performed in his final public appearance.[58] Having recently learned of a purported war atrocity affecting children, he immediately penned his own text, a strikingly unorthodox artistic confrontation with the unmitigated horrors of war. Here perhaps more than in any other work of the period, he makes a strong emotional investment, as he alternates between the innocent, the menacing, and the ironic (paradoxically recalling Schubert's "Erlkönig").

Probably intended to resemble the poem, "L'Enfant," from Victor Hugo's collection *Les Orientales,* the text is cast as a childlike imploration to Santa Claus from traumatized children who have lost their homes in the war. Here Debussy attempted, in part, to explode the still current myth of "heroic, storybook children" (extending back to the Napoleonic Wars), and rather faces the sordid reality.[59] To do so, ironically, he uses the German lied as a model (perhaps unconsciously), for it is ineluctably suggested through the vivid piano accompaniment (immediately recalling "Erlkönig") and an emotionally charged imagery that is rare in his work. Here anti-German content is perversely expressed within a German stylistic framework, the effect being not one of parody, but rather inversion, or subversion, of a national genre (Example 3).

Debussy thus again dialogically undermines his own myth of French cultural purity. Ironically, in other aspects he manifests obeisance to the dogma of French classicism he had attacked. For striking here is the clarity and balance of form—ternary with refrain—as well as the rhythmic and metric clarity and frequently defined tonality, suggesting the naïve certainties of childhood. These qualities, which Debussy had previously abhorred, are indeed those that the critic for *Action française* perceived in Debussy's late style, although removed from its textual context.

Debussy was ardently patriotic, as we have noted, but it was consistently on his own terms, for he continued critically, or intellectually, to accept or reject specific elements of wartime myth. While he did so in a relatively overt manner through the manipulation of current symbols in the series of compositions we have just examined, he did so more covertly in another, abstract series. Here he boldly squares off against the wartime paradigm of classicism, defining his own, and in the interests of authenticity, at times betraying his own conscious, or verbal

Example 3. Debussy, "Noël des enfants qui n'ont plus le maison"

doctrine. Among such works one might, of course, include his Piano Etudes of 1915, but here I shall focus rather on his late sonatas, beginning with that for Cello and Piano.

In this composition, above all, we may locate the discursive complexity that Bakhtin identified in all "great art," or the dialogical interplay of voices that immediately confounds monologic consciousness. For in this, as in other sonatas of the period, Debussy practices his unorthodox classicism, continuing to define himself against his contemporaries, and particularly the rivals d'Indy and Saint-Saëns.[60] Clearly at issue here is his treatment of sonata form, which he had previously derided, considering it as synonymous with the rigid German mold that d'Indy taught at the Schola Cantorum. But Debussy now audaciously reclaims the genre as endemically French, referring back to its origins, as we noted in his prose, as simply an instrumental piece. In adopting this definition, Debussy was again defining his approach in opposition to the norm, or contestably demonstrating what a sonata doesn't necessarily have to be. Ironically here embracing "la grande musique," he, like his progenitors at the Société Nationale de Musique, was convinced that this form, which carried Germanic connotations, could be filled with and redefined by French content.[61]

According to Jacques Durand, it was after hearing Saint-Saëns's Septet (of 1881) at the Concerts Durand that Debussy conceived his idea of writing a set of sonatas for different combinations of instruments. As a composer always responding to his contemporaries, Debussy was probably also aware that Saint-Saëns (who was similarly published by Durand) was now writing a series of instrumental sonatas. Hence Debussy projected six sonatas; however, increasingly weakened by cancer, he would succeed in producing only three before his death in 1918. In writing them he was certainly also aware of the many French classicizing sonatas now being composed, and performed at the Société Nationale as well as at the Société Musicale Indépendante.[62] But such rivalry provided him with yet another occasion to accept or reject specific elements of the dominant conception of classicism, along with the ideological connotations it carried.

The first of the set, the Sonata for Cello and Piano, is a highly personal statement, a work that Debussy originally considered entitling *Pierrot fâché avec la lune* (Pierrot angry with the moon). This was meant to refer not only to the theater of eighteenth-century France, but to Debussy himself, who now personally identified with the sad figure of Pierrot. Significantly, for eighteenth-century French artists, including Watteau and Couperin, Pierrot had become a symbolic embodiment of man's dissatisfaction with his own desire. In addition, Pierrot was traditionally an incarnation of paradox, as well as of the ineffability and illusory nature of all appearance.[63]

Debussy, in fact, had made reference to the figure of Pierrot several times already, in works like his *Fêtes galantes* (to poems of Verlaine), of 1882.[64] But now the trope was particularly meaningful, for Debussy was painfully aware of the paradox of his recent creative evolution, and of the transience of his own personal identity. As someone who had come from the social margins, had arrived in society, yet was ill at ease there, and who had rejected his academic training, but now found himself embracing it, the irony was unmistakable and acrid.[65]

However, there was yet another paradox that Debussy himself did not clearly perceive, for in certain respects his approach approximates the description of a sonata by the scholiste pianist Blanche Selva. In her 1914 book, *Quelques mots sur la sonate* (Several words on the sonata), she describes the genre as follows:

> In the sonata, where tonality can be compared with the place of action, the themes are the characters possessing word, gesture, and movement within it. The rhythm is the gesture and the melody the word. The characters or themes all converge, by their gestures or words, in the general action, which is the work. Through interpretation, the character-theme should be presented from the start, with all the habitual rapidity of gestures, the timbre of the voice, the accent of the speech.[66]

This is precisely what Debussy does in an arrestingly literal sense, for his "character" appears immediately, with his own distinctive traits, and thereafter remains omnipresent. But the character here seems anachronistic—out of place—for the opening material is far different from what one would expect in a sonata and has even been described as evocative of French Trouvère melodies (Example 4). Also, as opposed to the conventional sonata, the concentration throughout the first movement is not on a harmonic goal (in the traditional sense) but rather on the unfolding of the protagonist in all his facets. (Revealingly, the markings in the score include "largement déclamé" as "vocal" instructions to the "character.") And in place of either traditional lyric continuity or conventional thematic development, ideas are rather juxtaposed—a practice frequently denounced in the period as "boche."[67]

Hence, while the development section does impart tension, again the techniques are not those of the Schola, nor is Debussy's treatment of the recapitulation, which is thematic, but not tonal. In short, Debussy has perversely written a sonata-form first movement that dialogically

Example 4. Debussy, Sonata for Cello and Piano

invokes and violates the standard classic model of wartime France. But in keeping with the now dominant aesthetic (particularly as articulated by the Action Française) the proportions, if the not the content, is classic as Debussy himself was proud to point out. Attempting judiciously to distinguish his classicism from that of "the mold," he observed, "I like its proportions and its form that is almost classical in the good sense of the word."[68]

Just as mordant and original melodically is the Sonata for Violin and Piano, which Debussy composed and premiered himself in his last public appearance before his untimely death. Here, perversely, given the dominant conception of the "purity" of French culture, to which he ascribed in his prose, Debussy employs melodies and sonorities that suggest the Oriental, or the non-Western. Of course, this was not the first time that Debussy, after having denounced foreign influences on the French in print, then paradoxically turned again to the nonWestern for melodic and harmonic inspiration. Yet here even more paradoxical is that, once more "arguing against" his own statements, he subjects his material to academic procedures he had once satirized, such as augmentation and diminution.[69] Moreover, the first movement ironically begins and ends in G minor, employing conventional contrasts and logical development, and the last movement of the work recalls the first, in the franckiste or scholiste manner.

However, the sarcasm here is directed not at the Schola, but rather honestly, dialogically, at himself—at his own inner battle with the Conservatoire training he had naïvely rejected. As Debussy said of the work, "you can read between the lines; you will see the traces of that image of the perverse which drives us to choose the very idea we should have rejected." As Rollo Myers points out, Debussy also observed that the mood which emerged in this sonata was far different from his own mood at the time, the former being "full of life, almost joyous." Debussy went on to muse that this may be proof of "how little a man's own feelings are concerned with what is occupying the brain": here the creative and the conscious were again ineluctably at odds.[70]

Increasingly, Debussy was creatively rediscovering certain components of his academic training, a phenomenon that would similarly characterize his wartime Sonata for Flute, Viola, and Harp. But here he employs themes that contemporaries perceived as recalling not only Gregorian chant in their length and rhythmically amorphous quality, but, again, French Troubadour and Trouvère melodies.[71] He is, then, in a highly unorthodox sense, invoking the theme of "Latin culture," but in a manner that approaches it from an historical perspective, free of the later eighteenth-century model. Yet at the same time the sonorities and nondirectional effect created by the texture, harmonic language, and rhythm, distinctly suggest the non-Western element (Example 5).

Equally heterodox is the thematic structure: Not only does Debussy employ no less than six different thematic ideas in the course of the movement, but they return, juxtaposed and treated sectionally, without significant variation, and in a substantially different order. And in spite of the incorporation of minuet and rondo elements in the following movements, he mixes these largely later eighteenth-century Germanic genres with stylistic features that recall the French baroque.

Example 5. Debussy, Sonata for Flute, Viola, and Harp

Not only does he invoke baroque dance styles, and emphasize the period's syntactical traits, but again in the manner of Couperin, he gives the movements theatrical titles—Pastoral, Interlude, and Finale.[72]

Debussy was indeed promoting French tradition, but not subserviently or slavishly, in the dominant manner, and with an irony that he himself appreciated, as he now played with his own academic past. His final acceptance of this past, and his public acknowledgment that he did wish to enter the canon, in spite of his disdain for models and schools, became patent in his very last public gesture. As early as 1914, Debussy's candidacy for the prestigious Institut de France had been proposed, and received strong support from members in several different cultural fields. For this was the year that the chair of the organist, Charles-Marie Widor, became available, since Widor had been named the permanent secretary of the Académie des Beaux-Arts. But during most of the war there were no elections at the Institut de France, and when all believed that the war would soon end, Debussy's wife contacted Widor on his behalf. She indicated her husband's willingness to submit his candidacy for election at that time, and asked Widor about the specific procedures that would have to be followed.[73]

But Saint-Saëns was strenuously opposed, and hence the proposal was further delayed, although most French contemporaries generally assumed that Debussy would, in fact, be elected. However, when he finally sent his official letter of candidacy to the Institut de France, on March 17, 1918, ironically hopeful of becoming an academic authority, he was already on the verge of death. Even in these final days, however, Saint-Saëns continued to do all he could to prevent Debussy's elevation to the rank of "immortal," and thus his entry into the canon.[74]

It is noteworthy that both composers firmly believed they embodied the "French classical tradition" and is indeed an indication of how contentious conceptions of it remained in wartime France. And while Debussy sketched only one blatantly patriotic work, (his cantata *Ode à la France*), and Saint-Saëns produced many propagandistic compositions, Debussy was by no means any less engaged. However, he insisted on expressing his political and artistic beliefs and nationalism in his own terms, through a rigorous intellectual evaluation of French wartime myth, including so-called French classicism. If this required him to ignore or confront the centripetal cultural forces of wartime, or even to contradict himself, this was less important than achieving personal authenticity. For Debussy, who had scrupulously constructed and reconstructed his creative identity throughout his lifetime, was now irrefragably aware of the multiplicity of "personal truth." His resultant capacity to undermine his own discourse led Debussy, in addition, to the brink of what for many theorists inherently constitutes "the modern" in art.

The result was a series of compositions that manifest an "inner dialogy," and hence are semiotically complex and multivalent in meaning, accommodating diverse construals even in his lifetime. For Debussy's political investment did not destroy his aesthetic integrity, and like all great art, as Bakhtin perceived, it could be both political and apolitical. Discourse and dialogy were unequivocally present at the moment when Debussy conceived these works—there was a situation of interlocution, a context, that made them specific "utterances" in their period. But the discourse has since become abstract text, and entered other "environments": the works are now autonomous, removed from their original communicative context and "speaking subject." This, as we have seen, was Debussy, the intellectual, not only exposing stereotypes, but intervening in language," or "speaking truth to power," and at the same time, unflinchingly, to himself.[75]

NOTES

1. Matei Calinescu, "Modernism and Ideology," in *Modernism: Challenges and Perspectives,* ed. Monique Chefdor, Ricardo Quionones, and Albert Wachtel (Urbana: University of Illinois Press, 1986), pp. 90–91. On Bakhtin's theories of the dialogical, see Tzvetan Todorov, *Mikhail Bakhtin: The Dialogical Principle* (Minneapolis: University of Minnesota Press, 1984). On Bakhtin's resonance across the disciplines see Amy Mandel, ed., *Bakhtin in Contexts Across the Disciplines* (Evanston, Ill.: Northwestern University Press, 1995).

2. See Julien Benda, *La Trahison des clercs* (Paris: B. Grasset, 1927).

3. Edward Said, *Representations of the Intellectual* (New York: Pantheon, 1994), pp. xv and 20.

4. On the political and cultural divisions in France immediately preceding the war, see Jane F. Fulcher, *French Cultural Politics and Music from the Dreyfus Affair to the First World War* (New York: Oxford University Press, 1999), pp. 216–19. In the months before the outbreak of war, military authorities had squared off against the Socialists and Syndicalists. On this, as well as on the subsequent forced reconciliation of political factions in the interests of national solidarity (referred to by Pioncaré as "l'Union sacrée") see Maurice Agulhon, *La République,* vol. 1 (Paris: Hachette, 1990), pp. 260–62.

5. Fulcher. *French Cultural Politics,* pp. 4–7 and 120–26.

6. Modris Eksteins, *Rites of Spring: the Great War and the Birth of the Modern Age* (Boston: Houghton Mifflin, 1989), pp. 223–36; Pascal Ory and Jean-François Sirinelli, *Les Intellectuals en France de l'Affaire Dreyfus à nos jours* (Paris: A. Colin, 1986), pp. 62–66.

7. See Maurice Agulhon and André Nouschi, *La France de 1914 à 1940* (Paris: Nathan, 1974), p. 5, and Agulhon *La République,* vol. 1, pp. 257–58.

8. On the referencing of the war in myth, see Eksteins, *Rites of Spring,* p. 179. On history as the core of identity in England, see Eric Hobsbawm and Terrence Ranger, eds., *The Invention of Tradition* (Cambridge, Eng.: Cambridge University Press, 1983), p. 12.

The theme of the war as an impetus for the return to the past is developed extensively by Jay Winter in his *Sites of Memory. Sites of Mourning: the Great War in European Cultural History* (Cambridge, Eng.: Cambridge University Press, 1995).

9. Eugen Weber, *Action Française: Royalism and Reaction in Twentieth-Century France* (Stanford, Calif.: Stanford University Press, 1962), pp. 9–11.

10. David Carroll, *French Literary Fascism, Nationalism, Anti-Semitism, and the Ideology of Culture* (Princeton, N.J.: Princeton University Press, 1995), pp. 35, 72–73, and 83.

11. Ibid., pp. 16 and 40; Michel Winock, *Le Siècle des intellectuals* (Paris: Seuil, 1997), pp. 37–38. Also see Christophe Prochasson and Anne Rasmussen, *Au nom de la patrie. Les Intellectuals et la première guerre mondiale (1910–1919)* (Paris: Editions de la Découverte, 1996), p. 280.

12. See Christopher Green, *Cubism and its Enemies. Modern Movements and Reaction in French Art, 1916–1928* (New Haven, Conn.: Yale University Press, 1987), pp. 14, 153, and 190; Prochasson and Rasmussen, *Au nom de la patrie*, p. 180.

13. See Jean Darnaudet, "Grétry," *Action française* 1 Jan. 1917; Martha Hanna, *The Mobilization of Intellect: French Scholars and Writers during the Great War* (Cambridge, Mass.: Harvard University Press, 1996), p. 9.

14. Prochasson and Rasmussen, *Au nom de la patrie*, p. 272.

15. On the conflicts over the "French tradition" within both educational institutions and performance societies in the prewar period, see Fulcher, *French Cultural Politics*, pp. 140–53.

16. See Michel Duchesneau, "La Musique française pendant la guerre 1914–1918. Autour de la tentative de fusion de la Société Nationale et de la Société Musicale Indépendante," *Revue de musicologie* 82, 1 (1996): p. 133.

17. On the enduring popularity of Wagner in France throughout the prewar period see Frédérique Patureau, *Le Palais Garnier dans la société parisienne 1875–1914* (Liège: Margada, 1991), pp. 281–84.

18. Brochure and statutes of the Ligue pour la Défense de la Musique Française, 10 March 1916, preserved in Maurice Ravel, *Lettres autographes*, Bibliothèque Nationale, Département de la Musique. As Duchesneau points out in "La Musique française pendant la guerre," p. 130, despite its claims to be aesthetically unbiased, the league still emphasized France's "Latin roots."

19. Tenroc was not only chief editor of the *Courrier musical*, but went on to write for *Comœdia* and the *Petit parisien*. See Piero Coppola, *Dix-sept ans de musique à Paris 1922–1939* (Geneva: Slatkine, 1982), p. 114.

20. Although not presenting itself as political, the league's very language recalls that of the Action Française, for it advocated a battle against *les trusts suspects*, which since the Dreyfus Affair generally implied the non-French and particularly the Jews.

21. These festivals were founded by the organizers of the journal, with the assistance of the members of the league. See Duchesneau, "La Musique française," p. 128.

22. On Ravel's position, see Jane F. Fulcher, "The Composer as Intellectual: Ideological Inscriptions in French Interwar Neoclassicism," *The Journal of Musicology* 27, 2 (Spring 1999): pp. 214–18.

23. On Debussy's independent stance with regard to factions, see Fulcher, *French Cultural Politics*, pp. 179–86.

24. Ibid., p. 193.

25. Mme Bach-Sisley, ed., *Pour la musique française. Douze causeries* (Paris: Editions Georges Grès et Cie., 1917).

26. Claude Debussy, Preface to ibid., p. v. *"s'agit de mauvais herbes qu'il faut arracher sans pitié, comme un chirurgien coupe une jambe où montre la gangrène."*

27. Ibid., p. vi. *"Retrouvons notre liberté, nos formes: les ayant inventées pour la plupart, il est juste que nous les conservions; il n'est pas de plus belle. Ne nous essoufflons plus à écrire des symphonies, pour lesquelles nous tendons nos muscles sans résultat bien appreciable . . . préferions-leurs l'opérette."*

28. Debussy, like Maurice Barrès, believed that all constraints, including those of form, should arise from the national past: true liberty lies in recognizing history's necessities. See Fulcher, *French Cultural Politics*, p. 182.

29. Ibid., pp. 157 and 172.

30. See Jean Darnaudet, "La Musique française: Claude Debussy," *Action française* 1 and 15 August 1915.

31. Ibid., 15 August, 1915. *"C'est le système d'art qui sacrifie l'ensemble au detail, qui vient supléer à l'idée absente ou défaillant par la multiplication et les refinements de la sensation, qui se rattrape de la faiblesse ou de l'indécision des lignes et des formes généales sur la prodigalité des menues touches et nuances."*

32. Ibid.

33. On Debussy's writings concerning Rameau and the classic model of the Schola, see Fulcher, *French Cultural Politics*, pp. 184–86 and 190–94.

34. Debussy, Preface to Bach-Sisley, ed., *Pour la musique française*, p. vii.

35. François Lesure, ed., Richard Langham Smith, trans., *Debussy on Music* (New York: Alfred A. Knopf, 1977), p. 322.

36. Claude Debussy, *Lettres, 1884–1918*, ed. François Lesure (Paris: Hermann, 1980), p. 265. *"Il faudra nettoyer ce microbe de la fausse grandeur, de la laideur organisée, dont nous ne sommes pas aperçus qu'elle était simplement de la faiblesse . . . . Vous êtes assurément un de ceux qui pourront combattre victorieusement ces autres 'gaz' aussi mortel que les autres [sic], contre lesquelles nous n'avions pas de masques."*

37. Debussy, *Lettres*, p. 265. *"C'est si beau d'être de son pays, d'être attaché à sa terre comme des plus humbles paysans."*

38. Ibid., p. 264. Letter to Robert Godet, 14 October, 1915. *"Strawinsky [sic] lui-meme incline dangereusement du coté de Schoenberg."*

39. Ibid. On the place of Rameau in Debussy's own personal canon (as well as that of the "Debussystes," his followers) see Fulcher, *French Cultural Politics*, pp. 185–86.

40. On Bruneau's Republican conception of the French canon and the place of Rameau within it see ibid., *French Cultural Politics*, pp. 42–43, and Jane F. Fulcher, "The Concert as Political Propaganda in France and the Control of 'Performative Context,'" *The Musical Quarterly* 82, 1 (Spring 1998): 47–51.

41. Debussy's contribution was then published by Durand the following year with the inscription *"Pour rendre hommage à S. M. le Roi Albert de Belgique et à ses soldats."* On the dating of the composition as November 1914 see Jurgen Vis, "Debussy and the War. Debussy, Luther, and Janequin," *Cahiers Debussy*, 15 (1991): 43.

42. On the commercial and commemorative images of the war, see Jay Winter, *Sites of Memory*, especially Chapter 1.

43. The tonalities are E-flat, D, and F.

44. See Vis, "Debussy and the War," p. 44. He notes the march reference in the section marked "grave et soutenue."

45. Léon Vallas, *Achille-Claude Debussy* (Paris: Presses Universitaires de France, 1944), p. 251. As Marc Ferro has incisively observed, "the cameras that recorded the war never show men in the process of dying . . . they only show the image of the dead." See Marc Ferro, "Cultural Life in France, 1914–1918," in *European Culture in the Great War. The Arts, Entertainment, and Propaganda, 1914–1918*, ed. Ariel Roshwald and Richard Stites (New York: Cambridge University Press, 1999): 298.

46. See Lawrence Kramer, *Music as Cultural Practice 1800–1900* (Berkeley: University of California Press, 1990), pp. 9–10.

47. *"Qui reste à sa place/Et ne danse pas/De quelque disgrace/Fait l'aveu tout bas."*

48. Vallas, *Debussy*, p. 259.

49. Significantly, Gounod was a strong supporter of Debussy when the latter won the Prix de Rome. Paradoxically, the movement is dedicated to a "foreigner," Serge Koussevitsky.

50. On Debussy's social trajectory and on his settings of Villon, see Fulcher, *French Cultural Politics*, pp. 170–84.

51. Charlot was a nephew of Debussy's editor, Durand; Debussy had worked with him in 1914. Vis, "Debussy and the War," p. 32.

52. Debussy praised Janequin's "Bataille de Marignon" in a review of a performance in March 1914 in the *Revue musicale SIM*. On it, see ibid., p. 36.

53. On *Le Feu* see Winock, *Le Siècle des intellectuels*, p. 142.

54. Debussy's previous use of musical quotations includes his reference to the music of the "Garde Républicaine" in "Fêtes" (from the *Nocturnes*) and his interweaving of popular chansons in "Rondes du printemps" (from the orchestral *Images*), as well as numerous examples in his piano *Preludes*. On his reference to Luther and to the "Marseillaise," see Vallas, *Debussy*, pp. 255–56 and Vis, "Debussy and the War," p. 36.

55. D'Indy similarly made reference to this myth in his *Symphony No. 3*. According to the composer, there was an implicit program, although it was not published, but rather "explained" by his supporters. The purported contents of the movements are "1—La Mobilisation du Marne; 2—La Gaiété du front; 3—L'Art latin et l'Art boche; 4—La Victoire avec hymne." See d'Indy's undated letter to Guy Ropartz concerning the work in *Lettres Autographes*, Bibliothèque Nationale, Département de la Musique.

56. On the sketches, revisions, and "mood" of the work see Vis, "Debussy and the War," pp. 32–33.

57. Respect for the "letter" of tradition, or "historical authenticity," was rather characteristic of the Schola Cantorum.

58. On Debussy's last public appearance, at the Société Musicale Indépendante, see D. E. Inghelbrecht, "Mouvement contraire," *Souvenirs d'un musicien* (Paris: Bomat, 1947), p. 144. In addition to performing the "Noël" (which was written in early 1915), Debussy also performed his Sonata for Violin and Piano on this occasion.

59. On the myth of "heroic" children, see Ferro, "Cultural Life in France," p. 299.

60. For a discussion of the dialogical interplay of voices, as opposed to "monologic consciousness," see James Clifford, *The Predicament of Culture. Twentieth-Century Ethnography, Literature, and Art* (Cambridge, Mass.: Harvard University Press, 1988), p. 38.

61. The Société Nationale de Musique was a performance society begun by innovative young French composers in 1871, in the wake of the Franco-Prussian War, with the goal of "meeting and defeating" the Germans on their own grounds—that is, in the large abstract forms, but now imbued with French content and spirit.

62. Saint-Saëns's wartime sonatas were published in 1921. On Debussy's rivalry with Saint-Saëns, see Jacques Durand, *Quelques souvenirs d'un éditeur de musique*, 2e série (1910–1924) (Paris: A. Durand et Fils, 1925), p. 78.

63. Wilfred Mellers, *François Couperin and the French Cultural Tradition* (London: Faber and Faber, 1987), p. 144.

64. Pierrot is also referred to in Debussy's early settings of Banville, dating from 1880–1882.

65. On Debussy's reference to the commedia dell'arte as "an expression of painful duality, symbolized by the adopted costume and the fixed features of the mask," see Paul

Roberts, *Images: The Piano Music of Claude Debussy* (Portland, Ore.: Amadeus Press, 1996), p. 98.

66. Blanche Selva, *Quelques mots sur la sonate* (Paris: Delaplane, 1914), p. 56.

67. Again, Debussy is here returning to the original goals of the Société Nationale (on whose board he served) of redefining the Germanic genres from within—through the use of "French content."

68. Edward Lockspeiser, *Debussy, His Life and Mind* (New York: Cambridge University Press, 1978), p. 212.

69. On Debussy's previous satirical use of these "academic" procedures in his "Rondes du printemps" see Fulcher, *French Cultural Politics*, pp. 187–88.

70. Rollo Myers, *Modern French Music from Fauré to Boulez* (New York: Praeger, 1971), p. 101.

71. Lockspeiser, *Debussy*, p. 180. The work was written in 1915 and premiered at the Société Musicale Indépendante on 21 April 1917.

72. Ibid., p. 179.

73. Vallas, *Debussy*, p. 249. See Charles-Marie Widor, *Fondations. Portraits de Massenet, à Paladilhe* (Paris: Durand, 1927), pp. 6–7.

74. Vallas, *Debussy*, p. 250.

75. On the potential of discourse to be both political and apolitical, see Calinescu, "Modernism and Ideology," p. 89. Also see Clifford, *The Predicament of Culture*, pp. 38–41, and Caryl Emerson and Gary Morson, *Mikhail Bakhtin. Creation of a Prosaics* (Stanford, Calif.: Stanford University Press, 1990), pp. 51–52, as well as the references to Said in note 3.

PART II

The Context

✦

Debussy, Fauré, and d'Indy and

Conceptions of the Artist

The Institutions, the Dialogues, the Conflicts

Gail Hilson Woldu

When Debussy wrote to congratulate Gabriel Fauré on his appointment in 1905 as director of the Conservatoire national de musique et de déclamation, he alluded playfully to the anticipated stir that the appointment would create in French musical circles: ". . . But if they've decided to put 'the right man' at the head of our Conservatoire, what's going to happen? And oh! won't traditional old dust be shaken up!"[1] Debussy was right: Throughout his tenure, Fauré shook up years-old administrative and curricular dust at the Conservatoire, and forced France's most prestigious school of music, if not its most forward thinking, to reconceive its ideas about musical artistry. Clearly, Fauré cannot alone be credited with redefining the roles and goals of the artist at the Conservatoire or, by extension, in early twentieth-century France; a diversity of musicians, critics, and cultural institutions was responsible, key among whom, in addition to Fauré, were Debussy, Vincent d'Indy, the Conservatoire, the Schola Cantorum, and the Institut de France, each contributing to the swirl of debate and controversy on artistry that consumed musical France between 1880 and 1930.[2]

The Institutions

The Schola Cantorum

D'Indy and his Schola Cantorum were always embroiled in the most heated of these disputes. Transformed in 1894 from a school of religious music to a college of music, d'Indy's Schola reflected the primacy he accorded religion in art and in all aspects of life, as well as his unique view of art and artistry.[3] Because d'Indy believed that religion was the foundation of all art, it is little surprising that the Schola in the late nineteenth and early twentieth centuries was devoted to the study of religious music and centered in particular on the work of Palestrina. For d'Indy all art existed but to glorify and serve God, and he deemed religious art the most exalted form of creative expression. This credo—that all art must be a manifestation of one's religious faith and devotion—was ubiquitous in d'Indy's writing, interviews, and public talks, appearing as an omnipresent refrain no matter the context of the discourse.

D'Indy based the Schola's curriculum on the principles of his mentor and friend, César Franck, whom d'Indy dubbed "the grandfather" of the Schola. Instruction included primary and advanced levels for vocalists, instrumental musicians, and composers. Instruction in the primary level for students of vocal and instrumental music comprised a series of études, which d'Indy likened to "warm-up exercises in a military drill," whose goal was to ensure technical proficiency.[4] These included for singers exercises in articulation, diction, and rhythm, and scales and vocalizing to strengthen the voice. Primary-level instrumentalists studied orchestral passages from the works of Bach, as well as those from other eighteenth- and nineteenth-century composers. This study was supplemented with that of newly composed concertos, each of which posed specific technical difficulties for the various orchestral instruments. Instruction in the second phase assumed pupils' technical proficiency, focused on artistic and spiritual development, and introduced students to a range of musical literature that considered a variety of periods and styles.

The program in composition was the Schola's most comprehensive and most controversial.[5] In it d'Indy's signature ideology is clear: that students could seek the title of creative artist only after they had mastered the many facets of their art. As in the programs in vocal and instrumental music, instruction was stepwise: students were taught to consider rhythm, melody, notation, and musical form in historical succession, from the monodic period through the late nineteenth century, and then taught to compose in the style of a particular period or composer. Medieval monodies and motets; eighteenth-century fugues, canons, suites, and sonatas; eighteenth- and nineteenth-century symphonies; and the dramatic works of Rameau, Gluck, Gounod, Beethoven, Liszt, and Wagner were staples in the repertory. Not surprisingly, the prerequisites for pursuing this historical and theoretical journey were many: to be admitted to d'Indy's composition class, students had first to possess diplomas in plainchant and in counterpoint, and to have attended the first-year class in composition taught by Auguste Serieyx.

Opinion on the Schola in the early twentieth century was divided. Some praised the innovations of the curriculum, touting d'Indy's unflagging commitment to giving young musicians a multifaceted education in music. Others, responding no doubt to the unsavory aspects of d'Indy's cultural and personal politics as well as to the dogma of d'Indy's writing on music, attacked d'Indy personally and cast a wary eye on the Schola's programs and goals. In each camp comparisons between the Schola and the Conservatoire abounded.[6] Pierre Lalo of *Le Temps*, for example, was as consistently supportive of d'Indy's initiatives at the Schola as he was condemnatory of the curriculum at the Conservatoire in the years preceding Fauré's tenure as director.[7] Former Schola student and music critic Louis Laloy, on the other hand, was on occasion equivocal in his assessment of d'Indy's programs and he sometimes wrote unflattering comments about d'Indy.[8]

In his first published critique of the Schola, Lalo wrote in 1899 that Paris could expect excellent results from the Schola, hailing d'Indy's approach to teaching singers the art of singing as he decried the results of vocal instruction at the Conservatoire.[9] In 1909 Lalo rejected the complaints of those who called instruction at the Schola narrow and tyrannical and again applauded d'Indy's curriculum, writing that it exposed students to all styles and periods of music without seeking to impose any one point of view about the music studied.[10] Musicologist and former Conservatoire student Emile Vuillermoz voiced a similar view in another comparison of the Schola and the Conservatoire, also written in 1909. He denigrated the teaching of music history at the Conservatoire—a course he alleged was widely disregarded by the students—nodded approvingly at the serious, scholarly tenor of the Schola's courses, and wrote enthusiastically about the Schola's concerts, many of which resurrected forgotten works of pre–nineteenth-century composers.[11] Critic Jean Marnold of *Le Mercure de France* shared many of Lalo's and Vuillermoz's views, especially his negative assessment of vocal instruction at the Conservatoire and praise for the Schola's methodical program in voice.[12] Like Lalo also, Marnold commended the "intellectual" climate that d'Indy fostered and called the Schola the artistic center of musical France. Above all, Marnold lauded the teaching repertoire at the Schola, writing:

> There is no other place in Paris, or perhaps even the world, where in six months one could have heard, as we heard this year, several of Bach's cantatas, all of Beethoven's string quartets and some of his most beautiful piano sonatas . . . complete acts from the operas of Lully, Rameau, and Gluck, forgotten or almost forgotten works of seventeenth- and eighteenth-century clavecinists and organists, songs of Carissimi, lieder of Schumann and Schubert, organ chorales of Bach and Franck, [and] Mozart's Requiem. At the Schola a lot of music is performed and it is simply the best music.[13]

Laloy, who began his studies at the Schola in 1899, was more guarded. Many of his comments were equally positive and negative, and he was as likely to praise the programs at the Schola for their attempts to remediate curricular deficiencies of the Conservatoire as he was to disparage d'Indy for his "baronial" classroom demeanor and his inflexible style of teaching.[14] While Laloy lauded the Schola as being the only place in France to learn about music before 1600, he hinted that this instruction might impede the study of modern music.[15]

Debussy disagreed with the tenets of the Schola. The musical intellectualism in vogue at the beginning of the twentieth century, embodied for many in the Schola, appealed little to him and he denounced in particular "the narrow traditions of German and Germanized pedagogues."[16] Debussy was known for his public condemnation of "academic music" and the brand of pedantry associated with d'Indy's Schola, which in his view attached too much importance to the formulaic craft of writing music.[17] Unlike d'Indy, who believed that discipline in music—realized in a graduated and meticulously planned course of study—and musical artistry were inextricably bound, Debussy thought that discipline was found in freedom and not, as he wrote, in the "formulas of a decayed philosophy."[18]

The Conservatoire National de Musique et de Déclamation

If the Schola's curriculum under d'Indy was alternately heralded and derided for its rigor and seriousness of purpose, the Conservatoire's curriculum under Fauré—fashioned in large measure after d'Indy's program and "proof" of Fauré's approval—was almost universally applauded. Among critics and the musical elite in Paris, the words *rigor* and *intellectual* came to mean rigid and pedantic with reference to d'Indy's Schola; by contrast, those same words were synonymous with a finely tuned and balanced academic structure in discussions about the Conservatoire.[19] During his tenure as director, from 1905–1920, Fauré effected important reforms in the Conservatoire's curriculum that moved the nation's most prestigious school of music from being little more than a training ground for composers and performers who aspired to the Parisian stage to a college of music, like d'Indy's Schola, where students learned the history and theory of music as they perfected the art of performance.[20] The most significant of Fauré's curricular reforms were implemented during his first year as director. As a professor of composition at the Conservatoire during the administration of perhaps the least distinguished of the Conservatoire's directors, Théodore Dubois, Fauré was keenly aware of his institution's shortcomings. He disapproved the curricular emphases on theatrical music and competitions, and he repudiated the repertory of the annual student recitals. Because he had "certainly thought often about the Conservatoire's program of instruction,"[21] Fauré was quick to change deficient areas—in particular those in voice and music history—and make them conform to his sense of artistry.

Instruction in voice at the Conservatoire was a laughingstock through most of the nineteenth century. From the moment of their matriculation, singers began preparing for the yearly competitions— and a place on the Parisian stage. Without first having learned either the fundamentals of vocal production—scales, vocalizations, and exercises in diction—or how to sight-read a simple song, student singers were taught florid and technically difficult arias from the works of Ambroise Thomas, Rossini, and Meyerbeer, all of which, not surprisingly, were staples in the concert repertory and at the Opéra. According to critics, the fault lay with the Conservatoire's system of competitions and the goals of vocal instruction, both of which pushed students to attempt a repertory far beyond their technical abilities. Critic and former Conservatoire student Gaston Carraud wrote in 1905 that students' voices become "progressively weaker with more practice, . . . given that instruction in vocal technique, diction, and style are nonexistent . . . big classical arias, which should be reserved for the most mature talents, [are] study pieces for beginners."[22] Lalo agreed, writing also in 1905 that student singers at the Conservatoire "know nothing. Apart from a few competition arias, they know nothing at all about music . . . Moreover, the students are not taught to sing . . . The voice classes have not produced a singer with a well-placed voice capable of reciting a phrase or singing on key for ten years."[23] For this, Lalo faulted the voice faculty, "all former theater singers, who are for the most part musicians of most distressing mediocrity who know nothing about music, and for whom the theatre alone exists."[24]

Fauré's vision of vocal artistry would not allow this. Beginning in 1905, he mandated that voice professors expand their teaching and performance repertory beyond grand opera and nineteenth-century French opera to include works of Cimarosa, Monteverdi, Handel, Pergolesi, Schubert, and Schumann. Moreover, Fauré required voice students to begin their instruction with preparatory exercises and vocalizations.[25] In 1917, well into his tenure as director, Fauré created a special competition for students in these preparatory classes and forbade first-year students from performing music from the concert repertory at their first examinations in January.[26] Fauré's commitment to works written before 1800 was also seen in the changed repertory of the public recitals, which beginning in 1906 came to include works of Renaissance and Baroque composers. Not only did Fauré change the repertory of these recitals, which came to include performances of entire symphonies, concertos, and scenes from operas, he also made the programs compact and unified.[27]

Fauré's desire that Conservatoire students acquire a comprehensive understanding of the many facets of their art is seen particularly clearly in his revisions to the music history class. What had been an "independent and optional course that Conservatoire students did not bother to attend" became through Fauré's initiatives a required course, with students dismissed from the Conservatoire if they did not attend.[28] Fauré summoned musicians from the vocal and instrumental ensemble classes to instructor Bourgault-Ducoudray's music history class to provide musical illustration of the genres taught, which included rondeaux, motets, liturgical dramas, mass movements, and sonatas of the seventeenth and eighteenth centuries. In this way, the Conservatoire's young musicians came to acquire an understanding of musical chronology and stylistic development as they made music together and studied the literature and musical practices of many periods.

Debussy wrote a lot about France's premier school of music, both in his own name and under the guise of Monsieur Croche. He spent many years at the Conservatoire, entering as a boy of eleven and later winning the Grand Prix de Rome, which, although sponsored under the aegis of the Institut de France, was the official *grand prix* in composition for the students at the Conservatoire. His words about the Conservatoire were rarely complimentary. Although Debussy acknowledged that the school was an institution where "some subjects are taught excellently,"[29] he more often spoke impassionedly against the education he received there. He was especially critical of the Conservatoire's instruction in harmony, asserting that "the teaching of harmony seems to me altogether faulty. I can assure you that I did very little when I attended the harmony classes."[30] More important, this criticism underscored his belief that all standardized instruction in harmony was both useless and harmful. He advocated "the suppression of the study of harmony as practiced at school" because it forced composition to conform "to such a point that all musicians, with but few exceptions, harmonize in the same manner."[31] These words must also be understood in the context of Debussy's feelings about music education in France and, specifically, in French conservatories. He thought that French schools of music were unprogressive and conventional, and he decried the internal cabals among faculty and administrators that hindered learning. In particular, he disdained the textbook approaches to composition adhered to at the Conservatoire and at the Schola that resulted in students' uniformity of thinking about music and, even worse, their writing in the same "approved" styles. While he wrote a bit less disparagingly of the Schola than of the Conservatoire, he nonetheless said that students at both schools "must follow the same routine, whether they have the genius of a Bach or the gifts of a Chopin."[32]

D'Indy's opinions about the Conservatoire are complicated because of his long, often overlapping, professional affiliation with it and with his own Schola. He had served on the Commission of 1892, a state-appointed board charged with proposing reforms to the Conservatoire's curriculum, in the years immediately preceding the creation of the Schola, and he had recommended exhaustive changes to the Conservatoire's programs in solfège, composition, and vocal and instrumental music.[33] His four-part proposal to the Commission was rejected but it ultimately became the foundation for the curriculum d'Indy implemented at the Schola. Of greater significance are d'Indy's appointments at the Conservatoire, as professor of the orchestra class (1912) following the resignation of Paul Dukas, and as professor of conducting (1914), that coincided with his years as director of the Schola. These appointments were made during Fauré's tenure as director, and d'Indy and Fauré enjoyed a collegial professional relationship. In the years preceding Fauré's tenure, however, d'Indy frequently attacked the Conservatoire for its emphases on competition and virtuosity were ideologically at variance with his notions about artistry and the type of instruction he deemed most conducive to creating musical artists. In 1895 he criticized the curriculum, writing that "teaching at the

Conservatoire, in all areas, in no way responds to the advances made in the art of music for some twenty years . . . Studies there are conducted entirely haphazardly in most classes [and] the teaching there is of a fashion neither logical nor well thought out."[34] Later, in 1909, d'Indy recalled the inadequacy of his instruction as a student at the Conservatoire and ridiculed succeeding students' lack of musical sophistication. He wrote:

> In my time there were even some teachers of composition at the Paris Conservatoire who did not thoroughly understand their own craft, and were therefore totally incapable of imparting it to others . . . [students] were completely ignorant of all the music of the sixteenth and seventeenth centuries, and of a great part of the work of the eighteenth; they usually regarded Bach as a bore, and Gluck's style was the butt of their wittiest jokes. [35]

The Institut de France: Competition for the Prix de Rome

The Institut de France, which included the Académie des Beaux-Arts, was unlike the Schola Cantorum and the Conservatoire in that it was not an institution that one entered in order to become a scholar or to hone one's skills as a virtuoso performer.[36] Instead, it was hallowed ground for a range of professionals, including artists across the disciplines, already recognized by their peers and the State for outstanding accomplishment in their field. A curious assemblage of musicians and composers occupied the coveted *fauteuils* of the Institut in the late nineteenth and early twentieth centuries, among them Fauré, Dubois, Saint-Saëns, Jules Massenet, and, lesser known to us, Charles Lenepveu, Emile Paladilhe, and Ernest Reyer.

Chief among the Institut's charges was the direction and oversight of various competitions, of which the Prix de Rome was preeminent. Competition for the *grands prix*, held each in sculpture, engraving, painting, architecture, and composition, was strictly regulated by the Académie, and comprised preliminary and final tests, both determined and presided over by members of the Académie. The competition in music had its own rules and requirements in addition to those set for the other *grands prix*. These special criteria were hotly contested in the early twentieth century, especially in the wake of the so-called "scandal of 1905" that saw Ravel "fail" a preliminary examination. Lalo, in a characteristic tirade, denounced the selection process of the jurors, the composition of the audience for the final competition, and the exclusion of the press, writing that "matters would proceed in a different manner if those who know music and are unconcerned with the petty intrigues of the Conservatoire and the Institut attended the meetings of the Rome competitions: the competitors would have a safeguard; the jury, surveillance. But that is precisely what displeases the Institut: it wants no one to judge its judgments."[37]

It is little surprise that Debussy, Fauré, and d'Indy complained bitterly about the Prix de Rome, each condemning its examinations, adjudication, and dramatic cantata. In this, they agreed with Saint-Saëns and the journalists who at the beginning of the twentieth century criticized the competition and advocated a variety of reforms.[38] Debussy, a Prix de Rome laureate, was relentless in his attacks. His Monsieur Croche called the competition the most ridiculous of the ridiculous institutions in France and he asked: "is not the academic detachment of the gentlemen of the Institute, who decide which among a number of young persons shall be an artist, astonishing in its ingenuousness? What do they know about it? Are they so sure of being artists themselves? On what then do they base their claim to control so enigmatical a destiny?"[39] D'Indy's criticism was focused more narrowly on his disdain of all competition. From his familial correspondence of the 1870s to his published writing of the 1930s, d'Indy denounced the policies and pernicious influences of all competitions in music.[40] Like Debussy, he despised the theatrical cantata of the Prix de Rome, believing that symphonic works and music based on folk tunes were more suitable for the competition's final composition.[41] Fauré's concerns were two: (1) the competition's not being reserved exclusively for Conservatoire students; and (2) the competition's "immutably static, illegitimate, and odious" cantata.[42] Like Saint-Saëns, Fauré envisioned a competition in composition open only to the Conservatoire's students, overseen entirely by the Conservatoire's administration and faculty, and reflective of the institution's educational ideals and goals. He explained these ideas to Lalo in 1907:

> You know every French person can hope to compete for the prix de Rome, as access to this competition *is not reserved exclusively* for Conservatoire students. Thus the competition cannot be called "Concours du Conservatoire . . ." If the Rome competition takes the place of a competition in composition at the Conservatoire, is it surprising that our students devote themselves excessively to the cult of the cantata, which keeps them away from other more noble and more interesting genres, and leads them to mistreat the voice? [43]

Fauré's model carried with it two significant changes. First, it would remove the cantata, with its banal and melodramatic texts, as the centerpiece of the competition. In its place students would be permitted to write a vocal, orchestral, or chamber work. Second, Fauré's competition would restrict adjudication to those professionally qualified. His reference to the cantata's dramatic character is important. With its roots in theatrical traditions where larger-than-life dramatic situations generated a similarly grandiose musical style, the cantata had become an anachronism by the early twentieth century—a cliché for a musical style of composition no longer in vogue. The notion of French music as theatre was abhorrent to Fauré and he saw the competition's cantata as a hindrance to the progression of French composition because it reinforced the notion that young composers ought aspire only to the stage, and it discouraged them from cultivating other genres.

Conceptions of Musical Artistry

Debussy, Fauré, and d'Indy were active at the same time, affiliated with the same institutions, and as a consequence they shared some notions about the state of music in France. All three spoke against the Prix de Rome; all three argued in favor of curricular revision at the Conservatoire. The coalescence ends here, by and large, for the men had very distinct thoughts on artistry and the path best suited to becoming an artist. In many ways, Fauré and d'Indy embraced similar pedagogical ideals, this attributable in part to their professional roles at the Conservatoire and at the Schola, and the close working relationship the two enjoyed while Fauré was director of the Conservatoire. Because both were responsible for conceiving and implementing curricula, Fauré and d'Indy were obliged to think about practical and efficacious ways of creating the artists they desired. By contrast, Debussy, who was never a classroom teacher or an administrator, had the luxury of thinking and writing about the art of the musician from the idealistic perspective of the composer.

At the heart of d'Indy's thinking about musical artistry is the importance he attached to the connection between religion and art. Whatever the nature of d'Indy's discourses on music—women's roles in music, competitions in music, an education in music—religion becomes the focal point. In this sense, his writing on music is as much proselytism as it is commentary and analysis. He believed that "man was placed on earth to know, love, and serve God" and that "the artist should have but one goal: to know, love, and serve art."[44] D'Indy held religious art as the most exalted of all creative expression and proclaimed again and again that "Love and Faith can alone conceive and produce an immortal work."[45]

Central to d'Indy's thinking on the artist was his belief that the consummate musician—in his eyes, the artist—was skilled at his instrument as well as knowledgeable about the history of music, the history of musical style, and the history of music theory. In his convocation address of October 1900 to the Schola, d'Indy told his institution's students and faculty that being a musician involved more than knowing how to play an instrument well or how to write a competition cantata, and that while these studies are "certainly components of an education in music, they can hardly be considered art."[46] He explained that the goal of the Schola, unlike that of the Conservatoire, was to produce artists and not competition winners, and disdained the emphasis that his rival placed on producing prize-winning, virtuoso performers. For d'Indy, the goal of the Schola was to produce "virtuoso artists" who viewed the craft of the musician as more than technical brilliance.[47] He wrote many sermonlike essays on musical artistry that often included diatribes on virtuosity. Although he opposed the excesses of virtuoso performance and the virtuoso esprit, d'Indy nonetheless distinguished between good and bad virtuosity. To d'Indy, bad virtuosos were little more than "musical circus clowns" who sought and won success through technical acrobatics. Good virtuosos, on the other hand, were "simple and faithful servants of music": masters of the technical components of their instrument as well as masters of interpretation, the latter made possible only through an understanding of musical style and the history of music.[48] D'Indy proposed six steps to becoming a good virtuoso: (1) complete mastery of one's instrument; (2) deep understanding of the works one performs; (3) knowledge of the various styles in the history of music; (4) understanding of musical accent and its expressive possibilities; (5) scrupulous respect for the original text of a composition; and (6) refusal to perform bad music.[49]

Fauré's conception of artistry is crystallized in an interview for *Le Figaro* on the day of his formal nomination as director of the Conservatoire. Asked to address the course he envisioned for his institution, Fauré responded:

> I want to be the auxiliary to an art that is at once classical and modern, which sacrifices neither current taste to established tradition, nor tradition to the vagaries of current style. But that which I advocate above all else is liberalism: I do not want to exclude any serious ideas. I am not biased toward any one school and I censure no genre that is the product of a well-conceived and sincere doctrine.[50]

The word *liberalism* was well chosen. Fauré's understanding of musical artistry bore an implicit tolerance for a diversity of ideas, whether popular or not. In his first years at the Conservatoire, Fauré was considered to be a dictatorial tyrant—a Robespierre—whose curricular and administrative changes displeased defenders of the old regime under directors Ambroise Thomas and Dubois.[51] His new curriculum, if founded largely on that already in place at the Schola, was radical in its novelty for the Conservatoire, which throughout the late nineteenth century and the beginning of the twentieth century had been a bastion of conservatism, rigidity, and inflexibility—all of the pejoratives assigned incorrectly to the Schola. The respect that Fauré commanded as a composer, his reputation as a fair and empathic teacher, and his undogmatic manner allowed him to "shake old dust" and effect revolutionary reforms that transcended the Conservatoire's walls and extended to Parisian concert halls.

We can observe the results of Fauré's sense of artistry by turning again to the curricula he devised in voice and in the ensemble programs. The voice competitions of 1906, the first of Fauré's tenure, were similar to those of 1905 and earlier: they consisted largely of excerpts from the work of Gluck, Handel, and French operas of the mid-nineteenth century.[52] The women's competition of 1906, however, was distinguished by its performance of Schubert's "Gretchen am Spinnrade."[53] This inclusion of a genre outside of opera and oratorio was remarkable, and was the first indication of Fauré's mandate to voice instructors to expand their teaching and performance repertoire. By 1907 *morceaux de style* became equal partners with the omnipresent *morceaux de bravoure*, and operatic works and oratorios by composers of the eighteenth century outnumbered operatic works by French composers of the nineteenth century. This is an important turnaround, given the repertoire of previous competitions. Between 1897 and 1905 excerpts from the operas of Meyerbeer dominated the Conservatoire's voice competitions: fourteen performances of excerpts from *Le Pardon de Ploërmel*; eleven from *L'Africaine*; seven from *Les Huguenots*; and two from *Le Prophète*.[54] "Valse de l'ombre" from the second act of *Le Pardon de Ploërmel* was a particular favorite among teachers, students, and judges: it was performed in all but two years of Dubois's term as director (1896–1905) and it was the first-prize-winning aria in 1900, 1901, and 1903.[55] The precedents established in 1906 and in 1907, which saw performances from Lully's *Atys* and, remarkably, from Wagner's *Die Walkyrie* and *Tannhaüser*, continued throughout the Fauré years: lieder and *mélodies* became staples of the competition repertoire, as did works of the sixteenth and seventeenth centuries and operas by nineteenth-century German, Italian, and Russian composers.[56]

The repertoire of the ensemble class concerts also became increasingly focused on works of the sixteenth through eighteenth centuries, especially chamber music of French and Italian composers; in addition, early nineteenth-century lieder assumed prominence. As examples, the eighteenth century was highlighted in April and May 1906, with performances of works by Corelli, Marcello, Handel, and Mozart; the years 1907, 1909, and 1915 showcased a variety of periods and compositional styles, including performances of music by Lalande, Lekeu, Monteverdi, Schumann, and Rameau.[57]

These are the tangible aspects of Fauré's conception of artistry—the acts that we can note and quantify. Others are less readily apparent. Fauré, unlike d'Indy, wrote no how-to manuals on any facet of his opinions concerning artistry, nor did he catalogue his views on art and the artist's spirit in volumes, essays, interviews, and articles. We are thus left to construct his aesthetics for ourselves, piecing together what we glean from his correspondence and the testimony of his students. The often-cited words of Fauré to his son Philippe are especially revelatory. Stated with Fauré's quintessential elegance and grace, we find in these words a philosophy on music that seeks to sublimate our daily experiences and exalt them through the art of music alone. This aesthetic, much like Fauré's music, is by turns complex and almost too facile: "For me, art—and in particular music—exists to raise us as far as possible above ordinary existence."[58]

Debussy wrote that he belonged to no school and that he had no disciples.[59] The Scholists' congruence of ideal did not comport with the importance he attached to individual expression; indeed, Debussy asserted that musicians must be "detached from every school, every clique" as the "enthusiasm of a circle spoils an artist," transforming his unique gifts into "the mere expression of his circle."[60] These beliefs—that an artist must have free rein over his ideas and a distinctive style—were the hallmarks of Debussy's conception of musical artistry, seen in his disdain of labels that pigeonhole artistic expression and manifest above all else in his rejection of musical pedagogy's formalized prescriptions. In this sense, as in many others, Debussy's ideas collided with d'Indy's. Where d'Indy's artistry was controlled by rules, Debussy's was inspired by spontaneity. He voiced his "no rules" credo repeatedly in his writing, affirming it vehemently to distinguish his thinking from that of the pedants and musical intelligentsia: "To some people, rules are of primary importance . . . I love music passionately, and because I love it, I try to free it from barren traditions that stifle it . . . It must never be shut in and become an academic art."[61] In a particularly virulent repudiation of d'Indy's ideas about art and religion, Debussy wrote:

It is really inconceivable by what miraculous process the two words art and rule ever came to be associated . . . Do not let us confuse respect, which is merely a virtue, with art—that most beautiful of religions, built on love and egoism unashamed.[62]

Debussy's and d'Indy's divergent opinions of artistry are numerous enough to tally. Debussy believed that "music should humbly seek to please"; d'Indy believed that "music should serve."[63] Debussy condemned musical intellectualism; d'Indy flaunted his scholarly understanding of music. Fauré's aesthetic is more difficult to define. He embraced many of Debussy's and d'Indy's ideals, and fashioned them into a curriculum at the Conservatoire intended to create the musician's musician: one who was technically skilled, grounded in the history of his art, and open to a diversity of ideas about music.

In his congratulatory letter to Fauré on his appointment as director of the Conservatoire, Debussy spoke of stirring up—and ultimately removing—the old dust of antiquated tradition. In a similar vein, Debussy also wrote: "If ever a man of genius tries to shake off the heavy yoke of tradition, he is overwhelmed with ridicule."[64] This statement might apply equally to d'Indy, Fauré, and Debussy, for each was criticized or mocked for his new and unconventional ideas: d'Indy, the most rebuked of the three, for his unflinching convictions—and the dogma of his doctrine—that an education in music need consist in more than knowing how to play an instrument well; Fauré, for his bold curricular reforms at the conservative Conservatoire; and Debussy, for his refusal to conform to rules.

NOTES

1. "Mais si on se decide à mettre 'l'homme qu'il faut' à la tête de notre Conservatoire, que va-t-il arriver? Et que de vieille poussière traditionelle à secouer!" François Lesure, ed., *Claude Debussy: Lettres 1884–1918* (Paris: Hermann, 1980), p. 139.

2. Among the many excellent, recent studies of music in France between 1880 and 1930 are Jane F. Fulcher, *French Cultural Politics and Music: From the Dreyfus Affair to the First World War* (New York: Oxford University Press, 1999); Steven Huebner, *French Opera at the Fin de Siècle: Wagnerism, Nationalism, and Style* (New York: Oxford University Press, 1999); and Jann Pasler, "Paris: Conflicting Notions of Progress," in *Music and Society: The Late Romantic Era*, ed. Jim Samson (Englewood Cliffs, N.J.: Prentice Hall, Inc., 1991).

3. See Vincent d'Indy, "L'Art en place et à sa place," in *La Tribune de Saint-Gervais* September 1897, pp. 139–40; October 1897, pp. 157–159; December 1897, pp. 187–189; January 1898, pp. 17–18; February 1898, pp. 40–42; and March 1898, pp. 65–68.

4. D'Indy mentioned "des mouvements d'asspoulissement dans l'exercice militaire" in "Une Ecole d'art répondant aux besoins modernes," *La Tribune de Saint-Gervais* (November 1900). This article presents a comprehensive overview of d'Indy's goals for the Schola.

5. See *Cours de composition musicale* (Paris: Durand et Fils. In two volumes, published between 1903 and 1950). Written in collaboration with Auguste Serieyx, this four-volume treatise is d'Indy's exploration of the skills necessary to learning and understanding the craft of composition. See as well Gail Hilson Woldu, "Le Conservatoire et la Schola Cantorum: une rivalité résolue?" in *Le Conservatoire de Paris: des ménus-plaisirs à la cité de la musique, 1795–1995*, ed. Yves Gérard and Anne Bongrain (Paris: Buchet et Chastel, 1996), pp. 235–59, for an overview of the controversies surrounding the composition class.

6. Of the many articles written at the beginning of the twentieth century about the Conservatoire and the Schola Cantorum, the following are particularly important: Pierre Lalo, "L'Œuvre de la Schola Cantorum," *Le Temps*, 11 April 1899; Pierre Lalo, "Les Jeunes Musiciens et l'enseignement de M. d'Indy," *Le Temps*, 23 March 1909; Louis Laloy, "Une Nouvelle École de musique: le cours de M. Vincent d'Indy," *Revue d'histoire et de critique musicales* (November 1901), pp. 393–98; Jean Marnold, "Le Conservatoire et la Schola," *Le Mercure de France* (July 1902), pp. 105–115; Emile Vuillermoz, "La Schola et le Conservatoire," *Le Mercure de France*, 16 September 1909, pp. 234–43.

7. See Lalo, "L'Œuvre de la Schola Cantorum" and "Les Réformes du Conservatoire," *Le Temps*, 22 August 1905.

8. See Louis Laloy, *La Musique retrouvée, 1902–1927* (Paris: Desclée de Brouwer, 1974), pp. 68–92.

9. See Lalo, "L'Œuvre de la Schola Cantorum": "Une école de musique a été ouverte de laquelle on peut attendre d'excellents résultats, où l'on enseigne à des élèves deja nombreux le contrepoint, la composition, l'orgue, le solfège, le chant, où les noms des principaux professeurs garantissent la valeur des leçons et la pureté de la doctrine . . . L'enseignement du chant mérite une mention particulière. Aux temps anciens les cantors était la plupart du temps des musiciens excellents. Ces chanteurs exercés, comprenant le latin, élevés dans une tradition forte et suivie, trouvaient spontanément, à l'aspect de la ligne mélodique, la juste cadence, le rythme et l'accent expressif. Le mot de maîtrise avait alors tout son sens. Aujourd'hui, presque partout, les chanteurs connaissent à peine les premiers éléments de la musique, se bornent à solfier sans style et sans art,—trop heureux encore lorsqu'ils solfient juste,—et achèvent de défigurer le plainchant, déjà mutilé et altéré, par leur exécution martelée, pesant, massive et monotone, et pas d'intolerables ralentissements qui les obligent à couper les périodes musicales . . . Ici encore la Schola a fait œuvre de renovation."

10. Lalo, "Les jeunes musiciens": "J'ai plaisir à voir ainsi prendre possession d'eux-mêmes les disciples de M. Vincent d'Indy; à constater que cet enseignement porte de tels fruits; à reconnaître, ainsi que je l'avais espéré, que cette éducation si forte, et que certains ont coutume de pretendre étroite et tyrannique, est au contraire celle qui soit le mieux laisser intacte la nature et la personnalité, qu'elle nourrit chacun de principes et de savoir, sans imposer à personne une manière et une empreinte; et que cette discipline sévère, fondée sur l'étude approfondie de toutes les formes et de toute la musique, est plus propice à l'indépendance que ne sont d'autres enseignements auxquels on est trop volontiers tenté de prêter un esprit plus libre, parce qu'on les voit incomplète et superficiels." This is an extraordinary comment, given the widespread criticism of d'Indy's dogmatism.

11. Emile Vuillermoz, "La Schola et le Conservatoire": "Le Conservatoire oublie facilement l'utilité de l'histoire de la musique; un simple cours libre, ignore des trois quarts des élèves, y répand les bienfaits de la rétrospection: la Schola voulut aussitôt faire reposer toute son esthétique sur des considérations historiques. Ses premiers travaux furent féconds. Paris étonné apprit les noms d'une dizaine d'ancêtres de génie dont il ne soupçonnait pas l'existence, et plus d'un prix de Rome, enveloppé d'un manteau couleur de muraille, se glissa, le soir, dans la salle de concerts de la rue Saint-Jacques, pour y assister à la résurrection de quelques glorieux primitif enseveli jusqu'ici dans le linceul de poussière d'une bibliothèque."

12. Jean Marnold, "Le Conservatoire et la Schola," p. 112: "Au point de vue de l'enseignement du chant, on forme au Conservatoire des chanteurs par des procédés de psittacismes. C'est toujours la vieille méthode empirique, à laquelle il est temps de substituer enfin une méthode rationnelle, scientifique et moderne, sans peine de faillité artistique . . . Les 'humanités' musicales n'y sont enseignées à personne, c'est-à-dire que l'enseignement normal du style et du chant avec base solide de connaissances historiques et démonstrations par l'étude raisonnée et coordonnée des compositeurs est encore à instituer. C'est une faculté de musique qu'il s'agirait de créer au lieu d'une série de petits 'beuglants' superieurs. Pour mieux juger de cette infériorité, il suffit de voir, par opposition, ce que M. Vincent d'Indy a créé rue Saint-Jacques. Aux serinettes du Conservatoire on a substitué l'enseignement des styles et l'histoire des styles. On y étudie méthodiquement et l'on y interprète, en tâchant de faire revivre leurs styles, Handel ou Bach, dans le même esprit qu'à la Sorbonne on explique et on traduit Montaigne et Rabélais . . ."

13. Louis Laloy, "Le Conservatoire et la Schola,", p. 105: "Il n'y a pas un autre endroit à Paris, peut-être au monde, où l'on puisse entendre en six mois, comme on le put faire cette année, plusieurs *Cantates* de Bach, tous les *Quatuors* à cordes de Beethoven avec les plus belles de ses *Sonates* pour le piano . . . des actes entiers d'opéras de Lully, de Rameau et de Gluck, des œuvres ignorées ou quasi des clavécinistes ou organistes des XVIIe et XVIII siècles, des airs de Carissimi, des lieder de Schumann et de Schubert, des *chorals* d'orgue de Bach et de César Franck, le *Requiem* de Mozart . . . A *la Schola*, on joue beaucoup de musique et seulement de la bonne musique."

14. See "Une Nouvelle Ecole de musique" in which Laloy gives a detailed description of the teaching of music history at the Schola and observes, on p. 395: "On voit que le cours de M. Vincent d'Indy n'a pas son equivalent ailleurs: l'histoire et la composition musicales n'ont jamais été unies d'une aussi étroite alliance." See also "Schola Cantorum" in *La musique retrouvée* where Laloy mocked the religious and ideological emphasis of the Schola, writing that the institution was "une école de morale, non moins que de musique" and sneered at d'Indy's "air de baron féodal." See pages 76 and 82.

15. See *La Musique retrouvée*, pp. 75–78, and in particular Laloy's observation that "l'étude du passé est utile et même indispensable, pour faire comprendre l'état actuel, mais à condition qu'on suive le cours du temps sans s'arrêter en route."

16. See Léon Vallas, *The Theories of Claude Debussy, musicien français*. Trans. Maire O'Brien (New York: Dover Publications, 1967; originally published in 1929), p. 17.

17. Ibid., pp. 12–14.

18. Ibid., p. 18.

19. A comprehensive discussion of the Conservatoire under Fauré is found in Gail Hilson Woldu, "Gabriel Fauré as Director of the Conservatoire National de Musique et de Déclamation, 1905–1920," Ph.D. diss., Yale University, 1983. Of those who disapproved Fauré's appointment, see Jules Combarieu, "M. Gabriel Fauré et la direction du Conservatoire," *La Revue musicale*, 1 July 1905, pp. 351–52.

20. See especially Gaston Carraud, "Pour le Conservatoire," *Le Mercure musical,* 15 July 1905, p. 199: "Pour le Conservatoire, le théâtre seul existe; toute musique qui n'est point de théâtre y est considerée comme un genre inférieur, on n'y cherche à former que des compositeurs de théâtre, des chanteurs de théâtre, on pourrait presque dire: des violinistes, des pianistes de théâtre."

21. On the day of his nomination as director of the Conservatoire, he told *Le Figaro* that he had "souvent réfléchi à l'enseignement du Conservatoire." See André Nede, "Le nouveau director du Conservatoire," *Le Figaro,* 14 June 1905.

22. Carraud, "Pour le Conservatoire," p. 195: "Dans les classes de chant, on constatera que les voix, quelquefois excellentes à un premier concours, vont diminuant toujours, par une phenomène excessivement prodigieux, à mesure qu'elles sont plus exercées, l'enseignement de la technique vocale étant nul, aussi bien que celui de la diction et du style: et l'on s'amusera, mieux qu'on ne l'avait encore fait, des gaietés d'un règlement qui considère les grands airs classiques, par exemple—qui devraient être reservés aux talents les plus mûrs—comme des Etudes pour les commençants."

23. Pierre Lalo, "Les Réformes du Conservatoire," *Le Temps,* 22 August 1905: "Pour les chanteurs . . . ils ne savent rien. Hormis quelques air de concours, ils ignorent toute la musique." He goes on to write: "Ils sont incapables de solfier, de déchiffrer à lire ouvert la mélodie la plus facile."

24. Ibid.: ". . . les professeurs de chant, tous anciens chanteurs de théâtre, pour la plupart musiciens d'une affligéante médiocrité, qui ignorent tout de la musique, et pour qui le théâtre seul existe . . ."

25. See Gail Hilson Woldu, "Gabriel Fauré, directeur du Conservatoire: les réformes de 1905," *Revue de musicologie* 70, no. 2 (1984): pp. 206–207.

26. Ibid.

27. Ibid., pp. 210–15.

28. Lalo wrote that Bourgault-Ducoudray's course had been "un cours libre et facultatif, où les élèves du Conservatoire se dispensaient d'assister." See Lalo, "Les Réformes du Conservatoire." See as well Woldu, "Gabriel Fauré," pp. 208–209.

29. See Vallas, *Theories of Claude Debussy,* p. 26.

30. Ibid.

31. Ibid., p. 26.

32. Ibid., p. 24.

33. See Constant Pierre, *Le Conservatoire national de musique et de déclamation. Documents historiques et administratifs* (Paris, 1900), pp. 373–94.

34. See F. Raoul Aubry, "Enquête sur la réforme du Conservatoire," *L' Echo de Paris,* 6 August 1895: "L'enseignement du Conservatoire, dans toutes ses branches, ne répond nullement au mouvement qui s'est accompli dans l'Art musical depuis une vingtaine d'années . . . Les études y sone menées tout à fait arbitrairement dans la plupart des classes; l'enseignement n'y est donné d'une façon ni logique ni raisonnée."

35. Vincent d'Indy, *César Franck.* Trans. Rosa Newmarch (London: John Lane, The Bodley Head, 1929; originally published in 1909), pp. 247–48.

36. An excellent discussion of the Institut de France is found in Paul Landormy, "L 'Institut de France et le Prix de Rome," *Encyclopédie de la musique et dictionnaire du Conservatoire* (Paris: Librairie Delagrave, 1925), pp. 3479–575.

37. Pierre Lalo, "Les concours du Prix de Rome en 1905," *Le Temps,* 11 July 1905: "Les choses iraient d'autre façon si quelques personnes familières avec la musique et indifférentes aux petites intrigues du Conservatoire et de l'Institut assistaient aux séances du concours de Rome: les concurrents auraient une garantie, le jury une surveillance. Mais

c'est tout justement ce qui déplait à l'Institut: il ne veut point qu'on puisse juger ses jugements . . ."

38. In the 30 October 1896 meeting of the Conseil Supérieur, the Conservatoire's governing and policy-making board, Saint-Saëns proposed the creation of a competition for musical composition at the Conservatoire, open only to Conservatoire students. According to Saint-Saëns, this special competition would not take the place of the Prix de Rome, but afford the Conservatoire's composition students the unique opportunity to compete among themselves in a contest overseen and regulated entirely by the Conservatoire. Nothing came of this proposal, although it was revisited (and tabled) during the Conseil's meeting of 24 February 1899. See Archives Nationales AJ^{37}195, 5*.

39. Claude Debussy, "Monsieur Croche the Dilettante Hater," in *Three Classics in the Aesthetic of Music* (New York: Dover Publications, 1962; from the English translation of Noel Douglas, 1927), p. 11.

40. See Vincent d'Indy, "Les Concours: l'opinion de M. Vincent d'Indy," *La Belgique musicale*, 28 January 1897: ". . . je considère l'institution des concours, *telle qu'elle est actuellement mise en pratique*, comme éminemment préjudiciable au développement artistique d'une nation." See also Vincent d'Indy, "L 'Institut jugé par ceux qui n'en sont pas," *Le Figaro*, 28 October 1895, p. 2: "Je suppose qu'il est trop tard maintenant pour vous développer ce que je pense des concours de l'Institut et spécialement de celui intitulé: Concours du Prix de Rome, dont l'inutilité est flagrante et qui exerce même, de mon sens, une influence des plus délétérée sur l'enseignement artistique de notre pays."

41. See Vincent d'Indy, "Les Écoles regionales de musique," *La Revue provinciale*, 15 March 1902.

42. See Philippe Fauré-Frémiet, *Gabriel Fauré: Lettres intimes* (Paris, 1951), p. 138 : ". . . le concours de Rome représente une formule de composition immuablement la même, et bâtarde: la Cantate, et tant qu'on s'en tiendra à cette formule, nos élèves s'efforceront de piocher ce genre faux et néfaste."

43. "Vous savez que tout Français peut espérer à concourir pour le Prix de Rome, l'accès de ce concours n'étant pas réservé exclusivement aux élèves du Conservatoire—Donc, ce concours ne peut s'appeler: 'Concours du Conservatoire . . .' Si le concours de Rome tient lieu de concours de composition du Conservatoire, quoi de surprenant à ce que nos élèves se consacrent à outrance au culte de la Cantate qui les tient éloignés de plusieurs autres genres plus nobles et plus intéressants, et les entraîne à maltraiter la voix?" Letter contained in Jean-Michel Nectoux, *Gabriel Fauré: Correspondance* (Paris: Flammarion, 1980), pp. 267–68.

44. Vincent d'Indy, "L'Education musicale de la jeune fille," *La Revue du foyer*, 15 May 1913, p. 55: ". . . l'homme a été placé sur la terre pour connaître Dieu, l'aimer et le servir . . . l'artiste ne doit avoir qu'un but, connaître, aimer et servir l'art."

45. See d'Indy, *César Franck*, p. 250.

46. See d'Indy, "Une Ecole d'art," p. 303: ". . . ces études font évidemment partie de l'enseignement musical, mais elles ne constituent point l'art . . ."

47. See Ibid. See as well Jean Marnold, "Le Conservatoire et la Schola": "Dans cette 'Ecole de musique répondant aux besoins modernes,'—selon le mot du maître qui en est l'âme, Vincent d'Indy—on n'a pas d'autre but, d'autre pensée que l'art. On n'y recherche pas le succès; on n'y exhibe point de virtuoses."

48. Vincent d'Indy, "Le Virtuose," *Le Monde musical*, June 1925, p. 212: ". . . le mauvais virtuose est donc en somme et ne peut être qu'une sorte de clown musical qui doit chercher le succès dans une succession d'acrobaties. C'est généralement comme ça qu'ils font et il y a beaucoup de gens qui viennent voir ces virtuoses comme acrobates, mais ne disons pas qu'ils sont de grands musiciens, nous nous tromperions. Le bon virtuose, lui,

ne pense qu'à se constituer en simple et fidèle serviteur de la musique, tandis que le mauvais se sert lui-même de cette sainte musique pour arriver à la notoriété et à la fortune."

49. Ibid., pp. 211–12: "Le première condition c'est de savoir son métier . . . Deuxième condition: c'est la connaissance approfondie de l'oeuvre à l'exécuter, de sa construction, de sa manière d'être, des modifications d'interprétation qu'elle peut subir . . . La troisième condition c'est la commaissance des divers styles qui existent dans l'histoire musicale . . . la quatrième condition: c'est l'assimilation des intentions expressives de l'auteur manifestées par la place des accents musicaux . . . la cinquième condition, on devrait à peine en parler: c'est le respect scrupuleux du texte original . . . Quant à la sixième condition, elle est la plus grave, mais j'avoue qu'elle me paraît tout à fait indispensable au bon virtuose. C'est celle de refuser d'interpréter de la mauvaise musique . . . La mauvaise musique ne doît être propagée, ne doit pas exister, par conséquent, vous, bons interprètes, vous ne devez pas la produire au jour."

50. "Je désire être l'auxiliare d'un art à la fois classique et moderne, qui ne sacrifie ni le goût actuel aux saines traditions, ni non plus les traditions aux caprices de la mode. Mais ce que je préconise surtout, c'est le libéralisme: je ne veux exclure aucune conception sérieuse. Je n'ai pas de parti pris d'école et je n'excommunie aucun genre pourvu qu'il provienne d'une doctrine réfléchie et sincère." Quoted in Néde, "Le nouveau directeur du Conservatoire."

51. See Gail Hilson Woldu, "Gabriel Fauré as Director of the Conservatoire," pp. 1–12. See as well Philippe Fauré-Frémiet, *Gabriel Fauré* (Paris, 1957), pp. 92–93. Here, we are told that Dubois is alleged to have said to Fauré: "Monsieur, le Conservatoire, comme son nom l'indique, est pour *conserver la Tradition*."

52. See Woldu, "Gabriel Fauré as Director," Appendix D.

53. On the performance of "Gretchen am Spinnrade," see Alfred Bruneau, "Les Concours du Conservatoire," *Le Matin*, 20 July 1906; Pierre Lalo, *Le Temps*, 7 August 1906; and the anonymously published "Concours de fin d'année du Conservatoire," *La Revue musicale*, 1 August 1906, pp. 363–64.

54. See Woldu, "Gabriel Fauré as Director," Appendix D.

55. See the following articles by Arthur Pougin entitled "Concours du Conservatoire," *Le Ménestrel*: 24 July 1898, p. 238; 23 July 1899, p. 236; 22 July 1900, p. 229; 21 July 1901, p. 228; 20 July 1902, p. 229; 26 July 1903, p. 234; and 23 July 1905, p. 236.

56. These performances from Wagner's operas marked the first such in the Conservatoire's voice competitions. See "Gabriel Fauré as Director," Appendix D.

57. See Archives Nationales AJ^{3}783, 5c.

58. "Pour moi l'art, la musique surtout, consiste à nous élever le plus loin possible au-dessus de ce qui est." Letter of 31 August 1908 to son Philippe Fauré-Frémiet, contained in Jean-Michel Nectoux, *Gabriel Fauré: Correspondance*, p. 275.

59. See Vallas, *Theories of Claude Debussy*, p. 20.

60. Ibid., p. 18.

61. Ibid., p. 10.

62. Ibid., p. 24.

63. Ibid., p. 13. See as well Vallas, "Une école répondant," p. 305: ". . . le vrai but de l'art est d'enseigner, d'élever graduellement l'esprit de l'humanité, de *servir*, en un mot, dans le sens du sublime: *dienen*."

64. See Vallas, *Theories of Claude Debussy*, p. 18.

Debussy, Mallarmé, and "Les Mardis"

Rosemary Lloyd

Sylvain d'haleine première
Si ta flûte a réussi
Ouïs toute la lumière
Qu'y soufflera Debussy.

Woodlander from when the world was young
If your flute was once inspired,
Listen to the radiance it acquired
When Debussy gave it tongue.

It was on the twenty-first of December 1894 that Debussy sent the following brief invitation to the poet Stéphane Mallarmé: "Dear Master, need I tell you what a joy it would be to me if you were willing to encourage with your presence the arabesques that a possibly blameworthy pride has led me to believe your faun's flute dictated."[1] Publishing the score of his *Prelude to the Afternoon of a Faun* in the following year, Debussy clarified that it was "a very free illustration of Mallarmé's beautiful poem; it makes no claim to be a synthesis of the poem. It consists rather of a series of backdrops on which the desires and dreams of the faun move in the warmth of the afternoon."[2] Ironically, it was in this poem more than any other that Mallarmé had resolved to take back from music what he believed belonged to poetry: as he explained to the journalist Jules Huret, he had attempted "to set alongside the alexandrine [that is: the traditional twelve-syllable line common to classical French poetry] in all its finery a kind of running game strummed around it, as if, you might say, it were a musical accompaniment written by the poet himself and allowing the official line to come out only for the special occasions."[3] Nevertheless, if Mallarmé believed he had already set his poem to music, his initial doubts about Debussy's enterprise were removed by the performance. According to the composer, writing some sixteen years after the event: "Mallarmé came to my apartment, with an air of impending doom, adorned with his tartan wrap. After listening, he remained silent for a long moment and then said to me: 'I wasn't expecting anything like that! That music extends the emotion of my poem, and situates its décor more passionately than color could.'"[4] In a letter to Debussy, Mallarmé was just as enthusiastic: "What a marvel! Your illustration of 'The Afternoon of a Faun' offers no dissonance with my text, except that it goes further, truly, in nostalgia and light, with finesse, uneasiness, and richness."[5] Indeed, the lack of dissonance in the thinking of these two major figures of the late nineteenth century is exceptionally striking.

Debussy, who had been from adolescence an enthusiastic and discriminating reader of contemporary poetry and fiction, had set Mallarmé's poem "Apparition" to music as early as 1882, but their first meeting, so it seems, took place only in 1890, when the minor writer André-Ferdinand Herold made it possible for Mallarmé to hear Debussy's settings of five poems by Baudelaire. At the time when they first met, therefore, Mallarmé was in his late forties, an established figure, at least among the artists and intellectuals, while Debussy, who was twenty years younger, was at the outset of his career. Their friendship would never be close, but there was a relationship founded on mutual respect and on some striking similarities of esthetics and personality. It was moreover a relationship that flourished above all in the atmosphere of Mallarmé's "Mardis." From then until Mallarmé's death in 1898, Debussy could be found from time to time at these Tuesday evening gatherings of the poet, which attracted a wide variety of writers, musicians and artists to drink punch, to talk, and above all to listen to Mallarmé.

This group of writers, artists, journalists, and musicians shared a passion for contemporary art, an interest in renewing outworn artistic conventions, and an openness to what the West perceived as the esthetics of Japan and China. The poets among them were, for the most part, particularly concerned with ways of finding correspondences between inner and outer worlds, through the power of suggestion and evocation rather than through description and statement. In addition, many were enthusiastically experimenting with the possibilities opened up by the development of free verse, a development Mallarmé reports in his Oxford and Cambridge lectures of 1894.

It was at these Tuesday evening gatherings that Debussy could have met, for instance, the irascible Whistler, whose prickly temper Mallarmé almost alone of his friends could subdue, and of whom Debussy was later to note: "I was dubbed the 'Whistler of music'"[6]; the witty and flamboyant Irish writer, Oscar Wilde; the painters Renoir, Monet, Degas, and Redon; the sculptor Rodin, who was to exclaim on Mallarmé's death that Nature would never find again the mold from which she had cast him; the young writers André Gide (known to his friends at this stage as "the symbolist"), and Paul Valéry, who was later to describe Debussy as a "monster." And he could have heard Mallarmé hold forth on subjects as diverse as esthetics and politics, music and painting, free verse and the naturalist novel. André Gide, looking back at these gatherings when he came to write his autobiography, describes Mallarmé's contribution to them in the following terms: "Certainly Mallarmé prepared his conversations, which were often not much different from his most polished 'divagations' but he spoke with such art and in a tone that had so little of the doctrinal about it that it seemed as if he had just that instant invented each new proposition, which he didn't affirm so much as seem to submit it for your consideration, almost interrogatively."[7]

Among those who gathered at these Mardis, Debussy would have found many friends and acquaintances met in other literary circles or at such nightclubs as Le Chat noir. Both he and Mallarmé had a profound sense of the importance and value of friendship, and while retaining a certain inapproachability to many, they were capable of exceptional devotion, charm, and warmth to those they truly valued. The brilliant young writer Pierre Louÿs, who became Debussy's closest friend, was a frequent presence at the Tuesday evening gatherings, although his first experience of one was negative enough for him to write in his diary: "Mallarmé pontificates unbearably."[8] He soon succumbed, however, to the charm of the older poet, who was to describe him as "precise, fleeing, gemlike, and musical."[9] Louÿs had made his own copy of Mallarmé's 1887 edition of *Poésies*, which the poet, who relished the task of writing occasional verse, inscribed with the following quatrain:

Louÿs, ces vers recopiés	Louÿs, when you these poems repeat,
Ô svelte enchantement, la Stance	O suave enchantment, the Stance
Fleurit et rit mieux de ses pieds	Flourishes and laughs better at its feet
Que dans une autre circonstance.	Than in another circumstance.[10]

It was to Louÿs that Debussy wrote, in February 1895: "I am working on things that will be understood only by the little children of the twentieth century; they alone will see that 'clothes maketh not the musician' and they will tear the veils off idols, revealing that underneath there is nothing but a sad skeleton."[11] Although later on Debussy was to qualify their relationship as "absurd and chimerical, and what's more incomprehensible"[12] he continued to sign his letters to Louÿs as "your unchangeable." Their heated debates about Wagner and more generally about the nature and function of art would, moreover, have provided Louÿs an opportunity to raise with Debussy points debated by Mallarmé both at the Tuesday gatherings and in the newspaper articles he devoted to music and ballet.

André Poniatowski, the businessman and writer who admired Debussy and gave him both moral and material support, was also one of Mallarmé's circle. Despite the apparent difficulty of fitting such a name to a French metrical pattern, Mallarmé sent Poniatowski's wife the following rhyming address:

Princesse Poniatowska	Princess Poniatowska
Traîneau—vingt-deux Avenue	Take your sleigh to twenty-two
du Bois et ne pense qu'à	Avenue
rayer la glace chenue	Du Bois, thinking only of how far
	You can stripe the hoary ice
	anew.[13]

In a letter of 1892, Debussy expressed his gratitude to Poniatowski in the following terms: "Anyway, whatever happens, I will always be grateful to you for having had, in a country as utilitarian as this, the fantasy of remembering me, and helping me to climb back out of the back hole my life has so often been. It will give me the courage to go on in spite of everything." [14]

Among writers who frequented both Debussy and Mallarmé was one of the poet's oldest friends, Paul Verlaine, whose mother-in-law had been the composer's first piano teacher. Moreover, Verlaine's brother-in-law Charles de Sivray played an important role in introducing Debussy to the writers and intellectuals who gathered at Le Chat noir. For all their differences in personality and esthetics, Mallarmé and Verlaine had been close friends since their early twenties, and Mallarmé, perhaps more than any other contemporary, understood and appreciated the importance of Verlaine's poetic experimentation, encouraging him and delighting in his manipulation of verse forms that draw at least some of their charm from their unpredictability and their lack of adherence to the standard prosodic laws.[15]

Another of those in Mallarmé's circle, the symbolist poet Henri de Régnier, acted as an intermediary between Debussy and Maeterlinck to obtain permission to set *Pelléas et Mélisande* to music, and Régnier's group of poems "Scènes au crepuscule," from *Poèmes anciens et romanesques*, inspired the initial title for what later became Debussy's *Nocturnes*. In September 1893, Debussy played his *Prelude to the Afternoon of a Faun* for Régnier. Recounting this episode in a letter to their mutual friend Ernest Chausson, Debussy wrote: "I put on my very best behavior and played *The Afternoon of a Faun* which he found as hot as in an oven and whose shivers he praised! (Just try to add that up for me!) Moreover, when he talks about poetry, he becomes deeply interesting, and reveals a truly refined sensitivity."[16] Writing in his unpublished diary, which also offers many insights into Mallarmé's Mardis, Régnier described Debussy's playing on this occasion in the following terms:

> He played his "Afternoon of a faun" with a quite exceptional languorous fury. He looks Italian, with an intelligent face, black, almost frizzy hair. It's his stay at the villa Médicis that left on him the southern stamp. There's a kind of charm in seeing him speak a little through his nose, something free and brusque about him. There is in him a hint of the Calabrese shepherd mixed with an orchestral player.[17]

Régnier was one of Mallarmé's most devoted disciples, the one who, perhaps, together with Valéry, received the most informative letters concerning his own poetry, and who was most profoundly influenced by what he believed to be Mallarmé's aesthetics. In responding to the journalist Jules Huret's enquiry on contemporary literature, Régnier asserted: "It's owing to Stéphane Mallarmé, to the example set by his works and the influence of his splendid talks that I am what I am, and I believe the tradition that he represents together with Villiers de l'Isle-Adam is the closest to the genius of classicism."[18] His diary entries are richly informative of what Edouard Dujardin termed the heroic period of the Mardis. In a comment jotted down in his diaries in November 1890 he sums up their charm in the following words: "Nothing will replace for me those evenings at Mallarmé's house where in addition to the delicious, perfect presence of the master of the house, you have the chance to meet an intelligent company."[19]

Listening to the master of the house, Debussy would have recognized that many of the writers and artists Mallarmé valued were those he himself admired, and that they shared many convictions about the role and nature of art. His setting of poems by Baudelaire had attracted the poet's attention, for however much the young Mallarmé had had to struggle to break free from Baudelaire's influence, he continued to admire him greatly. Debussy, moreover, had not only been inspired to set to music particular poems from *Les Fleurs du mal*, but had taken for his own and adapted for his own purposes Baudelaire's assertion in his letter to Arsène Houssaye that serves as a preface to the prose poems, according to which he wanted to create "a poetical prose, without rhythm or rhyme, supple and chaotic enough to adapt itself to the lyrical movements of the soul, to the undulations of reverie, to the leaps of the conscience."[20] These are precisely the terms Debussy takes up in a letter of 1885, asserting that he wants to create a kind of music that is "supple and chaotic enough to adapt itself to the lyrical movements of the soul, to the caprices of reverie."[21]

The passion for the writings of Edgar Allan Poe was also something they shared. Following Baudelaire's influential translation of Poe's prose works (he reluctantly refused to translate the verse, saying that to do so would be to strip Poe's achievement of the sensual delight of rhyme and rhythm), Mallarmé had translated Poe's poetry, and in conjunction with Manet, had produced a beautiful edition of "The Raven." In a questionnaire of 1889, Debussy had given Poe and Flaubert as his favorite prose writers.[21] His letters include frequent allusions to the American writer and his works, and according to André Suarès, he worked for some time on a symphony inspired by Poe's tales in general, and in particular by "The Fall of the House of Usher."[23]

Debussy's enthusiasm for the poet Jules Laforgue, whose work exerted a profound influence on him,[24] would also have touched a cord in Mallarmé, for, although the two poets were not personal friends, "Crise de vers" pays tribute to the vital role Laforgue played in the development of free verse: "Jules Laforgue introduced the unmistakable charm of the incorrect line of verse."[25] Moreover, commenting on the collection of interviews Huret published under the title of *Enquête sur l'évolution littéraire*, Mallarmé drew the journalist's attention to what he saw as a significant lacuna: he had failed to mention Laforgue, who, Mallarmé argued, was one of the principal poets in the development of symbolism.[26]

Finally, Mallarmé, who was a close friend of the poet Théodore de Banville, would have appreciated Debussy's early ambition of setting to music Banville's "heroic comedy" entitled *Diane au bois*. For all the differences in aesthetic that separate them, there are frequent traces of Banville's writing in Mallarmé's poetry, and he was profoundly moved by the older poet's death, confiding to Régnier "I've had tears in my eyes for two days now. I adored that man."[27]

Mallarmé may well have been more dubious about Debussy's project of setting to music Catulle Mendès's libretto, *Rodrigue et Chimène*, for although he and Mendès were friends over a long period, he regarded

Mendès's creative writing with a more questioning eye than his critical work. But Mendès was certainly seen at the time, as Huret's enquiry for instance suggests, as "one of the biggest and most complex figures of contemporary literature."[28] He was the author of numerous volumes of poetry, novels, and plays, and his libretto *Gwendoline* had been set to music by Chabrier in 1886. Debussy himself struggled in trying to work with what François Lesure has qualified as Mendès' "hefty" libretto, and he eventually abandoned the projected opera after confessing to his friend Robert Godet: "My life is sadly feverish because of that opera, in which everything is against me, and my poor little feathers whose color you love drop sadly to the ground."[29]

A more successful collaboration was with the Belgian violinist Eugène Ysaÿe, to whose quartet Debussy dedicated his own string quartet in 1893. Ysaÿe was also a close friend, with whom Debussy discussed various possibilities for producing *Pelléas et Mélisande*, clarifying for instance in a letter to him, "if this work has any merit, it is above all in the connection between the scenic movement and the musical movement."[30] Indeed, it was to Ysaÿe that Debussy originally dedicated his opera. It was Ysaÿe who, together with Chausson, gave the first public performances of the César Franck sonata for violin and piano that so famously inspired Marcel Proust, and they are known to have played the sonata in the studio of another of Mallarmé's artist friends, Auguste Rodin. The Ysaÿe quartet, consisting of the cellist Josef Jacob, the viola player Léon van Hout, and the violinist Mathieu Crickboom as well as Ysaÿe himself, were enthusiastic supporters of contemporary French and Belgian music. As members of the XX (together with Whistler, Félicien Rops, Manet, Rodin and Octave Maus, the secretary, all of whom were closely associated with Mallarmé) they arranged a concert Mallarmé heard in Brussels in early February 1890. Mallarmé's association with Ysaÿe was less close than that of Debussy, but all three had a mutual friend in Octave Maus, one of the leading figures of Belgium's "Libre esthétique" group. Maus, moreover, had organized a concert in Brussels on March 1, 1894, at which Ysaÿe had performed Debussy's quartet, as well as the *Proses lyriques* and *La Demoiselle élue*.

Not surprisingly, both Mallarmé and Debussy reveal complex reactions to the work of Richard Wagner. While Debussy's approach was necessarily different from the poet's, it is likely that he would have both understood and respected Mallarmé's hesitations about the German composer and would have realized how much that hesitation included a reluctant but profound admiration. Mallarmé was close to three of the most devoted French supporters of Wagner: Catulle Mendès, for whose lectures on Wagner Debussy played the musical illustrations; the poet, novelist, and music critic Judith Gautier, who is said to have inspired Parsifal; and the composer Augusta Holmès, whose role in drawing attention to Wagner from an early stage is attested to by Mallarmé's friend Henri Cazalis, and of whom Debussy was later to write in an obituary that "she has left numerous melodies that bear witness to a beautiful sensuality and an intense musicality."[31] Mallarmé devoted two pieces to Wagner, a memorial sonnet, and his "Reverie of a French Poet," and it is clear from contemporary records that he also talked about him at the Tuesday evening gatherings. André Fontainas, for instance, noted after one of these conversations in January 1895:

> The other evening, Mallarmé was saying [. . .] that the weak point in Wagner's theory lay in putting at the same rank poetry, music, and ballet. First, it seemed to him that Wagner nevertheless gave music an obvious predominance, such that poetry was subsumed into music, finding its starting point in music and returning to music,—whereas for Mallarmé the role of poetry was on the contrary the preponderant one. [. . .] But the serious objection is based on the nature of poetry and music on the one hand, and of ballet on the other. Ballet can no longer represent to a modern mind the traditional, regular, and plastic movement of the Ancients, and is in any case merely the materialized expression of what in the theater is conveyed by an author. [. . .] Poetry and music, on the contrary, create the fiction, give it birth, and far from being a means of expression, they are what is expressed, or ought to be, by the scenic representation or even just by the imagination aroused by reading. Moreover Mallarmé hates the word poetry being used without distinction and so randomly that it is stripped of all meaning.[32]

The prose piece entitled "Reverie of a French poet" suggests that Mallarmé was acutely aware that Wagner had, as he puts it, thrown down the gauntlet to poets, but he also conveys his conviction that the composer's use of music was such that it evoked in his audience an instant visceral reaction, not the slowly developed intellectual response that the reader of a complex literary text might experience after a long period of deciphering. "And that is why, O Genius! I, the humble writer subjected to an eternal logic, O Wagner, I suffer and blame myself, in the minutes stamped by lassitude, for not being one of those who, abandoning everything to find the final salvation, go directly to the edifice of your art, which for them lies at the end of the road."[33] Mallarmé saw Wagner's work rather as a temple halfway up the holy mountain, and presents himself as gazing beyond it, toward the menacing mountain peak. Debussy, who referred to the year 1889 as "that charming period when [he] was madly Wagnerian,"[34] offers a reaction that is more ambivalent, especially in the 1890s. Writing to Chausson in 1893 he makes the following vital point: "One of the things I'd like to see you abandon is the preoccupation with the 'underside,' by which I mean this: I think we've been thrown into this by the same R. Wagner, and that all too often we think of the frame instead of the painting, and sometimes the richness of the frame makes us blind to the poverty of the idea. [. . .] We would do better, so it seems to me, to take the opposite point of view."[35] The example he quotes to illustrate his meaning is indeed the sparse later sonnets of Mallarmé. Yet while he might call the German composer "that old poisoner"[36] he also refers, in a much later letter to Stravinsky, to "orchestral certainties I have encountered only in *Parsifal.*"[37] The articles he wrote for various periodicals in the first decade of the twentieth century reveal very much the same kind of doubt that we find in Mallarmé. He shares the poet's distrust of rules and blueprints when he asserts, "Wagner has left us diverse formulae to accommodate music to theater, formulae which one day will be seen as utterly useless,"[38] but, like Mallarmé, he is torn between admiration and irritation when he argues, "Wagner, to use some of that grandiloquence that is appropriate to him, was a beautiful sunset that was taken for a dawn."[39]

As such mutual friendships, interests, and judgments might suggest, Mallarmé and Debussy also shared numerous convictions about art more generally, sometimes to an astonishing degree. Occasionally, Debussy refers specifically to the poet, less as the source for a certain conviction, than as a proof of its validity, as when he remarks on the use of symbol and ornamentation: "we would do better to find a perfect outline for an idea and to add to it only those ornaments that are absolutely necessary. . . Look at the poverty of the symbol hidden in several of Mallarmé's last sonnets, where, however, the workmanship is carried to its highest limits." [40]

They were each somewhat dismissive of theory. Debussy asserted to the younger musician Charles Levadé (in addition to warning him that the triangle was not a sentimental instrument), that "the art of orchestration is learned more by listening to the noise of leaves moved by breezes than by consulting treatises in which the instruments are transformed into parts of the anatomy."[41] Mallarmé, too, while insisting in *Crise de vers* that prosody is "inflexible," wittily adds that it "alerts us to certain prudent acts, such as the hemistich, and sets forth what is the least we need to do to simulate versification, like those codes that warn us that abstaining from flying is, for example, the necessary condition for remaining upright. Exactly what you don't need to learn, because if you haven't worked it out for yourself beforehand, then that's enough to establish the pointlessness of trying to obey it."[42]

Mallarmé's scorn for a literature based on rules is paralleled by his condemnation of a literature confined to the anecdotal. This sentiment finds, moreover, an exact parallel in Debussy's remark to Poniatowski concerning the function of music: "There are those who want music to tell base anecdotes! As if the newspapers didn't perform this task wonderfully well already."[43] "*Naming* an object removes three-quarters of the pleasure of the poem, which comes from the happiness of guessing little by little; *suggesting* it, that's the dream,"[44] asserts Mallarmé, and, in his response to the young Marcel Proust's charges of obscurity: "I prefer to respond to this aggression by riposting that our contemporaries don't know how to read.—Except for the newspaper."[45] Equally, Debussy's comment to Chausson recalls many of Mallarmé's pronouncements: "truly music should have been a secret science, guarded by texts that were so hard and took so long to interpret that it would certainly have discouraged the flock of people who use it with the same insouciance as they use a pocket handkerchief!"[46] Jules Huret's enquiry on contemporary literature reports the poet insisting, "there must always be enigma in poetry, and the aim of literature—there is no other—is to evoke objects."[47] In his 1896 article entitled "Le Mystère dans les lettres" Mallarmé makes a similar point, which indeed sums up much of his earlier assertions about the need for art to be enigmatic:

> There must always be something secret in the depths of everything, I truly believe in something abstruse, whose meaning is closed and hidden, dwelling within the everyday: for as soon as you send the masses on the track of a reality that exists for instance on a sheet of paper in a certain piece of writing—not a reality in itself—but something that is obscure, then the masses grow restless, become a hurricane eager to attribute the darkness to whatever it may be, profusely and flagrantly. The masses' credulity faced with those who calm them down while at the same time lining their own purses, is excessive: and the one the masses designate as the devil's disciple will henceforth not be able to slip in a word without those very same masses, with an effort they would not have put into solving the enigma, shaking the fan of their skirts around them, and snorting: "Don't understand," even if the innocent in question were merely announcing an intention to blow his nose.[48]

For Debussy, like Mallarmé, art demands an act of interpretation on the part of its recipients, a willingness to enter into a domain different from the everyday, a determined resolution to seek out beauty not in the hackneyed and the simple, but in the demanding and the unexpected.

Equally, the importance the two men placed on silence within the work of art creates a striking parallel between them. Debussy, writing to Chausson in 1893, when he was working on *Pelléas et Mélisande,* asserts: "I made use, quite spontaneously, moreover, of a means that seems to me fairly rare, I mean silence (don't laugh) as an agent of expression and perhaps the only way of making the emotion of a phrase gain its true weight."[49] In his preface to the "Coup de dés", Mallarmé, for his part, was to emphasize the role of silence, indicated by the white space on the page to which he had always attached remarkable importance: "The 'white spaces' indeed take on importance, strike one straightaway; the versification demanded it, as a form of silence around it, ordinarily, to the extent that a piece, lyrical or having few syllables, occupies, in the middle, about a third of the sheet of paper." [50]

Both reveal a preference for a theater of the mind, Mallarmé insisting that full appreciation of a work of art, a poem, a play, or a ballet must come through the reader or viewer playing it out within his or her own imagination,[51] and Debussy arguing, "putting a work of art on the stage, however beautifully realized it may be, is almost always in contradiction with the inner dream that alternately gave it birth from the twin possibilities of doubt or enthusiasm."[52]

In terms of personality, there is also much that links the two men. As "L'Après-midi d'un faune" reveals, Mallarmé was acutely aware of the fragile and changing nature of desire, whose fluctuations the faun so amply and beautifully suggests. Debussy, in a letter to Poniatowski dated February 1893, explains this phenomenon at some length, with both wit and perspicacity:

> You can have a mad and sincere longing, almost a need, for a work of art, (a Velasquez, a Satsuma vase or a new kind of tie). What joy you feel when you first own it, it's truly a question of love. After a week, nothing, the object is there, you walk past it five or six days without even glancing at it. Only after an absence of several months do you meet it again with an echo of passion . . . it's like the sun, which is wonderfully dear when April mornings first return, but which ends by wearing us over the long summer months. You could give the formula for desire in these words: everything comes from desire and everything returns to desire, which makes for a pretty kind of deception. The desire to be happy is exactly the same thing, you're never happy except in comparison to something else, and by limiting ourselves, some to a certain number of

millions, others to a certain number of children, on whose shoulders they usually place the burden of increasing their own glory.[53]

Musing on the impossibility of determining whether the nymphs he thought he had seen stemmed from reality, dream, or imagination, Mallarmé's faun turns to an image celebrated from antiquity: that of the bunch of grapes.

. . . *quand des raisins j'ai sucé la clarté*	When I have sucked the brightness from the grapes
Pour bannir un regret par ma feinte écarté,	to banish a regret my pretense brushes aside
Rieur, j'élève au ciel d'été la grappe vide	laughing, I lift to the summer skies the empty bunch
Et, soufflant dans ses peaux lumineuses, avide	and blowing into their luminous skins, eager
D'ivresse, jusqu'au soir je regarde au travers	for intoxication I gaze through them."[54]

Art, for both Mallarmé and Debussy, demands more than a purely physical response to the world or a mimetic re-creation of it. What is essential is, for instance, the transposition of the bunch of grapes into the notion of intoxication, suggested here by the faun's playful blowing into the empty grape skins. Art no longer has the function of representing the external world in any mimetic manner, but rather of summoning it into being through an evocation of our responses to it. According to Mallarmé, this meant that writers no longer had "the pretension of [. . .] including on the subtle paper of the volume anything other than, for example, the horror of the forest; not the intrinsic and dense wood of the trees."[55] This is a claim that finds a close parallel in one of the articles Debussy wrote for the *Revue blanche* in 1902, where he asserted that music "was not confined to producing Nature, more or less exactly, but rather to producing the mysterious correspondences which link Nature with Imagination"[56]

Both were great poets of the sea, Debussy drawing mainly on his memories of the time he spent in Jersey with Emma Bardec when he had left his wife Lilly; Mallarmé remembering both the sensual beauty of the Mediterranean, which he had seen in his twenties when he visited his friend Eugène Lefébure at Cannes, and his later trips to the Atlantic seen from the Normandy coast. In a letter to Pierre Lalo, who had written a hostile critique of "La Mer" in *Le Temps* of 15 October 1905, Debussy asserted: "I love the sea, I have listened to it with the passionate respect that it deserves"[57] and certainly his orchestral poem bears eloquent witness to the truth of that affirmation. Mallarmé's admiration for the sea is perhaps less passionately but no less intensely expressed, in his early poem "Brise marine," in his sonnet "A la nue accablante tue," and above all in the experimental "Un Coup de dés."

Both artists were great poets of love, not just of erotic passion, but of the whole gamut of emotions connected with love. A decade and a half after Mallarmé's death, his son-in-law, Edmond Bonniot, published the complete poetical works. This seems to have inspired Debussy to return to song-writing, setting to music three of Mallarmé's love poems: "Soupir," (Sigh), "Placet futile" (Futile Petition) and "Autre Evantail" (Another Fan). The first of these offers a depiction of a calm, even melancholy love, where the woman replaces the seductions of the flesh, those so eloquently evoked in the "Afternoon of a Faun," with the consolation given by a sister. Moreover, in this poem, the purely emotional landscape reflects the poet's longing for the perfection symbolized by the "azure," but here tinged with hope in the yellow ray of sun that lingers on the still water of the ponds. "Placet futile" focuses on a very different concept of love. Mallarmé described this playful pastiche of the gallant poetry of the eighteenth century as a Louis XV sonnet and wrote it at the request of the future society hostess Nina Gaillard. Its narrator begs to be appointed the shepherd of the princess's smiles, "so that love will paint him playing on a flute to send her flock to sleep."[58] Debussy may well have been attracted to this delightful poem for its evocation of the poetry of a past age (as for instance he was also to turn to works by the medieval poet Villon), for its humor, and for its representation of the poet as musician. If the first two poems deal on the one hand with playful gallantry and on the other with the melancholy love of two people who are bound more by friendship than erotic love, the third, "Autre Eventail" written for Mallarmé's daughter, Geneviève, is concerned with paternal love. It is primarily a fanciful response to his daughter's fan, a poem that takes pleasure in evoking Geneviève Mallarmé's beauty, her laughter, and her particular kind of quick-witted intelligence, all symbolized by the fan itself. Through a curious coincidence, Ravel, in the same year, had also set "Placet futile" and "Soupir" and at first Dr. Bonniot refused to give Debussy permission to publish his own settings, relenting only when Ravel intervened. Debussy offered a tongue-in-cheek explanation of this refusal when he suggested that the Mallarmé family, after the scandal aroused by Nijinsky's ballet based on the faun, feared he might also choreograph the love songs.

Mallarmé and Debussy were never close friends, but their aesthetics were very much in harmony, as the settings of the poems, and especially the response to the "Faune" reveal. As artists, they offer a striking vignette of the fin de siècle's fascination with suggestion, evocation, and allusion, and as men they symbolize the productive and energizing nature of such gatherings as Mallarmé's Mardis. As the poet's little quatrain for Debussy suggests, the musicality of Mallarmé's poetry finds a remarkable match in the radiance of Debussy's music.

NOTES

1. Claude Debussy, *Lettres 1884–1918*, réunies et présentées par François Lesure (Paris: Hermann, 1980), p. 70. All translations are my own except where indicated otherwise.

2. Quoted in Stéphane Mallarmé, *Correspondance*, ed. Lloyd James Austin, vol.7 (Paris: Gallimard, 1963–1984), p. 281.

3. Jules Huret, *Enquête sur l'évolution littéraire*, préface et notes de Daniel Grojnowski (Paris: Corti, 1999), p. 105.

4. Claude Debussy, *Lettres*, p. 190.

5. Mallarmé, *Correspondance: Lettres sur la poésie*, ed. Bertrand Marchal (Paris: Folio, 1995), p. 623.

6. Debussy, *Monsieur Croche, et autres écrits*, ed. François Lesure (Paris : Gallimard, 1987), p. 293.

7. André Gide, *Si le grain ne meurt* (Paris: Gallimard, 1928), pp. 263–4.

8. Pierre Louÿs, *Œuvres complètes, vol. 9* (Geneva: Slatkine, 1973), p. 293. Entry for 24 June 1890.

9. Mallarmé, *Correspondance*, vol. 5, p. 64.

10. Mallarmé, *Œuvres complètes,* ed. Bertrand Marchal, vol. 1 (Paris: Pléiade, 1998), p. 316.

11. Debussy, *Lettres*, p. 73.

12. Ibid., p. 135.

13. Mallarmé, *Œuvres complètes,* ed. Marchal, vol. 1, p. 268.

14. Ibid., p. 38.

15. On this, see my *Stéphane Mallarmé: The Poet and his Circle* (Ithaca, N.Y.: Cornell University Press, 1999).

16. Debussy, *Lettres*, p. 51.

17. Henri de Régnier, *Annales psychiques et occulaires* (unpublished diaries) Mss nouvelles acquisitions françaises, 14974–77, notebook 19 (Paris: Bibliothèque nationale).

18. Huret, *Enquête sur l'évolution littéraire*, p. 131.

19. Régnier, *Annales*, notebook for 1890.

20. Baudelaire, *Œuvres complètes, vol. 1* (Paris: Pléiade, 1975), pp. 275–76.

21. Debussy, *Lettres*, p. 12.

22. Ibid., p. 51.

23. Ibid.

24. See Lesure in ibid., p. 45.

25. Mallarmé, *Œuvres complètes* (Paris: Pléiade, 1945), p. 365.

26. Huret, *Enquête sur l'évolution littéraire*, p. 403.

27. Régnier, *Annales*, notebook, 1 November 1890 – 1 May 1891.

28. Huret, *Enquête sur l'évolution littéraire*, p. 287.

29. Debussy, *Lettres*, p. 32.

30. Ibid., p. 83.

31. Ibid., *Monsieur Croche*, p. 94.

32. André Fontainas, *De Stéphane Mallarmé à Paul Valéry: notes d'un témoin,* entry for 18 January (Paris: Edmond Bernard, 1928), p. 195.

33. Mallarmé, *Œuvres complètes*, (1945), p. 546.

34. Debussy, *Monsieur Croche*, p. 144.

35. Ibid., *Lettres*, p. 58.

36. Ibid., p. 78.

37. Ibid., p. 224.

38. Ibid., *Monsieur Croche,* p. 41.

39. Ibid., p. 67.

40. Ibid., *Lettres*, p. 58.

41. Ibid., p. 128.

42. Mallarmé, *Œuvres complètes*, pp. 361–62.

43. Debussy, *Lettres*, p. 40.

44. Huret, *Enquête sur l'évolution littéraire,* p. 103.

45. Mallarmé, *Œuvres complètes,* (1945), p. 386.

46. Debussy, *Lettres*, p. 51.

47. Huret, *Enquête sur l'évolution littéraire* p. 104.

48. Mallarmé, *Œuvres complètes*, p. 383.

49. Debussy, *Lettres*, p. 55.

50. Mallarmé, *Œuvres complètes*, ed. Marchal, vol. 1, p. 391.

51. Ibid., p. 300.

52. Debussy, *Monsieur Croche*, p. 200.

53. Ibid., *Lettres*, p. 39.

54. Mallarmé, *Œuvres complètes*, ed. Marchal, vol. 1, p. 24.

55. Ibid., pp. 365–66.

56. Debussy, *Monsieur Croche*, p. 62.

57. Ibid., *Lettres*, p. 145.

58. Mallarmé, *Œuvres complètes*, ed. Marchal, vol. 1, p. 8.

Debussy in Fin-de-Siècle Paris

CHRISTOPHE CHARLE
TRANSLATED BY VICTORIA JOHNSON

Describing fin-de-siècle Paris, the setting and the first site of the education and consecration of Debussy and his music, requires the mobilization of data drawn from urban, social, cultural, and political history. Indeed, at the turn of the century, Paris was a city so laden with contradictory images and so heavily populated by symbols and illustrious figures that the historian is in constant danger of relying on all-purpose explanations that might be valid for any creator, and which are therefore not specific to the case of Debussy. On the other hand, it would be equally reductive to enclose him in the tiny world of the avant-garde and of "geniuses," with its conventional elements of incomprehension and of scandal, of suffering and of solitude, elements that fail to convey the complexity of the social, intellectual, and musical trajectory of the composer of *Pelléas et Mélisande*. So powerful are the biographical stereotypes and the prefabricated rhetoric arising from the romantic tradition that even the best works on Debussy do not escape this sort of simplification, which therefore lacks the specificity of a particular epoch and place.

To guard against these pitfalls, one can progressively narrow the angle of vision—after sketching a panoramic view of the cosmopolitan city of Paris, with its immense possibilities and its equally great constraints, both of which exercised their effects on a musician who had received a meager lot in life in comparison to his closest colleagues and rivals. One can then narrow the scope of the field to the musical milieu and the elite public, a specific world that could facilitate the emergence of a professional composer like Debussy—or fail to do so. This approach reveals Debussy's room for maneuvering, again taking into account a musical trajectory at once typical and atypical with regard to the norms of the times. Finally, by means of a reconstruction of his itinerary through a city marked by strong social contrasts, one can uncover the contradictions of an artist who experienced social constraints on the most minute aspects of his musical and social inclinations. In the French musical world of the fin-de-siècle, liberation from inherited norms was largely incomplete. This particular lag between music and all other forms of art, which had themselves gained greatly in autonomy since the 1880s, explains the contradiction between the intellectual possibility of rebellion, of which many contemporary writers or artists whom Debussy knew and admired provided examples, and the social impossibility of going through with this rebellion, thanks to the private and public constraints that he felt particularly as the product of an unprivileged milieu.

Paris as a World of Art

Debussy's Paris, that of the period stretching from the 1880s to World War I, can be defined as a cosmopolitan city and even as the cosmopolitan city par excellence. No other European capital of the time could lay claim to such a concentration of wealth, culture, and creativity, and of institutions of education, exhibition, distribution, and communication. Without a doubt, London was more populated and richer thanks both to its city and to its port, which together dominated international commerce and tied London to the world's largest colonial empire and to an aristocratic season that attracted an opulent leisure class to the hotels of the West End each year. Nevertheless, the British capital was home to fewer theaters, newspapers, students, journalists, men of letters, and artists than Paris: in 1891, 2,485 men of letters and journalists were officially counted there, as opposed to more than 4,000 in Paris in 1896. While fifty-one percent of French journalists and men of letters resided in Paris in 1876, sixty-five percent did so in 1896. More than eighty percent of French books were published in the capital, and the big, popular daily papers represented, at the turn of the century, two-thirds of the total output of the press.[1]

The more recent European cultural capitals—Berlin, Brussels, St. Petersburg, Madrid, Rome, and Vienna, all with smaller populations—were even more firmly under the Parisian sway, importing huge quantities of Parisian comedies, operettas, paintings, and novels. In Vienna, for example, between 1885 and 1900, French works constituted a sixth of all theatrical performances.[2] Furthermore, universities, museums, and publishers from these European capitals were also in competition with other active centers within the same political space: Munich, Leipzig, and Cologne for the German capital;[3] Prague and Budapest for the Austro-Hungarian Empire. Moscow competed with St.

Petersburg for cultural innovation in Russia;[4] Barcelona competed with Madrid in Spain; and Milan, Florence, and Naples competed with Rome in Italy. In contrast, Paris exercised unmitigated domination within its national space, whether in matters of higher education, literature, or the arts.

This is why budding American and Russian artists, in search of instruction and of contacts with masters of painting, overwhelmingly chose to frequent the École des Beaux-Arts and the independent ateliers on both banks of the Seine. Later in their careers, they would exhibit their work in the salons of the French capital, where twenty percent to thirty percent of the artists showing their work at the beginning of the century were foreigners.[5] A stay in Paris was also de rigueur for a number of future writers, journalists, and poets from Italy, Spain, Central Europe, and Latin America. The encounters with Maeterlinck, D'Annunzio, the Ballets russes, and Stravinsky that were so important for Debussy were typical of the indirect effects of the cosmopolitan cross-fertilization to be found in Paris, an urban atmosphere without equivalent elsewhere in the world.[6]

Similarly, the leisure classes of America and Europe stampeded to the three great universal expositions of which Debussy was an eyewitness: those of 1878, 1889, and 1900, the best-attended of the century. They received, respectively, 16 million, 32 million, and 51 million visitors, as opposed to 5.6 million in attendance at the London exposition of 1886; 7.3 million at Vienna's exposition in 1873; and 11.6 million at Glasgow's in 1901.[7] These expositions nurtured the impression among Parisians in general, and among members of the Parisian artistic and literary world more specifically, that their city still constituted the center of civilization.

This national and international Parisian influence certainly did not originate in this epoch,[8] but it had reached its apogee at this time thanks to innovations imposed on the city and on French life in general since the Second Empire. The network of national and international railroads, centered on the capital, further facilitated the centralization and concentration of national and international elites. Paris therefore served as a second residence for an entire cosmopolitan leisure class, a class caricatured in *La Vie parisienne* (1866) by Jacques Offenbach, Henri Meilhac, and Ludovic Halévy. The English contingent, the most upper crust, practically doubled its numbers between 1872 and 1891.[9] In 1896, Paris harbored 11,951 British and 4,038 North Americans, the majority of whom lived in the fashionable districts.[10]

Indeed, in Paris, now expanded to include twenty arrondissements, the brutal work of tearing down old quartiers to make room for grand avenues—a process known as "Haussmanization," had created a city made to order for the upper classes, who were for the first time preserved from the constant dangers threatening them in the first two-thirds of the nineteenth century: epidemics linked to poor hygiene, urban overcrowding, and revolts and violence from the working classes. Like London, Paris now possessed its West End, composed of the eighth arrondissement, the sixteenth arrondissement, the western section of the ninth arrondissement, the seventeenth arrondissement, and the seventh arrondissement, on the margins of which Debussy and his family lived for a long time before the composer managed to force his way in after his second marriage, as we will see in more detail below.[11]

This city of parvenus and independently wealthy members of the bourgeoisie; of large, tree-lined avenues (while the old sections of Paris lacked sidewalks); of chiseled stone buildings graced by columns and balconies, with caryatids and marble statues displayed in their entrance halls, this city represented the success of its inhabitants, privileged by fortune and by birth. This part of Paris also attracted the majority of the creative minds in letters and arts who would ensure the reputation of these forty golden years of French culture, whether they acquired their fame during their lives or after. France's national glory, Victor Hugo, lived at this time on the avenue in the sixteenth arrondissement that bore his name even during his own lifetime, while Edmond de Goncourt received writers who cultivated aestheticist writing in his *grenier* at Auteuil, where he had created a living environment worthy of the aristocratic eighteenth century, source of inspiration for Paul Verlaine and Gabriel Fauré.[12] Paul Bourget, the fashionable novelist whose first poems Debussy set to music when the composer was embarking on his musical career, chose the Faubourg Saint Germain (rue Barbet de Jouy), as did Vincent d'Indy (avenue de Villars). Many of Debussy's friends, acquaintances, and celebrated contemporaries lived in the quartier de l'Europe and the plaine Monceau, the most bourgeois area of the seventeenth arrondissement: Stéphane Mallarmé, 89 rue de Rome; Fauré, and Debussy's boyhood friend Pierre Louÿs, boulevard Malesherbes[13]; and Emile Zola, 21 bis rue Bruxelles.

Following Voltaire's approach in his *History of the Century of Louis XIV,* one could depict turn-of-the-century Paris as an extraordinary city and an extraordinary epoch, in which Zola and Octave Mirbeau attended the first performance of a play by Ibsen at the Théâtre libre, after having defended *la nouvelle peinture* in the newspapers; where the young Léon Blum unceremoniously attacked, in *La Revue Blanche*, the venerable *Revue des Deux Mondes* and its director Brunetière, and where

Figure 1
Successive Addresses of Debussy and Some
Contemporary Writers and Musicians

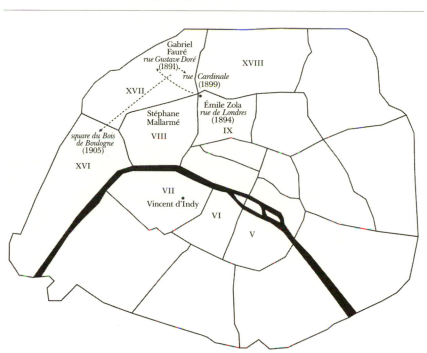

he sang the praises of the little avant-garde reviews in which Strindberg, Hauptmann, Nietzsche, and Tolstoy published, and which defended Postimpressionist painting.[14] It was also a moment teeming with masters, when the young Barrès, the young Bourget and the young Charles Péguy followed the courses of Taine at the École des Beaux-Arts and at the École libre des sciences politiques, and of Renan and Bergson at the Collège de France. And it was a singular intellectual conjuncture, when a firm belief in science, education, and the promotion of democracy confronted the reactionary return of certain writers and artists to Catholicism, spiritualism, elitism, or esotericism.

But this rosy myth also has its darker underside. Here we encounter less glorious images: an Académie française from which the real writers were excluded, from which they stayed distant, or where they underwent humiliating failures during elections of members. Over these writers the venerable assembly preferred dukes, boulevard writers, and conservative historians, and critics. This self-styled Athenian republic overwhelmingly preferred to commission academic paintings, while only grudgingly accepting certain bequests from collectors of modern paintings—bequests being fought over by foreign art lovers.[15] The press, astonishingly free in tone since the law of July 29, 1881, had largely been corrupted by financiers, as Maupassant showed ferociously in *Bel-Ami*. Philistine art critics snickered in their newspaper columns at the canvases of innovators. In this world capital of cultural innovation, the light (sometimes pornographic) press, like light theater and cafés-concerts, had many more readers or spectators than the learned reviews or the avant-garde theaters that programed northern European works. In the musical world of the time, we know the violence of the resistance to Wagner (for reasons more political than musical), the slightly ridiculous intensity of the Wagnermania of the Bayreuth pilgrims (among them the young Debussy, who was soon to repent of this idolatry), and the persistence of academicism and of the competitions that Debussy would ridicule, through Monsieur Croche, in his articles.[16]

To reduce the culture of Paris at the turn of the century to any one of these images would be equally misleading. The originality of Parisian cultural life, judged as it was by a whole range of public tastes, consisted precisely in the conflict-laden and difficult cohabitation of these thousands of creators, researchers, professors, and students, of Frenchmen and foreigners, of native Parisians and ambitious provincials. The interactions, disputes, polemics, and attacks (which sometimes went as far as duels) in this permanent struggle for survival and recognition created a specific and electric atmosphere, an atmosphere born of an exaggerated individualism, of durable and ephemeral friendships, and of likely and improbable encounters. This highly charged environment rendered even more necessary the invention of particular sites and modes of selection for purposes of survival and mutual assistance. Thus an Italian observer who had come to Paris in the beginning of the 1880s—the moment when Debussy was embarking on his musical career—writes:

> How grand and intoxicating is the triumph of genius in that city, a triumph scarcely noticed by her who receives the salutations of unknown admirers and offers and counsels from every part of the globe; how to the man unsuccessful in one direction, a hundred other roads remain open, if he be willing to lower to a very slight degree his pretension to glory; how the forgetful nature of that great city, which, not permitting anyone to rest upon one

triumph, obliges all to represent themselves continually at the contest, produces that marvelously busy life, those obstinately warlike old men, whose example inspires coming generations with the passion for work; and in fine, what an enormous quantity of unfinished work, of attempts, sketches, of material spoiled by some, but not useless to others, and of praiseworthy creations in all fields, but condemned to die where they arise, because they are crushed by the abundance of something better.[17]

Though he was not familiar with this text, Debussy wrote a letter soon after returning from a sojourn at the Villa Medici that conveys the same sense of disarray. He confirms, in this letter, the power of the pressure exercised by the cultural metropolis over his old musician friends. They were all putting on the airs of Rastignac in this "bazaar of success":

Even my own friends created the impression of being important personages: Vidal very busy, grudgingly granting me the favor of lunching with him! Leroux giving me an audience in the street between two rendezvous! Pierné! I don't dare even go to see him. All those people treating Paris like a conquered city! And you have to see how malleable they are, how they have lost their pretty indignations of days gone by. Now I ask myself how I am going to manage, with my exaggerated savagery, to find my way and assert myself in the middle of this "bazaar of success" and I foresee lots of trouble, offenses beyond number.[18]

In the 1880s, at the end of a century of revolutions and of successive regimes, a century that saw the laborious birth of democracy and of parliamentary government, France was caught up in a liberal and conflict-ridden political climate, a climate unique in contemporary Europe and born of the final convulsions in a struggle against all forms of authority, whether intellectual, moral, educational, religious, or political. The other cultural and political capitals of Europe were still far from having completed this metamorphosis at this time, situated as they were in monarchical states where official religion dictated law, law which for example, could, even in the liberal climate of England in the 1890s, block performance of Oscar Wilde's *Salome* (because it was still forbidden to perform plays based on sacred texts). *Salome* was therefore premiered in Paris by Sarah Bernhardt.

This intellectual and political climate, free from almost all constraints, formed the basis of the Parisian claim to represent the avant-garde and to be the center of the international intellectual and artistic world. In 1871 this city had dared to secede from the official government (a vivid and painful memory for Debussy, whose father had been imprisoned for his participation in the Commune).[19] A majority in this city had voted for the extreme radical left, making life difficult for the central authorities who refused to give the town a normal municipal regime. The city rallied equally quickly to the putschist General Boulanger out of disgust with scandals involving the bourgeois republicans. It experienced a wave of anarchist assassinations at the beginning of the 1890s, then anti-Semitic unrest during the Dreyfus Affair. On the other hand, the city also served as headquarters for mobilization in Dreyfus's favor. Moderation and indifference were less common here than elsewhere.

We know the attraction exercised by anarchism on the symbolist milieux frequented by Debussy through the "Librairie de l'art indépendant" and the review *Entretiens politiques et littéraires*.[20] The spirit of derision and disrespect current in the Montmartre cabarets, less political but sometimes even more devastating, is another manifestation of this anarchism, of which Debussy was a devotee during the years 1889–1892. He kept this tone and spirit his whole life, as is evidenced by the most ferocious passages of his letters, his ironic musical chronicles in *La Revue blanche* and the impertinent answers he sometimes made to his interviewers, even after he had become famous. Thus in a letter of 1893, when he was still largely unknown to the general public, Debussy pitilessly derides the strategies of seduction employed by Gustave Charpentier, the rising star in music at the turn of the century:

> There's also a new star on the musical horizon called Gustave Charpentier, destined, it seems to me, to achieve glory, riches, and complete freedom from aesthetic considerations. He's taking over from Berlioz, who was, in my opinion, an inveterate practical joker who came to believe in his own jokes. Charpentier hasn't even got Berlioz's moderately aristocratic nature. He's a man of the people: to the extent, it seems, of creating an opera called *Marie* and set in Montmartre. The work that has just endeared him to the populace is called *La Vie du poète*. The faded romanticism of the title tells us something about it, but what you cannot possibly imagine is the work's total absence of taste—what you might call "the triumph of the Brasserie." It smells of tobacco and there are whiskers all over it.[21]

Eight years later, endowed with an avant-garde column widely read in the milieux of Dreyfusard and Germanophile intellectuals, the author

of *Monsieur Croche,* inspired by the irreverent tone of the cabarets and
satirical journals, is able to satisfy his caustic spirit in public:

> There has been in the last few weeks a big delivery of German con-
> ductors. This is less grave than an epidemic, but it makes much
> more noise . . . a conductor being multiplicable by ninety . . .[22]

The irreverence shown here toward Germany, France's neighbor
and musical rival, was hardly reserved for foreign cultures. Debussy displays the same irreverence toward French institutions —in particular
toward that French obsession with rules with which the Republic had
so far been unable to break, an irreverence witnessed by the following
charge, which appeared in the *Revue musicale SIM* in 1912:

> For a long time we have been caught up in a mania for adminis-
> trating the least administrable things in the world, and necessarily
> this mania ends by invading art! If one wishes to make music, one
> immediately founds a society where contradictory elements gen-
> erally end up neutralizing one another. One wishes to learn music?
> One has a choice between the Conservatoire and the Schola
> Cantorum, where no matter whether one is as much a genius
> as Bach or as gifted as Chopin, one must submit to the same rules
> as everyone else.[23]

This anti-institutional temper is not merely the expression of personal discontent on the part of a composer who has been mistreated by
the official theaters and by the public. Debussy's writing here takes up
and extends to the musical world, less liberated than the other arts, all
the critical reflections produced over the previous thirty years or so by
Flaubert, Zola, Mallarmé, André Antoine, and other less well-known
writers against the prizes, the academies, the schools, and the cultural
institutions that since Napoleon, or perhaps even since Louis XIV, continued to claim jurisdiction over literature, art, theater, and poetry, at
precisely the moment when the demand for freedom was the order of
the day in the cultural sphere.

Unfortunately for the musical arts, independence from this domination was even harder to secure than in other domains: the vast majority
of musicians, unlike writers, did not dispose of the resources of the
press. Nor did they have access to a blossoming art market, as did
painters, nor, a devoted new public, as did playwrights, alternatives
that permitted them to escape the protection of the state, the constraints
of the official theaters, and public commissions. While the republican

state had liberated the press and indirectly multiplied its readers thanks to free, mandatory education; while it had adopted a more liberal policy regarding the exhibition of *beaux-arts*, its musical policy remained in step with the monarchical and imperial tradition. Dominated by a provincial political class whose members were educated in the humanities and occasionally in classical aesthetics, but who were virtually ignorant with regard to music, the Third Republic reformed its higher musical institutions very late and even then only negligibly. Indeed, these institutions concerned only a tiny elite and a very small audience, hardly of strategic importance to a regime with a rural base of political support. Composers—particularly those like Debussy and his contemporaries, who wished to be innovators and not follow the tastes of the average audience or to solicit official commissions[24]—had to find other means of making themselves heard. Essentially this meant using the arena then known as *le monde*—that is to say, the leisure class of the fashionable quarters.

High Life in Paris

This leisure class was the product of two new features of turn-of-the-century Parisian society. With the help of the urban transformations sketched above, this class had regrouped itself outside the traditional center and the declining former aristocratic neighborhoods. To the west, the average rents were between 1,025 francs a year for the most chic neighborhood (Champs-Élysées) and 434 francs a year for the Monceau area, while in the working-class neighborhoods on the city's periphery, one had to spend on average only between 55 and 75 francs a year.[25] The attraction exercised by the new bourgeois neighborhoods is evidenced by the increase in the population of the Champs-Élysées district, which climbed from a base of 100 in 1861 to 205, the Chaillot district to 233, and the Monceau district to 420, while the old bourgeois and aristocratic neighborhoods in the center stagnated or declined.[26] The west of Paris was also increasingly the location of choice for foreign residents: The biggest contingents of British and North and South Americans permanently residing in Paris were recorded in the eighth and the sixteenth arrondissements. There they found modern buildings with the latest comforts and the proximity of green spaces (the Parc Monceau, the Bois de Boulogne, the promenade of the Champs-Élysées, and the Champ de Mars), as well the possibility of individual residences such as were generally home to the well-to-do in English and American cities.

This region of Paris also accommodated holders of recently acquired fortunes who came in search of social distinction and cultural activities affording social prestige. In the absence of a political elite to set the tone, as would have been the case in a monarchy with its court, and in the absence of a nobility that was as unified and sure of itself as England's, the social milieu that was called at the time *le monde*, *le High Life*, or *le Tout-Paris*—the uncertainty of the vocabulary is itself the sign of the fluid boundaries of the leisure class—was a composite ensemble of circles and coteries who competed to influence cultural and artistic activities and launch new fashions. Proust has given us the best account of the complexity of this world. Seen from afar, it appeared unified, while in fact this society of independently wealthy individuals, by and large liberated from the cares of moneymaking, made a pastime, at worst, of the futile and the trivial (fashion, knickknacks, horses, sports, cars, yachts, and leisure activities) and at best, of the patronage of the arts and letters. This patronage, modeled on a bygone aristocratic age, was practiced now by nonaristocrats. It played a role of great importance, particularly for those art forms that disposed of few alternative audiences and sources of support.

There were still many literary salons, but their function had become peripheral for most writers. Recognition and audiences were now reached through reviews, newspapers, and success on the stage or in publication, as well as through the circles of mutual admiration furnished by cafés and literary dinners. Similarly, though some upper-class art lovers were able to facilitate the breakthrough of this or that painter who had been mistreated by the salons or by official institutions, there were other paths as well. Favorable reviews by men of letters, the assistance of enterprising merchants in the conquest of foreign markets, or the mutual assistance of private exhibitions were just as helpful to the careers of painters or sculptors. State commissions also continued to play a role.[27]

Live music, on the contrary, was an easy prey for the salons of turn-of-the-century Paris. The state was ineffectual in this domain and public venues were scarce.[28] More than letters and the visual arts, music fit easily into the private space of townhouses or of the huge bourgeois apartments of the "world where one is bored." In this society, peopled by *belles âmes* devoted to the quest for pleasure and haunted by the ephemeral nature of a lifestyle oriented to the search for the new and instantaneous, the art of passing time that is music was the entertainment par excellence—music because that is the way things were done, music because it was the simplest means of attaining the illusion of communion above and beyond the multiple divisions, subtle but nevertheless very important, that ran through this *monde*.

Debussy, whose social origins in no way predisposed him to integrate himself into the *monde*, was forced very early to plunge into this universe so difficult to understand for a new arrival both to music and the dominant class. His first experiences with high society, products of unintentional biographical chance, present a kaleidoscope of images that faithfully capture the diversity of the *monde* of the epoch. The cosmopolitan aspect of this *monde* appeared in the form of his first patroness, the Russian Baroness Nadezhda von Meck,[29] while the frivolousness of wealthy young men is illustrated by his brief friendship with the prince André Poniatowsky. Born into the imperial nobility, first officer, then military attaché, a lover of horse races and a member of aristocratic clubs, Poniatowsky became an international speculator and tried to launch Debussy in the United States.[30] The world of the nouveaux riches of the bourgeois Republic was personified by the proprietor of Chenonceaux, Marguerite Wilson, daughter of a gas magnate of English origin, sister of a racketeering deputy who was himself the son-in-law of the president of the Republic, Jules Grévy, and who was to precipitate the fall of the latter through a notorious traffic in official decorations.[31] On a more modest scale, one finds among recent arrivals to the bourgeoisie the composer Ernest Chausson, son of a building entrepreneur, and the financier Étienne Dupin—both music lovers, friends, and benefactors of Debussy. The enlightened amateur was also present in the salons of Escudier and of Saint-Marceaux, where one performed music as much as one listened.[32]

As historians of society life have shown,[33] the social relations of this universe were founded on asymmetry except at those moments when the musicians socialized exclusively among themselves: physical proximity made social distance felt only more keenly. On a smaller scale, these relations reproduced the universe of the court.[34] Ostensibly there to be admired by the audience assembled by the mistress of the house, the artist was expected to conform to the conventions of the private space in which he was a mere guest, while the rest of the participants were there by birthright, kinship, or social position. The applause that an artist received, the praise and tips given, the notoriety gathered from soirée to soirée before he appeared on more important stages, gradually opened up other salons and the public space in general (for example, through engagements in France and abroad or mentions in the press). But this success in *le monde* presupposed that the artist was willing to accept the basic rules of *savoir-vivre*, comportment and seduction in effect in the circle in which he had been received. All musicians knew that they were rarely appreciated for themselves, independent of these conventions passed down by aristocratic tradition. Many submitted to them, performing or composing the music expected of them because it was the price of certain success with members of high society, that least cultivated and most numerous of audiences.

The annual publication *Tout Paris*, in which the mistresses of households found the addresses of the musicians who would grace their soirées, recorded 116 composers in 1903,[35] while the general census of the Seine region in 1896 gives a number three times as high as this for composers active in Paris. The majority of these chose to reside in the fashionable districts that were also home to this audience of elites.[36] Less than half of these society composers (forty-one) received an entry in the *New Grove Dictionary of Music and Musicians*, which indirectly proves their submissiveness with regard to the dominant taste, itself fairly different from today's musical taste. Even among the forty composers elected for posthumous celebrity by musicologists, the majority had to conform to the rituals of salon music, from those most well-known to Debussy (Fauré, Saint-Saëns, Charles de Bériot) to the more obscure (Raoul Pugno, Cécile Chaminade, Francis Thomé).[37]

Debussy himself was forced to take part in this social game beginning in 1893–94. He was wholly conscious of his function:

Indeed, I no longer recognize myself! I'm to be found in the salons executing smiles, or else conducting choruses at the house of Countess Zamoïska! Oh yes, and while I'm immersing myself in the beauty of these choruses of Magnanarelles I tell myself it's a just punishment for this dreary music to be flayed by fearless society ladies. Then there's Mme de Saint-Marceaux, who's discovered that I'm a first-rate talent! It's enough to make you die laughing. But really you'd have to be a hopelessly weak character to be taken in by all this rubbish. It's so fatuous![38]

Despite his legitimate fear of entrapment, it must be acknowledged that there was hardly any alternative for a musician such as Debussy, who was not a virtuoso, who rejected as much as possible commercial music of all kinds (in spite of propositions in this regard made to him by his friend Pierre Louÿs[39]) and who had, in addition, no official post. To exist symbolically outside the French tradition handed down by the Conservatoire, as well as outside the currents of Wagnerism and Italian verismo; to survive financially without abandoning the demanding activity of composition—this was impossible without such self-interested, high-society sources of support.[40] The musical salon afforded opportunities to meet influential figures who could open the door to theaters. It also brought the wages always appreciated by a chronic debtor. Above all it provided a circle of admirers greater than that formed by the composer's own musical or literary friends. The salon permitted Debussy's breakthrough after decisive performances of his earliest works in the concerts of the elite, though he did not immediately take this route toward public recognition, and never did so with enthusiasm. In the beginning, everything distanced him from this path: first, his lack of *savoir-vivre*, the product of a milieu and education that was anything but bourgeois; second, his friendships among the literary avant-garde, for whom a hatred of all things socialite and bourgeois was one of the articles of faith. To them this world was encapsulated in the Boulevard, that is to say, in the district of theaters, newspapers, and fashionable cafés where favors, gossip, and wit were exchanged for one another. Thus Debussy wrote at the age of twenty-five, "Seeking the attention of *boulevardiers*, socialites, and other vegetables—my God, how tiresome."[41]

After the long period of asceticism in which *Pelléas* was created, after the many disappointments brought by constantly mismatched romances and associations arising from Debussy's precarious social position between the bohemian world and the bourgeoisie, between musical ambition and poverty, between snobbery and the lack of means to satisfy it, the power of constraint won out, as is indicated by the compromises he was forced to accept between 1903 and his death. He turned his back more and more on previously held beliefs born from his contact with the model of the absolute artist embodied by Mallarmé and his circle. In his famous letter to Verlaine on the *poètes maudits*, Mallarmé sketches the field of tensions in which the poet (and the musician) were caught in a new society dedicated to mass cultural consumption:

> At bottom, I consider the contemporary epoch an interregnum for the poet, who has no need to get mixed up therein: the times are too obsolete and full of preparatory effervescence for the poet to do anything other than work cryptically with an eye to the future, from time to time send his calling card—verses or sonnet—to the living to avoid being lambasted by any who suspect him of knowing they don't exist. Solitude is the necessary accompaniment of this kind of attitude . . .[42]

Even if in the beginning Debussy had initially found inspiration in this very demanding Mallarméan ideal when he had some of his works published in a luxurious limited subscription edition, a practice dear to the poet of rue de Rome, it was hardly practicable for composing live music.[43] Mallarmé himself, in the paragraph preceding this passage, admitted to having had to make several compromises with the century. From the moment Debussy wished to get *Pelléas* performed, he too had to play the dominant social game. Once he gained recognition thereby, he sought the social status that went hand in hand with it. This move was manifested in his private life by his divorce and his subsequent remarriage to a woman who was not just a music lover, but also a true product of the *monde* on which he had so recently heaped his disdain. It became harder and harder to maintain the old ethic of purity, as we will shortly see in his relations with his publisher and in his new lifestyle, which was precisely that of the *monde*.

High Music and High Life

Now that we have situated Debussy in the diverse social universes that directly or indirectly influenced him, we must examine how he situated himself within them given what was possible in the musical world and in the social world in general—either by necessity linked to his inherited advantages and disadvantages, or by strategy, positive or negative, conscious or unconscious. Contrary to the idealism flaunted in the world of art and especially in the more spiritual world of music, the public and private writings of Debussy and of his contemporaries reveal a full consciousness of the constraints, possibilities, and impossibilities encountered by the composer on the road to fame. The logic of his trajectory obliged him to decide between the ideal of artistic identity born of his frequenting the world of the poets, and his social identity, shaped by the growing frustrations and unfulfilled aspirations that were produced by this misleading intimacy with a world where he would always be an intruder. Without this audience, Debussy's music, that which he held most dear, could not exist. The Mallarméan or Flaubertian model of the artist, of art for art's sake, entails making, as Flaubert puts it, "two parts of one's life." This life was possible only under two conditions, which were fulfilled differently by the two authors: One was to do away with all economic recompense for symbolic production thanks to an independent income (Flaubert). The second was to force oneself to take on a second career (Mallarmé was a teacher of English). In the second case one counted on the recognition of the "happy few" or of posterity, thanks to the durability conferred by the printed word and the intimate colloquy between the author and reader, listener and coterie.

Debussy assayed this route, but could not keep to his course, both for the economic reasons already sketched and because access to the public before the age of mechanical reproduction was by necessity socially mediated in ways that were much more constraining than those affecting books. This discrepancy between live music and elite literature was aggravated by that between Debussy's artistic ideal, grounded in a deep disdain for the very public on which he depended, and his social ideal, whose values and tastes were those both of "good society" and of the majority of his colleagues and musician friends, who were less stringent with regard to artistic creation than Debussy. In this respect, Debussy was not an exception: like almost all artists—even those of the avant-garde—he aspired to the bourgeois lifestyle, the bohemian lifestyle and its attendant poverty serving only as a youthful phase or an indication of failure. In Debussy's case, a return to the bohemian lifestyle would constitute a return to his point of departure despite the sacrifices undertaken by him and his family, given their initial modest resources. This double discrepancy at the moment when success seemed just within reach produced a premature illusion of having arrived and a refusal to face the truth of the situation. Both facts are conveyed to us, in all their incontrovertible dryness, by the account books of Debussy's income and outlay during the last fifteen years of his life.

Biographers have already noted the striking contrast between Debussy's standard of living before and after 1904. Following simple causality, they explain this by referring to the change in the social position of a man who had become a famous musician and also the lover, then husband, of Madame Bardac, niece of the fabulously wealthy financier Osiris. This explanation accords too much power to external factors and to the weakness of character of a man who was frequently at a loss in the face of material difficulties, a man who played upon these problems in order to get sympathy and ask for help without shame. In fact, when Debussy adopted this new lifestyle for the reasons elaborated above, he did more than give in to bourgeois conformism—he lost all sense of reality and proportion. As he himself pointed out, to rent a townhouse situated in a private square on one of the most opulent avenues of western Paris, the avenue du Bois de Boulogne (today avenue Foch), is to go far beyond a will for social revenge or for the satisfaction of the snobby tastes of a bourgeois mistress (later his wife).[44] One need only mention the names and social positions of the Debussys' neighbors. On the same sidewalk, at No. 40, was the townhouse of the famous aristocrat Count Boniface de Castellane, who was married to a wealthy American. The successful playwright Georges Feydeau lived at No. 50; and at No. 60 lived the art dealer and owner of the *Revue blanche*, Alfred Natanson. In 1903, at No. 64 (the address of the section of the building that included the Debussy household) lived the Marquis and the Marquise de Barral-Montferrat, Count Stanislas Potocki, several independently wealthy English and Americans, a businessman named Adolphe Bontoux (member of the club of the Union artistique), several members of the royal family of Serbia, Karageorgewitch, and a family of rich Russians, the Kouznetzoff.[45] In this cosmopolitan, noble, propertied [46] and leisured village, the presence of a composer with no hope of an inheritance and rich only in debts—even if he were married to a member of the bourgeoisie—was a social incongruity felt by Debussy himself. In a letter to Ingelbrecht, Debussy speaks of the "'cocktail' habitués of the avenue du Bois de Boulogne" and complains in a letter to his editor:

> This avenue du Bois de Boulogne smelling of Brazilians and Americans, not much ancient feel here! I also come back to my landlord, the English alcoholic, who'll have no compunction throwing me out if ever he finds a millionaire adventurer![47]

If one excepts the heirs of bourgeois families (Chausson, Dukas) or of noble families (Vincent d'Indy), none of the well-known musicians of the period adopted as sumptuous a lifestyle. The repeated complaints in the *Correspondance*, the temptation of suicide, the advances agreed to by the publisher Durand or by friends, and the attempts made by his wife in 1910 to take out loans—all reveal the financial abyss that the Debussys' new society lifestyle was digging. It was never filled. In a letter of September 5, 1913, to Victor Segalen, the composer writes that he is thinking of "moving to the suburbs in order to have more peace and a house that is less ridiculously costly."[48]

Though Debussy's earnings increased appreciably after the relative success of *Pelléas*, they were still far smaller than his expenditures. His townhouse rent was 8,000 francs per year, eight times the rent that Debussy had paid for his previous apartment at 58 rue Cardinet.[49] This rent was in the highest bracket for Parisian elites of the day. It was justified by a private garden of 640 square meters (6,000 square feet) and a floorplan of 146 square meters (1,500 square feet) on the ground level. Between the basement, the ground floor, and the second and third floors, the townhouse included eighteen rooms and outbuildings (wine cellar, shed, stables). For the maintenance of such a residence, one must calculate in the cost of keeping several servants (at least 2,000 francs), the family's food (3,000 francs), their clothing (3,000 francs), and various other expenditures, such as taxes, travel, books, newspapers, furniture, and Debussy's beloved knickknacks (at least 4,000 francs)—in total, an approximate budget of at least 20,000 francs a year. This figure represented, at the time, the salary of a very senior functionary or the interest from about 400,000 francs in principal.[50] To complicate the situation further, Debussy had to pay 4,800 francs a year in alimony to his ex-wife.

This overall indirect estimation of Debussy's budget can be confirmed by the annual total of the advances agreed to by the publisher Durand for his favorite author (see Table 1). For the seven years for which detailed accounts have survived, we find an average of more than 16,000 francs a year in advances. Even if we allow that the revenues accruing to the former Madame Bardac[51] and Debussy's supplementary sources of income (the rights to foreign performances, orchestra conducting, wages from society soirées, revenues from articles, etc.) permitted him to approach the estimated sum of 20,000 francs, three indicators show that Debussy seriously overestimated the probable increase in his income when he settled on his new address.

The proof that Debussy's real expenditures exceeded his total income lies in the fact that the deficit in his account with his principal publisher was already around 12,850 francs in 1907[52]—that is, almost six months' worth of his estimated expenses after only three years in his new life. There were probably further debts to other merchants that would have to be added to this deficit, as well as the legal fees relating to the divorce.

Table 1

Debussy's Advances on Rights and Account Deficits (in Gold Francs)
with the Publisher Durand

Dates cover April 1 to March 31 of the following year.

Year	Amount of advance	Deficit in account
1907/08	17,300	12,850
1908/09	20,150	13,750
1909/10	8,800	11,800
1910/11	11,266.65	27,066.65
1911/12	16,800	42,866.65
1912/13	16,300	39,166.65
1913/14	23,800	49,688.30
Average	16,345.23	28,169.75

Indeed, in 1911 the deficit, which had remained for four years in the same bracket, doubled brutally, even though Debussy had by then multiplied his sources of income (invitations abroad, rights on performances abroad, ballet music, articles in the newspapers, honoraria for sitting on juries). When he started suffering from cancer in 1909 (a source of additional expenditures), Debussy even had to give up the vacation that he had taken regularly since 1901. In spite of this attempt to economize, the deficit on his author's account increased more than sixfold: at the time of his death in 1918, it had reached 66,080.30 francs. This rising tide of debt was certainly still higher in reality; a bill at his English tailors in Paris for 1,963 francs, no doubt one among many, still had not been paid when Debussy died,[53] even though the publisher Durand served as a veritable banker to his composer, notably with regard to the payment of Lily Texier's alimony and by providing no-interest loans. Durand even served as Debussy's host during the holidays.[54]

All this was a result of his failure to honor his most fruitful contracts and to find a dramatic success comparable to that of *Pelléas et Mélisande*. If he hoped to pay off his debts and maintain his sumptuous lifestyle, Debussy would have had to complete the operatic works he had promised, for which he had been paid in advance by Durand but had never finished, and which were therefore never performed. Debussy would also have had to achieve with these works a success identical to or greater than that which had greeted *Pelléas et Mélisande*, for which one can calculate the earnings from the accounts of the Opéra Comique as follows: the total amount of receipts for performances in 1902 reached 113, 627 francs; if one applies the usual rate of six percent of the gross income for the composer, that represents 6,817 francs, to which would be added 25,000 francs for the rights to the orchestral score.[55] Even then, Debussy would have had just barely enough to repay his debts and to dispose of a little surplus.

However, if one sets aside Massenet and composers of operettas, no composer of lyric works at the time had enjoyed this kind of success on a permanent basis. This was even more so since the lyric stage had become more and more dominated by Italian and Wagnerian operas. Of the thirty-two lyric works created at the Opéra between 1902 and 1914, fourteen were the work of German or Italian musicians. French works that were performed often fell within traditional or Wagnerian currents hostile to Debussy, which explains his retreat to the new modernist stage of the Théâtre des Champs-Élysées.[56] The scathing diatribes against foreign musicians[57] in which Debussy's articles abounded were not simply, as is usually claimed, the expression of a newfound enthusiasm for nationalism. They convey instead his conscious sense that despite a promising beginning, his failure on the French stage was partly the result of a persistent attachment of the public to foreign productions, to the detriment of French music or more particularly of music that, like his, upended its conventions. These foreign productions were not simply distasteful to him; they actually subjected him to daily difficulties, even though in 1913 he was the eighth most frequently performed composer in concerts.[58] Hence the paradox: Here was a musician, who saw himself more and more as French, being compelled to depend on income from abroad. This situation reached a dramatic pitch when World War I blocked all possibility of foreign income. The result: a renewed deterioration of his accounts just as his health worsened seriously.

Conclusion

This contextualization of Debussy in turn-of-the-century Paris strips away a conventional, idealized, and romantic vision and permits us to measure at one and the same time the potentialities offered by the world capital of the avant-garde and the difficulties encountered by an artist who rejected the well-trodden paths of ordinary careers and who tried to maintain his course against the social and economic constraints that conspired to divert him from it. This tension did not make a romantic hero of Debussy, as his daily life, which could not be more bourgeois, plainly shows. Instead it submitted him to contradictory pressures and to permanent and painful decisions between social survival and musical ambition. Just when the success of *Pelléas et Mélisande* seemed to pry loose the financial vise of his first forty years, Debussy himself walked into a new trap by acquiescing to the fallacious prestige of a life too bourgeois for his real income. The historian does not become a moralist in so stating. With the exception of Erik Satie, almost all Debussy's contemporaries were doing the same. It was as if the musicians of the elite could live anywhere other than in a totally sheltered world. This was not a matter of fate, but simply because in the sharing of profits of an activity that is still rare, the musical creator who was neither a virtuoso nor holder of public prebends, depended more than did painters or men of letters on an elite audience, and was even less well provided for than they. One can easily imagine a less tragic end to Debussy's life only if, enjoying a longevity like that of Ravel, he had been able to draw on the real and immense profits that recorded music brought to all the intermediaries who siphoned off their tithe on his music throughout the twentieth century.

NOTES

1. Christophe Charle, *Les Intellectuels en Europe au XIXè siècle, essai d'histoire comparée* (Paris: Le Seuil, 1996), pp. 160–63.

2. Calculated on the basis of statistical data from *Statistisches Jahrbuch der Stadt Wien für das Jahr* (Vienna: Verlag der Wienermagistrat, 1885, 1895 and 1900).

3. Christophe Charle, *Paris fin de siècle* (Paris: Le Seuil, 1998), Chapter 1; *Metropolis Berlin, Berlin als deutsche Hauptstadt im Vergleich europäischer Hauptstädte, 1870–1939*, ed. Gerhard Brunn and Jürgen Reulecke (Bonn-Berlin: Bouvier Verlag, 1992).

4. Eva Bérard, ed., *Saint Petersbourg: une fenêtre sur la Russie 1900–1935* (Paris: Editions de la Maison des sciences de l'homme, 2000).

5. Lois Marie Fink, *American Art at the Nineteenth-Century Paris Salons* (Cambridge, Eng.: Cambridge University Press; and Washington, D.C.: National Museum of American Art, Smithsonian Institution, 1990); *Annuaire statistique de la ville de Paris 1899*; and Charle, *Paris fin de siècle*, pp. 42–45.

6. This is shown by several partial analyses in André Kaspi and Antoine Marès, eds. *Le Paris des étrangers depuis un siècle*, (Paris: Imprimerie nationale, 1981): Mario Carelli, "Les Brésiliens à Paris de la naissance du romantisme aux avant-gardes," pp. 287–98; Christiane Séris, "Microcosmes dans la capitale ou l'histoire de la colonie intellectuelle hispano-américaine à Paris entre 1890 et 1914," pp. 299–312; François Livi, "Le 'saut vital': le monde littéraire italien à Paris (1900–1914)," pp. 313–27; see also Pascale Casanova, *La République mondiale des lettres* (Paris: Le Seuil, 1999), Chapter 4.

7. Claude Tapia, "Paris, ville des Congrès de 1850 à nos jours," in *Le Paris des étrangers depuis un siècle*, ed. Kaspi and Marès, p. 39. More than 480,000 British and North Americans and more than 426,000 people from Germanic countries attended the Universal Exposition of 1900 (*Album de statistique graphique 1900* [Paris: Imprimerie nationale, 1906], Fig. 46).

8. An indicator is the increase in the number of travel guides published on Paris in the second half of the eighteenth century. See Gilles Chabaud, "Les guides de Paris: une littérature de l'accueil?," in *La Ville promise. Mobilité et accueil à Paris, fin XVIIè-début XIXè siècle*, ed. Daniel Roche (Paris: Fayard, 2000), p. 81.

9. See Christophe Leribault, *Les Anglais à Paris au 19è siècle* (Paris: Paris-Musées, 1994), p. 48, following Jacques Bertillon, *Origine des habitants de Paris, lieu de naissance des habitants de Paris en 1833 et en 1891. Les Etrangers à Paris, leur origine et leurs professions* (Paris, 1895) and Brigitte de Montclos, *Les Russes à Paris au XIXe siècle, 1814–1896* (Paris: Paris-Musées, 1996).

10. Paris 1896 census.

11. After the failure of their business at Saint-Germain-en-Laye, Debussy's parents settled in Paris at 11 rue de Vintimille (ninth arrondissement) near the Place Clichy, at the end of the 1860s; in the 1870s they lived in cramped quarters on a courtyard at 59 rue Pigalle (ninth arrondissement), then at 13 rue Clapeyron (eighth arrondissement) and 27 rue de Berlin near les Batignolles, streets located in the neighborhoods between "popular" and "bourgeois" Paris. François Lesure, *Claude Debussy. Biographie critique* (Paris: Klincksieck, 1994), pp.14, 19, 27. Debussy himself lived in the same sector of Paris until 1894: 42 rue de Londres (ninth arrondissement; rent was 120 francs). As his fame grew, he gravitated toward northwest Paris, in the Plaine Monceau district: 10 rue Gustave-Doré (seventeenth arrondissement; rent was 450 francs), then 58 rue Cardinet (rent was 1,000 francs) almost at the corner of the boulevard Malesherbes, equidistant between Gabriel Fauré (living at 154) and one of his patrons, Mme de Saint-Marceaux, who owned

a townhouse at No. 100 (*Archives de Paris D1P4*, respectively, boxes 1221, 268, 115, 651, 525, 188).

12. Deborah L. Silverman, *Art Nouveau in Fin-de-Siècle France: Politics, Psychology, and Style* (Berkeley, Calif.: University of California Press, 1989), Chapter 1.

13. The latter lived successively at the following addresses: 8 rue Rembrandt (eighth arrondissement, in 1893); 1 rue Grétry (second arrondissement, in 1895); 11 rue de Chateaubriand (eighth arrondissement); 147 boulevard Malesherbes (seventeenth arrondissement, in 1897), 29 rue de Boulainvilliers (sixteenth arrondissement, in 1902). Drawn from the *Correspondance de C. Debussy et P. Louÿs (1893–1904)*, selected and annotated by Henri Borgeaud (Paris: José Corti, 1945).

14. See for example, *L'Œuvre de Léon Blum*, vol. 1 (Paris: Albin Michel, 1954), p. 3 and p. 211 (articles that first appeared in *La Revue Blanche* in March 1894 and August 1897).

15. Pierre Vaisse, *La Troisième République et les peintres* (Paris: Flammarion, 1995), pp. 161–64, on the Caillebotte bequest. On the vogue for French art in the United States: Albert Boime, "Les magnats américains à la conquête de l'art français," *L'Histoire*, 44 (1982): 38–48; in Germany: *Von Manet bis Van Gogh. Hugo von Tschudi und die Kampf um die Moderne* (Berlin: Nationalgalerie, 1996).

16. Myriam Chimènes, "Elites sociales et pratiques wagnériennes: de la propagande au snobisme," in *Wagner zum Wagnérisme. Musik, Literatur, Kunst, Politik*, ed. Anegret Fauser and Manuela Schwartz (Leipzig: Leipziger Universitätsverlag, 1999), pp. 155–97; Claude Debussy, *Monsieur Croche et autres écrits*, ed. François Lesure (Paris: Gallimard, 1971), especially pp. 54, 140–41, 247.

17. Edmond de Amicis, *Studies of Paris*, (trans. W. W. Cady, (New York: Putnam, 1882), p. 273. *"Le triomphe de l'intelligence est si grand et si enivrant dans cette ville, qu'à peine est-il salué par elle, qu'il reçoit des saluts d'admirateurs inconnus, et des offres de toutes les parties du monde. À l'homme tombé sur une voie, cent autres voies restent ouvertes, pour peu qu'il se résigne à abaisser d'un seul degré ses prétentions à la gloire. La nature oublieuse de la grande ville, qui, ne laissant personne s'endormir sur un seul triomphe, oblige tous les compétiteurs à se représenter continuellement au combat, produit ces vies merveilleusement productrices, ces vieillesses obstiné- ment batailleuses, dont l'exemple inspire la passion du travail aux générations suivantes; et enfin, nulle part on ne trouve autant de travaux inachevés, d'essais, de plans, de créations estimables, mais condamnées à périr où elles sont nées, parce qu'elles sont écrasées par l'abondance du mieux."* In Edmond de Amicis, *Souvenirs de Paris* (Paris: Hachette, original edition, 1880), p. 247.

18. *"Mes amis même m'ont fait l'effet de personnages considérables; Vidal très occupé, m'ac- cordant péniblement la faveur de déjeuner avec lui! Leroux me donnant audience dans la rue entre deux rendez-vous! Pierné! Celui-là, je n'ose même pas y aller. Enfin tous ces gens-là traitant Paris en ville conquise! et il faut voir comme ils sont souples, comme ils ont perdu leurs belles indigna- tions d'antan! (. . .) Maintenant je me demande comment je vais faire, avec ma sauvagerie exagérée, pour trouver mon chemin et me débattre au milieu de ce 'Bazar au succès' et je pressens des ennuis, des froissements sans nombre."* Letter to Hébert of 17 March 1887. In Claude Debussy, *Correspondance 1884–1918*, ed. François Lesure, p. 55.

19. Lesure, *Claude Debussy. Biographie critique*, pp. 16–17.

20. Ibid., p. 117; Georges Jean-Aubry, Introduction to the *Correspondance de C. Debussy et P. Louÿs (1893–1904)*, p. 8; Richard D. Sonn, *Anarchism and Cultural Politics in Fin de Siècle France* (Lincoln and London: University of Nebraska Press, 1989).

21. *"Il se lève aussi à l'horizon musical un jeune astre du nom de Gustave Charpentier qui me paraît destiné à une gloire aussi productrice qu'inesthétique. Celui-là prend la succession de Berlioz qui fut, je crois, un prodigieux fumiste qui arriva à croire lui-même à ses fumisteries; Charpentier a en moins la nature assez aristocratique de Berlioz; il est peuple et cela au point de*

faire, paraît-il, un opéra qui s'appellera Marie *et se passera à Montmartre, l'œuvre qui vient de le vouer à l'admiration des foules s'appelle* La Vie du Poète. *Ce titre d'un romantisme culotté nous dit déjà quelque chose, mais ce que vous ne vous figurez pas, c'est le manque de goût dont témoigne cette œuvre, c'est comme on pourrait dire le triomphe de la Brasserie. Ça sent la pipe et il y a comme des cheveux sur la musique.*" Letter to André Poniatowsky, February 1893. In Debussy, *Correspondance*, p. 72. Translation from *Debussy Letters*, François Lesure and Roger Nichols, eds., Roger Nichols, trans. (Cambridge, Mass.: Harvard University Press, 1987), p. 41.

22. Debussy, *Monsieur Croche*, p. 31, excerpt from *La Revue blanche* of 15 April 1901. This period does indeed mark the apogee of the presence of German conductors in Paris: See Joëlle Caullier, "Les chefs d'orchestre allemands à Paris entre 1894 et 1914," *Revue de musicologie* vol. 67, no. 2 (1981): 191–209, especially 197.

23. Debussy, *Monsieur Croche*, p. 213; first appeared in the *Revue musicale SIM*, December 1912.

24. See Jane F. Fulcher, *French Cultural Politics and Music from the Dreyfus Affair to the First World War* (New York: Oxford University Press, 1998), pp. 26–27.

25. *Annuaire Hachette 1897* (Paris: Hachette, 1897), p. 131.

26. Maurice Halbwachs, *Les Expropriations et le prix des terrains à Paris (1860–1900)* (Paris: Rieder & Cornély, 1909), pp. 96 and 140.

27. Cynthia and Harrison White, *Canvases and Careers*, (New York: John Wiley & Sons, 1965); Vaisse, *La Troisième République*, Chapters 8 and 9.

28. Myriam Chimènes, "Le Budget de la musique sous la IIIe République," in *La Musique du théorique au politique*, ed. Hugues Dufourt and Joël-Marie Fauquet (Paris: Klincksieck, 1991), pp. 261–312; ibid., "La Musique dans les salons de la Belle époque aux années cinquante," in *Musique et musiciens au Faubourg Saint-Germain*, ed. Jean Gallois (Paris: Délégation à l'action artistique de la ville de Paris, 1996), pp. 88–101.

29. Lesure, *Biographie,* pp. 43–45.

30. Prince Poniatowski, *D'un siècle à l'autre*, (Paris, Presses de la Cité, 1948), pp. 200–38.

31. Eric Anceau, *Dictionnaire des députés du Second Empire* (Rennes: Presses universitaires de Rennes, 1993), p. 367.

32. Myriam Chimènes, "Debussy à travers le journal de madame de Saint-Marceaux (1894–1911)," *Cahiers Debussy* no. 3 (1976): 5–10; Jean-Michel Nectoux et al., *Les Saint-Marceaux: une famille d'artistes en 1900*, Les Dossiers du Musée d'Orsay, no. 49 (Paris: Réunion des Musées nationaux, 1992).

33. Anne Martin-Fugier, *La Vie élégante ou la Formation du Tout-Paris 1815–1848* (Paris: Fayard, 1990), reissued by Le Seuil, "Points," (1993); Maurice Agulhon, *Le Cercle dans la France bourgeoise, 1810–1848, étude d'une mutation de sociabilité* (Paris: A. Colin, École des hautes études en sciences sociales, 1977); Cyril Grange, *Les Gens du Bottin Mondain 1903–1987, y être c'est en être* (Paris: Fayard, 1996).

34. See Norbert Elias, *Mozart: Portrait of a Genius* (Berkeley, Calif.: University of California Press, 1993).

35. Debussy, despite *Pelléas et Mélisande*, is not yet in here.

36. Twenty-eight lived in the ninth arrondissement, twenty-five in the seventeenth, twenty-three in the eighth, thirteen in the sixteenth, and only eleven on the Left Bank (primarily in the seventh and the sixth), according to *Tout Paris, annuaire de la société parisienne* (Paris: La Fare, 1903).

37. Debussy alludes to this last composer in a letter of 5 September 1908, to Francisco de Lacerda: ". . . a piano on which the same young girls can linger innocently over the latest thought from Francis Thomé." In *Debussy Letters*, ed. Lesure and Nichols, p. 196; see also Debussy, *Correspondance*, p. 242.

38. *"Je ne me reconnais plus! On me voit dans les salons, exécutant des sourires, ou bien je dirige des chœurs chez la comtesse Zamoïska! (oui monsieur !) et je me pénètre de la beauté du chœur des* Magnanarelles *en me disant que c'est la juste punition à une triste musique que d'être écorchée par d'impavides mondaines. Il y a aussi Mme de Saint-Marceaux qui m'a découvert un talent de premier ordre! Tout cela est à mourir de rire. Mais vraiment il faudrait être d'âme bien faible pour se laisser prendre dans cette glu. Et la bêtise de tout cela!"* Letter to Ernest Chausson of 5 February 1894, in Debussy, *Correspondance*, p. 96. Translation in Lesure and Nichols, *Debussy Letters*, p. 64.

39. See the letter from Pierre Louÿs of 24 July 1896: "My dear Claude, your mistake (if you are making one) is to believe that you are a musician accessible exclusively to the elite, when in fact you have everything you need to be the favorite musician of the squares and casinos . . ." Cited by Lesure, *Biographie*, p. 169.

40. As Jane Fulcher has shown, Debussy drew more and more on tradition, but it was a tradition reinvented by him independently of official musical instruction (J. Fulcher, *French Cultural Politics*, pp. 187–94).

41. *"Chercher à avoir la considération des boulevardiers, gens du monde et autres légumes, mon Dieu, que ça doit être ennuyeux."* Letter to Hébert of March 17, 1887. In Debussy, *Correspondance*, p. 56.

42. Letter from Mallarmé to Paul Verlaine of 16 November 1885, in Stéphane Mallarmé, *Correspondance complète*, (Paris: Gallimard,1991), pp. 587–88.

43. Lesure, *Biographie*, pp. 105 and 130. In 1889, he organized a subscription in order to publish his *Poèmes de Baudelaire* (150 copies sold at 12 francs each [1,800 francs]); in 1892, a new subscription sale at 160 copies, with a cover illustrated by Maurice Denis, for *La Damoiselle élue*.

44. "To struggle on one's own is nothing! But to struggle when one has a family is becoming odious! Add to this the domestic requirements of a former luxury which they do not understand has become impossible to sustain. As for me, I struggle only in the name of a certain point of honor—perhaps false, but which I can explain by saying that I don't want to be reproached one day for having accepted the current situation only in order to exploit it to my own profit (charming irony of the situation!)." Letter to his publisher Durand of 15 July 1913, cited by Lesure, *Biographie*, p. 368.

45. According to *Tout Paris 1903* and *Archives de Paris*, file D1P4/134 (1900).

46. Most of the inhabitants of the square owned their townhouses, while Debussy rented his from an Englishman, André Fairbairn, who lived at Brighton (according to the *Annuaire des propriétaires et des propriétés de Paris* [Paris, 1909] and the archive file cited in note 45).

47. *"Ah! cette avenue du Bois-de-Boulogne, qui sent le Brésilien, l'Américain, c'est cela qui manque de passé. Je revois aussi mon propriétaire alcoolique anglais, qui ne manquera pas de me mettre à la porte si jamais il trouve le rastaquouère et son million!"* Letters of 30 September 1915, and 9 August 1912. In Debussy, *Correspondance*, p. 309. Translation in Lesure and Nichols, *Debussy Letters*, p. 302 and p. 309.

48. Cited in Debussy, *Correspondance*, n. 8.

49. The rental value and the description of the grounds are furnished in the notebooks of the property register of the *Archives de la Seine* (file D1 P4/134 [square du Bois de Boulogne] et D1P4/188 [rue Cardinet]). In *Les Elites de la République (1880–1900)* (Paris, Fayard, 1987), p. 383, I showed that the median rent paid by a businessman stood at around 9,500 francs and those of a senior functionary at around 3,800 francs. Anatole France, almost the neighbor of Debussy (villa Saïd), a famous critic and successful author, was owner of a simple house with a rental value of 3,000 francs. The composer Vincent

d'Indy contented himself with an apartment on the avenue de Villars that cost 4,000 francs a year.

50. I am basing these estimations on the expenses of the wealthy families cited by Marguerite Perrot in *Le Mode de vie des familles bourgeoises 1873–1953* (Paris: A. Colin, 1961), especially p. 168. It is likely that a musician would have higher expenses for clothing and transportation than the average bourgeois family, but on the other hand he could save on food and evenings out, as he would frequently be hosted by others, and his transportation would sometimes be reimbursed, all of which would offset the additional expense.

51. The Debussys nevertheless maintained separate accounts, which does not permit us to determine the proportion in which the ex-Madame Bardac contributed to the household expenses. In 1907, the latter inherited a yearly income of 5,000 francs from her uncle Daniel Iffla Osiris.

52. Bibliothèque nationale de France, département de la musique, Institut de recherche sur le patrimoine musical français, Centre Claude Debussy, archives de la maison Durand à Asnières, photocopies of Debussy's account sheets. I gratefully acknowledge the help of Myriam Chimènes, researcher at the CNRS, who gave me access to unpublished data.

53. Lesure, *Biographie*, p. 387.

54. Debussy thus writes, with longing, about the estate of Bel-Ebat, near Fontainebleau, a property belonging to Durand which Debussy had visited (August 1903): "The estate of Bel-Ebat is beautiful . . . I contemplate with stupefaction how much it would take in author's rights to procure such an estate for myself!" In Debussy, *Lettres à son éditeur*, ed. Jacques Durand (Paris: Durand, Dorbon aîné, 1927), p. 12.

55. Information given by Jules Martin, *Nos artistes annuaire des théâtres et concerts 1901/1902* (Paris: Ollendorff, 1901), pp. 390–91, and receipt figures (1902) for *Pelléas et Mélisande* at the Opéra Comique taken from Jann Pasler, "Opéra et pouvoir: forces à l'oeuvre derrière le scandale du Pelléas de Debussy" in *La Musique et le pouvoir*, ed. Hugues Dufourt and Joël-Marie Fauquet (Paris: Aux amateurs de livres, 1987), pp. 173–74. The price of the rights to the orchestral score is noted in Lesure, *Biographie*, p. 269.

56. Frédérique Patureau, *Le Palais Garnier dans la société parisienne 1875–1914* (Liège: Mardaga, 1991), pp. 451–53. On the increase in imports of German musical editions and the decline in French musical exports: see Annick Devriès-Lesure, "Le commerce de l'édition musicale française au XIXè siècle. Les chiffres du déclin," *Revue de musicologie* 79, no. 2 (1993): 263–96.

57. Debussy, *Monsieur Croche*, pp. 34–35, 41, 77–78, 138, 190, 233–34, 241.

58. Evelyne Hurard, "Aperçu sur le goût musical à Paris en 1913" in *L'Année 1913. Les Formes esthétique de l'oeuvre d'art à la veille de la première guerre mondiale*, ed. Liliane Brion-Guerry (Paris, Klincksieck, 1971), pp. 521–22.

PART III
Documents

✤

Debussy's Paris
Conservatoire Training

JOHN R. CLEVENGER

When the ten-year-old Achille-Claude Debussy entered the Paris Conservatoire as an aspiring pianist in the autumn of 1872, he was an impoverished, nearly indigent youngster with barely two years of private piano lessons under his belt. Home-schooled and ignorant, with his father temporarily imprisoned following the recent Commune uprising in Paris, his prospects in life must have seemed dim. But by the time Achille (Debussy was known as Achille throughout his student years) graduated twelve years later in the summer of 1884, he had become an accomplished accompanist and a prize-winning composer, with bright prospects for a successful musical career. Clearly, Debussy's time at the Conservatoire transformed him. His only formal musical training, in fact his only formal education of any sort, could only have had a lasting impact upon his life.

Yet Achille's career as a Conservatoire pupil was uneven at best, at times even turbulent. Constantly subject to disciplinary action for poor attendance and more than once seeing his studies in a particular area terminated because of poor showings in the all-important year-end competitions, Debussy evidently found himself in imminent danger of expulsion at least once. Some of his scholastic problems undoubtedly stemmed from his painful situation at home, compounded by ordinary adolescent ennui. But a more fundamental cause may well have been the inevitable conflicts that any visionary and keenly original artist would have with the entrenched instructional doctrines of a venerable institution so firmly rooted in tradition. To survive academically, Debussy played along to an extent with the Conservatoire's established instructional orthodoxy. At the same time, he gradually learned his craft, finding ample opportunities for experimentation, generally in song settings of new poetry outside the purview of the Conservatoire. After twelve years of effort and not a little tribulation Debussy emerged, ultimately, well along the path to achieving stylistic mastery—at once despite and because of what he had learned at the Conservatoire.

Much about Debussy's stormy tenure as a Conservatoire pupil can be gleaned from a thoroughgoing examination of the relevant documents contained in the AJ[37] series devoted to the Conservatoire of the Archives Nationales in Paris. What follows is a comprehensive collation, in tabular form with accompanying commentary, of all the pertinent information about Debussy's Conservatoire studies contained in these records: his courses, professors, and classmates; the piano pieces he learned in his piano class; all extant semester reports; and his experiences in the competitions. Beyond serving as a basic reference resource and clearing up certain factual inaccuracies found in previous biographical accounts of Debussy's Conservatoire studies, this compilation is intended to yield insights into how Debussy was regarded by the very professors whose teachings he would have to repudiate in order to find his distinctive compositional voice. It is hoped that the secure documentary foundation established by this collation will make possible a fuller appreciation of Debussy's trying—but in the end triumphant—student years.

Courses and Professors

Debussy's complete course registrations, including audits, are provided in Table 1, which also identifies his professors and specifies the class meeting times, where available.

Debussy's participation in René Baillot's instrumental ensemble class and the date of his abortive audit in César Franck's organ class were only first reported recently by François Lesure.[1] But the exact dates of Debussy's spotty participation in the instrumental ensemble class, as indicated by René Baillot's semester reports (see Table 4c), differ from those reported by Lesure.[2] Debussy, who would never show much interest in chamber music generally, attended the class regularly in 1874–1875 but then dropped out midway through the fall 1875 semester. He skipped the class entirely for the next three years, finally returning only to attend irregularly in the spring 1879 semester. Upon the termination of Debussy's piano studies with Antoine Marmontel in the summer of 1879, the requirement that Debussy take the instrumental ensemble class would have lapsed. Given the lack of administrative interest in chamber music at the Conservatoire during this period, the course must have been peripheral to the overall instructional program anyway, which may explain why Debussy was able to get away with such a poor attendance record.

As for the organ class, given Franck's stature as a composer—surely higher than that of Debussy's composition professor, Ernest Guiraud—it is perhaps unfortunate that Franck and Debussy did not see eye to eye. Moreover, in the apt words of Christopher Palmer, "it is difficult to imagine an instrument more antipathetic to the Debussyan sensibilities than the organ."[3] As a result, Debussy, who entered the class as an auditor in the fall of 1880, decided to stop attending it after about six months.[4]

Upon graduating from Albert Lavignac's solfège class in the summer of 1876, Achille audited Emile Durand's harmony and accompaniment class for a year, 1876–1877, before taking it as a regular student in 1877–1878. Previous authors have been unaware of this audit, while also erroneously treating the class as a regular harmony class, ignoring the accompaniment component. With the implementation of Director Ambroise Thomas's curricular reforms in the fall of 1878, the class changed to instruction in harmony

tion pupils, students must have felt no compulsion to attend, given the lack of both semester examinations and competitions. Indeed, in his article on Debussy's early songs, Charles Koechlin, who had been a Conservatoire pupil in the 1890s, confirms that "many of the pupils did not attend his [Bourgault-Ducoudray's] course."[6] Because Debussy was prone to skip classes anyway, and because he never mentioned Bourgault-Ducoudray in his later correspondence (as he surely would have had he attended the class, in view of its unconventional content), it seems entirely possible that he did not attend the music history class even once.

alone, and Debussy remained in it for two more years, taking Auguste Bazille's piano accompaniment class simultaneously with Durand's harmony class in 1879–1880. Thus Debussy spent four years studying harmony with Durand, not three, as previously thought, and he spent three years studying accompaniment, two of them with Durand, and not just one year with Bazille, as has been reported.[5]

It is uncertain when or if Debussy attended Louis Bourgault-Ducoudray's music history class. This class was considered a marginal area of instruction at the Conservatoire during this period, and no registration records were maintained for it. Even though the class was supposedly obligatory for harmony and composi-

Table 1
Courses and Professors[1]

1872–1873	Antoine Marmontel: *Piano* (M W F 11:30–1:30)	Albert Lavignac: *Solfège* (T Th Sa 9–11)		René Baillot: *Ensemble Instrumental*[2] (no times listed)
1873–1874				
1874–1875				
1875–1876				
1876–1877		Emile Durand: *Harmonie et Accompagnement*[3] (T Th Sa 9–11; audit)	Bourgault-Ducoudray: *Histoire Générale de la Musique* (?)[4] (Th 4–5)	Baillot: *Ensemble Instrumental*
1877–1878		Durand: *Harmonie et Accompagnement*		
1878–1879		Durand: *Harmonie* (no times listed; probably T Th Sa 9–11)		
1879–1880	Auguste Bazille: *Accompagnement au Piano* (no times listed)			
1880–1881	César Franck: *Orgue*[5] (M 9–10, T F 2–3; audit)	Ernest Guiraud: *Composition* (T F 9–11)		
1881–1882				
1882–1883				
1883–1884				

Table 1 continued

1. Sources: Archives Nationales documents AJ^{37} 96*–107* (unpaginated), AJ^{37} 158*/2–5 (unpaginated), AJ^{37} 159*/1–5 (unpaginated), AJ^{37} 160*/1–4 (unpaginated), AJ^{37} 284: 442 and 599, AJ^{37} 285: 139 and 279–80, and AJ^{37} 286: 471 and 637.

2. Although all instrumental pupils who had won an award in the competitions were expected to take this course, Baillot's semester reports show that Debussy attended it only in 1874–1875, the beginning of fall 1875, and spring 1879. See Archives Nationales documents AJ^{37} 285: 139 and 280 and AJ^{37} 286: 471.

3. Although Debussy is listed as an auditor in this class in 1875–1876 in both Archives Nationales documents AJ^{37} 99* (unpaginated) and AJ^{37} 158*/5 (unpaginated), a schedule conflict with his solfège class, which met at the same times, would have made this impossible. Therefore these listings must have been erroneous, perhaps representing an initial intention that had to be abandoned when the conflict became apparent. That Durand gave Debussy permission to audit the class that year is confirmed by an inscription, dated 4 November 1875, found in Archives Nationales document AJ^{37} 368/4b*: 69. Another, seemingly less likely possibility is that the meeting times for one or the other class had been changed from those shown in Archives Nationales document AJ^{37} 99* (unpaginated), and that Debussy did in fact audit the harmony and accompaniment course in 1875–1876.

4. By regulation, all harmony and composition students were expected to take this three-year course, but no registration records were maintained.

5. Debussy attended this class for at most six months.

Debussy's classmates are listed in Tables 2a to 2g. The lists of auditors must be regarded with some caution, since the Conservatoire's registration records are inconsistent and sloppy with respect to auditors. The total numbers of pupils in each of the classes in a particular area and the comparative listings of the awards they received, shown at the bottom of each class roster, are useful in assessing the relative popularity and success of Debussy's professors.

The class rosters and related archival documents also confirm that Debussy did, in fact, begin composing during the 1878–1879 school year. This was both his last year in Marmontel's piano class and his first year in Durand's regular harmony class, as reported by his friend and classmate at the time, Paul Vidal. In a verbal account of his memories of Debussy's youth, Vidal recalled that he was Debussy's classmate in both Marmontel's piano class and Durand's harmony class that year, and that he and Debussy, who had just turned sixteen, quickly became close friends. According to Vidal, he, Debussy, and three of their friends, Gabriel Pierné (another student in Marmontel's class), Edmond Missa (an auditor in Marmontel's class), and Henri Passerieu (a singing pupil who was not a classmate of Debussy), liked to gather in the Messageries hotel, where they tried out Debussy's earliest compositions. Vidal's memory, while a little foggy in other particulars, is certainly clear on this point: the Conservatoire's registration records indicate that 1878–1879 was Vidal's first and only year with Debussy in both Marmontel's piano class and Durand's harmony class, and that Missa audited Marmontel's class that year, as shown in Tables 2a and 2d; and a separate document indicates that Passerieu was enrolled at the Conservatoire only from the fall of 1878 through the fall of 1879.[7] Because the first composition of Debussy mentioned by Vidal, the song "Madrid," bears the inscription, "A mes bons Amis, P. Vidal et Passerieu" ("To my good Friends, P. Vidal and Passerieu"), it therefore had to be composed during the 1878–1879 school year.[8]

Table 2a

Class Rosters: Marmontel, *Piano*, 1872–79[1]

	1872–1873	1873–1874	1874–1875
Pupils	Dolmetsch, V.; 5th year: *1st certificate.*	Dolmetsch; 6th year: no prize.	Dolmetsch; 7th year: *2nd prize.*
	Guerout, L.; 5th year: no prize.	Guerout; 6th year: no prize.	Desgranges; 4th year: no prize.
	Rieffler, T.; 5th year (expelled).	Desgranges; 3rd year: *2nd prize.*	Rouveirolis; 4th year: no prize.
	Spinetti; 5th year (resigned).	Rouveirolis; 3rd year: no prize.	**Debussy; 3rd year: *1st certificate.***
	Desgranges, F.; 2nd year: *2nd certificate.*	Ardaillon; 2nd year (expelled).	Lemoine; 3rd year: *1st certificate.*
	Lapuchin, J.; 2nd year (resigned).	**Debussy; 2nd year: *2nd certificate.***	Mestres; 3rd year: *2nd certificate.*
	Rouveirolis, P.; 2nd year: *2nd prize.*	Lemoine; 2nd year: *2nd certificate.*	Wiernsberger; 3rd year: no prize.
	Ardaillon, E.; 1st year: not admitted.	Mestres; 2nd year: no prize.	Guiard; 2nd year: not admitted.
	Debussy; 1st year: not admitted.	Wiernsberger; 2nd year: not admitted.	Hugonnenc; 2nd year (resigned).
	Lemoine, L.; 1st year: no prize.	Guiard; 1st year: not admitted.	Thomas; 2nd year: no prize.
	Mestres, E.; 1st year: no prize.	Hugonnenc; 1st year: not admitted.	Braud, P.; 1st year: not admitted.
	Wiernsberger, J.; 1st year: not admitted.	Thomas, J.; 1st year: not admitted.	Loyer; 1st year: not admitted.
			Sujol, A.; 1st year: not admitted.
Auditors	Fanelli, S., Guiard, E., Henry, Loyer, R.	(no auditors listed)	Pierné, G., Piffaretti, F., Thibaud, A.
Marmontel's totals	12 pupils, 4 auditors; 1 2nd prize, 1 1st certificate, 1 2nd certificate.	12 pupils; 1 2nd prize, 2 2nd certificates.	13 pupils, 3 auditors; 1 2nd prize, 2 1st certificates, 1 2nd certificate.
Mathias's totals	11 pupils, 1 auditor; 1 2nd prize.	10 pupils; 1 1st prize, 1 2nd prize, 1 1st certificate, 1 2nd certificate.	12 pupils; 1 2nd prize, 1 1st certificate, 1 2nd certificate.

Table 2a continued

	1875–1876	1876–1877	1877–1878
Pupils	Desgranges; 5th year: no prize. Rouveirolis; 5th year: no prize. **Debussy; 4th year: no prize.** Lemoine; 4th year: (on leave). Mestres; 4th year: *1st certificate.* Wiernsberger; 4th year: *2nd certificate.* Guiard; 3rd year: not admitted. Thomas; 3rd year: no prize. Braud; 2nd year: *2nd certificate.* Loyer; 2nd year: not admitted. Sujol; 2nd year: not admitted. Bellaigue, C.; 1st year: *1st certificate.* Castellanos; 1st year: not admitted. Pierné; 1st year: not admitted. Thibaud; 1st year: *1st prize.*	**Debussy; 5th year: *2nd prize.*** Lemoine; 5th year (resigned). Mestres; 5th year: no prize. Wiernsberger; 5th year (resigned). Guiard; 4th year: *2nd certificate.* Thomas; 4th year: no prize. Braud; 3rd year: no prize. Loyer; 3rd year: no prize. Sujol; 3rd year: no prize. Bellaigue; 2nd year: *2nd prize.* Castellanos; 2nd year: no prize. Pierné; 2nd year: not admitted. Jimenez, J.; 1st year: *1st prize.* Martinet, J.; 1st year: no prize. René, C.; 1st year: not admitted.	**Debussy; 6th year: no prize.** Braud; 4th year: *1st certificate.* Loyer; 4th year: no prize. Bellaigue; 3rd year: *1st prize.* Castellanos; 3rd year: no prize. Pierné; 3rd year: *2nd prize.* Martinet; 2nd year: *2nd certificate.* René; 2nd year: no prize. Dowell; 1st year: no prize. Landry, L.; 1st year: not admitted. Piffaretti, F.; 1st year: not admitted. Roger, J.; 1st year: not admitted.
Auditors	Chabert, Delloye, Loret.	Lefebvre, L.	(no auditors listed)
Marmontel's totals	15 pupils, 3 auditors; 1 1st prize; 2 1st certificates; 2 2nd certificates.	15 pupils, 1 auditor; 1 1st prize, 2 2nd prizes, 1 2nd certificate.	12 pupils; 1 1st prize, 1 2nd prize, 1 1st certificate, 1 2nd certificate.
Mathias's totals	13 pupils; 2 2nd prizes.	14 pupils, 1 auditor; 2 1st prizes, 2 1st certificates.	12 pupils; 1 1st prize, 1 2nd prize, 1 1st certificate, 1 2nd certificate.

Table 2a continued

Pupils	**1878–1879** **Debussy; 7th year: no prize.** Braud; 5th year: no prize. Loyer; 5th year: no prize. Pierné; 4th year: *1st prize.* Martinet; 3rd year (on leave). René; 3rd year: *2nd certificate.* Landry; 2nd year: *2nd prize.* Piffaretti; 2nd year: no prize. Roger; 2nd year: not admitted. Courras, J.; 1st year: not admitted. Grand-Jany, A.; 1st year: not admitted. Lefebvre; 1st year: not admitted. Mesquita, C.; 1st year: *2nd prize.* Vidal, P.; 1st year: not admitted.
Auditors	Aubry, G., Cru, C., Leroux, X., Leveaux, A., Lewicki, Missa, J., Wintzweiller.
Marmontel's totals	14 pupils, 7 auditors; 1 1st prize, 2 2nd prizes, 1 2nd certificate.
Mathias's totals	14 pupils; 1 1st prize, 2 1st certificates.

1. Sources: Archives Nationales documents AJ[37] 96*–102* (unpaginated), AJ[37] 158*/2–5 (unpaginated), and AJ[37] 159*/1–3 (unpaginated); Constant Pierre, "Dictionnaire des lauréats" in *Le Conservatoire National de Musique et de Déclamation: documents historiques et administratifs* (Paris: Imprimerie Nationale, 1900), pp. 684–872.

Table 2b

Semester Reports: Lavignac, *Solfège*, 1872–76[1]

	1872–1873	1873–1874	1874–1875	1875–1876
Pupils	Köbler; 6th year: no prize. Destefani, C.; 3rd yr: *3rd medal.* Thomas, J.; 3rd year: no prize. Trubert; 3rd year: not admitted. Hainl, G.; 2nd year (resigned). O'Kelly, H.; 2nd year: not adm. Pierné, G.; 2nd year: *3rd medal.* Stupuy, A.; 2nd year: no prize. **Debussy; 1st year: not adm.** Prioré, G.; 1st year: no prize. Vasseur, E.; 1st year: *3rd medal.*	Destefani; 4th year: *2nd medal.* Thomas; 4th year: *3rd medal.* O'Kelly; 3rd year: *3rd medal.* Pierné; 3rd year: *1st medal.* Stupuy; 3rd year: *1st medal.* **Debussy; 2nd year: *3rd medal.*** Prioré; 2nd year: *3rd medal.* Vasseur; 2nd year: no prize. Guiard; 1st year: not admitted. Honnoré; 1st year: no prize. Lemaire; 1st year: not admitted. Loyer; 1st year: not admitted.	Destefani; 5th year: *1st medal.* O'Kelly; 4th year: *2nd medal.* **Debussy; 3rd year: *2nd medal.*** Prioré; 3rd year (resigned). Vasseur; 3rd year: *2nd medal.* Guiard; 2nd year (resigned). Honnoré; 2nd year: no prize. Lemaire; 2nd year: no prize. Loyer; 2nd year: no prize. Grand-Jany; 1st year: *2nd medal.* Vizentini; 1st year: no prize.	O'Kelly; 5th year: *1st medal.* **Debussy; 4th year: *1st medal.*** Vasseur; 4th year (expelled). Honnoré; 3rd year: *3rd medal.* Lemaire; 3rd year: no prize. Loyer; 3rd year: *3rd medal.* Grand-Jany; 2nd year: *1st medal.* Vizentini; 2nd year: no prize. Flacière; 1st year: not admitted. Lafleurance; 1st year: no prize. Paquotte; 1st year: not adm.
Auditors	Ardaillon, E., Courtin, Grand-Jany, A., Guiard, E., Honnoré, L., Lemaire, G., Loyer, R., Vizentini, E.	Grand-Jany, Vizentini.	Flacière, Lafleurance, L., Paquotte.	Aubry, G., Bonniol, P., Corrodi, Franck, J., Hielard, Laforge, T., Nogent, L., Pré, Samary, H., Winkler.
Lavignac's totals	11 pupils, 8 auditors; 3 3rd medals.	12 pupils, 2 auditors; 2 1st, 1 2nd, and 4 3rd medals.	11 pupils, 3 auditors; 1 1st medal, 4 2nd medals.	11 pupils, 10 auditors; 3 1st medals, 2 3rd medals.
Alkan's totals	16 pupils, 4 auditors; 3 2nd medals.	12 pupils, 3 auditors; 3 1st, 2 2nd medals, and 1 3rd medal.	11 pupils; 3 1st medals, 2 3rd medals.	10 pupils, 10 auditors; 1 2nd medal, 1 3rd medal.
Gillette's totals	13 pupils, 1 auditor; 1 3rd medal.	9 pupils, 1 auditor; 1 2nd medal.	10 pupils, 3 auditors; 1 1st medal, 1 3rd medal.	14 pupils, 1 auditor; 1 1st medal, 1 2nd medal.
Decombes & Marmontel fils's totals	*Decombes:* 12 pupils, *Marmontel fils's* 3 auditors; 1 2nd medal.	*Decombes:* 11 pupils, 2 auditors; 1 1st medal.	*Marmontel fils:* 9 pupils, 2 auditors; 1 1st medal.	*Marmontel fils:* 9 pupils, 1 auditor; 1 3rd medal.
Rougnon's totals	—	?; no medals.	?; 1 3rd medal.	?; 1 1st medal, 1 2nd medal.

1. Sources: Archives Nationales documents AJ37 96*–99* (unpaginated) and AJ37 158*/2–5 (unpaginated); Pierre, "Dictionnaire des lauréats" in *Conservatoire National,* pp. 684–872.

Table 2c

Class Rosters: Durand, *Harmonie et Accompagnement*, 1875–78[1]

	1875–1876	1876–1877	1877–1878
Pupils	Lapuchin, J.; 6th year: no prize. Lemoine, L.; 4th year: (on leave). Falkenberg, T.; 2nd year: *2nd prize.* Choisnel, M.; 1st year: not admitted. Desgranges, F.; 1st year: not admitted. Dusautoy, C.; 1st year: (expelled). Lemaire, G.; 1st year: not admitted. Piffaretti, F.; 1st year: no prize. Sablon, A.; 1st year: (on leave). Tanera; 1st year: not admitted. Thomas, J.; 1st year: not admitted.	Lemoine; 5th year: *2nd prize.* Falkenberg; 3rd year: *1st prize.* Choisnel; 2nd year: *2nd certificate.* Desgranges; 2nd year: (resigned). Lemaire; 2nd year: no prize. Piffaretti; 2nd year: *2nd certificate.* Sablon; 2nd year: (on leave). Thomas; 2nd year: no prize. Delloye; 1st year: not admitted. Hillemacher; 1st year: *1st certificate.* Pierné; 1st year: not admitted. Thibaud; 1st year: not admitted.	Lemoine; 6th year: no prize. Choisnel; 3rd year: (on leave). Lemaire; 3rd year: no prize. Piffaretti; 3rd year: *2nd prize.* Sablon; 3rd year: (resigned). Delloye; 2nd year: not admitted. Hillemacher; 2nd year: *1st prize.* Pierné; 2nd year: *1st certificate.* Thibaud; 2nd year: not admitted. **Debussy; 1st year: no prize.** Fezandié; 1st year: no prize. Grand-Jany; 1st year: *2nd prize.*
Auditors	**Debussy;**[2] Delloye, Destefani, C., Gal, J., Hillemacher, L., Honnoré, L., Köbler, O'Kelly, H., Pierné, G., Tavant, Thibaud, A.	Adour, P., Braud, P., **Debussy,** Forter, Frêne, E., Grand-Jany, A., Honnoré, Kaiser, H., Loyer, Schwab, Wiernsberger, J.	Adour, Banès, A., Braud, Cibert, Domergue, E., Forter, Frêne, Honnoré, Kafka, Kaiser, Landry, L., Loyer, Wintzweiller.
Durand's totals	11 pupils, 12 auditors; 1 2nd prize.	12 pupils, 11 auditors; 1 1st prize, 1 2nd prize, 1 1st certificate, 2 2nd certificates.	12 pupils, 13 auditors; 1 1st prize, 2 2nd prizes, 1 1st certificate.
Duprato's totals	10 pupils, 3 auditors; 1 1st certificate.	7 pupils; no prizes.	11 pupils; no prizes.

1. Sources: Archives Nationales documents AJ[37] 99*–101* (unpaginated), AJ[37] 158*/5 (unpaginated), and AJ[37] 159*/1–2 (unpaginated); Pierre, "Dictionnaire des lauréats" in *Conservatoire National*, pp. 684–872.
2. Although Debussy is listed as an auditor in this class in 1875–1876 in both Archives Nationales documents AJ[37] 99* (unpaginated) and AJ[37] 158*/5 (unpaginated), a schedule conflict with his solfège class, which met at the same times, would have made this impossible. Hence Debussy almost certainly did not attend the class this year. See Table 1.

Table 2d

Class Rosters: Durand, *Harmonie*, 1878–80[1]

	1878–1879	1879–1880
Pupils	Choisnel; 4th year: *2nd prize*. Lemaire; 4th year: (resigned). Piffaretti; 4th year: no prize. Pierné; 3rd year: no prize. Thibaud; 3rd year: no prize. **Debussy; 2nd year: no prize.** Fezandié; 2nd year: no prize. Grand-Jany; 2nd year: no prize. Adour; 1st year: not admitted. Honoré, L.; 1st year: not admitted. Kaiser; 1st year: no prize. Vidal, P; *1st prize*.	Piffaretti; 5th year: no prize. Pierné; 4th year: no prize. Thibaud; 4th year: not admitted. **Debussy; 3rd year: no prize.** Grand-Jany; 3rd year: *1st prize*. Adour; 2nd year: (resigned). Honoré; 2nd year: no prize. Kaiser; 2nd year: no prize. Bonheur; 1st year: not admitted. Courras; 1st year: not admitted. du Pontavice; 1st year: not admitted. Landry; 1st year: not admitted. Savard, A.; 1st year: not admitted. Verlé; 1st year: not admitted.
Auditors	Bonheur, R., Courras, J., Davison, H., Domergue, d'Orellana, du Pontavice, Forter, Frêne, Landry, Plantevignes, J., Souquet-Basiège, L., Trago, J.,; Wintzweiller.	(no auditors listed)
Durand's totals	12 pupils, 13 auditors: 1 1st prize, 1 2nd prize.	14 pupils: 1 1st prize.
Savard's totals	8 pupils: 1 1st certificate.	9 pupils: 1 1st prize, 1 1st certificate, 1 2nd certificate.
Dubois's totals	12 pupils, 7 auditors: 1 1st prize, 1 2nd prize, 1 2nd certificate.	12 pupils: 1 2nd prize, 1 2nd certificate.
Duprato's totals	11 pupils, 2 auditors: no prizes.	12 pupils: no prizes.

1. Sources: Archives Nationales documents AJ[37] 102*–103* (unpaginated) and AJ[37] 159*/3–4 (unpaginated); Pierre, "Dictionnaire des lauréats" in *Conservatoire National*, pp. 684–872. This table is a continuation of Table 2c, as Durand's harmony class in 1878–1879 was a continuation of his harmony and accompaniment class the year before.

Table 2e
Class Roster: Bazille, *Accompagnement au Piano*, 1879–80[1]

1879–1880

Pupils

- Boulsagol; 2nd year: no prize.
- **Debussy**; 1st year: *1st prize.*
- Kaiser, H.; 1st year: *1st prize.*
- Archainbaud, Mlle M.; 2nd year: not admitted.
- Bonis, Mlle M.; 2nd year: no prize.
- Vacher-Gras, Mlle F.; 2nd year: not admitted.
- Baudéan, Mlle M.; 1st year: not admitted.
- Chrétien, Mlle H.; 1st year: *2nd prize.*
- Lefrançois, Mlle M.; 1st year: *1st certificate.*
- Prat, Mlle I.; 1st year: not admitted.

Totals

10 pupils; 2 1st prizes, 1 2nd prize, 1 1st certificate.

Table 2f
Class Roster: Franck, *Orgue*, 1880–81[2]

1880–1881

Pupils

- Papot, Mlle M.; 5th year: (resigned).
- Chapuis, A.; 3rd year: *1st prize.*
- Sourilas, P; 2nd year: no prize.
- Ganne, G.; 1st year: not admitted.
- Pierné, G.; 1st year: *2nd prize.*

Auditors

- Bemberg, Bessand, **Debussy**, Jeannin, P., Le Borne, Mélodia, J.

Totals

5 pupils, 6 auditors; 1 1st prize, 1 2nd prize.

1. Sources: Archives Nationales documents AJ[37] 103* (unpaginated) and AJ[37] 159*/4 (unpaginated); Pierre, "Dictionnaire des lauréats" in *Conservatoire National*, pp. 684–872.
2. Sources: Archives Nationales documents AJ[37] 104* (unpaginated) and AJ[37] 159*/5 (unpaginated); Pierre, "Dictionnaire des lauréats" in *Conservatoire National*, pp. 684–872.

Table 2g

Class Rosters: Guiraud, Composition, 1880–84[1]

	1880–1881	1881–1882	1882–1883	1883–1884[2]
Pupils	Debussy; 1st year: no prize in fugue competition.	Debussy; 2nd year: 2nd certificate in fugue comp.; failed Prix de Rome prelim.	Debussy; 3rd year: no prize in fugue competition; 1st 2nd Rome prize.	Debussy; 4th year: 1st grand Rome prize.
	Bonis, Mlle M.; 1st year: no prize in fugue competition.	Piffaretti; 2nd year: no prize in fugue competition.	Piffaretti; 3rd year: no prize in fugue competition.	Honnoré; 3rd year: not admitted to fugue competition.
	Piffaretti, F.; 1st year: no prize in fugue competition.	Jeannin; 2nd year: no prize in fugue competition.	Jeannin; 3rd year: no prize in fugue competition.	Souquet-Basiège, L.; 1st year: no prize in fugue competition; failed Prix de Rome preliminary.
	Jeannin, P.; 1st year: 2nd prize in fugue competition.	Honnoré, L.; 1st year: not admitted to fugue competition.	Honnoré; 2nd year: not admitted to fugue competition.	Courras, J.; 1st year: not admitted to fugue competition.
Guiraud's totals	4 pupils; 1 2nd prize in fugue competition.	4 pupils; 1 2nd certificate in fugue competition.	4 pupils; 1 1st 2nd Rome prize.	4 pupils; 1 1st grand Rome prize.
Delibes's totals	4 pupils; no prizes.	4 pupils, 2 auditors; 1 1st prize in fugue competition.	2 pupils; 1 2nd 2nd Rome prize.	4 pupils; 1 2nd cert. in fugue comp.; 1 1st 2nd Rome prize.
Massenet's totals	16 pupils, 10 auditors; 2 1st prizes, 1 1st cert., 1 2nd cert. in fugue comp.; 1 1st 2nd Rome prize, 1 2nd 2nd Rome prize, 1 Rome prize hon. mention.	14 pupils; 2 2nd prizes, 1 1st cert., 1 2nd cert. in fugue comp.; 1 1st grand Rome prize, 1 2nd 1st grand Rome prize, 1 Rome prize hon. mention.	11 pupils; 2 1st prizes, 1 2nd prize, 1 1st certificate, 1 2nd certificate in fugue competition; 1 1st grand Rome prize.	10 pupils; 1 1st prize, 1 2nd prize, 1 1st certificate in fugue competition; 1 2nd 2nd Rome prize.

1. Sources: Archives Nationales documents AJ37 104*–107* (unpaginated), AJ37 159*/5 (unpaginated), AJ37 160*/1–3 (unpaginated), and AJ37 258/3a: 49–59; Pierre, "Dictionnaire des lauréats" in *Conservatoire National*, pp. 684–872; *Le Ménestrel* 48 (1881–1882): 246.

2. The following year, the size of Guiraud's class more than doubled to ten pupils, as against twelve in Massenet's class and five in Delibes's class. This was clearly a result of Debussy's winning the Prix de Rome in 1884. See Archives Nationales documents AJ37 107* (unpaginated) and AJ37 160*/4 (unpaginated).

Piano Pieces Played

The prepared pieces that Debussy played during his years in Marmontel's piano class, as well as his admission examination piece and the one work he is known to have played for his instrumental ensemble class, are listed in Table 3. Where available, the degree of difficulty for each piece, as assigned by Marmontel, is shown in brackets in the table. In his piano pedagogy treatise, Marmontel specifies the degrees of difficulty as follows: 1–4, very easy (*très facile*); 4–8, easy (*facile*); 8–12, intermediate between easy and rather moderate difficulty (*intermédiaire entre facile et la petite moyenne force*); 12–15, progressive between the first degree of rather moderate difficulty and more brilliant moderate difficulty (*progressif entre le premier degré de la petite moyenne force et la force moyenne plus brillante*); 15–20, progressive between moderate difficulty and attaining virtuosity (*progressif entre la difficulté moyenne et atteignant la virtuosité*); 20–25, progressive from this order of difficulty to very difficult (*progressif de cet ordre de difficulté au très-difficile*); 25–30, from very difficult to transcendent virtuosity (*du très-difficile à la virtuosité transcendante*); and 30–35, maximum difficulty (*maximum du difficile*).9

Marmontel's difficulty rating for Carl Maria von Weber's *Aufforderung zum Tanze*, 15–25, or moderately difficult to very difficult, makes Achille's successful performance of the work for the October 1872 admission examination all the more impressive. Debussy's rapid progress in his first three years in the piano class, which enabled him, starting in the fall of 1875, when he was just thirteen years old, regularly to negotiate works rated by Marmontel as 25–35, or of transcendent virtuosity to maximum difficulty, is also remarkable.

Indeed, what stands out the most about these pieces, taken as a group, is their virtuosic character. Piano instruction at the Conservatoire throughout the nineteenth century was oriented first and foremost toward turning out virtuosos. Hence flashy pianistic technique was emphasized over musicality in the competitions, and this pervasive emphasis undoubtedly influenced Marmontel's choice of pieces during the school year. This is why the particular works of Johann Sebastian Bach that Debussy was assigned, the Toccata in G minor (BWV 915), which he played for the January 1873 semester examination, and the *Chromatische Fantasie* (from BWV 903), which he played for the January 1875 semester examination, are among Bach's more florid and technically difficult keyboard compositions. Debussy's early perceptions about the music of Bach, then, may have been distorted somewhat through these youthful contacts with pieces that contain unusually heavy doses of what he would later call "divine arabesque."[10]

Bach's Toccata in G minor and his *Chromatische Fantasie* are both replete with what might be called "proto-arabesques." Although the florid melodic figurations are all more or less tightly constrained and regularized by meter and harmonic rhythm, they involve duple against triple polyrhythms, affording a freely flowing sense to the rhythm. Also, the frequent use in both pieces of flowing triplet figurations and primarily conjunct motion calls to mind melodic usages that Debussy would favor throughout his compositional career. The only missing ingredients of full-fledged Debussyan arabesque, in fact, are frequent syncopations or tied notes and irregular harmonic rhythm, both of which would serve to obscure further the perception of a regular meter. This technical similarity between keyboard works of Bach that Debussy played as a student and one of his most elemental compositional preoccupations in later life represents an important technical link between Debussy's style and that of Bach.

By the same token, most of these compositions were traditional mainstays of the piano repertory at the time; with only a few exceptions, they contain little or no music of an especially innovative nature. The exceptions,

though, are important. Both the Finale from Robert Schumann's *Faschingsschwank aus Wien* (Op. 26), which Debussy played for the January 1879 semester examination, and Frédéric Chopin's Ballade No. 1 in G minor (Op. 23), which he played for the July 1875 competition, contain untraditional musical usages that may have proved suggestive for Debussy.

The conclusion of Schumann's *Faschingsschwank aus Wien* contains, at mm. 297–304, a rather simple incipient instance of hexatonicism, based on an augmented triad, that is comparable to early usages of Debussy. The most prominent employment of hexatonicism of Debussy's early oeuvre, near the end of his 1883 song, "Pantomime," bears a striking resemblance to this passage of Schumann. It may therefore be plausibly asserted that this work of Schumann was a possible source of hexatonicism in Debussy's early oeuvre—although similar usages occur in certain French works that Debussy is known to have loved, such as especially Edouard Lalo's *Namouna*. Other, more general stylistic similarities of Schumann's piano music to Debussy's music may also be noted, but none can be specifically postulated as a direct outgrowth of Debussy's piano studies. The only other work of Schumann that Debussy is known to have learned in Marmontel's class, the first movement of Schumann's Piano Sonata No. 2

in G minor (Op. 22), which he played for the 1877 competition, contains primarily bravura passages, exhibiting no important Debussyan characteristics.

As indicated in Table 3, Debussy is known to have played some twenty-three compositions during his years in Marmontel's class, aside from Weber's *Aufforderung zum Tanze*, which he performed for the admission examination. Of these twenty-three works, by far the greatest number—seven—were composed by Chopin. By contrast, Debussy played two pieces each of Bach, Wolfgang Amadeus Mozart, Weber, Ignaz Moscheles, Schumann, and Stephen Heller; and he played one piece each of Ludwig van Beethoven, Felix Mendelssohn-Bartholdy, Johann Baptist Cramer, and Sigismond Thalberg. This disparity may reflect either Debussy's enthusiasm for Chopin's piano music or the esteem in which this music was held by Marmontel and at the Conservatoire generally at the time, or possibly both. Either way, given that Debussy was virtually immersed in the music of Chopin during his years in the class, it seems logical that he would have drawn from this prolonged contact with the works of the Polish master a deep and lasting formative influence.

Marcel Dietschy reports that Debussy once claimed, in a conversation with André Gide that was related by André Gauthier, to have "come entirely from Chopin's

Ballade No. 4."[11] Whether or not Debussy actually made the statement, and whether or not it was reported accurately, it would not be far wide of the mark to assert that an elemental formative influence indeed occurred, but stemming from Chopin's first, rather than fourth, Ballade.[12] For the passage from the first Ballade at mm. 67–90 contains several stylistic features that are virtually indistinguishable technically from usages Debussy would employ throughout his compositional career. Most obviously, but also most trivially, Chopin's frequent use of enriched chords was taken up by not just Debussy but virtually all French composers of the latter half of the nineteenth century. Other features found in the passage that may have proved suggestive to Debussy include subtonic nullifications, nested reiterations, a combination of successive two-against-three polyrhythms and relatively frequent syncopations or tied notes, resulting in another good example of proto-arabesque, and some limited developmental formal aspects. But the most notable connection of this passage to Debussy's later style lies in an indefinable tenderness that results in part from the compositionally deft combination of these various features. The touchingly evocative music at mm. 80–90, in particular, may have revealed for the first time to Debussy a little-explored realm of expressive potential that could be opened up, to some degree, even within an essentially syntactical harmonic context.

As shown in Table 3, archival records list only one piece played by Debussy during his time in Baillot's instrumental ensemble class. With the clarinetist Faustin-Stanislas-Anselme Perpignan and the cellist Marie-Jeanne Gatineau, he played the third movement from Beethoven's Trio No. 4 in B-flat major (Op. 11) for the June 1875 semester examination.[13] This variations movement is standard Beethoven fare; it exhibits no links to Debussy's later compositional style. Performing it would undoubtedly have left Achille nonplussed.

Table 3
Piano Pieces Debussy Played[1]

1872–1873	*October 1872 Admission Examination:* Carl Maria von Weber *Aufforderung zum Tanze*, Op. 65 [15–25]	*January 1873 Examination:* Johann Sebastian Bach Toccata in G minor, BWV 915 *During Fall Semester:* Johann Baptist Cramer Concerto [?][2] [8–25]	*June 1873 Examination:* Ignaz Moscheles Concerto No. 1 in F major, Op. 45 [8–20]
1873–1874	*January 1874 Examination:* Wolfgang Amadeus Mozart Fugue [from K. 394?] *During Fall Semester:* Mozart Rondo [?][3]	*June 1874 Examination:* Ignaz Moscheles *Tre Allegri di bravura*, Op. 51 No. 2, "La Leggerezza" [around 25]	*July 1874 Competition:* Frédéric Chopin Concerto No. 2 in F minor, Op. 21 First movement
1874–1875	*January 1875 Examination:* Johann Sebastian Bach *Chromatische Fantasie*, from BWV 903 [25–35]	*June 1875 Examination:* Frédéric Chopin Rondo in E-flat major, Op. 16 [20–30] *For Instrumental Ensemble Class:* Ludwig van Beethoven Trio No. 4 in B-flat major, Op. 11 Third movement (Variations)	*July 1875 Competition:* Chopin Ballade No. 1 in G minor, Op. 23 [20–30]
1875–1876	*February 1876 Examination:* Carl Maria von Weber Sonata No. 3 in D minor, Op. 49 [20–35] Third movement (Rondo)	*June 1876 Examination:* Stephen Heller Sonata No. 3 in C major, Op. 88 [25–35] Second movement (Scherzo)	*July 1876 Competition:* Ludwig van Beethoven Sonata No. 32 in C minor, Op. 111 [25–35] First movement

Table 3 continued

	January Examination:	*June Examination:*	*July Competition:*
1876–1877	*January 1877 Examination:* Robert Schumann *Faschingsschwank aus Wien*, Op. 26 [25–35] Fifth movement (Finale)	*June 1877 Examination:* Felix Mendelssohn-Bartholdy Concerto No. 2 in D minor, Op. 40 [25–35]	*July 1877 Competition:* Schumann Sonata No. 2 in G minor, Op. 22 [25–35], First movement
1877–1878	*January 1878 Examination:* Stephen Heller *Variationen über "Warum" von Schumann*	*June 1878 Examination:* Frédéric Chopin Sonata No. 3 in B minor, Op. 58 [25–35] Second movement (Scherzo) *During Spring Semester:* Sigismond Thalberg Sonata in C minor, Op. 56	*July 1878 Competition:* Carl Maria von Weber Sonata No. 2 in A-flat major, Op. 39 First movement [20–35]
1878–1879	*February 1879 Examination:* Frédéric Chopin Sonata [No. 2 in B-flat minor, Op. 35][4] [25–35]	*June 1879 Examination:* Chopin *Fantaisie*, Op. 49	*July 1879 Competition:* Chopin *Allegro de concert*, Op. 46 [25–35]

1. Sources: Archives Nationales documents AJ^{37} 195/1*: 314 and 331, AJ^{37} 206*/1: 21, 58, 128, 167, 177, 241–42, 276, and 342, AJ^{37} 206*/2: 28, 98, 136, 214, and 247, AJ^{37} 223/4 (unpaginated), AJ^{37} 233/1 (unpaginated), AJ^{37} 238*/2: 3, 9, 11, 17, 22, 25, and 34, AJ^{37} 241/1d (unpaginated), AJ^{37} 245*: 82, AJ^{37} 247/3 (unpaginated), AJ^{37} 251*/1–2 (unpaginated), AJ^{37} 283: 385 and 552, AJ^{37} 284: 90, 238, 380, and 566, AJ^{37} 285: 103, 259, 387, and 569, AJ^{37} 286: 97, 263, 421, and 589, AJ^{37} 307*: 81, 189, 257, 431, 645, 713, and 789, and AJ^{37} 308*: 63 and 125; Antoine Marmontel, *Art classique et moderne du piano*, vol. 2 (Paris: Heugel, [1876]). Where available, Marmontel's difficulty ratings, ranging from 1–4 = very easy to 30–35 = maximum difficulty, are shown in square brackets.

2. Concertos rated intermediate in difficulty (8–20) and thus appropriate for Debussy's first semester: No. 1 in E-flat major, Op. 10; No. 2 in D minor, Op. 16; No. 3 in D major, Op. 26; No. 4 in C major, Op. 38; No. 5 in C minor, Op. 48. Concerto No. 7 in E major, Op. 56 is rated moderately difficult (12–25). See Marmontel, *Art classique*, vol. 2, pp. 35 and 62–63.

3. Most likely possibility: Rondo in F major, K. 494, which Marmontel rates as moderately difficult (12–25) and thus approximately as advanced as the other pieces Debussy played around this time. Marmontel rates the Rondo in D major, K. 485, as easy to moderate (4–15), thus probably too easy for Debussy at this point, and he makes no mention at all of the Rondo in A minor, K. 511. See Marmontel, *Art classique et moderne*, vol. 2, pp. 25 and 64. Less likely possibilities include the rondo movements from the following sonatas: B-flat major, K. 281; D major, K. 284; C major, K. 309; D major, K. 311; F major, K. 533; C major, K. 545.

4. Marmontel rates only Chopin's second and third sonatas as very difficult (25–35), and thus appropriate for Debussy at this advanced stage of his studies. See Marmontel, *Art classique et moderne*, vol. 2, p. 107. Because Debussy had already played a movement from Chopin's third sonata for the June 1878 examination and he would not have played another movement from the same work at a later examination, it is very likely that he prepared a movement from the second sonata for the February 1879 examination. Records indicate, however, that he missed the examination because of a sore thumb.

Semester Reports: Performance, Solfège, Harmony

All of Debussy's extant semester examination reports, some of which have been published previously,[14] are provided in Tables 4a to 4g.[15] In the tables, occasional illegible words in some of the reports are indicated by question marks enclosed in angle brackets; slashes indicate line breaks where the lack of punctuation or capitalization may obscure the meaning.

Much more than just a dry record of his semester examinations, Debussy's semester reports represent the Conservatoire's official view of one of its most rebellious pupils, who would go on to become perhaps its most illustrious graduate. In these reports are found frequent remarks attesting to Achille's lack of punctuality, carelessness, and even disruptive behavior at certain points in his studies, traits that are probably just as indicative of an independent teenager's rebellion against authority as they are symptomatic of a budding genius's rebellion against established doctrines. Alongside mundane observations about examination trials well or poorly carried out, the reports contain seemingly prescient statements about Debussy's potential for greatness. They also contain a few intriguing reactions on the part of Debussy's professors and other examination committee members to

his profound originality, which Debussy could not hide completely no matter how hard he tried—if he did, in fact, try to hide this most salient aspect of his genius.

As Table 4a shows, Debussy's pianistic talent was recognized from the outset. Marmontel found his youngest pupil to be "charming," using the word in each of his first three reports. Remarking that Debussy was blessed with "much ability" and a "true artist's temperament" (June 1873), he correctly forecast that Debussy would become "a great artist" (January 1873) and "a distinguished musician" (January 1874). Altogether, five prognostications that Achille would have a "future" were made by Marmontel and the other examination committee members during Debussy's first year alone. Through Debussy's third year in the class, 1874–1875, the reports remained mostly positive, except for Henri Duvernoy's complaints, beginning in January 1875 and continuing the following year, about Debussy's frequently vague or uneven rhythm.

As Table 4b shows, Lavignac similarly and repeatedly acknowledged Debussy's musical gifts in his reports for the first two years of Debussy's solfège class. According to Lavignac, Debussy was "marvelously

singing skills had reached such an advanced level that, as Lavignac remarked in his June 1875 report, he had risen to the head of the class.

As Table 4c shows, Debussy also managed to ingratiate himself somewhat with Baillot during his first year in the instrumental ensemble class. In his first semester report on Debussy in January 1875, Baillot described Achille as both "willing" and "rather able," but "inexperienced in ensemble music"—not surprisingly, since Debussy had never before played in groups. Hence there is nothing to indicate that Debussy was anything but a model pupil throughout his first three years at the Conservatoire.

As Tables 4a–4c show, however, Debussy evidently grew bored with his studies during his fourth year at the Conservatoire in 1875–1876. In their reports that year, both Marmontel and Lavignac chastised Achille for his lack of punctuality, carelessness, and inattentive study, Marmontel's February 1876 report being typical: "good pupil, intelligent, studious. But a little mischievous and careless. Must study more carefully." Indeed, Debussy's lackluster attitude definitely impinged on his piano playing that year, as the negative reports of most of the commentators in February and June of 1876 make clear. Although his sight-reading remained strong, Debussy's playing was generally

gifted" (January 1873), a "very excellent pupil," "intelligent," and "hard-working" (June 1874). But Lavignac also pointed to Debussy's initial total lack of knowledge of the elementary principles of music theory—a topic that had apparently been largely ignored during his two years or so of private piano lessons before entering the Conservatoire. At his first semester examination in January 1873, judging by the remarks of the other committee members, Achille must have failed to answer any of the theory questions correctly; and he missed or even skipped the written portion of the June 1873 examination. Lavignac's January 1874 report indicates that he had asked Debussy to concentrate on the theory principles the previous semester; to the detriment of his sight-singing, Whereas Debussy again failed the theory portion of that examination, the deficiency was largely corrected by the time of the June 1874 test, as the remarks of the other commentators reveal. Meanwhile, his sight-singing and dictation skills had steadily improved, attracting frequent comments of "very good" at the same examination. In his third year in the solfège class in 1874–1875, Debussy's progress continued. Although he remained a little slow for the principles, according to Lavignac's January 1875 report, Debussy's dictation and sight-

criticized for poor rhythm and lack of clarity. In the solfège class, Debussy proved himself to be no longer blissfully ignorant but instead actively disdainful of theoretical principles, as Lavignac's June 1876 report indicates. But Achille's "remarkable intelligence" and facility for sight-singing and dictation were applauded by the instructor in the January and June 1876 reports, and Debussy would graduate with a first medal in solfège at the end of the year, as detailed in the following section. For his part, Baillot could only angrily report Debussy's desertion of the instrumental ensemble class a month or two into the school year in the fall of 1875; Achille would never again attend the class regularly.

As Table 4a shows, following Debussy's single difficult year in the piano class in 1875–1876, his final three years under Marmontel went more smoothly. Marmontel reported in June 1877 that Debussy "had renounced his carelessness and developed a taste for work," adding with evident satisfaction that he was "content with his progress and his musical intelligence." As detailed in the following section, the summer of 1877 indeed marked the high point of Debussy's piano studies at the Conservatoire, for he would win second prize in the piano competition that July. Marmontel's ensuing reports were almost invari-

ably positive, except for his criticism in the June 1878 report of Debussy's "very great unevenness" of rhythm, a negative view that Henry Fissot certainly shared, writing that Debussy's performance was "not good enough" for a second prizewinner. Despite Marmontel's best efforts, Debussy's playing really did not improve at all in his final two years in the class.

As Tables 4d and 4e show, Debussy revealed his troublemaking side in Durand's harmony and accompaniment classes. Like both Marmontel and Lavignac, Durand immediately recognized Debussy's "excellent musical ability" (January 1878), extolling the youngster's "musical instinct" and "accompanist-sight-reader's temperament" (June 1878), but he also repeatedly chaffed at Achille's carelessness and mischievousness. Debussy was, in Durand's words, "a pupil very gifted for harmony" (June 1879), and his ill behavior may be taken as an indication that he could hardly stand being force-fed the Conservatoire's stiff and antiquated harmony doctrine. Yet given Maurice Emmanuel's purely negative assessment of the interactions between Durand and Debussy,[16] it is important to note that during Debussy's final year in his regular harmony class, 1879–1880, Durand had nothing but good things to say about his most original pupil. That Durand's final two, laudatory semester reports on Debussy have previously been overlooked by scholars has helped to obscure the fact that Durand and Debussy eventually got along pretty well. Durand's June 1880 description of Debussy as a "quite gifted pupil, whose progress is very great this year," for example, is hardly indicative of a teacher who detests his pupil or underestimates his ability. Furthermore, the assessments of Debussy's harmony realizations by the other commentators during all three years were generally positive, the only exception being Thomas's criticism of Debussy's realizations for the June 1879 harmony examination as "too affected" and "not natural."

Debussy's talent as a sight-reader is indicated by several reports, including Marmontel's June 1879 report for Achille's final semester examination for the piano class ("excellent sight-reader"), shown in Table 4a; Durand's January 1878 report for his first semester examination for harmony and accompaniment class ("much aptitude for sight-reading"), shown in Table 4d; and Bazille's June 1880 report. In the only substantive semester examination report that was preserved for Debussy's piano accompaniment class, shown in Table 4f, Bazille provided an interesting assessment of Debussy's all-around practical musical abilities at this relatively advanced stage of his studies: "great facility / good sight-reader / very good fingers (could work more) / good harmonist a little prone to fantasy—much initiative and verve." By the summer of 1880, apparently, Debussy's considerable musical gifts, together with his harmonic originality, had really begun to assert themselves.

Table 4a.
Semester Reports: Marmontel, *Piano*, 1872–79[1]

Examination Date/ Pieces Played	Commentator	French Original	English Translation
29 January 1873: Bach, *Toccata* in G minor, BWV 915 (Cramer Concerto during semester)	Marmontel	<u>Charmante organisation</u> / deviendra un grand artiste / progresse d'une façon merveilleuse	<u>Charming facility</u> / will become a great artist / progress in a marvelous fashion
	Thomas	va bien	pretty good
	Bazin	de l'avenir	[he has] a future
	Duvernoy	Enfant intelligent. Joli son.—a plus de mesure	Intelligent boy. Pretty sound.—has more rhythm [than some of the other pupils, whom Duvernoy criticizes for a lack thereof]
11 June 1873: Moscheles, Concerto No. 1 in F major, Op. 45	Marmontel	<u>Charmant enfant</u>. beaucoup de moyens. véritable tempérament d'artiste. grand avenir.	<u>Charming boy</u>. much ability. true artist's temperament. great future.
	Thomas	pass[able].	passable
	Bazin	(de l'avenir)	([he has] a future)
	Sauzay	a de l'avenir / joli son	has a future / pretty sound
	Duvernoy	<?> de l'avenir. Lecture passable.	<?> [he has] a future. Sight-reading passable.
23 January 1874: Mozart, Fugue [from K. 394] (Mozart Rondo during semester)	Marmontel	Charmant enfant / véritable tempérament d'artiste. Deviendra un musicien distingué. beaucoup d'avenir.	Charming boy / true artist's temperament. Will become a distinguished musician. much future.
	Thomas	va bien. intelligent.	pretty good. intelligent.
	Sauzay	<u>Gentil</u>	<u>Nice</u>
	Duvernoy	Bonne organisation musicale. Ira bien.—de joli doigts. Pas mal lu.	Good musical aptitude. Will be okay.—good fingers. Not badly read.

Table 4a continued

Examination Date/ Pieces Played	Commentator	French Original	English Translation
23 June 1874: Moscheles, *Tre Allegri di bravura*, Op. 51, No. 2, "La Leggerezza"	Marmontel	Charmante nature musicale. je désire beaucoup le faire concourir.	Charming musical nature. I desire much to have him compete.
	Thomas	va bien—pas mal lu.	pretty good—not badly read.
22 January 1875: Bach, *Chromatische Fantasie*, from BWV 903	Marmontel	élève très intelligent et studieux. beaucoup d'avenir.	very intelligent and studious pupil. much future.
	Thomas	passable—trop vite.	passable—too fast.
	Duvernoy	Jeu trop vite. Vague dans la mesure.	Playing too fast. Vague rhythmically.
22 June 1875: Chopin, *Rondo* in E-flat major, Op. 16	Marmontel	véritable tempérament d'artiste. charmant enfant / très intelligent. très studieux.	true artist's temperament. charming boy / very intelligent. very studious.
	Thomas	[morceau:] passable [lecture:] assez bien	[prepared piece:] passable [sight-reading:] rather good
	Duvernoy	Mesure mal assise. bonne organisation musicale. Très bien lu.	Rhythm poorly established. good musical aptitude. Very well read.
	Sauzay	assez bien lu	rather well read
2 February 1876: Weber, Sonata No. 3 in D minor, Op. 49, Third movement (Rondo)	Marmontel	bon élève, intelligent, studieux. Mais un peu brouillon et étourdi. Devrait étudier avec plus de soin.	good pupil, intelligent, studious. But a little mischievous and careless. Must study more carefully.
	Thomas	pas mal—étourdi!	not bad—careless!
	Duvernoy	Il presse trop. Elève intelligent.	He rushes too much. Intelligent pupil.
	Fissot	Difficile pour lui.—intelligent—lit bien.	Difficult for him.—intelligent—reads well.
	Sauzay	pas de netteté	no clarity

Table 4a continued

Examination Date/ Pieces Played	Commentator	French Original	English Translation
20 June 1876: Heller, Sonata No. 3 in C major, Op. 88, Second movement (Scherzo)	Marmontel	Ne tient pas du tout ce que j'espérais. étourdi, inexact, il pourrait beaucoup mieux.	Has not achieved at all what I had hoped for: careless, not punctual, he could do much better.
	Thomas	passable. pas de mesure.	passable. no rhythm.
	Duvernoy	Jeu intelligent.—Mesure pas <?>. Lecture. bien lu.	Intelligent playing.—Rhythm not <?>. Sight-reading. well read.
	Fissot	Manque de mesure. trop de faiblesse de mesure. Lecture pas mal.	Lacks rhythm. too much rhythmic weakness. Sight-reading not bad.
	Sauzay	joli son et bon rythme / le seul bien lu	pretty sound and good rhythm / the only one reading well
31 January 1877: Schumann, *Faschingsschwank aus Wien*, Op. 26, Fifth movement (Finale)	Marmontel	Je suis beaucoup plus content de cet enfant, qui s'était endormi sur ses premiers succès.	I am much more content with this boy, who fell asleep on his first successes.
	Thomas	va bien.	pretty good.
	Duvernoy	Joli sentiment musical.	Pretty musical feeling.
	Fissot	Manque de <?>—Manque de clarté—pas en progrès—joli son.	Lacks <?>—Lacks clarity—not in progress— pretty sound.
21 June 1877: Mendelssohn-Bartholdy, Concerto No. 2 in D minor, Op. 40	Marmontel	a renoncé à son étourderie et pris gout au travail / je suis content de ses progrès et de son intelligence musicale.	has renounced his carelessness and developed a taste for work / I am content with his progress and his musical intelligence.
	Thomas	[morceau:] assez bien [lecture:] passable	[prepared piece:] rather good [sight-reading:] passable
	Duvernoy	Bon sentiment musical. <?> mécanisme.—a bien lu.	Good musical feeling. <?> mechanism.— read well.
	Fissot	Pas mal.—assez bien lu	Not bad.—rather well read

Table 4a continued

Examination Date/ Pieces Played	Commentator	French Original	English Translation
25 January 1878: Heller, *Variationen über "Warum" von Schumann*	Marmontel	étudie beaucoup mieux / moins emporté que par le passé. / intelligent deviendra un artiste s'il veut s'astreindre à plus de réflexion.	is studying much better / less impetuous than in the past. / intelligent will become an artist if he wishes to restrain himself to more reflection.
	Thomas	assez bien	rather good
	Fissot	poignet assez facile—pas mal	rather flexible wrist—not bad
20 June 1878: Chopin, Sonata No. 3 in B minor, Op. 58, Second movement (Scherzo) (Thalberg Sonata in C minor, Op. 56 during semester)	Marmontel	a beaucoup mieux étudié cette année / a des qualités d'exécution, mais aussi des inégalités très grandes.	has studied much better this year / has performing qualities, but also very great unevenness.
	Thomas	[morceau:] assez bien [lecture:] passable	[prepared piece:] rather good [sight-reading:] passable
	Duvernoy	assez bien. bien lu.	rather good. well read.
	Fissot	poignet lourd—pas mal—pas assez bien pour un 2d p[rix]—lecture bonne.	heavy wrist—not bad—not good enough for a 2nd prize—good sight-reading.
4 February 1879: Chopin, Sonata [No. 2 in B-flat minor, Op. 35]	Marmontel	a du talent. Sa légèreté de caractère a pris fin. je me <?> de son travail et de ses progrès. Il est malheureusement foulé le pouce.	has some talent. His carelessness of character has ended. I am <?> with his work and his progress. He has unfortunately sprained his thumb.
	Thomas	malade	ill

Table 4a continued

Examination Date/ Pieces Played	Commentator	French Original	English Translation
19 June 1879: Chopin, *Fantaisie*, Op. 49	Marmontel	a progressé et conscieusement étudié toute l'année. excellent lecteur / a des qualités et de l'esprit / n'a plus qu'une récompense à obtenir.	has progressed and conscientiously studied the whole year. excellent sight-reader / has some qualities and spirit / has only one more recompense to obtain.
	Thomas	[morceau:] assez bien [lecture:] assez bien.	[prepared piece:] rather good [sight-reading:] rather good
	Duvernoy	a très bien lu.	read very well.
	Fissot	pas mal—bien lu	not bad—well read
	Herz	va bien [lecture:] très bien.	pretty good [sight-reading:] very good.

1. Sources: Archives Nationales documents AJ[37] 195/1*: 314–15 and 330–31, AJ[37] 206*/1: 20–21, 58, 128, 167, 241–42, 276, and 342, AJ[37] 206*/2: 28, 98, 136, 213–14, and 247, AJ[37] 223*/4 (unpaginated), AJ[37] 233/1 (unpaginated), AJ[37] 238*/1 (unpaginated), AJ[37] 238*/2: 3, 9, 11, 17, 22, 25, and 34, AJ[37] 238*/3 (unpaginated), AJ[37] 260/13 (unpaginated), AJ[37] 283: 385 and 551–52, AJ[37] 284: 89–90, 237–38, 379–80, and 565–66, AJ[37] 285: 103, 259, 387, and 569, AJ[37] 286: 97, 263, 421, and 589, AJ[37] 307*: 81, 97, 189, 257, 337, 431, 503, 579, 645, 713, 789, and 855, AJ[37] 308*: 63 and 125.

Table 4b

Semester Reports: Lavignac, *Solfège*, 1872–76[1]

Examination Date	Commentator	French Original	English Translation
17 January 1873	Lavignac	Est tout nouvellement dans ma classe et ne connaît que trois clefs. Il est merveilleusement organisé et deviendra un excellent élève.	Has just now entered my class and knows only three clefs. He is marvelously gifted and will become an excellent pupil.
	Thomas	[dictée:] assez bien [théorie:] nul [lecture:] assez bien	[dictation:] rather good [theory:] zilch [sight-singing:] rather good
	Marmontel	dictée assez bien. principes nuls. assez bien lu.	dictation rather good. principles zilch. rather well read.
	Prumier	[Dictée:] assez bien [Principes:] nul [Solfège:] passable	[Dictation:] rather good [Principles:] zilch [Solfège:] passable
	Vervoitte	[Principes:] faible [Dictée:] assez bien [Clefs:] bien	[Principles:] weak [Dictation:] rather good [Clefs:] good
18 June 1873	Lavignac	Sera un très bon élève l'année prochaine. Depuis le dernier examen, il a appris toutes les clefs, et fait souvent des dictées réussies.	Will be a very good pupil next year. Since the last examination, he has learned all the clefs, and often takes dictation successfully.
	Thomas	[dictée:] absent [théorie:] absent [lecture:] assez bien.	[dictation:] absent [theory:] absent [sight-singing:] rather good.
	Marmontel	Lecture—bien. // Bonne classe.	Sight-singing—good. // Good class.
	Bazin	[lecture:] assez bien	[sight-singing:] rather good
	Prumier	[Solfège:] passable	[Solfège:] passable
	Vervoitte	[Clefs:] très bien	[Clefs:] very good

Table 4b continued

Examination Date	Commentator	French Original	English Translation
16 January 1874	Lavignac	Depuis la rentrée, je l'ai fait appliquer surtout à la théorie, qui était très faible l'année dernière. De là vient que la lecture est un peu en retard, mais comme il est très bien doué je suis persuadé qu'il s'y mettra rapidement.	Since the beginning of the school year, I have had him apply himself above all to theory, which was very weak last year. Because of that, the reading is a little behind, but as he is quite gifted, I am convinced that he will get it rapidly.
	Thomas	[dictée:] bien [théorie:] mal [leçon:] assez bien.	[dictation:] good [theory:] poor [sight-singing:] rather good
	Prumier	[Dictée:] Bien [Principes:] Moyen [Solfège:] Passable	[Dictation:] Good [Principles:] Average [Solfège:] Passable
	Vervoitte	[Principes:] faible [Dictée:] bien [Clefs:] très bien	[Principles:] weak [Dictation:] good [Clefs:] very good
	Weckerlin	[Lecture:] Bien [Dictée:] Bien [Réponses:] mal	[Sight-singing:] Good [Dictation:] Good [Responses:] bad
11 June 1874	Lavignac	Très excellent élève. Intelligent, travailleur et fort bien organisé musicalement. Je compte sur lui pour se distinguer au concours.	Very excellent pupil. Intelligent, hard-working, and quite gifted musically. I am counting on him to distinguish himself at the competition.
	Thomas	[dictée:] très bien [théorie:] bien [leçon:] bien	[dictation:] very good [theory:] good [sight-singing:] good
	Marmontel	Très bien lecture, dictée et théorie.	Very good sight-singing, dictation, and theory.
	Prumier	[Dictée:] très Bien [Principes:] Bien [Solfège:] Bien	[Dictation:] very Good [Principles:] Good [Solfège:] Good
	Vervoitte	[Principes:] bien [Dictée:] bien [Clefs:] très bien	[Principles:] good [Dictation:] good [Clefs:] very good
	Weckerlin	[Solfège:] très bien [Dictée:] très bien [Principes:] bien	[Sight-singing:] very good [Dictation:] very good [Principles:] good

Table 4b continued

Examination Date	Commentator	French Original	English Translation
15 January 1875	Lavignac	Excellent lecteur; oreille parfaitement sûre; encore un peu en retard pour les principes.	Excellent sight-singer; perfectly sure ear; still a little slow for the principles.
	Thomas	[dictée:] très bien [théorie:] bien [lecture:] assez bien	[dictation:] very good [theory:] good [sight-singing:] rather good
	Prumier	[Dictée:] très Bien [Principes:] Bien [Solfège:] Bien	[Dictation:] very Good [Principles:] Good [Solfège:] Good
	Vervoitte	[Principes:] bien [Dictée:] très bien [Clefs:] très bien	[Principles:] good [Dictation:] very good [Clefs:] very good
	Weckerlin	[Lecture:] très bien [Dictée:] très bien [Principes:] bien	[Sight-singing:] very good [Dictation:] very good [Principles:] good
9 June 1875	Lavignac	Organisation musicale complète, et travail sérieux. Tient avec Destefani la tête de la classe.	Complete musical facility, and serious work. With Destefani is at the head of the class.
	Thomas	[dictée:] très bien [théorie:] très bien [lecture:] bien.	[dictation:] very good [theory:] good [sight-singing:] good.
	Vervoitte	[Principes:] très bien [Dictée:] très bien [Clefs:] très bien	[Principles:] very good [Dictation:] very good [Clefs:] very good
	Weckerlin	[Dictée:] très bien [Réponses:] très bien [Lecture:] très bien	[Dictation:] very good [Responses:] very good [Sight-singing:] very good

Table 4b continued

Examination Date	Commentator	French Original	English Translation
19 January 1876	Lavignac	Intelligence remarquable. Admirablement organisé, mais ne travaille pas assez, et se fie beaucoup trop à sa facilité.	Remarkable intelligence. Admirably gifted, but does not work enough, and relies much too much on his facility.
	Thomas	[dictée:] parfait [théorie:] bien [lecture:] assez bien	[dictation:] perfect [theory:] good [sight-singing:] rather good
	Marmontel	très bien les trois épreuves.	very good all three trials.
	Prumier	[Dictée:] Parfaite [Principes:] Bien [Solfège:] Bien	[Dictation:] Perfect [Principles:] Good [Solfège:] Good
	Vervoitte	[Principes:] bien [Dictée:] très bien [Clefs:] bien	[Principles:] good [Dictation:] very good [Clefs:] good
	Weckerlin	[Dictée:] Parfait [Principes:] Bien [Lecture:] Bien	[Dictation:] Perfect [Principles:] Good [Sight-singing:] Good
9 June 1876	Lavignac	Parfait pour la lecture et la dictée. Encore étourdi pour la théorie, quoiqu'il la comprenne fort bien.	Perfect for sight-singing and dictation. Still careless about theory, although he understands it quite well.
	Thomas	[dictée:] parfait [théorie:] passable [lecture:] bien	[dictation:] perfect [theory:] passable [sight-singing:] good
	Marmontel	Dictée parfaite, théorie assez bien, lecture parfaite.	Dictation perfect, theory rather good, sight-singing perfect.
	Prumier	[Dictée:] très Bien [Principes:] très Bien [Solfège:] Bien	[Dictation:] very Good [Principles:] very Good [Solfège:] Good
	Weckerlin	[Solfège:] presque très bien [Dictée:] très bien [Théorie:] pass[able].	[Sight-singing:] almost very good [Dictation:] very good [Theory:] passable

1. Sources: Archives Nationales documents AJ[37] 195/1*: 298–99 and 341–42, AJ[37] 206*/1: 8–9, 36, 114, 148, and 250–51, AJ[37] 233/3 (unpaginated), AJ[37] 239*/3 (unpaginated), AJ[37] 240/1 (unpaginated) and 2 (unpaginated), AJ[37] 260/13 (unpaginated), AJ[37] 283: 313–14 and 435–36, AJ[37] 284: 11, 155, 299, and 461, AJ[37] 285: 19 and 153, AJ[37] 307*: 62, 118, 151, 211, 306, 374, 460, and 524.

Table 4c

Semester Reports: Baillot, *Ensemble Instrumental*, 1874–75, 1879[1]

Examination Date	Commentator	French Original	English Translation
30 January 1875	Baillot	Bonne volonté, assez habile, mais inexpérimenté dans la Musique d'Ensemble.	Willing, rather able, but inexperienced in Ensemble Music.
26 June 1875: Beethoven, Trio No. 4 in B-flat major, Op. 11, Third movement (Variations)	Baillot	assez bien. peu Expérimenté. bonne volonté.	rather good. little Experienced. willing.
29 January 1876	Baillot	A cessé de suivre la classe depuis deux mois, sans motif.	Has stopped attending the class for the last two months, without any reason.
24 June 1876	Baillot	M[essieu]rs Debussy et Rouveirolis ont abandonné la classe sans excuser.	Messieurs Debussy and Rouveirolis have abandoned the class without an excuse.
8 February 1879	Baillot	noter: M[essieu]rs Pierné, Martinet, Fresne, Debussy ne se sont pas présentés à la classe.	Note: Messieurs Pierné, Martinet, Fresne, Debussy were not present in the class.
21 June 1879	Baillot	pas exact. a peu travaillé pendant ce semester.	not punctual. has worked little during this semester.

1. Sources: Archives Nationales documents AJ[37] 206*/1: 139–40, 176–77, 239–40, and 283–85, AJ[37] 206*/2: 220–21 and 252–53, AJ[37] 284: 442 and 599, AJ[37] 285: 139 and 279–80, and AJ[37] 286: 471 and 637.

Table 4d

Semester Reports: Durand, *Harmonie et Accompagnement*, 1877–78[1]

Examination Date	Commentator	French Original	English Translation
19 January 1878	Durand	Excellente organisation musicale, beaucoup d'aptitude pour la lecture; mais bien de l'étourderie.	Excellent musical ability, much aptitude for sight-reading; but quite a bit of carelessness.
	Thomas	[basse:] assez bien [chant:] assez bien [basse chiffrée:] passable [partition:] passable	[given bass:] rather good [given melody:] rather good [figured bass:] passable [score reading:] passable
	Delibes	pas mal.	not bad.
19 June 1878	Durand	Avec son instinct musical et son tempérament d'accompagnateur-lecteur, Debussy serait un excellent élève s'il était moins brouillon, moins léger.	With his musical instinct and his accompanist-sight-reader's temperament, Debussy would be an excellent pupil if he were less mischievous, less unsteady.
	Thomas	[basse et chant:] assez bien [basse chiffrée:] assez bien [partition:] assez bien	[given bass and given melody:] rather good [figured bass:] rather good [score-reading:] rather good
	Delibes	ensemble pas mal.	altogether not bad.

1. Sources: Archives Nationales documents AJ[37] 206*/2: 90–91 and 135, AJ[37] 234*/4 (unpaginated), AJ[37] 286: 73 and 235–36, AJ[37] 307*: 726 and 834.

Table 4e
Semester Reports: Durand, *Harmonie*, 1878–80[1]

Examination Date	Commentator	French Original	English Translation
30 January 1879	Durand	Bonne organisation musicale—Un peu moins brouillon cette année.	Good musical aptitude—A little less mischievous this year.
	Thomas	passable.	passable.
20 June 1879	Durand	Elève très bien organisé pour l'harmonie mais d'une étourderie désespérante.	A pupil very gifted for harmony but of a distressing carelessness.
	Thomas	Pas mal—trop recherché. pas naturel.	Not bad—too affected. not natural.
23 January 1880	Durand	Elève bien organisé, en voie de progrès.	Quite gifted pupil, on the path of progress.
	Thomas	bien	good
18 June 1880	Durand	Elève bien organisé dont les progrès sont très grands cette année.	Quite gifted pupil, whose progress is very great this year.
	Thomas	va bien	pretty good

1. Sources: Archives Nationales documents AJ[37] 206*/2: 210, 250, and 325–26, AJ[37] 206*/3: 23, AJ[37] 286: 395–96 and 563, AJ[37] 287: 81 and 261, AJ[37] 308*: 26, 132, 205, and 317.

Table 4f

Semester Reports: Bazille, *Accompagnement au Piano*, 1879–80[1]

Examination Date	Commentator	French Original	English Translation
4 February 1880	Thomas	[basse chiffrée:] passable [chant à accomp.:] passable [grande partition:] assez bien [transposition:] passable [morceau:] passable	[figured bass:] passable [melody to accompany:] passable [full score:] rather good [transposition:] passable [piece:] passable
	Delibes	[basse chiffrée:] assez bien [chant:] bien [partition:] pass[able]. [accompagnement:] médiocre	[figured bass:] rather good [melody:] good [score:] passable [accompaniment:] mediocre
21 June 1880	Bazille	grande facilité <u>bon lecteur / très bons doigts</u> (pourrait travailler d'avantage) / <u>bon</u> harmoniste un peu fantaisiste—beaucoup d'initiative et de verve.	<u>great facility good sight reader / very good fingers</u> (could work more) / <u>good</u> harmonist a little prone to fantasy—much initiative and verve.
	Thomas	[b. ch.:] bien [ch. donné:] assez bien [transposition:] assez bien [exécution:] bien [grande partition:] assez bien	[given bass:] good [given melody:] rather good [transposition:] rather good [performance:] good [full score:] rather good
	Delibes	[basse chiffrée:] bien [chant donné:] très bien [grande partition:] bien [transposition:] bien [exécution à vue:] très bien	[figured bass:] good [given melody:] very good [full score:] good [transposition:] good [performance at sight:] very good

1. Sources: Archives Nationales documents AJ[37] 206*/2: 343, AJ[37] 206*/3: 26–27, AJ[37] 234*/4 (unpaginated), AJ[37] 287: 273, AJ[37] 308*: 245 and 321.

Semester Reports, Composition

The semester reports for Debussy's composition class, shown in Table 4g, contain occasional expressions of bewilderment on the part of examination committee members confronted with even the milder side of Debussy's compositional originality. They also provide important data regarding which compositions Debussy wrote for his composition class.

In his very first semester report on Debussy in January 1881, Guiraud noted that the eighteen-year-old was "intelligent" and showed promise as a composer. At this examination, Debussy's Andante cantabile for piano four-hands was played, along with a song (perhaps "Nuit d'étoiles," which was Debussy's first published composition, or else another early song that was similarly not unduly radical stylistically—"fresh and rather simple," as Théodore Dubois described it) and the ubiquitous instrumental fugue.[17] The remarks of the various committee members about the Andante cantabile underscore the fact that Achille, though he was already showing signs of originality, composed rather awkwardly at the time: "long—clashes" (Thomas); "some originality" (Léo Delibes); "1st motive rather good—too long as a whole—tonality too long forgotten" (Dubois). The latter remark of Dubois, in particular,

points to Debussy's emerging tendency to obscure tonality, a fundamentally significant technical trait underlying his greatest masterworks that would be perhaps his single most important contribution to the history of style. At the June 1881 examination, Guiraud again described Debussy simply as "intelligent" and a "good pupil." But Dubois's more substantive comments suggest that at this point in his studies Achille, rather than being a misunderstood genius, was simply an inexperienced aspiring composer who had much to learn. Criticizing Debussy's piece for chorus and orchestra—almost certainly *Hélène*—as being "twisted—too modulatory," Dubois concluded that the adolescent was on a "bad path" in his development as a composer.

When Debussy's operatic duet, "Églogue," which is replete with enriched sonorities but otherwise not overly untraditional, was performed at the January 1882 examination, Guiraud commented that Achille was "intelligent, but needs to be bridled." Guiraud evidently perceived that an important part of his role in guiding Debussy's development as a composer would be helping his young charge to learn to control his more radical compositional impulses. At the June 1882 examination, Debussy's *Intermezzo* for orchestra was played in an arrangement for piano four-hands. Guiraud's rather glum assessment of Debussy's modest progress that semester and his "poorly balanced" nature was in keeping with the tenor of the rest of his report for his "sad class" as a whole. Dubois's surprisingly positive report, "ingenious—in progress," indicates how original such a seemingly tame composition as the *Intermezzo* was taken to be by the tradition-bound Conservatoire professoriat. The piece was, however, apparently the only purely instrumental work explicitly inspired by a poetic subject (Heinrich Heine's *Lyrisches Intermezzo*) that Debussy would offer for such official scrutiny.

There would remain only two more composition examinations, since Debussy was admitted to the final round of the Prix de Rome competition each of the following two summers, precluding his taking part in the June semester examinations. (Debussy had participated for the first time in the preliminary round of the 1882 Prix de Rome competition, but he had failed the trial.) In the January 1883 examination, two unknown pieces for orchestra of Debussy, or perhaps two movements of the same work, were played, again

probably arranged for piano four-hands. Guiraud, while acknowledging that Debussy had at least made progress, described his pupil as having a "bizarre but intelligent nature," remarking that he still "writes music poorly."

By far the most fascinating reports of all of Debussy's semester examinations in composition are those for the February 1884 test, as Achille was about to begin what would be his final semester at the Conservatoire. At this examination, a "Ballet"—almost certainly the second movement from Debussy's *Première Suite d'orchestre*, which was clearly inspired by Guiraud's work of the same title[18]—was performed. The piece obviously raised eyebrows, for no less than three of the commentators used the word *strange* to describe the piece: "always strange" (Thomas); "strange—original" (Delibes); "strange color, well orchestrated" (Dubois). An opportunity to examine the various movements of Debussy's *Première Suite d'orchestre*, if and when the manuscripts can be recovered, would represent an important next step for Debussy research. A performance of this work would be interesting indeed.

Table 4g
Semester Reports: Guiraud, *Composition*, 1880–1884[1]

Examination Date/ Compositions Evaluated	Commentator	French Original	English Translation
31 January 1881: fugue; Andante cantabile; song ("Nuit d'étoiles"?)	Guiraud	Intelligent / Promet un compositeur	Intelligent / Promises a composer
	Thomas	[composition:] Morceau à 4 mains long— duretés.... Romance passable.	[composition:] Piece for 4 hands long— clashes.... Romance passable.
	Réty	fugue. Debussy fait entendre un Andante à 4 mains et une mélodie.	fugue. Debussy has an Andante for 4 hands and a song performed.
	Delibes	Marche à 4 mains. de l'originalité	March in 4 hands. some originality
	Dubois	Andante piano à 4 mains—1er motif assez bien— trop long comme ensemble—tonalité oubliée trop longtemps—Romance—fraîche et assez simple	Andante piano 4-hands—1st motive rather good—too long as a whole—tonality too long forgotten—Romance—fresh and rather simple
27 June 1881: fugue; *Hélène*	Guiraud	Intelligent. Bon élève.	Intelligent. Good pupil.
	Réty	fugue. chœur avec orchestre	fugue. chorus with orchestra
	Dubois	morceau ch[oeu]r. et orch[es]tre—tortillé— trop modulé—mauvaise voie.	piece for chorus and orchestra—twisted—too modulatory—bad path.
11 January 1882: fugue; "Eglogue"	Guiraud	Intelligent, mais a besoin d'être bridé. Est revenu de voyage assez tard, et n'a pu encore beaucoup travailler cette année.	Intelligent, but needs to be bridled. Returned from traveling rather late, and has still not been able to work much this year.
	Réty	fugue. Debussy fait entendre une Eglogue, duo pour ténor et soprano.	fugue. Debussy has an Eglogue, duet for tenor and soprano, performed.

Table 4g continued

Examination Date/ Compositions Evaluated	Commentator	French Original	English Translation
26 June 1882: fugue; Intermezzo for orchestra	Guiraud	Quelques progrès. Nature mal équilibrée, mais intelligent. Arrivera, je crois. // En somme, triste classe. Peu d'espérance, parmi mes auditeurs. Ceux qui me paraissent organisés musicalement étant encore trop peu avancés en harmonie pour que je puisse les recevoir à la rentré.	Some progress. Poorly balanced nature, but intelligent. He will arrive, I hope. // In sum, sad class. Little hope, among my auditors. Those who seem musically gifted to me being still too little advanced in harmony for me to receive them [into my class as regular pupils] at the beginning of the next school year.
	Réty	fugue. Intermezzo pour orchestre.	fugue. Intermezzo for orchestra.
	Dubois	orchestre—ingénieux—en progrès.	[piece for] orchestra—ingenious—in progress.
9 January 1883: fugue; two pieces for orchestra (perhaps two movements of an unidentified but partially extant work dated 2 January 1883)	Guiraud	Nature bizarre, mais intelligente. Ecrit mal la musique. A fait cependant des progrès.	Bizarre but intelligent nature. Writes music poorly. However, has made progress.
	Thomas	[fugue:] assez bien.	[fugue:] rather good
	Réty	fugue. 2 pièces (pour orchestre) composées par M Debussy.	fugue. 2 pieces (for orchestra) composed by M Debussy.
26 June 1883: (none)	Guiraud	A concouru à l'Institut.	Competed at the Institut.
	Réty	Debussy a concouru pour le grand Prix de Rome.	Debussy has competed for the grand Prix de Rome.

Table 4g continued

Examination Date/ Compositions Evaluated	Commentator	French Original	English Translation
1 February 1884: fugue; *Première Suite d'orchestre*	Guiraud	2d Grand prix de Rome / Travail un peu irrégulier	2nd grand Rome prize / Work a little uneven
Second movement (Ballet)	Thomas	Fugue à 4 mains—passable. la fin est bien. Ballet—orch.—toujours étrange.	Fugue in 4 hands—passable. the end is good. Ballet—orchestra.—always strange.
	Réty	Fugue pour orchestre (au Piano à 4 mains), Air de ballet (Orchestre).	Fugue for orchestra ([played] on the Piano in 4 hands), Air de ballet (Orchestra).
	Delibes	fugue pour orchestre. bien. fantaisie orchestre. étrange—original.	fugue for orchestra. good. orchestral fantasy. strange—original.
	Dubois	fugue à 4 mains—Bien. Ballet—orchestre—couleur étrange, bien orchestré—cet élève à tous les examens présente des morceaux ayant trop la même couleur.	fugue for 4 hands—Good. Ballet—orchestra—strange color, well orchestrated—this pupil at every examination presents pieces having too much the same color.
16 June 1884:	Thomas	(En loge)	(In sequestration)
(none)	Réty	Absent : M. Debussy, en loge pour le concours de Rome.	Absent: M. Debussy, in sequestration for the Rome competition.

1. Sources: Archives Nationales documents AJ^{37} 206*/3: 91, 126–27, 186, 255–56, and 306, AJ^{37} 207*/1: 41, 125–26, and 152–53, AJ^{37} 234*/4 (unpaginated), AJ^{37} 237*/1 (unpaginated), AJ^{37} 287: 451 and 619, AJ^{37} 288: 83, 241, 405, and 565, AJ^{37} 289: 81, AJ^{37} 308*: 426, 528, 578, 738, and 880, AJ^{37} 309*: 88 and 146.

Competitions

Debussy's experiences in the competitions are summarized in Table 5. The notes of Director Thomas, who presided over the juries for the in-house competitions, that is, the competitions other than the Prix de Rome competition, are provided in Table 6. In Table 5, Debussy's rankings relative to the other contestants are specified for the first time, as accurately as can be determined from existing archival sources.[19] Although the basic results of Debussy's competitions have been known for decades, this additional information is worth considering, primarily because it shows how poorly Debussy—who would, after all, go on to become one of the greatest French composers who ever lived—placed in most of these competitions.

During Debussy's twelve-year stint as a Conservatoire pupil, he took part in in-house competitions in six different areas—piano, solfège, harmony and accompaniment, harmony, accompaniment at the piano, and fugue—plus the Prix de Rome competition, run by the Institut de France. Of the in-house competitions in which he participated, only the piano competitions were carried out publicly. Indeed, the piano competitions, which involved the performance of a prepared piece or movement as well as the execution at first sight

of a specially composed short work, often received considerable attention. Besides the competition judges, family and friends of the competitors, the general public, and reporters from the press would all attend. Camille Bellaigue, who was Debussy's classmate in Marmontel's class for three years, from the fall of 1875 until the summer of 1878, when he graduated with the first prize and the brand-new Erard grand piano that came with it,[20] vividly describes his first piano competition in 1876:

One morning in July, about twenty of us—some almost children, still in shorts and sailor shirts; others in tail-coats; still others, already almost men, in frock-coats—were gathered in the artists' wing of the Société des Concerts, waiting for the little stage door to open for each of us in turn. How many times we had seen this stage, on Sundays, filled entirely by the famous orchestra, illuminated, like the hall, as if for a celebration! Now it was necessary to appear there completely alone, only our master following us, under the stingy, cold, and almost funereal twilight that fell from the glazed ceiling. Funereal himself, in the great central box, Ambroise Thomas presided over the impassive jury. The competition piece finished, one went on to the sight-reading of another piece, composed for the occasion, in manuscript, and intentionally strewn with harmonic and enharmonic stumbling blocks, but for the most part, in other respects, at least at this period, not very formidable. Before this final test, from up in the box, a lamentable voice [that of Thomas] let fall these words: "Marmontel, here is the tempo," which was followed by three or four beats of a metronome.[21]

Thomas's notes for Debussy's first two piano competitions in 1874, at which he played the first movement from Chopin's Second Concerto in F minor; and in 1875, at which he played Chopin's first *Ballade* in G minor, were not preserved. But in view of Debussy's young age—he was not quite twelve at the time of his first competition—he did quite well in these competitions, receiving the second certificate in 1874 and the first certificate in 1875. In the 1876 piano competition, which took place during the summer following his most difficult year in the class, Achille had to play the first movement from Beethoven's Sonata No. 32 in C minor. As shown in Table 6, Thomas, while taking note of an awkwardly handled trill, reacted rather favorably to Debussy's performance overall, even briefly considering him for the second prize. However, Debussy ended up receiving no votes from the competition panel. Achille had scored above the fiftieth percentile among all contestants in each of these first three competitions. But he had evidently played Chopin's effusive and tuneful first *Ballade* more convincingly for the 1875 competition than he had played the stridently rhetorical movement of Beethoven, a composer he always disliked, for the following year's competition.

Debussy's greatest success as a piano student came in the 1877 competition, when he won second prize. Playing the virtuosic first movement from Schumann's Second Sonata in G minor, he received strong praise from Director Thomas, as shown in Table 6: "On fire— [he has] fingers." But Achille did not fare well in his final piano competitions the following two summers. Having already received the second prize, the only recompense he could henceforth obtain in the piano competitions was first prize; therefore it would be theoretically possible for Debussy to have played quite well in these competitions, yet receive no award. However, while Debussy's sight-reading remained as strong as ever, his playing of the first movement from Weber's Second Sonata in A-flat major in 1878 was criticized by Thomas

According to Vidal, Debussy's father "wanted to exploit him, make an infant prodigy out of him, and for a time it worked; but when the composer in him awoke, he sent the piano and the harmony books to the devil and did only what he wanted to, treating his father with ill-disguised rancor. His father has found it practically impossible to forgive the abandonment of the lucrative virtuoso career he'd dreamed of and has only just begun to recognize him as a composer, and that only from the time he started winning prizes for it."[23] Hence Debussy became a composer not because he had to, but because he wanted to.

The solfège competitions involved two separate closed-door sessions held on different days. At the first session, the students had to answer a series of elementary theory questions in writing, and then notate two melodic dictation exercises, which had been specially composed for the occasion and which were sung by a female singing pupil. At the second session, each student had to perform a specially composed sight-singing exercise, usually involving frequent changes of clef, and transpose another exercise, also at sight. Although initially he had been weak in elementary theory, Achille ultimately had mastered the subject by concentrating on the principles of theory during his second year, at the behest of Lavignac. And his natural musical gifts

as "mediocre" stylistically and his playing of Chopin's *Allegro de concert* in 1879 as "not very clean" and "ordinary." Indeed, Debussy actually placed lower relative to the other competitors in his last two piano competitions than he had in any of his first four. Moreover, in the 1879 competition, he received no votes whatsoever from the jury. Given that Debussy's ranking in this last contest was the lowest of all six of his piano competitions, the cruel barb made by the reviewer for the *Revue et gazette musicale*, that he had made "progress in reverse" during his last year in Marmontel's class, was probably justified.[22] By regulation, two such consecutive failures resulted in the termination of his piano studies in the summer of 1879.

Although it might thus seem apparent that Debussy turned to composition only because he had failed as a pianist, the testimony of Vidal, perhaps his closest friend at the time, indicates otherwise. The evidence is found in a 12 July 1884 letter to Henriette Fuchs, the director of the La Concordia choral society for which Debussy was then serving as accompanist. Vidal, upon hearing that Debussy had just won the Prix de Rome, asserts that Achille's decline as a pianist, as well as his failures in the harmony competitions around the same time (to be discussed later in this section), had in fact been caused by his burgeoning interest in composition.

Melodic Dictation

Debussy's written answers for the 1876 Solfège Competition, containing his earliest known autograph signatures

always shone through when it came to taking dictation or singing at sight. Indeed, the youngster scored higher in the solfège competitions relative to the other contestants than in any other in-house competitions except for the 1880 accompaniment at the piano competition. At Debussy's final solfège competition in 1876, his efforts were crowned not only by the first medal, but by Thomas's positive characterization of the teenager as a "good musician," as shown in Table 6. Debussy's written responses for that final solfège competition are given in facsimile, along with a transcription and translation of the theory questions and answers, in the illustration below.[24] Besides indicating the level of difficulty of the melodic dictation exercises that were used and providing a sample of what sorts of materials were taught in the elementary theory component of the course, these documents contain Debussy's earliest known autograph signatures, dating from just before his fourteenth birthday.

(Text continues on pg. 348.)

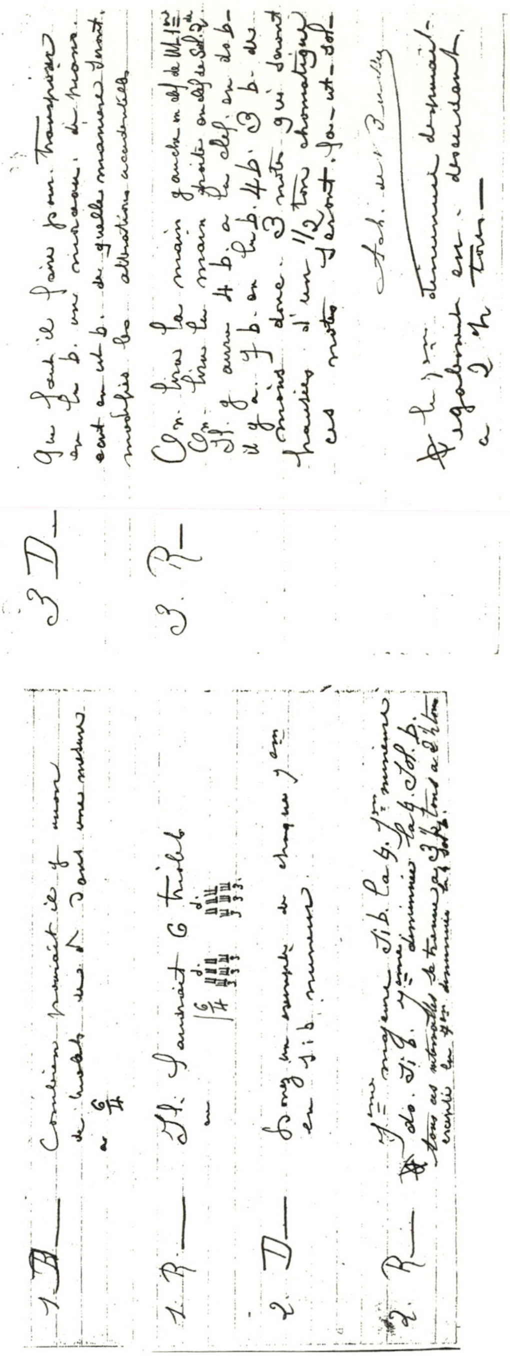

Theory Questions

Transcription/Translation of Theory Questions and Answers[1]

3. D[emande]	*Que faut il faire pour transposer en la un morceau de piano en uts et de quelle manière seront modifiées les alterations accidentelles?*	
Question		What must be done to transpose a piano piece in C-flat into A-flat, and in what manner will the accidentals be modified?
3. R[éponse]	*On lira la main gauche en clef de ut 1ere. On lira le main droite en clef de sol 2de. Il y aura 4♭ a la clef en do—il y a 7♭ en la♭. 4♭. 3♭. —de moins donc 3 notes qui seront haus[s]ées d'un ½ ton ch[r]omatique ces notes seront fa–ut–sol.*	
Answer		One will read the left hand in the C clef on the 1st line [soprano clef]. One will read the right hand in the G clef on the 2nd line [treble clef]. There will be 4 flats in the clef in C-flat—there are 7 flats in A-flat. 4 flats. 3 flats. — hence at least 3 notes that will be raised by a chromatic half step these notes will be F–C–G.
1. D[emande]	*Combien pour[r]ait il y avoir de triolets de ♪ [croches] dans une mesure à 6/4?*	
Question		How many eighth note triplets would there be in a 6/4 measure?
1. R[éponse]	*Il y aurait 6 triolets*	
Answer		There would be 6 triplets
2. D[emande]	*Don[n]ez un exemple de chaque 7ème [des trois espèces de septième] en [dans le ton de] si♭ mineur.*	
Question		Give an example of each of the three species of seventh in B-flat minor.
2. R[éponse]	*7ème majeure si♭ la♮. 7ème mineure do si♭. 7ème diminuée la♮ sol♭. tous ces intervalles se tienne a 3 ½ tons a 2½ tons excepté la 7ème diminuée la♮ sol♭.†*	
	† La 7ème diminuée [?] egalement en descendant a 2½ tons.	
Answer		Major 7th B♭ A♮. Minor 7th C B♭. Diminished 7th A♮ G♭. all these intervals contain from 3½ steps to 2½ steps, except the diminished 7th A♮ G♭.†
		† The diminished 7th [?] similarly in descending to 2½ steps.

1. The questions as actually asked, as discerned from other competitors' papers, are shown using brackets. Debussy's awkward orthography and occasionally incorrect grammar are maintained. An illegible word is indicated by a question mark enclosed in brackets.

The single harmony and accompaniment competition in which Debussy participated in 1878 involved, like the solfège competitions, two separate, closed-door trials held on different days, one for harmony and the other for accompaniment. In the harmony trial, carried out during a grueling sequestration that lasted from 6 A.M. until midnight, the contestants had to realize in four voices a given bass and melody that had been composed for the occasion. Following the judgment of the harmony realizations by the jury the next morning, the accompaniment trial was held the following afternoon. It involved the realization at sight of a specially prepared figured bass and the reduction at sight of an excerpt from an orchestral score. Debussy's performance in this competition, in which he placed no better than eighth out of nine total contestants and received no votes whatsoever from the competition panel, can probably best be described as dismal. As shown in Table 6, Thomas felt that Debussy was weaker in harmony than in accompaniment. He characterized each of Debussy's harmony realizations as "not very natural" (though he subsequently changed his mind about the given bass), which indicates that Achille either had not yet mastered the Conservatoire's stilted harmonic precepts or else simply experienced trouble in trying to conform to the expected scholastic style.

The harmony competitions were identical to the harmony component of the harmony and accompaniment competitions, requiring a 6 A.M. to midnight sequestration, during which a specially composed given bass and given melody had to be realized in four voices. Debussy again did rather poorly in the two harmony competitions in which he participated in 1879 and 1880, ranking above the fiftieth percentile only in the latter competition. Indeed, Achille received no votes whatsoever in the 1879 competition and just one vote, for the second certificate, the lowest award accorded, in the 1880 competition. That he had at least improved slightly by his final harmony competition is indicated by Thomas's comments, shown in Table 6, that Debussy's two realizations were "not bad," and his brief consideration of awarding the teenager a second certificate. But the improvement was too little and came too late: according to regulation, Debussy's matriculation in the harmony class was terminated because of his failure to win any award that year.

The accompaniment at the piano competition, in which Debussy competed in 1880, involved several tasks, and was indeed quite different from the accompaniment component of the harmony and accompaniment competition in which he had taken part two years before. There were five separate trials in the 1880 competition: (1) realization at sight of a specially prepared figured bass; (2) improvised accompaniment of a specially composed given melody; (3) transposition at sight of a piece; (4) reduction at sight of an excerpt from an orchestra piece; and (5) accompaniment at sight of an instrumental melody. Debussy, a fine sight-reader with a superb capacity for reducing orchestral scores, excelled at most of these tasks, and this would be the only in-house competition in which he ranked an unequivocal first. As indicated in Table 6, Thomas nonetheless hesitated to award Debussy the first prize, seeming to prefer the second prize. By regulation, Debussy could have been expelled if he had failed to win any award at this competition—an expulsion that would almost certainly have put an end to his compositional career before it could begin.[25]

The fugue competitions, like the harmony competitions, involved a 6 A.M. to midnight sequestration, during which the contestant had to compose a school fugue based on a subject written for the occasion. Although Debussy managed to win a second certificate in 1882, he ranked well below average in each of the three fugue competitions in which he participated in 1881 through 1883. In fact, Achille actually ranked lower in comparison to his fellow competitors in all three of these fugue competitions than he had in either

of the harmony competitions in which he had participated in 1879 and 1880. Furthermore, in the 1881 and 1883 fugue competitions, Debussy received no votes whatsoever from the competition jury. Thomas's lukewarm responses to Debussy's 1882 and 1883 efforts, shown in Table 6, indicate that Achille was no master of the school fugue, at least when he had to write one in a single day. Nonetheless, Debussy's poor showings in the fugue competitions should not be taken as evidence for the oft-repeated claim that he was a "vertical composer" who could not write counterpoint, for his *Fugue d'école*, composed as a class assignment probably in 1883 or 1884, demonstrates considerable mastery of the fugue medium. The *Fugue d'école* also exhibits important foreshadowings of Debussy's later style (particularly in its heavy use of Bachian proto-arabesques), while representing a direct point of stylistic contact between Debussy's music and the contrapuntal music of Bach.

The Prix de Rome competitions, administered by the Institut de France, presented, of course, the most arduous challenges of all. The contest was comprised of both preliminary and final rounds; by regulation, at most six competitors were admitted to compete in the final round, based on their rankings in the preliminary round.[26] During the six days of sequestration of the preliminary round, competitors were required to compose, without the use of a piano, a four-voice fugue on a given subject, identical to that required for the Conservatoire fugue competitions, and a choral work with orchestra. In the final round, the competitors who passed the preliminary round were sequestered for twenty-five days, granted access to a piano, and required to compose and orchestrate a cantata, the libretto for which was chosen as part of a preliminary poetic competition.[27] That this was no mean feat for such a short period of time probably explains why the sequestration was extended to thirty days beginning in 1899.[28]

The form of the cantata was determined largely by the structure of the supplied text, which was tightly regulated. According to Article 25 of the regulatory code in force when Debussy competed for the Prix de Rome in the early 1880s, the poem, which was selected through a preliminary poetic competition, had to be "a lyrical scene, for two or three characters. This scene must provide material for a more or less developed aria or solo for each character, for a duet, and moreover, a trio, if the scene is for three voices, as well as recitatives linking these various pieces." According to Article 29, the music for the scene had to be written, insofar as possible, for unequal voices. An instrumental introduction should precede the scene, and the trio, if

present, could involve some vocal ensemble passages without accompaniment.[29]

About a week and a half after the twenty-five-day sequestration for the final round had ended (during this interval, singers had to be lined up and rehearsals conducted), the cantatas were performed twice with piano four-hands accompaniment. An initial performance took place in the Conservatoire for the musical section of the Académie des Beaux-Arts; a second performance took place in the Institut's lavishly appointed Left Bank palace, this time for all the sections of the Académie combined. Journalists attended this definitive performance, which was also open to the public. After the second playing, a final judgment was rendered by majority vote.

During Debussy's time, the competitors were lodged in the Conservatoire building itself, not the Palais d'Institut, as previously, or the château de Compiègne, as subsequently.[30] Even the preliminary round was trying, as an early May 1887 letter of Gustave Charpentier indicates:

What a frightful thing these [preliminary] competitions are. I am required to bring my bed, a chair, a worktable, a lamp, a sufficient provision of kerosene, and a night pot, this last item . . . is totally necessary, seeing as how we are allowed access to the bathrooms only two or three times per day. We go into sequestration Saturday at 10 A.M. and come out the following Friday at 10 A.M.; the judgment takes place the next day at 10 A.M. So that after having woodshedded for seven straight days, we must still spend the night reducing our choruses for the piano and recopying our fugues. . . . And all that to end up possibly failing—this is not funny.[31]

But the final round, of course, was much more difficult. The conditions of the sequestration, for which each contestant was paid 100 francs to cover expenses,[32] were less than comfortable, as a press account of the 1887 competition explains:

Formerly, the studios were installed under the cupola of the Institut de France. Since 1864, they have been transferred to the Conservatoire in the Poissonnière suburb, next to the concert hall. Small, narrow, and shallow, [the rooms] are sumptuous, according to the administration; on the cracked and split ceiling runs a tangle of bizarre lines; the walls have the chaste nudity of olden

times; all that one can do is to sweep up after every trial, so that the candidates do not find, in the dust of their elders, an old chord or a forgotten organ point. In return, they are free to furnish their studios as they see fit. . . . They are even permitted to put their feet on ice and to light up the mind with champagne. At noon, the candidates, followed by their chaperones, go down to the dining hall: the menu is served by Brébant, who is the restaurant-keeper of music. After lunch, the short walk down the corridor; any conversation is closely monitored. Then one goes back upstairs and begins working again fiercely. The candidates for the Prix de Rome are kept under a veil of secrecy; only at 7 in the evening can they receive their friends in the large courtyard.[33]

In his recently published second set of memoirs, Alfred Bruneau, who took part in two Prix de Rome competitions, placing second in 1881 (the year before Debussy first entered the fray), describes the sequestration in similarly colorful terms:

The sequestration at this time [was not held], as at present, in the Château de Fontainebleau, where the candidates enjoy a relatively tranquil liberty, . . . but at the Conservatoire, where they were shut up behind the bars of the narrow and gloomy lofts opening their sinister windows above the entrance of the Saint-Eugène church. We would bring in a bed, a table, a chair, some ruled paper, a pen, and some ink, scanty furniture; we would curse the church organ that would fill the little street with its triumphant fracas, preventing us from working when we most felt like it. . . . Our brief recreations that were granted to us in the morning and evening in the small courtyard . . . had the same character of mystifying turbulence. The passersby, bewildered, stopped short at the exceptional spectacle of these ball players, comically dressed, tumultuous and provocative, these strange prisoners furiously shaking the bars of their cage.[34]

According to Marguerite Vasnier, Debussy hated being cooped up in such conditions for so long. During one of her family's regular evening visits with an unhappily sequestered Achille, she inquired why his windows had bars. He replied, "It's because they consider us no doubt to be ferocious beasts."[35] To make matters worse, the time pressures on the contestants were enormous, as a reviewer of the 1883 competition

points out: "Inspiration must come by the minute, during these hours at their disposal—hours that allowed them scarcely enough time to trace the innumerable signs of the musical language that must be thought, reasoned, combined. These hours seemed short to them, and more than one has been seen to flee from them not without anxiety, for at the Rome competition, under pain of being eliminated, the first condition is to 'finish'."[36]

According to both Marguerite Vasnier and Vidal, Debussy was anything but eager to participate in the Prix de Rome competitions, for to win the prize would mean a two-year sojourn in Rome. In his 12 July 1884 letter to Fuchs, Vidal notes that Debussy had already been to Rome with the von Mecks and detested it, and that he had had to persuade Achille, after he failed the preliminary round in 1882, to enter the competitions in 1883 and 1884.[37] Indeed, Debussy signed up last or next to last for each of the three Prix de Rome competitions in which he competed.[38] As is now well known, the secret reason for Debussy's hesitancy had to do more with his fear of separation for two years from his lover, Marie Vasnier.

Debussy did not do especially well in the preliminary rounds of the Prix de Rome contests. His fugues for these preliminary rounds, which were again written under severe time pressure, were no better than those he composed for the fugue competitions, and his choral compositions, which are surprisingly unconstrained stylistically, were undoubtedly too radical for the tastes of the judges. But in the final rounds, Achille's innate compositional ability asserted itself. His 1883 Prix de Rome cantata, *Le Gladiateur*, is a cred-

itable musical-dramatic setting that surely earned for him, besides his second-place finish in the competition and a cash prize of between 200 and 1000 francs,[39] a measure of respect from Guiraud. And Debussy's win of the coveted first grand Rome prize in 1884 with his well-known cantata, *L'Enfant prodigue*, did nothing less than launch his career.[40]

Table 5
Competitions[1]

Year		
1874	*Concours de Piano:* 2nd certificate (ranked 7th of 15 competitors), Chopin, Concerto No. 2 in F minor, Op. 21, First movement	*Concours de Solfège:* 3rd medal (ranked 12th of 35 competitors)
1875	*Concours de Piano:* 1st certificate (ranked 4th of 14 competitors), Chopin, *Ballade No. 1 in G minor,* Op. 23	*Concours de Solfège:* 2nd medal (ranked 7th to 10th of 36 competitors)
1876	*Concours de Piano:* no prize (ranked no better than 8th of 18 competitors and received no votes), Beethoven, Sonata No. 32 in C minor, Op. 111, First movement	*Concours de Solfège:* 1st medal[2] (ranked 3rd of 27 competitors)
1877	*Concours de Piano:* 2nd prize (ranked 5th of 21 competitors), Schumann, Sonata No. 2 in G minor, Op. 22, First movement	
1878	*Concours de Piano:* no prize[3] (ranked no better than 9th of 17 competitors), Weber, Sonata No. 2 in A-flat major, Op. 39, First movement	*Concours d'Harmonie et Accompagnement:* no prize (ranked no better than 8th of 9 competitors and received no votes)
1879	*Concours de Piano:* no prize[2] (ranked no better than 8th of 14 competitors and received no votes), Chopin, *Allegro de concert,* Op. 46	*Concours d'Harmonie:* no prize (ranked no better than 14th of 26 competitors and received no votes)

Table 5 continued

Year		
1880	Concours d'Accompagnement au Piano: 1st prize[2] (ranked 1st of 7 competitors)	Concours d'Harmonie: no prize[2] (ranked no better than 11th of 25 competitors)
1881	Concours de Fugue: no prize (ranked no better than 8th of 14 competitors and received no votes)	
1882	Concours de Fugue: 2nd certificate (ranked 7th of 12 competitors)	Concours de Rome, Concours d'essai: failed (ranked no better than 6th of 7 competitors)
1883	Concours de Fugue: no prize (ranked no better than 8th of 11 competitors and received no votes)	Concours de Rome, Concours d'essai: passed (ranked 4th of 6 competitors)
		Concours de Rome, Concours définitif: 1st 2nd grand prize (ranked 2nd of 5 competitors)
1884	Concours de Fugue: absent	Concours de Rome, Concours d'essai: passed (ranked 4th of 9 competitors)
		Concours de Rome, Concours définitif: 1st 1st grand prize (ranked 1st of 5 competitors)

1. Sources: Pierre, Conservatoire National, 733; Archives Nationales documents AJ[37] 251*/1–3 (unpaginated), AJ[37] 252*/1 (unpaginated), AJ[37] 258/3a: 52–59, and AJ[37] 364/4 and 5 (unpaginated).

2. Final competition in this subject by regulation. A pupil's studies in a particular area were terminated upon winning the first prize, losing two consecutive competitions after winning a prize, or failing to obtain any prize in three straight competitions.

3. If not by regulation, at least by practice, no pupil could win an award of equal or lesser value to his or her highest previous prize in a given competition. But the voting totals for the 1878 and 1879 piano competitions recorded in Archives Nationales document AJ[37] 251* (unpaginated) indicate that Debussy did not play well enough to receive any recompense in these competitions, even were this not the case.

Table 6
Director Thomas's Notes on Debussy's In-House Competitions[1]

Competition/ Result	Piece(s) or Trial(s)	French Original	English Translation
Piano, 1874: second certificate	*Prepared piece:* Chopin, Concerto No. 2 in F minor, Op. 21, First movement *Sight reading:* piece by Fissot	(no notes preserved)	—
Piano, 1875: first certificate	*Prepared piece:* Chopin, *Ballade* No. 1 in G minor, Op. 23 *Sight reading:* piece by Cohen	(no notes preserved)	—
Piano, 1876: no prize	*Prepared piece:* Beethoven, Sonata No. 32 in C minor, Op. 111, First movement *Sight reading:* piece by Fissot	Mauvais trille / trop court. com-passé—D'assez bonnes choses. Passable (2 P)???	Bad trill / too short. stiff—Some rather good things. Passable ([second prize])???
Piano, 1877: second prize	*Prepared piece:* Schumann, Sonata No. 2 in G minor, Op. 22, First movement *Sight reading:* piece by Dubois	A[ssez]. B[ien]. / En feu—des doigts. A[ssez]. B[ien]. (2 P)?	Rather good / On fire—[he has] fingers. Rather good ([second prize])?
Piano, 1878: no prize	*Prepared piece:* Weber, Sonata No. 2 in A-flat major, Op. 39, First movement *Sight reading:* piece by Fissot	Sec—dur—accomp[agnemen]ts trop forts—style médiocre. A[ssez]. B[ien].	Dry—harsh—too strong accompaniments—mediocre style. Rather good
Piano, 1879: no prize	*Prepared piece:* Chopin, *Allegro de concert*, Op. 46 *Sight reading:* piece by Fissot	pas très net. ordinaire. très Bien ??	not very clean. ordinary. very Good ??
Solfège, 1874: third medal	*Dictation:* two melodies by Thomas *Theory questions* *Sight singing:* lesson by Thomas	(no notes preserved)	—

Table 6 continued

Competition/ Result	Piece(s) or Trial(s)	French Original	English Translation
Solfège, 1875: second medal	*Dictation*: two melodies by Thomas *Theory questions* *Sight singing*: lesson by Thomas	(no notes preserved)	—
Solfège, 1876: first medal	*Dictation*: two melodies by Thomas *Theory questions* (three) *Sight singing*: lesson by Thomas	Bien B[ien]. B[ien]. B[ien]. Bon musicien. (1)	Good Good. Good. Good. Good musician. ([first medal])
Harmony and Accompaniment, 1878: no prize	Realization of given bass by Delibes	~~peu naturel~~ / quelques bons passages / pass[able].	~~not very natural~~ / some good passages / pass[able].
	Realization of given melody by Delibes	peu naturel. Pass[able]., quelques fautes	not very natural. Pass[able]., some errors
	Realization of figured bass by Dubois	A[ssez]. B[ien].	Rather good
	Orchestral score reduction: excerpt from Herold's *Mosières*	Pass[able].	Pass[able].
Harmony 1879: no prize	Realization of given bass by Guiraud	(no notes preserved)	
	Realization of given melody by Guiraud		
Harmony, 1880: no prize	Realization of given bass by Delibes Realization of given melody by Delibes	Pas mal ordinaire / pas mal 2-acc?	Not bad ordinary / not bad [second certificate]?

Table 6 continued

Competition/Result	Piece(s) or Trial(s)	French Original	English Translation
Accompaniment at the Piano, 1880: first prize	Realization of figured bass by Dubois	Très Bien	Very Good
	Accompaniment of given melody by Thomas	A[ssez]. Bien	Rather Good
	Transposition at the second below of the Trio, No. 15 from Mozart's *Idomeneo*	A[ssez]. Bien	Rather Good
	Accompaniment of Vieuxtemps's Fourth Violin Concerto, Finale	A[ssez]. Bien	Rather Good
	Reduction of orchestral accompaniment of the Duet, No. 3 from Halévy's *Le Dilettante d'Avignon*	A[ssez]. Bien	Rather Good
		(1re P)? / (2e P)	([first prize])? / ([second prize])
Fugue, 1881: no prize	Fugue on given subject by Thomas	(no notes preserved)	—
Fugue, 1882: second certificate	Fugue on given subject by Thomas	Monotone quelques passages (2d acc)	Some passages monotonous ([second certificate])
Fugue, 1883: no prize	Fugue on given subject by Thomas	Un peu cherché et prétentieux—pas mal	A little affected and pretentious—not bad
Fugue, 1884 (absent)	—	—	—

1. Sources: Archives Nationales documents AJ37 247 (unpaginated), AJ37 251*/1–3 (unpaginated), AJ37 252*/1 (unpaginated), AJ37 255*/3: 7, 49, 89, and 131, and AJ37 257*: 7, 105, 205, 207, 285, and 325.

NOTES TO THE COMMENTARY

1. François Lesure, *Claude Debussy: Biographie critique* (Paris: Klincksieck, 1994), pp. 32 and 48.

2. Furthermore, all instrumental pupils who had received any award in the competitions were expected to attend the instrumental ensemble class, not just those who had received a first or second prize or a first certificate, as Lesure states, following Article 27 of the 1870 regulatory emendations, which were never implemented. Indeed, Debussy himself began attending the class in the fall of 1874, after receiving a second certificate in the piano competition the previous summer. See Lesure, *Biographie*, p. 32 and Constant Pierre, *Le Conservatoire National de Musique et de Déclamation: documents historiques et administratifs* (Paris: Imprimerie Nationale, 1900), p. 372.

3. Christopher Palmer, *Impressionism in Music* (New York: Charles Scribner's Sons, 1973), p. 104.

4. Archives Nationales document AJ^{37} 159*/5 (unpaginated). In a March 4, 1894 concert review in the Belgian journal *L'Art moderne*, Debussy is reported—probably based on his own statement—to have studied with Franck for "barely . . . six months." See Lesure, *Biographie*, p. 48, n. 7.

5. Archives Nationales documents AJ^{37} 99*–103* (unpaginated), AJ^{37} 158*/5 (unpaginated), and AJ^{37} 159*/1–4 (unpaginated).

6. Charles Koechlin, "Quelques anciennes mélodies inédites de Claude Debussy," *Revue musicale* 7 (1926): 135, n. 1.

7. Passerieu entered the singing class of Saint-Yves Bax on 4 November 1878, and he was expelled from the institution on 1 December 1879, as shown in Archives Nationales document AJ^{37} 348* (unpaginated).

8. Paul Vidal, "Souvenirs d'Achille Debussy," *Revue musicale* 7 (1926): 11–13.

9. Antoine Marmontel, *Art classique et moderne du piano*, (Paris: Heugel, [1876]), vol. 2, pp. 7–8.

10. In a letter to Victor Segalen, Debussy reports that he had been introduced to Bach's music by Antoinette Mauté, who, he writes, played Bach's music "as is no longer done now, putting life into it." Quoted in Lesure, *Biographie*, p. 20.

11. Marcel Dietschy, *A Portrait of Claude Debussy*, ed. and trans. William Ashbrook and Margaret G. Cobb (Oxford: Clarendon, 1990), p. 24, n. 6.

12. Naturally, Debussy may well have played the fourth *Ballade* and quite a number of other works of Chopin of his own volition, both during his years in Marmontel's piano class and later, as would also be the case with compositions of Bach and Schumann, not to mention Franz Liszt.

13. Archives Nationales document AJ^{37} 206*/1, 177.

14. Léon Vallas undertook the first investigation of these materials, considering only the semester reports of Debussy's professors. Lesure's treatment of these documents also includes some but not all reports of other examination committee members. See Léon Vallas, "Achille Debussy jugé par ses professeurs du Conservatoire," *Revue de musicologie* 34 (1952): 46–49 and Lesure, *Biographie*, pp. 23–74 passim.

15. Emile Réty's minutes for all of Debussy's examinations are contained in Archives Nationales documents AJ^{37} 195*/1* passim, AJ^{37} 206*/1–3 passim, and AJ^{37} 207*/1 passim. Thomas's notes on most of Debussy's examinations are contained in Archives Nationales

documents AJ³⁷ 307*–309* passim. Other semester reports are contained in the following Archives Nationales documents (page number citations within these documents are provided in the footnotes to the various segments of Table 4). For the piano examinations, Marmontel's notes are in AJ³⁷ 283–86; François Bazin's notes are in AJ³⁷ 223*/4; Henri Duvernoy's notes are in AJ³⁷ 238*/1; Henry Fissot's notes are in AJ³⁷ 238*/2; Henri Herz's notes are in AJ³⁷ 238*/3; and Charles-Eugène Sauzay's notes are in AJ³⁷ 233/1. For the solfège examinations, Lavignac's notes are in AJ³⁷ 283–85; Marmontel's notes are in AJ³⁷ 239*/3; Bazin's notes are in AJ³⁷ 223*/4; Antoine Prumier's notes are in AJ³⁷ 240*/1; Vervoitte's notes are in AJ³⁷ 240*/2; and Jean-Baptiste-Théodore Weckerlin's notes are in AJ³⁷ 233/3. For the instrumental ensemble examinations, Baillot's notes are in AJ³⁷ 284–86. For the harmony and accompaniment and regular harmony examinations, Durand's notes are in AJ³⁷ 286–87 and Léo Delibes's notes are in AJ³⁷ 234*/4. For the accompaniment at the piano examinations, Bazille's notes are in AJ³⁷ 287 and Delibes's notes are in AJ³⁷ 234*/4. And for the composition examinations, Guiraud's notes are in AJ³⁷ 287–89; Delibes's notes are in AJ³⁷ 234*/4; and Théodore Dubois's notes are in AJ³⁷ 237*/1.

16. Maurice Emmanuel, "*Pelléas et Mélisande*" *de Debussy: étude et analyse* (Paris: Mellottée, 1950), pp. 17–18.

17. Debussy wrote a total of at least six fugues for the composition class, one of which was played at each of the six composition semester examinations in which he participated. Judging from the unexpected sophistication and quality of the only such piece known to still exist, the so-called *Fugue d'école*, it is a shame that more of these in-class fugues were not preserved. They represent an important missing link in Debussy's compositional development, the significance of which is tantalizingly hinted at by the *Fugue d'école*. Debussy's extant competition fugues are markedly inferior to the *Fugue d'école*,

probably because they had to be written under severe time constraints, and possibly also because they had to be more stylistically subdued.

18. That the four movements of Debussy's suite, entitled "Fête," "Ballet," "Rêve," and "Bacchanale," call to mind those of both Guiraud's first orchestral suite of 1872, "Prélude," "Intermezzo," "Andante," and "Carnaval," and his second suite of 1886 (which had probably not, however, been written yet), "Petite Marche," "Divertissement," "Rêverie," and "Finale," points up how strongly Debussy was influenced at first by his composition professor.

19. Information on competition trials, numbers of contestants, and voting is found in Archives Nationales documents AJ³⁷ 247 passim, AJ³⁷ 251*/1–3 passim, AJ³⁷ 252*/1 passim, AJ³⁷ 255*/3 passim, AJ³⁷ 257* passim, AJ³⁷ 258/3a: 52–59, AJ³⁷ 364/4 and 5 passim, and AJ³⁷ 365*/1 passim.

20. As occasionally happened, two first prizes were accorded in the piano competition for boys in 1878. Only one piano was given away, however; it went to Bellaigue, not the first prizewinner from Georges Matthias's class. See Archives Nationales document AJ³⁷ 386/5: 34–35.

21. Camille Bellaigue, *Souvenirs de musique et de musiciens* (Paris: Nouvelle Librairie Nationale, 1921), p. 42.

22. Lesure, *Biographie*, p. 37.

23. Roger Nichols, *Debussy Remembered* (London: Faber, 1992), p. 24.

24. These materials are held, together with the written responses of other competitors, in Archives Nationales documents AJ³⁷ 204/78c and d (unpaginated).

25. As Article 60 of the Conservatoire's 1878 regulatory code states, "Every pupil who, after three years of studies, has not been admitted to compete is removed from the rolls. Ceasing likewise to

belong to the Conservatoire are those pupils who, having competed three times, have not won any prizes or certificates, and those who, after having obtained an award, have competed twice without success." See Pierre, *Conservatoire National*, p. 263. Debussy had won no awards in the 1878 and 1879 competitions.

26. Ibid., p. 277.

27. Alfred Bruneau, "Souvenirs inédits," *Revue internationale de musique française* 7 (February 1982): 37.

28. Pierre, *Conservatoire National*, p. 277, n. 1.

29. Ibid., p. 277. The preliminary poetic competitions, which involved a cash prize of 500 francs, were often hotly contested, with thirty or more entries frequently being submitted. See *Le Ménestrel* 50 (1883–1884): 78 and Archives Nationales document AJ³⁷ 259/1 (unpaginated).

30. Although some confusion has reigned in previous biographical literature on this point, archival documents make clear that the contestants had been lodged at the Institut from 1803 until 1864, when they began to be sequestered inside the Conservatoire building itself. See the brief history supplied on the title page of Archives Nationales document AJ³⁷ 258/2.

31. Françoise Andrieux, *Gustave Charpentier, lettres inédites à ses parents: la vie quotidienne d'un élève du Conservatoire, 1879–1887* (Paris: Presses Universitaires de France, 1984), p. 104.

32. Archives Nationales documents AJ³⁷ 53/12b (unpaginated) and AJ³⁷ 56/1 (unpaginated).

33. Andrieux, *Charpentier lettres*, p. 109, n. 1.

34. Bruneau, "Souvenirs," 35–37. An 1881 letter from Réty to the police commissioner, requesting that street musicians be kept off the streets surrounding the Conservatoire so as not to hinder the competitors' concentration during their sequestration, underscores the severity of the noise problems with which the contestants had to

contend at that time. See Archives Nationales document AJ³⁷ 258/4 (unpaginated).

35. Marguerite Vasnier, "Debussy à dix-huit ans," *Revue musicale* 7 (1926): 21.

36. Charles Darcours, "Notes de musique," *Le Figaro* (27 June 1883): 6.

37. Vasnier, "Debussy à dix-huit ans," 21; François Lesure, "Debussy de 1883 à 1885 d'après la correspondance de Paul Vidal à Henriette Fuchs," *Revue de musicologie* 48 (1962): 99–100.

38. Debussy signed up last in 1882 and 1884, and second-to-last (but on the same day as the last entrant) in 1883. In 1884, the year Debussy won the award, he signed up late indeed, inscribing his name on the register on 6 May, only one day before inscription was to be closed, four days before the preliminary round was to begin, and a full two weeks after the first contestants had signed up. See Archives Nationales documents AJ³⁷ 258/1 (unpaginated) and AJ³⁷ 258/3a: 52–59.

39. Between 1871 and 1890, winners of the second prize or a certificate in the competition received varying amounts in this range, as indicated in Archives Nationales document AJ³⁷ 53/12d (unpaginated).

40. The circumstances surrounding the adjudication process for the 1883 and 1884 competitions are described in Lesure, *Biographie*, pp. 61 and 69.

"Le Cas Debussy"

Reviews and Polemics About the Composer's

"New Manner"

Brian Hart

The following readings feature documents from 1908 to 1910, the high point of the period known as *debussysme*. In the years following the premiere of *Pelléas et Mélisande*, Debussy and his music became subject to vigorous dispute as supporters and opponents argued whether the composer's influence was good for French music—and if so, *which* Debussy should serve as model? The composer's perceived change of style starting with *La Mer* alienated some of the strongest supporters of *Pelléas*. A number of defenders, who wanted Debussy to produce more "symbolist" works, turned away; others, however, enthusiastically embraced the new sound. Louis Laloy, a close friend, became the spokesman for the latter. In an influential article, Laloy described *Pelléas* as the summation of Debussy's "first manner" and *La Mer* as the beginning of the composer's "new manner," i.e., his full maturity.[1] Many fights between the opposing camps of Debussy supporters broke out in the years around 1910, as will be evident below.

We begin with reviews of *La Mer* and *Rondes de printemps* by two of the most prominent and respected critics of the day, Pierre Lalo (1866–1943) and Gaston Carraud (1864–1920). Lalo wrote for the daily *Le Temps*, Carraud for the republican paper *La Liberté*; each also contributed articles to various journals. Both critics had strong credentials: Lalo, the only son of Edouard Lalo, was well-versed in literature and philosophy; while Carraud, a former composer, won the Prix de Rome in 1890. The two shared conservative sympathies: both favored d'Indy and the Schola Cantorum and detested the music of Debussy's supposed followers, especially Ravel. Lalo and Carraud exemplify the admirers of *Pelléas* who detected an unwelcome change of style and goal in *La Mer*. In his "first manner" Debussy freely and spontaneously expressed feelings inspired by nature. Now, said the critics, he has converted his style into a compositional system; the music of Debussy's "new manner" flows not from the genuine and instinctive communication of feelings but from a methodical and impersonal application of stylistic "formulas" based on his earlier procedures. Their attitude hardened with subsequent works, such as the orchestral *Images*.

The majority of this section is devoted to excerpts from a book that appeared in 1910 entitled *Le Cas Debussy*. In an attempt to draw attention to their journal *Revue du temps présent*, editors C.-Francis Caillard and José de Bérys sought to clarify Debussy's position in French music. Adopting the premise that it was now dominated by a "quarrel of Debussyists and anti-Debussyists," which in its intensity recalled the eighteenth-century battle between the Gluckists and Piccinnists (pp. 3, 129), Caillard and Bérys offered readers articles and commentaries by a diverse group of intellectuals which the editors hoped would produce a definitive judgment on Debussyism—namely that the composer's influence was neither important nor lasting, but simply a product of fashionable snobbery and chasing after novelty. *Le Cas Debussy* presents a valuable example of the anti-Debussyist perspective on the debate over the future of French music and the role of Debussy and his disciples in it.

Pierre Lalo: Two Reviews of *La Mer*
"La Mer, suite de trois tableaux symphoniques — Les qualités et les défautes de la Mer"*

Le Temps, 21 January 1908

Lalo reviewed La Mer *three times. Excerpts of his analysis of the 1905 premiere in* Le Temps *have been widely reprinted, especially the concluding line "I do not hear, I do not see, I do not feel the sea."*[2] *His later articles, both from 1908, provide more precise explanations of the critic's discomfort with Debussy's work. In the opening of the review of the second performance of* La Mer *(conducted by the composer), Lalo summarizes what he appreciates about Debussy's art and fears is being lost.*

La Mer is the most recent important work by M. Debussy. The premiere left me with a feeling of keen disappointment, which yesterday's

---

* "Music: *La Mer*, suite of three symphonic pictures — its virtues and faults"

performance did nothing to erase. In this work I seem to sense a change in M. Debussy's art and even more in his nature and sensibility—and this change is not auspicious. What seduces, enchants, and captivates in M. Debussy's music is an intensity, a freshness, a delicacy of feeling which is extraordinary—so natural, so unobtrusive, and so immediate that the impression produced by these objects passes through every bar of his music; and when listening to this music, we feel the same shiver that we would if we saw the objects themselves. . . . Recall *L' Après-midi d'un faune*. Recall the three parts of the *Nocturnes*: "Nuages," "Fêtes," and "Sirènes." Recall how the first movement gives us subtle sensations of the night, wind, and clouds passing through the sky; how from the second movement we carry away the dazzling and delicate impression of dances, light, and distant uproar; and how the third movement evokes the spectacle of waves plated in silver by the moon, in the midst of which one hears a mysterious song. Remember the most picturesque scenes in *Pelléas*: the grotto, where a few chords and a rhythmic pattern in the orchestra are enough to paint the whole night and the whole sea; and the exit from the subterranean depths, in which some notes in the harps and winds express all the joy of returning to the light, in the open air and under the clear sky. And the composer creates this striking and penetrating painting with the most delicate, light, natural, and refined means; it appears that the feeling expresses itself, in a language which is marvelously spontaneous, discreet, and profound.

This freshness and naturalness of feeling is what I no longer find in *La Mer*, and this is why the piece touches me less. . . .

A slightly modified version of the rest of the review appears in the second paragraph of the Courrier musical *review below.*

"Les Grands Concerts," Le Courrier musical 11

(15 November 1908), pp. 641–42

Here Lalo discusses La Mer *for a third time, after a performance at Concerts Lamoureux (conducted by Camille Chevillard, who also led the premiere). The author conflates and modifies passages from the previous articles in* Le Temps *to present his most lucid and reasoned explanation for his dislike of* La Mer *and the perceived change in Debussy's style.*

Of *Till Eulenspiegel, Sheherazade*, and other works performed in concert these last two weeks, I have nothing to say; they are too well known.

But I do still have things to say about Debussy's *La Mer*, which M. Chevillard played last Sunday. The case of M. Debussy and the evolution that seems to be taking place in his style are interesting things to consider, both as phenomena in themselves and for the ramifications they can have on future works by the composer of *Pelléas*. I must confess that from first hearing *La Mer* has disappointed me and, instead of passing away, this feeling has deepened and the reasons for it are becoming clearer. M. Debussy's most precious virtue, his most marvelous gift in his pictorial works (for we must set aside certain scenes of *Pelléas et Mélisande* which have a strong and profound humanity and whose beauty is of a superior order) is—or was up to this point—freshness, naturalness, and spontaneity of feeling. I no longer find these in *La Mer*; it seems to me that he wanted to feel instead of truly and naturally feeling, and that he wanted to express what he didn't feel or at best now felt only halfway. For the first time, when hearing one of M. Debussy's musical landscapes (so to speak), I have the impression not of being in front of Nature—as I did with *Nuages* or the grotto scene of *Pelléas*—but in front of a copy of Nature. An extraordinarily skillful and refined copy, but a copy nonetheless. For the first time I have the impression that M. Debussy found composition to be a duty instead of a pleasure, at least at certain moments.

It is not that the music of *La Mer* seems less precious than in M. Debussy's other works; on the contrary, never before perhaps has it been as ingenious or as full of striking details, surprising harmonies, or new and piquant timbral effects. You could say that M. Debussy has never written his music with so much care and ingenuity. But this is precisely the problem: there seems to be too much care, too much ingenuity; the system and method have become visible. Instead of indulging in the free-flowing charm of his sensibility as before, M. Debussy seems to have wanted to control it and convert it into formulas—he wanted to write "like Debussy" according to the rules and show how it must be done. So light, fleeting, and ungraspable up to now, his art has become precise, hardened, fastened in place, and nearly stiff. It goes without saying that I'm exaggerating: the fault I think I find in *La Mer* is not as striking as I've made it out to be, but it exists all the same. The abundance and accumulation of ingenious details harms the effect of the whole: all this display crushes the delicate sensibility that made M. Debussy's preceding works so rewarding, and the marvelous freshness of feeling disappears. A surprising thing happens: the pictorial movements, in which M. Debussy strove to evoke the spectacle of the objects depicted, do not give the impression of Nature but simply seem like ingenious and curious pieces of music. It would be a great shame if the signs that seem to appear in *La Mer* marked the beginning of an evolution in which M. Debussy lost his delightful creative spontaneity to become a composer who writes by formulas. I exaggerate again, wantonly overstating the case in order to explain more easily the minor faults of M. Debussy's latest *magnum opus*. One can listen to it with great pleasure—especially the second movement, "Jeux de vagues," which has a suppleness and fluidity that remind us of the Debussy of before. Let's wait for the next work: time will tell.

Gaston Carraud: Review of *Rondes de printemps* (1910)

In this review of the premiere of Rondes de printemps *(conducted by the composer), Carraud divides Debussy's admirers into musicians and music lovers, asserting that only non-musicians can take pleasure in* La Mer, Rondes, *and Debussy's other post-Pelléas works. The latter point elicited a sharp response from Maurice Ravel, who condemned Carraud and Lalo as "music scribblers" who were deaf to the poetry in* Rondes.[3] *Carraud's review implicitly criticizes Louis Laloy's defense of Debussy's "new manner"; in response, Laloy published an even more detailed apologia.[4] Léon Vallas paraphrases selections from Carraud's review in his biography of the composer.[5]*

"Le Mois: mars," *S.I.M.* 6 (April 1910), pp. 265–68

M. Claude Debussy's *Rondes de printemps* forms part of a collection of *Images* for orchestra along with *Ibéria*, heard recently at Concerts Colonne, and *Gigue triste* [*Gigues*], which has not yet been performed. *Ibéria* itself constitutes a small triptych, three brief pieces which contrast in color and design; the *Rondes*, on the other hand, is a single developed movement in which form and musical substance offer a perfect unity. At the Châtelet, the welcome given to *Ibéria* was as mixed as the public itself.[6] At the Salle Gaveau, where one was among musicians, one could sense some restraint in the success of the *Rondes de printemps*; the applause was directed more to the composer than to the work itself. It really must be said that everything M. Debussy has written after *Pelléas et Mélisande* has disappointed a large number of his early admirers. To be sure, another faction displays a growing enthusiasm for him, to the point of maintaining that only now has he begun his period of conscious maturity; *Pelléas* should be considered the last work of his youth. I think it's a little early for us to settle this question: we lack distance as well as the foresight to know what a genius who is this original and perenially fresh *will do*. But one can explain these differences of opinion by distinguishing two groups of people who love the music of M. Debussy: musicians and sensitive listeners on the one hand, painters and men of letters on the other (I'm speaking of course not only about professionals, but also about those who think and feel as musicians, painters, or writers do). It is the former who are drawing back from their favorite composer or rather expect other things from him; for while the form of his works always remains musical, the same can no longer be said of the emotion they express—and this is something to which *littérateurs* and painters must remain quite indifferent. To tell the truth, the emotion has disappeared. There was nothing like this emotion anywhere in music: in its mysterious unity it enveloped a host of sensations of surprising intensity, precision, delicacy, and novelty; the soul focused the evidences of the senses. In *Rondes* the sensations only exist, and it seems that they have shrunk and grown heavy at the same time, and they appear to have lost their freshness and originality. Instead of blending, they clash. Now it is the artificial method of musical technique that creates the unity, not feeling: built upon a single theme, virtually according to the principles of—*horrors!* . . .—the nurslings of the Schola, the *Rondes de printemps* does not give the same impression of cohesion that one finds in the works of M. Debussy's "first manner," with their multiplicities of different themes.[7]

By a strange phenomenon, the music of M. Debussy today reflects that of his own imitators. M. Ravel has been reproached (more than he should) for resembling M. Debussy, and now it's M. Debussy who starts to resemble M. Ravel. To be sure, there is still a distance between them. Compare M. Ravel's principal composition to date, the *Rapsodie espagnole*, with *Ibéria*, which occupies no more than a secondary rank among M. Debussy's works; nevertheless, in the latter piece you will detect a different power and different subtlety of musical construction, a different personality, and above all a different poetry. Nothing M. Ravel has ever written can approach the central part of *Ibéria* and the marvelous shading of nuances that connect it to the last section; nor can anything of his compare with the ingenious scheme of the *Rondes de printemps*. It is just that M. Debussy's structure—and this is again one of those things that matters only to musicians—has become more visible and more strained. In earlier compositions, his writing had an admirable tastefulness because of its transparent concision, but now it stresses and overwhelms; at times his coloring becomes coarse without gaining in boldness. In the past, to make the emotions more extraordinary, he employed an astonishing sobriety of means, and his infinite refinement dissolved into an impression of naturalness and simplicity.

Today, the accumulation and complication of means does a poor job of concealing what is dry, trifling, superficial, and petty in the conception. This music remains the work of an incomparable artist, but it deserves its title *Images* a little too much: and one senses the science, method, and effort in it.

Selections from Le Cas Debussy, ed. C.-Francis Caillard and José de Bérys

Paris: Bibliothèque du *Temps Présent*, 1910.
Page numbers given in parentheses indicate pages in original book.

Une Opinion de M. Debussy (interview by Maurice Leclercq)

The book opens with a previously unpublished interview that Debussy gave to the newspaper L'Éclair *in response to a 1908 questionnaire on Wagner's influence in France. Debussy denies the existence of a "Wagner school" because modern composers have neither the time nor the inclination to form schools or gather disciples. His response is consistent with his own well-known efforts to avoid becoming the leader of a group of followers. Caillard and Bérys, however, contend that Debussy is either a hypocrite or has changed his mind, for he has in fact become the leader of a school, "perhaps the most intransigent one has ever known in music." (2). The central passage of the interview goes as follows:*

Today all musicians and artists are self-absorbed, very self-absorbed. Their most pressing concern is to avoid with great care any appearance of influence in their compositions.

The admiration for beautiful works lives on; in fact, there have never been as many admirers as today. There are so many one could almost choke on them. But since one can simultaneously and with great fervor admire two beautiful works that are completely opposed in inclination, to call a person an admirer is not the same as calling that person a disciple. *There are no more disciples.*

There are no longer leaders of schools who can influence the work of musicians of succeeding generations. To be the leader of a school implies a special technique—not just some procedures, but his own doctrine—*his* grammar. Now, the musician (or the contemporary artist) who has achieved great notoriety is preoccupied with only one thing: to produce individual works, works that do new things as much as possible. He no longer has time to gather disciples or develop the grammar that allowed him to gather them in the first place.

This is the case with all modern celebrities, Wagner as well as others. (4–5)

M. Claude Debussy et le snobisme contemporain

Caillard and Bérys then reprint an extended and strongly anti-Debussyist article that first appeared in their journal in October 1909. Raphaël Cor, a writer on philosophy, dismisses Debussy's art as a passing fashion which takes interest only in fleeting harmonic and timbral novelties instead of "deep," "moving," and "profound" expressions conveyed by melody. As a result, Cor contends, Debussy's music is fundamentally insignificant and ephemeral. His supporters, e.g., Laloy, adhere to another contemporary fashion, that of admiring a chosen artist uncritically and denigrating anyone who opposed that person's art or could be seen as a rival. Cor criticizes Pelléas *and subsequent works at length, contending, like Lalo and Carraud, that Debussy has adopted a systematic approach to his supposedly "spontaneous" compositions. The unrelenting assault on Debussy in this article—a "masterpiece of deep misunderstanding" according to Marcel Dietschy[8]—concludes by insinuating that people praise Debussy principally in order to attack Wagner, but by doing so they render a disservice to French national art.*

I am not afraid to agree with M. Debussy's admirers and say he is a musician "without parallel." . . . I think his originality results from a very curious method of composition in which he uses all the elements of sound but seems to want to avoid blending them into a properly musical result. There are notes and sounds, but there is no music. (7–8) . . .

In truth, you will have said almost everything about M. Debussy's music when you say that which it is not. His originality is profoundly negative. Take out rhythm, melody, and emotion, and you will just about have it. What remains can have its charms: a sort of diffuse harmony, a murmuring and subtle monotony, still quite capable of pleasing delicate ears.

Besides, let us praise M. Debussy for his sincerity. Having planned to abolish melody, he, far from making a mystery about it, is not afraid to proclaim it openly. A superfluous declaration, to be sure, since the plan reveals itself clearly in whatever he composes. I do not know if melody and rhythm are obsolete, as he has said, but you would certainly search for them in vain in his music.* Truly, he has become a virtuoso at juggling a motive. At the most, one finds here and there the beginnings of melodies that start up, become elusive, and dissolve. In this fluid milieu, every musical thought seems to soften and vanish. It's like

---

* Save, it is true, for some works of his youth; these, on the contrary, have a violent and frankly excessive rhythm. [Cor]

a rain of sounds, a slow and monotonous rain, something infinitely diluted and amorphous. At first, you let this novelty seduce you: it's a kind of new little enchantment. Drowsiness takes hold of you, and it is not without sweetness. The music works on you like a narcotic. You feel scattered in this musical vapor in which you bathe; you relish the delights of a slow suffocation. And besides, the process seems delicate and discreet; you revel in these chords that are veiled like a secret . . . But how short-lived this initial pleasurable astonishment is! When you repeat a secret indefinitely, it quickly becomes obsessive, passing beyond the limits of the most tedious monotony. . . . With M. Debussy, [monotony] results from the impotence of an art addicted to endless repetition. It is the triumph of method. . . . Let us therefore say that what he composes is, if you will, "premusic"; and without disregarding the originality of this exciting and pretty art, let us at least be mindful not to make the ridiculous mistake of taking it too seriously. (16–19) . . .

We must take note of one more characteristic, since it is also one that explains his triumph: I mean this searching after the thin and slender, the infinitely small—a movement that dominates everywhere to some extent, especially in literature. This is how this art that has no grandeur clearly shows itself to be at one with its epoch. It amounts to a musical dust, a mosaic of chords. The composer splits hairs in every measure, advancing note by note, lingering over every tiny element. For lack of the supreme burst of an absent inspiration, we witness infinite quests for unusual sonorities—searches for which we cannot even say that the results are varied. To sum up: a subtle music, but one in which nothing lives or palpitates; a small and skillful model, but terribly barren and restricted—a Lilliputian art for the smallest-minded humans. (25) . . .

Above all else, the Debussyist craze clearly is a matter of fashion. That's the way we are in Paris—we have our fits of admiration, our little sicknesses of the season. One could say that M. Debussy has formed a sect in music. . . . These caprices of Parisian taste are, quite truthfully, very strange. One of its characteristics is always to go to extremes. . . . Note that if by chance a true genius happens to come into fashion, even our admiration goes to excess. Sometimes our admiration becomes an opportunity to disparage any rival . . .; and sometimes, under the pretext of doing justice to a great man, we exalt him uncritically, without discriminating between good and bad . . . And don't think that this need to take sides without mitigation or nuance indicates the presence of a vigorously original talent. No, rather it's because we are so poor at feeling that we yield to the temptation to exaggerate our judgments and thus acknowledge an artificial personality so cheaply.

And then, we are so afraid of being accused of lacking boldness! Paris is full of these salon critics for whom the fear of being behind the times preoccupies them more than anything. They push the cult of the exception and the rage for the elegant so far that by necessity they have come to regard talent in inverse ratio to success. [. . .] [F]or certain people who have very little confidence in their taste, popular success becomes a reason for suspicion. (30–33) . . .

By itself, [Debussy's] formula cannot be sustained for a long period. (Imagine the art of the miniaturist applied to the fresco.) It works best in short pieces, for when prolonged the formula quickly becomes tedious. [. . .] Is there anything more empty than his recent compositions, anything more coldly boring than, say, his *Hommage à Rameau*? (42–43) . . .

[Regarding *La Mer*:] Théophile Gautier . . . found himself more inspired by pictures than by nature itself. But at least his descriptions, which are so full of variety, had merit because of the richness of an incomparable palate. Nothing like that with M. Debussy, whose art is totally monochromatic. Really, in describing the sea, only he could succeed in giving us an impression of smallness—events within an aquarium, a tempest of ornaments, immensity in miniature. (44) . . .

[On Laloy's lavish praise of Debussy:] One could not offend good sense more resolutely, nor moreover render a more detestable service to French music. If our School shines today through originality and talent, one would think there would be a way to acknowledge the fact without lapsing into such clumsy and foolish exaggerations. . . . In spite of everything, a type of sincerity reveals itself. In this way everyone whom Wagner leaves cold but is hesitant to say so can seize a creditable excuse for making a confession and an admission. Having found a tiny art that suits and fits them, they draw from this discovery the courage that they had lacked. Now they unceremoniously repudiate the masterpieces they pretended to hear, though clearly the grandeur of these works escaped them. For them this provided an opportunity for a tardy candor; and with the same stroke they put an end to the most irritating of hypocrisies. Having put such a high premium on the sincerity of others, you won't be surprised if I am anxious above all to prove my own. Besides, such a duty is so far from seeming painful to me that I confess I received the keenest pleasure in conforming myself to it. (46–47)

Une Enquête de la *Revue du Temps Présent*

Inspired by the "success" of Cor's article, Caillard and Bérys now attempted to do for Debussy what L'Éclair had done with Wagner. They crafted an enquête *(questionnaire) designed to define Debussy's art and assess its legitimacy as a model for contemporary French music. The* enquête *consisted of the following three questions:*

What is the real importance of M. Claude Debussy and what should be his role in the evolution of contemporary music?

Is his an original individuality, or only an accidental phenomenon?

Does he represent a fruitful innovation, a model, and a direction capable of forming a school; indeed, should he form a school?

Caillard and Bérys sent the questions to one hundred musicians, philosophers, critics, and other literary figures in France, Belgium, and Germany. Only twenty-nine responded, most of whom either sided with Cor or took a noncommittal position. Some of the respondents are quite famous, others obscure:

Ernest Ansermet, Maurice Barrès, Albert Bazillas, Camille Bellaigue, Gaston Carraud, Albert Carré, Jean Chantavoine, A. Chéramy, Camille Chevillard, Arthur Coquard, Jules Ecorcheville, Maurice Fauqueux, Paul Flat, Funck-Brentano, Louis Ganne, Fernand Gregh, Siegmund von Hausegger, Camille Mauclair, Friedrich Mottl, G. de Pawlowski, Joséphin Péladan, Reynaldo Hahn, Robert Richard, Romain Rolland, Yvonne Sarcey, Edouard Trémisot, Jean d'Udine, Siegfried Wagner, Willy.

Excerpts from some of the most significant replies follow.

Ernest Ansermet

Conductor Ernest Ansermet's long response, an enthusiastic defense of Debussy, begins with a detailed rebuttal of Cor.

In the last few years, the music of M. Debussy has asserted itself to such a sovereign degree—sometimes with very unfortunate repercussions—that a reaction was inevitable. Besides, it speaks well of the vitality of French musical taste that having submitted strongly to the influence of a form of art, it quickly fears falling into a rut, regains self-control, and seeks to free itself from the rut. But to disown, ignore, or willfully forget this form of art is quite a different attitude, one I find deplorable; and I think M. Raphaël Cor has adopted this attitude rather thoughtlessly. (50) . . .

Melody! This is M. R. Cor's grand theme. But what does he mean by it? . . . Without speaking of the truly innovative forms in which M. Debussy clothes melody, his music contains an abundance of *melodies* in the most banal sense of the word. The same goes for rhythm. As for tonality, it might appear considerably enlarged and enriched in this music, but it is no less perfectly characterized. Never have I encountered any chords that appear to be randomly ordered and that lack a well-defined function. And I will add—and insist on it—that I do not know of any musician since Beethoven who has had not only as strong a sense of tonal unity as M. Debussy, but also as strong a need of it.

Melodic line, rhythm, tonal unity, formal balance, and clarity of the work—all of this, I do not hesitate to say, will show itself in M. Debussy's music to any mind capable of analysis or simply to any open mind; you only need time to get accustomed to the music. I need not add that the listener will also experience his diversity of expression, his orchestral richness . . ., and above all his constant evolution, which should dispell any notion of *a system*. (52–53) . . .

I can now respond to your questionnaire in a few words.

I find M. Debussy's work to be the most important musical phenomenon since Wagner and the Russians. Powerfully original work, it is so little accidental that one could have anticipated it if genius did not always surpass the highest extrapolations of logic. Indeed, this music clearly continues along the path both of Wagner and the Russians, enriching the style of the one with the discoveries of the others and making it supple; at the same time, the music remains the expression of a personality that strongly sums up the spirit of his own epoch and his own nation.

His influence is certain, neither to be wished for nor feared. To have such a personality close by is always a misfortune for people of average talents who are at high risk of being carried along in his tracks and swallowed up. Others will discern the part of his work that contains fruitful innovations and use it according to their genius. M. Debussy's considerable technical contributions have already made their impact on almost all of today's composers. I'm not speaking of M. Mahler, whose music I don't know well enough. But, to take one of the most curious cases, almost every page of [Strauss's] *Elektra* demonstrates what I have asserted. (54–55)

Camille Bellaigue

One of the more hostile and dismissive responses. Bellaigue was an influential conservative critic for the Revue des deux mondes, *a partisan of Verdi and strident opponent of Wagner and Debussy.*

"What is the real importance of M. Claude Debussy and what should be his role in the evolution of contemporary music?" I consider his importance minimal and I hope his role will be also.

"Is M. Debussy an original individuality?" Yes. "Only accidental?" One must hope.

"Does he represent a fruitful innovation?" No. "A model and a direction capable of forming a school; and indeed should he form a school?" No, and again no.

Your readers will have already found the reasons for and elaborations of these short answers in the excellent article by your collaborator M. Raphaël Cor. . . . (67)

Gaston Carraud

An example of the noncommittal answer.

Your questions seem premature; besides, for me the words *school* and *formula* have only a detestable meaning in art. No one could seriously raise any doubts about M. Debussy's present importance and originality. As for the rest—it's already hard enough to see clearly into the past; how then the future? (67)

Albert Carré

Director of the Opéra-comique at the time of the premiere of Pelléas et Mélisande.

The very brilliant position that M. Claude Debussy acquired from the beginning in the Art of music results from those features that proceed only from himself, and the only example I hope he gives his colleagues would be to demonstrate at what point "personality" adds to the superiority of an artist.

God protect us and protect French music from leaders of schools, from formulas and from imitators!

In art, imitation is never anything but making counterfeits, and a true artist must belong to only one school: his own. (68)

Arthur Coquard

A pupil and partisan of Franck, Coquard criticized Debussy's music for "powerlessness" and lack of "grandeur." He connects it with "neurasthenia," a word often associated with Debussyism at this time.

Is he an original individuality? How can anyone doubt it? Has he not created a new language for his own use, pouring out new formulas by handfuls and creating, if I may say so, a *musical neologism*? [This new language] is truly a prodigious inventor of harmonies, which are played like none before it, with chains of chords and unforeseen resolutions as well as the most refined "chiaroscuro" orchestral sounds. And yet he remains himself, precious and exquisite, irresistably seductive—"a musician without equal," in M. Raphaël Cor's singularly apt phrase, because he has almost no attachment to the past, lacking kindred and ancestors.

But personality and genius are two very distinct things. There are those who have invented plenty of formulas but remain in the second rank because they lack power and inspiration. [. . .] However audacious he was, do you think Bach ever dreamed of creating a "new style"? Mozart and Beethoven simply used the language of their day. Wagner himself was much more of an innovator, but he could not compare to M. Debussy in that respect. But the work of these masters blazes with a strength of invention, developmental power, and emotion that one must not expect from the composer of *Pelléas*.

Limited in this regard, M. Debussy's horizon is restricted from another perspective as well. Of the three essential elements that make up modern music—rhythm, melody, and harmony—M. Debussy has exploited only harmony. Now I admit that in this field his music is of great worth, and that among the numerous eccentricities one frequently finds progressions that are penetrating in their novelty and seductive in their pleasing boldness. But all of these beauties are of the same order and flow from the same method; this explains why a short work like the *Après-midi d'un faune* charms us from beginning to end while the works of longer breadth are distressingly monotonous despite the presence of certain exquisite and truly inspired pages. No strength or power in these interminable dialogues. One no longer finds tenderness and passion; in their place a sickly sentimentality stretches itself out, made to seduce neurotics at this time when neurasthenia flourishes. And grandeur, rapture . . . everything that is more noble in the human soul . . . where to find them, in these affected and languid pages? . . . It could be that M. Debussy will occupy in music history a position analogous to Verlaine and Mallarmé, poets who possessed originality but no power.

You can see that in my opinion M. Debussy is a musician with a singular and undeniable personality but one that is purely accidental. He could not create a school, since he is an exceptional and extraordinary talent. I think everyone agrees that imitations of him are doomed to nothingness. . . . (73–76)

Camille Mauclair

*Poet, novelist, and art critic, Mauclair (pseudonym of Camille Faust) counted
himself among Debussy's first admirers, and he continued to support the composer as long as he wrote in a "symbolist" manner. Like Coquard he tended to
see Debussy as a very original talent but not a profound genius. Mauclair's admiration did not extend to Debussy's self-styled followers, especially Louis Laloy,
with whom he feuded on several occasions. During one dispute (not involving
Debussy), Laloy accused his opponent of "universal incompetence" as a critic.
That Laloy's charge rankled is clear throughout Mauclair's response.[9]*

I was among those people who admired the skill and originality of
Claude Debussy at the time when his works encountered only indifference or derision when one deigned to play them at all. I joined the
ranks in 1892, and I can say there weren't many of us then! Overnight
Pelléas et Mélisande called forth thousands of "competent" admirers we
had never heard of, and they promptly took it upon themselves to show
us that we understood nothing about Debussy's genius. This makes it
very easy for me to tell you that in all honesty I find this deification of
a great artist to be ridiculous, and I absolutely refuse to make him
repugnant and grotesque—as these gentlemen are in the process of
doing—precisely because I took pleasure in Debussy long before they
discovered him.

Debussy is a superb musician. Debussyism is a detestable snobbery.
Pelléas is not what I find most remarkable in Debussy's work. That composition is an astonishing adaptation of one nature to another, a
marvelous imitation of the virtues and faults of a poet, a transposition
of personality. It is precisely for that reason that I prefer *Après-midi d'un
faune* when I look for Debussy in Debussy. This is why *Pelléas* is an
exceptional work: it is a tour-de-force that cannot be imitated or
renewed, and still less can it open up a new path. [. . .] Besides, *Pelléas*
is already several years old and we constantly await something else; the
few little works the composer has given us while we wait have not taught
us anything new about his creative powers. They repeat themselves,
and the unexpected charm of before has now become a charm that is
all too expected—even a method.

A school of opera stemming from *Pelléas* would be remarkable mostly
for the irresistible, solemn, and very aesthetic tedium that would be let
loose: emotion and life would be replaced by a comical mannerism, a
pseudo-mysticism as empty as it is turgid. A charming medieval tapestry
cannot serve as a fresco for the future, and this applies to the plays of
M. Maeterlinck as well as the lyrical drama of Debussy.

What mad passion has led people to want to build a school upon this moving sand? Everything in this capricious, cunning, and restless musician, who is smitten with the idea of fusing the arts and attains simplicity only by making things disconcertingly complex, shows how absurd this mania is. As for what the "competents" have written and the snobs have said about this fashion, I find it unjust to cause a composer to suffer when he must be the first one offended by all of this, since he is a man of taste. Most assuredly he perceives and conceives of sound in a special way, and that is reason enough to say of a musician that he is *inspired*; but this inspiration does not suffice to make that musician a complete genius, powerful and human. One can think that a man who realizes this and is intelligent and refined can create great and beautiful things, so long as he is not self-conscious about his emotion, listens to his heart, and devises noble subjects that have a great and lofty meaning or recognizes the same in true poets. We hasten to acknowledge that up to now he has produced works in which everything, faults and virtues alike, is uniquely his—exquisite pieces for piano, some interesting *mélodies*, one masterpiece each in the genres of string quartet and symphonic poem, and finally a singularly conceived drama in which sweet and violent pages shine within the monotony of an immense recitative. To acknowledge all of this is already to honor an artist among his colleagues in an epoch. But to transform him into a fetish, and to dare to deliver foolish speeches on his account in which, speaking about him in ecstatic tones, they go so far as to place the delicate harmonic knickknacks born of his expert hands next to the statues of Bach, Beethoven, and Wagner—this is buffoonery pure and simple. It is what I have called "Debussyitis," a type of musical influenza.[10] (88–90)

Romain Rolland

In addition to his work as a writer, Rolland was a professor of music history and a critic. Among his writings is a large novel, Jean-Christophe, *(1904–1912), a pungent commentary on the music of his day told through the eyes of a fictional German musician in Paris. In this response, Rolland lets Christophe speak for him.*

Please excuse me. Right now I have too much work to do to reply to your inquiries. My friend Christophe will answer for me. [. . .]

"I don't much like all your French music of today and I'm not crazy about your M. Debussy. But since you're so impoverished in artists, I can't understand why you argue about the greatest one you have.

"As for the question of knowing whether he will found a school and what the school will be worth, that's easy to answer:

"Every great artist has a school. Every school is disastrous.

"Wouldn't it therefore be better if there weren't great artists?"

—Jean-Christophe (96)

Jean d'Udine

Another prominent critic of the day, whose real name was Albert Cozanet, d'Udine became famous for his ardent promotion of Dalcrozian principles. This article impertinently attacks Debussy but recognizes his importance. Note a further comment on Laloy and the question of "competence."

I'll gladly respond to your questionnaire on *debussysme*, not because I think my opinion on this subject is *authorized* (no opinion is ever authorized) or because I think myself *highly competent* in this matter (no one dealing with art is ever competent, not even M. Laloy), but simply because it amuses me to do it, just as it amused M. Raphaël Cor to write his excellent article.

If I find this article excellent, it is undoubtedly because I harbor the same antipathy for M. Debussy's works as your collaborator. . . . I do like the *Nocturnes*, about which he didn't speak, but when it comes to *Pelléas*, the *Après-midi d'un faune*, and the insufferable *Damoiselle élue* (insufferable at least for me), I share the feelings of your collaborator in every respect. Many times in my own writings, I have clearly attested to my aversion for these stutterings; they seem to me to have brought to fruition the heights of monotony in sound. . . .[12] (99)

I will now respond in three words to your questionnaire.

¶ 1. "What is M. Claude Debussy's real importance . . . in the evolution of contemporary music?" Obviously an enormous importance, since almost all the helmsmen of quavers are now writing hypodebussy, when they aren't writing hyperdebussy.

"What should his role be?" See ¶ 3 below.

¶ 2. "Is his an original individuality, or only an accidental phenomenon?" Like M. Cor, I answer that M. Debussy is surely "without equal"; and if he is only an accident, he is in any case an accident that has momentous consequences, since he has disturbed the whole musical structure of his day.

¶ 3. "What *should* M. Debussy's role be? . . . Does he represent a fruitful innovation, a model and a direction capable of forming a school; and indeed should he form a school?" Not being privy to the secrets of the Apollonian will, I don't know if he *should* found a school; but I say that he *is the founder* of a school. As for whether I think this influence is fruitful or even if this composer is truly original—well, my outlook is too Darwinian to answer those questions with a prophecy. We will know in a century or two, and then, if you want, we can talk about it again in the Elysian Fields. All I wish is that in that delightful place they will play something other than *La Mer*—at least in our section! (101–02)

Willy

Another influential critic, Willy (one of several pseudonyms adopted by Henri Gauthier-Villars) had a guarded admiration for Debussy, though not for Ravel or Debussy's followers; he preferred d'Indy and the franckistes.

What use is there in arguing? M. Laloy tells us that only the spectacles of Nature and the music of C. Debussy make him "suffer by the strength of joy and the very excess of their beauty." Damn!

And then on the other hand, the only thing your pugnacious collaborator M. Raphaël Cor sees in *Pelléas* is a chain "of little superfluous sounds and arbitrary chords!" Damn again!

The Truth must lie in between this rapture and this slander!

God keep me from ever becoming a diehard Debussyist!

I have poked fun at the sacristans of this new cult many times, although I have never disrespectfully pulled the beard of the god himself. . . . In the commercialized work of the composer of the *Proses lyriques*, one can very judiciously sort out the meaningful creations from those that came from the bottom of the drawer that he put together with greater or lesser skill. . . .

One can perform a chemical analysis on certain works by Debussy's disciples and find only the bicarbonate of ninth chords on stepwise scale degrees, the acetate of dissonances in chains of major thirds, traces of unresolved appoggiaturas.... But one cannot deny the great value of a Debussy *"who has remained completely faithful to our French musical tradition,"* in the words of one of the most fervent admirers of *Pelléas*, M. Vincent d'Indy—whom no one, I believe, can accuse of incompetence or snobbery. . . .

And then, finally, to extend the limits of tonality, replace the everlasting major-minor dualism with a supple variety of modes, substitute a wave of glistening resonances for the rigid trilogy of perfect tonic, dominant, and subdominant chords—all that is quite something! (103–104)

In the next section, the editors reprint miscellaneous responses to Cor's article and the questionnaire from various journals, most of them little known. Caillard and Bérys close with an editorial (Le Secret de M. Debussy) *in which they agree with Cor that Debussy's music is fundamentally ephemeral. A representative passage follows.*

In sum, for what do people reproach him, with more vehemence and less injustice? Perhaps less for his methods, his innovations, and his originality than the uses to which he has wanted to put them; if we have understood correctly, what seems to have exasperated those who have raised their voices is not so much the art of M. Debussy but its totally artificial goal. They accuse him of *systématisme*. His means are but formulas, the only goal of his novelty is to surprise, his originality seeks but to astonish and produce a stupefying effect. His work would then be a bluff, his success a hoax, his audience a herd of snobs. Composer and admirers alike lack sincerity. And neither the enthusiasm nor its object are likely to live. . . .

Isn't it perhaps insufficient to respond, like his defenders do, that these new formulas have been used to enrich the musical language, in order to obtain a more workable and more nuanced "manner" and an expressiveness that is more penetrating, more intuitive for certain souls that are half-conscious, subconscious, indeed even unconscious? Isn't that a lot of philosophy for a little bit of music? (129–31) . . .

NOTES

1. Louis Laloy, "La Nouvelle Manière de Claude Debussy," *La Grande Revue* (10 February 1908): 530–35. For a recent translation, see *Louis Laloy (1874–1944) on Debussy, Ravel, and Stravinsky*, trans. and annotated by Deborah Priest (Brookfield, Vt., 1999), pp. 195–204.

2. Lalo, *Le Temps*, 24 October 1905. Debussy protested Lalo's review and the formerly warm personal relations between the two men deteriorated; by 1908 they were no longer on familiar terms. In a letter of 1909 Debussy dismissed Lalo as an "unsympathetic personality [. . .] one of those people who don't hear music for itself but for what it represents, to their ears, of traditions laboriously learned; and they can't change these without running the risk of no longer understanding anything at all . . ." See *Debussy Letters*, ed. François Lesure and Roger Nichols, trans. Roger Nichols (Cambridge, Mass., 1987), pp. 163–64, 192–94, and 212.

3. "A propos des *Images* de Claude Debussy," *Les Cahiers d'aujourd'hui* (February 1913): 135–38; trans. in *A Ravel Reader: Correspondence, Articles, Interviews*, comp. and ed. Arbie Orenstein (New York, 1990), pp. 366–68.

4. "Claude Debussy et le Debussysme," *S.I.M.* (15 August–September 1910): 506–19. For a translation, see *Louis Laloy*, trans. Priest, pp. 85–98.

5. *Claude Debussy: His Life and Works*, trans. Maire and Grace O'Brien (New York, 1973), pp. 198–99.

6. The Châtelet was the home of Concerts Colonne, which played to a mixed audience of musicians, music lovers, and members of the bourgeoisie who attended mostly out of social obligation (Romain Rolland characterized the latter as "fashionable society people who died of boredom but who would not have renounced the honor of paying dearly for a glorious boredom for anything in the world"; *Jean-Christophe: La Foire sur la place* (Paris, 1948), p. 692.) *Rondes* premiered at a special series of concerts at the Salle Gaveau arranged by publisher Jacques Durand; consisting exclusively of music by living and recently deceased French composers, these concerts played to a more specialized audience.

7. Debussy and his followers condemned composers at the Schola Cantorum for relying on cyclism and traditional developmental processes, which the Debussyists damned as sterile academic procedures. Carraud sarcastically suggests that basing *Rondes* on a single theme and appealing to musical technique rather than emotion to unfold it amounted to adopting the methods of the composers he disdained. Note the reference to Debussy's "first manner."

8. Marcel Dietschy, *A Portrait of Claude Debussy*, ed. and trans. William Ashbrook and Margaret G. Cobb (Oxford: Clarendon, 1994), p. 153.

9. Save, it is true, for some works of his youth; these, on the contrary, have a violent and frankly excessive rhythm. [Cor]

10. Laloy refers to this dispute in "Les partis musicaux en France," *La Grande Revue* (25 December 1907): 791.

11. Camille Mauclair, "La Debussyte," *Le Courrier musical* 15 (September 1905): 501–505.

12. D'Udine disputes two points from Cor's article but frames his retorts in ways to denigrate Debussy further. He rebuts the charge that Debussy is "insincere," for "contrary to you, I don't want to doubt M. Claude-Achille's very spontaneous joy in composing music that gives me no pleasure." (100) And to the allegation that Debussy does not write music, d'Udine responds, "Balderdash! [. . .] To say that M. Debussy's sonorous bread crumbs are not music *for the two of us*, since we get no pleasure from listening to them— I agree! But don't say that it's not music for MM. Lalo, Laloy, and probably Lalique, if it soothes their transcendental souls through the medium of their Eustachian tubes— after all, perhaps theirs are more delicate than ours." (100–101)

Index

✦

Index

Notes on the Contributors

Leon Botstein is President of Bard College, where he is also Leon Levy Professor in the Arts and Humanities. He is the author of *Judentum und Modernität* (Vienna, 1991) and *Music and Its Public: Habits of Listening and the Crisis of Modernism in Vienna, 1870–1914* (Chicago, forthcoming), as well as *Jefferson's Children: Education and the Promise of American Culture* (New York, 1997). He is also the editor of *The Compleat Brahms* (New York, 1999), music director of the American Symphony Orchestra, and Editor of *Musical Quarterly.*

Christophe Charle is professor of contemporary history at the Université de Paris-I Panthéon-Sorbonne and director of the Institut d'histoire moderne et contemporaine (of the Centre National de la Recherche Scientifique). His major books are *Les Elites de la République (1880–1900)* (Paris, 1987); *Naissance des "intellectuels" 1880–1900* (Paris, 1990); *A Social History of France in the Nineteenth Century* (Oxford, 1993); *La République des universitaires (1870–1940)* (Paris, 1994); *Intellectuels en Europe au XIXè siècle* (Paris 1996); *Paris fin-de-siècle, culture et politique* (Paris 1998); and *La crise des sociétés impériales, (1900–1940), histoire sociale comparée de l'Allemagne, de la France, et de la Grande-Bretagne* (Paris, 2001).

John R. Clevenger is lecturer in music theory at the University of California, Santa Barbara. His dissertation research on Debussy's Paris Conservatoire training and early stylistic development has been supported by a Jacob K. Javits National Graduate Fellowship and an AMS 50 Dissertation Fellowship. He received the Paul A. Pisk Prize for the best scholarly paper read by a graduate student at the Montreal meeting of the American Musicological Society in 1993. Clevenger contributed scores of thirteen unpublished compositions of Debussy for the Radio France Debussy 2000 cycle and oversaw the modern world première of Debussy's first Rome cantata, *Le Gladiateur,* in Chico, California, in 1997.

Jane F. Fulcher is Professor of Musicology at Indiana University. She has twice served as Directeur d'Etudes Associé at the Ecole des Hautes Etudes en Sciences Sociales in Paris, as well as serving as Directeur de Recherches at the Centre National de la Recherche Scientifique in Paris. She is the author of *The Nation's Image: French Grand Opera as Politics and Politicized Art* (Cambridge University Press, 1987); *French Cultural Politics and Music from the Dreyfus Affair to the First World War* (Oxford University Press, 1999); and *Composers, Intellectuals, and Politics in France from the First to the Second World War* (forthcoming). She is the recipient of research fellowships from The National Endowment for the Humanities, The American Council of Learned Societies, and the Wissenschaftskolleg zu Berlin.

David Grayson is Professor of Music (Musicology) at the University of Minnesota. He is the author of *The Genesis of Debussy's Pelléas et Mélisande* (Ann Arbor, 1986), and has contributed to three volumes on Debussy published by Cambridge University Press: The *Pelléas* volume in the Cambridge Opera Handbook series (1989), *Debussy Studies* (1997), and the forthcoming *Debussy Companion*. He is editing *Pelléas* for the Durand critical edition of Debussy's collected works and is on the editorial board of the *Cahiers Debussy*. He is also the author of *Mozart: Piano Concertos Nos. 20 and 21* (Cambridge, 1999) and is currently working on a performance history of Mozart's piano concertos.

Brian Hart is Assistant Professor of Music (Musicology) at Northern Illinois University. He has written several articles on aspects of the late romantic French symphony, including its place in Parisian concert life, governmental support for the genre, and the use of the symphony to communicate socio-political philosophies. He has recently completed an historical and analytical study of the symphony in France after Berlioz (ca. 1850–1920) which will appear in A. Peter Brown's forthcoming series, *The Symphonic Repertoire*, to be published by Indiana University Press.

Gail Hilson Woldu received her Ph.D. from Yale University and is Assistant Professor of Music at Trinity College in Connecticut. She has published numerous articles in French journals and books on Gabriel Fauré, the Paris Conservatoire, the Schola Cantorum, and music in Paris between 1870 and 1925. Professor Woldu was awarded a summer stipend from the National Endowment for the Humanities in 1998 to support her research on Vincent d'Indy.

Rosemary Lloyd is Rudy Professor of French at Indiana University. She received a National Endowment for the Humanities Fellowship to write *Mallarmé: The Poet and His Circle* (Cornell University Press, 1999). In addition to numerous articles on Mallarmé, she has translated a selection of his letters (University of Chicago Press, 1988) and is co-editor of the *Mallarmé Bulletin*. She is also the author of many books on nineteenth-century French literature.

Marie Rolf is Professor of Music Theory and Associate Dean of Graduate Studies at the Eastman School of Music. She is the editor of the critical edition of Debussy's *La Mer* (Durand, 1997) and is the author of articles on Debussy's music in *Debussy Studies* (Cambridge, 1997), the *Cahiers Debussy* (numbers 11, 12 and 13, in the new series), and *Perspectives on Music* (Austin, 1985). She is also the author of a seminal study on Debussy's orchestral manuscripts in *The Musical Quarterly* (Volume 70/4). She is a member of the editorial board for the *Œuvres complètes de Claude Debussy*, to which she was appointed in 1982.